Computing Essentials
2000–2001

INTRODUCTORY EDITION

Computing Essentials

2000–2001

INTRODUCTORY EDITION

Timothy J. O'Leary
Arizona State University

Linda I. O'Leary

Irwin
McGraw-Hill

Boston Burr Ridge, IL Dubuque, IA Madison, WI
New York San Francisco St. Louis Bangkok
Bogotá Caracas Lisbon London Madrid
Mexico City Milan New Delhi Seoul
Singapore Sydney Taipei Toronto

McGraw-Hill Higher Education

A Division of The ***McGraw-Hill*** *Companies*

COMPUTING ESSENTIALS, 2000–2001, INTRODUCTORY EDITION

Published by Irwin/McGraw-Hill, an imprint of The McGraw-Hill Companies, Inc. 1221 Avenue of the Americas, New York, NY, 10020.

This book is printed on acid-free paper.

domestic 1 2 3 4 5 6 7 8 9 0 BAN/BAN 0 9 0 9 8 7 6 5 4 3 2 1 0
international 1 2 3 4 5 6 7 8 9 0 BAN/BAN 0 9 0 9 8 7 6 5 4 3 2 1 0

ISBN 0-07-236247-2
ISSN 1067-8549

Vice president/Editor-in-chief: *Michael W. Junior*
Publisher: *David Kendric Brake*
Senior sponsoring editor: *Jodi McPherson*
Associate editors: *Beth Cigler, Steve Schuetz*
Developmental editor: *Erin Riley*
Senior marketing manager: *Jeff Parr*
Senior project manager: *Mary Conzachi*
Manager, new book production: *Melonie Salvati*
Freelance design coordinator: *Gino Cieslik*
Cover designer: *Francis Owens*
Senior supplement coordinator: *Marc Mattson*
Compositor: *Cecelia G. Morales*
Typeface: *10/12 ITC New Baskerville*
Printer: *The Banta Book Group*

INTERNATIONAL EDITION ISBN 0-07-116611-4

www.mhhe.com

Information Technology at Irwin/McGraw-Hill

At McGraw-Hill Higher Education, we publish instructional materials targeted at the higher education market. In an effort to expand the tools of higher learning, we publish texts, lab manuals, study guides, testing materials, software, and multimedia products.

At Irwin/McGraw-Hill (a division of McGraw-Hill Higher Education), we realize that technology has created and will continue to create new mediums for professors and students to use in managing resources and communicating information with one another. We strive to provide the most flexible and complete teaching and learning tools available as well as offer solutions to the changing world of teaching and learning.

Irwin/McGraw-Hill is dedicated to providing the tools for today's instructors and students to successfully navigate the world of Information Technology.

- **Seminar series**—Irwin/McGraw-Hill's Technology Connection seminar series offered across the country every year demonstrates the latest technology products and encourages collaboration among teaching professionals.
- **Osborne/McGraw-Hill**—This division of The McGraw-Hill Companies is known for its best-selling Internet titles Harley Hahn's Internet & Web Yellow Pages and the Internet Complete Reference. Osborne offers an additional resource for certification and has strategic publishing relationships with corporations such as Corel Corporation and America Online. For more information visit Osborne at www.osborne.com.
- **Digital solutions**—Irwin/McGraw-Hill is committed to publishing digital solutions. Taking your course online doesn't have to be a solitary venture, nor does it have to be a difficult one. We offer several solutions that will allow you to enjoy all the benefits of having course material online. For more information visit www.mhhe.com/solutions/index.mhtml.
- **Packaging options**—For more about our discount options, contact your local Irwin/McGraw-Hill Sales representative at 1-800-338-3987 or visit our Web site at www.mhhe.com/it.

Information Technology

BRIEF CONTENTS

CONTENTS

PREFACE

Introduction

The twentieth century not only brought us the dawn of the Information Age, but continued to bring us rapid changes in information technology. There is no indication that this rapid rate of change will be slowing—it may even be increasing. As we begin the 21st century, computer literacy will undoubtedly become prerequisite in whatever career a student chooses. The goal of *Computing Essentials, 2000–2001* edition is to provide students with the basis for understanding the concepts necessary for success in the Information Age. *Computing Essentials* also endeavors to instill in students an appreciation for the effect of information technology on people and our environment, and a basis for building the necessary skill set to succeed in this new, 21st century.

About the Authors

Tim and Linda O'Leary live in the American Southwest and spend much of their time engaging instructors and students in conversation about learning. In fact, they have been talking about learning for over 25 years. Something in those early conversations convinced them to write a book, to bring their interest in the learning process to the printed page. Today, they are as concerned as ever about learning, about technology, and about the challenges of presenting material in new ways, both in terms of content and the method of delivery.

A powerful and creative team, Tim combines his years of classroom teaching experience with Linda's background as a consultant and corporate trainer. Tim has taught courses at Stark Technical College in Canton, Ohio, Rocherster Institute of Technology in Upper New York state, and is currently a professor at Arizona State University in Tempe, Arizona. Tim and Linda have talked to and taught students from 8 to 80, all of them with a desire to learn something about computers and the applications that make their lives easier, interesting, and more productive.

Each new edition of an O'Leary text, supplement, or learning aid has benefited from these students and their instructors who daily stand in front of them (or over their shoulders). *Computing Essentials, 2000–2001* edition is no exception.

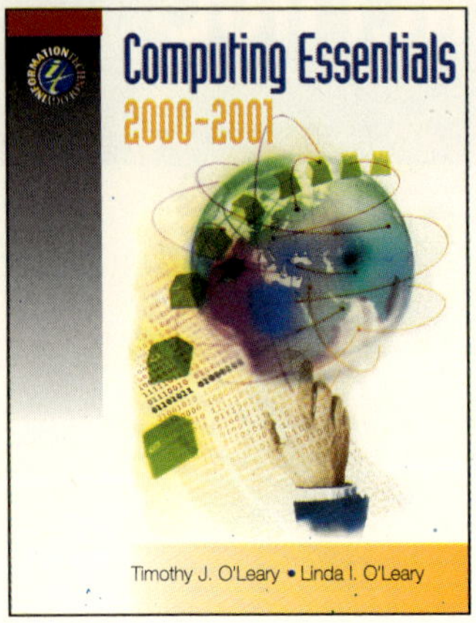

About Our Book

Times are changing, technology is changing, and this text is changing too. Do you think the students of today are different from yesterday? Mine are and I'll wager that yours are as well. On the positive side, I am amazed how much effort students put toward things that interest them and things they are convinced are relevant to them. Their effort directed at learning application programs and exploring the Web seems at times limitless. On the other hand, it is difficult to engage them in other equally important topics such as personal privacy and technological advances.

I've changed the way I teach and this book reflects that. I no longer *lecture* my students about how important certain concepts like microprocessors, input devices, and utility programs are. Rather, I begin by *engaging* their interest by presenting practical tips related to the key concepts, by *demonstrating* interesting applications that are relevant to their lives, and by *focusing* on outputs rather than processes. Then, I *discuss* the concepts and processes.

Motivation and relevance are the keys. This text has several features specifically designed to engage students and to demonstrate the relevance of technology in their lives. These elements are combined with a thorough coverage of the concepts and sound pedagogical devices.

What's New in this Edition?

- Reorganization of the early chapters of the text to allow for greater coverage of applications as well as system software.
- Chapter 2 now includes coverage of word processing, spreadsheets, databases, presentation graphics, integrated packages and suites, and browsers. The chapter emphasizes the features of the various programs and the output of each program.
- An exciting addition to our software coverage is a series of four, full-color pull-out guides that illustrate how each program works.
- Chapter 3 focuses on system software, including Windows 2000, Norton Utilities, and Outlook.
- One of the most significant enhancements to this edition is the integration of a three-level approach to learning in both the text and the supplements. Based upon a proven learning model, this three-level format is engineered to help students take ownership of the text material.

  Level 1 questions and exercises test recall of the basic information and terminology in the chapter.

  Level 2 questions and exercises review students' understanding of concepts and ability to integrate ideas presented in different parts of the chapter.

  Level 3 questions and exercises test students' critical thinking skills and ability to apply the concepts they have mastered to solve problems.
- Within the text material, we have incorporated new pedagogical features that follow the three-level approach and enhance both instruction and learning.

✔ In-text Concept Checks serve to reinforce text material by calling upon students to recall facts and concepts relating to what they have just read.

IT Making IT Work is a new feature that visually demonstrates how technology is applied in our everyday lives. Topics covered include TV Tuner Cards; Voice Recognition Systems; Music from the Internet; Home Networking; and Instant Messaging. These "gallery" style boxes combine text and art to take students step-by-step through technological processes that are both interesting and useful.

- The end of chapter material has been significantly revised in this edition. *Computing Essentials, 2000–2001* contains many more opportunities for students to test their knowledge. To facilitate student learning, the **Chapter Review** follows the three-level approach described above.

    Level 1 includes matching, true/false, multiple choice, and completion exercises.

    Level 2 includes short answer and concept mapping exercises.

    Level 3 includes critical thinking questions and problems.

- The **Testbank** follows the same three-level approach that is introduced in the text to provide a valuable testing and reinforcement tool. Each question is assigned a category: **Level 1,** definition, **Level 2** concept, and **Level 3** application. Also included are a text page reference and a rational for each question and answer.

For each chapter, the student **Online Learning Center** offers both a review of the text material, in the form of an **e-learning session,** and additional exercises organized around the following themes: Group/team projects, Internet/Web-related content, mini case studies of actual companies, and profiles of careers that are influenced by information technology. The content and activities for the exercises further establish O'Leary's three-level learning approach.

Resources for Instructors

We understand that, in today's teaching environment, offering a textbook alone is not sufficient to meet the needs of the many different instructors who use our books. To teach effectively, instructors must have a full complement of supplemental resources to assist them in every facet of teaching from preparing for class; to conducting and lecture; to assessing students' comprehension. *Computing Essentials, 2000–2001* offers a complete, fully integrated supplements package, as described below.

Instructor's Resource Kit

The Instructor's Resource Kit contains a printed Instructor's Manual and a CD-ROM containing the Instructor's Manual in both MS Word and .pdf formats; PowerPoint slides; and Brownstone's Diploma test generation software; and accompanying test item files for each chapter. The distinctive features of each component of the Instructor's Resource Kit are described below.

- **Instructor's Manual** The Instructor's Manual contains a schedule showing how much time is required to cover the material in the chapter; a list of the chapter competencies; tips for covering difficult material; and answers to the Concept Checks. Also included are references to corresponding topics on the Interactive Companion CD-ROM, answers to all the exercises in the Chapter Review section and answers to the On the Web Exercises. The manual also includes a helpful introduction that explains the features, benefits, and suggested uses of the IM and an index of concepts and corresponding competencies.
- **PowerPoint Presentation** Prepared by Alfred Zimermann of the University of Hawaii, the PowerPoint presentation is designed to provide instructors with a comprehensive resource for use during lecture. It includes a review of key terms and definitions, figures from the text, along with several new illustrations, anticipated student questions with answers, and additional resources which can be accessed in Internet-enabled classrooms. Also included with the presentation are comprehensive speaker's notes.
- **Testbank** The *Computing Essentials 2000–2001* edition testbank contains over 3,000 questions categorized by level of learning (definition, concept, and application). This is the same learning scheme that is introduced in the text to provide a valuable testing and reinforcement tool. The test questions are identified by text page number to assist you in planning your exams, and rationales for each answer are also included. Additional test questions, which can be used as pretests and posttests in class, can be found on the Online Learning Center, accessible through our supersite (www.mhhe.com/it).

Business Week Edition of *Computing Essentials*

An exciting new supplement with this edition of *Computing Essentials* is our *Business Week Edition.* With the purchase of a *Business Week Edition* of an Irwin/McGraw-Hill textbook, students will receive a 15-week subscription to *Business Week* for only $8.25 more than the price of the book alone. Professors who adopt the Business Week Edition will enjoy a complimentary subscription for a full year to *Business Week* magazine and complimentary access to the Business Week Resource Center Web site as well as Business Week Online through the duration of their subscription.

Students will also enjoy free access to the Business Week Resource Center Web site (www.resourcecenter.businessweek.com) for the duration of their magazine subscription. The Business Week Resource Center Web site contains a wealth of supplemental materials, including the Business Week Online Archives. Students will have instant access to any business topic from the past nine years of *Business Week*—from 1991 to 1999. From the Resource Center, students may also access Business Week Online (www.businessweek.com) for current issues, online-only features, and career tips. Access to these sites provides a marvelous opportunity to increase students' Internet literacy as instructors explore new ways to integrate the Web into a wide array of student exercises and research projects.

Interactive Companion CD-ROM

This free student CD-ROM, designed for use in class, in the lab, or at home by students and professors alike includes a collection of interactive tutorial labs on some of the most popular topics in information technology. By combining video, interactive exercises, animation, additional content, and actual "lab" tutorials, we expand the reach and scope of the textbook.

Digital Solutions to Help You Manage Your Course

PageOut—PageOut is our Course Web Site Development Center that offers a syllabus page, URL, McGraw-Hill Online Learning Center content, online exercises and quizzes, gradebook, discussion board, and an area for student Web pages. For more information, visit the PageOut Web site (www.mhla.net/pageout).

Online Learning Centers—The Online Learning Center that accompanies *Computing Essentials* is accessible through our Information Technology Supersite (www.mhhe.com/it). This site provides additional learning and instructional tools developed using the same three-level approach found in the text and supplements. This offers a consistent method for students to enhance their comprehension of the concepts presented in the text.

Online Courses Available—OLCs are your perfect solutions for Internet-based content. Simply put, these Centers are "digital cartridges" that contain a book's pedagogy and supplements. As students read the book, they can go online and take self-grading quizzes or work through interactive exercises. These also provide students appropriate access to lecture materials and other key supplements.

Online Learning Centers can be delivered through any of these platforms:

McGraw-Hill Learning Architecture (TopClass)

Blackboard.com

ECollege.com (formally Real Education)

WebCT (a product of Universal Learning Technology)

O'Leary Series Applications Lab Manuals

Available separately, or packaged with *Computing Essentials* is the O'Leary Series computer applications lab manuals for Microsoft Office. The O'Leary Series offers a step-by-step approach to developing computer applications skills and is available in both brief and introductory levels. The introductory level manuals are MOUS Certified and prepare students for the Microsoft Office User Certification Exam.

Skills Assessment

Irwin/McGraw-Hill offers two innovative systems to meet your skills assessment needs. These two products are available for use with any of our applications manual series.

ATLAS (Active Testing and Learning Assessment Software)—Atlas is one option to consider for an application skills assessment tool from McGraw-Hill. Atlas allows students to perform tasks while working live within the Microsoft applications environment. Atlas provides flexibility for you in your course by offering:

- Pre-testing options
- Post-testing options
- Course placement testing
- Diagnostic capabilities to reinforce skills
- Proficiency testing to measure skills

ATLAS is Web-enabled, customizable, and is available for Microsoft Office 2000.

SimNet (Simulated Network Assessment Product)—SimNet is another option for a skills assessment tool that permits you to test students' software skills in a simulated environment. SimNet is available for Microsoft Office 97 (deliverable via a network) and Microsoft Office 2000 (deliverable via a network and the Web). SimNet provides flexibility for you in your course by offering:

- Pre-testing options
- Post-testing options
- Course placement testing
- Diagnostic capabilities to reinforce skills
- Proficiency testing to measure skills

PowerWeb for Concepts

PowerWeb is an exciting new online product available for *Computing Essentials 2000–2001*. A nominally priced token grants students access through our Web site to a wealth of resources—all corresponding to the text. Features include an interactive glossary; current events with quizzing, assessment, and measurement options; Web survey; links to related text content; and WWW searching capability via Northern Lights, an academic search engine.

STUDENT'S GUIDE

Student's Guide to the O'Leary Learning System

At the end of last semester, some of my students stopped by my office to say they enjoyed the class and that they "learned something that they could *actually* use." High praise indeed for a professor! Actually, I had mixed feelings. Of course, it felt good to learn that my students enjoyed the course. However, it hurt a bit that they were *surprised* that they learned something useful.

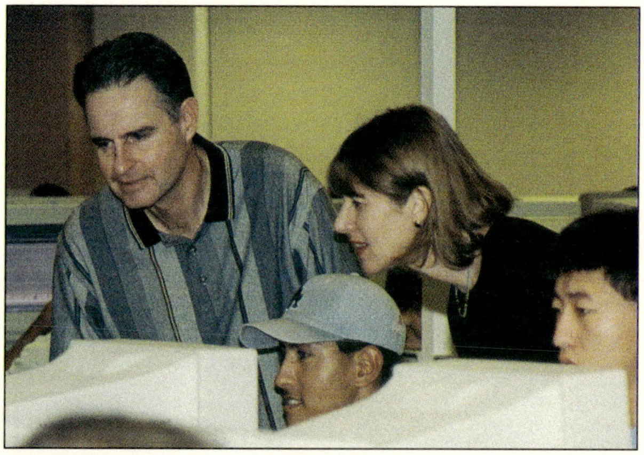

Here's my promise to you: *In the following pages you will find things that you can actually use now as well as provide a foundation to understand future technological advances.*

As you read the text, notice the "Tips" scattered throughout the book. These tips offer suggestions on a variety of topics from the basics of cleaning a monitor to how to make your computer run faster and smoother. Also, notice the "Making IT Work for You" sections that demonstrate some specific computer applications you might find interesting. For example, one demonstrates how to capture and use television video clips for electronic presentations and another shows how to capture, save, and play music from the Internet.

Many learning aids are built into the text to ensure your success with the material and to make the process of learning rewarding. On the pages that follow, we call your attention to the key features in the text. We also show you supplemental materials, such as the student Online Learning Center, that you should take advantage of to ensure your success in this course.

CHAPTER 8

The Internet and the Web

COMPETENCIES

After you have read this chapter, you should be able to:

1. **Describe Internet providers, connections, and protocols.**
2. **Discuss e-mail, mailing lists, newsgroups, and chat groups.**
3. **Describe Internet services: Telnet, FTP, Gopher, and the Web.**
4. **Describe electronic commerce including Web storefronts, electronic payment options, and Web auctions.**
5. **Discuss browsers, Web pages, and Web portals.**
6. **Compare the two types of search tools: indexes and search engines.**
7. **Discuss the two types of Web utilities: plug-ins and helper applications.**
8. **Describe intranets, extranets, and firewalls.**

Want to communicate with a friend across town, in another state, or even in another country? Perhaps you would like to send a drawing, a photo, or just a letter. Looking for travel or entertainment information? Perhaps you're researching a term paper or exploring different career paths. Where do you start? For these and other information-related activities, try the Internet and the Web. They are the 21st-century information resources designed for all of us to use.

The Internet is like a highway that connects you to millions of other people and organizations. Unlike typical highways that move people and things from one location to another, the Internet moves your *ideas* and *information.* Rather than moving through geographic space, you move through **cyberspace**—the space of electronic movement of ideas and information. The Web provides an easy-to-use, exciting, multimedia interface to

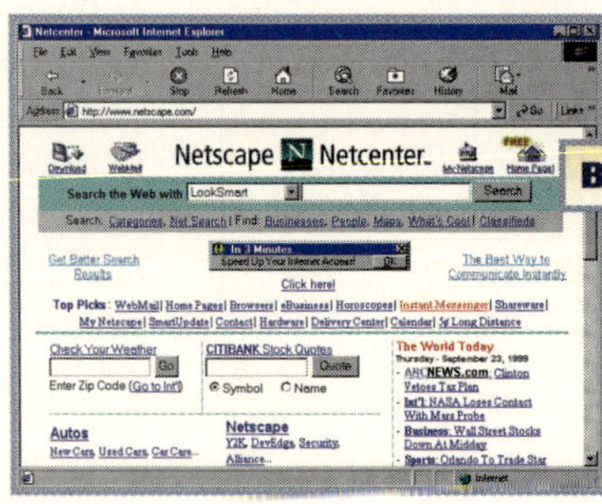

Browsers

172

Visual Chapter Openers

Each chapter begins with a unique presentation of text and graphics that introduces you to the key concepts in the chapter. A list of competencies will help you structure your reading of the chapter and keep you focused on the key points.

Key Terms

Throughout the text, the most important terms are presented in bold type and are defined within the text. You will also find a list of key terms at the end of each chapter and in the glossary at the end of the book.

Term	Description
FAQ	Frequently asked question
Flaming	Insulting, putting down, or attacking
Lurking	Reading news but not joining in to contribute
RFD	Request for discussion
Saint	Someone who aids new users by answering questions
Thread	A sequence of ongoing messages on the same subject

FIGURE 8-12
Selected discussion group terms

TIPS What if you don't know or have forgotten someone's e-mail address? You can go to e-mail address directories, also known as e-mail "white pages." These directories can be used much like you would use the telephone white pages. Here are three e-mail address directories you might try:

www.bigfoot.com

www.people.yahoo.com

www.infospace.com

Tips

Tips offer practical and timely advice on a variety of topics related to computers and information technology. These tips answer your questions about how to clean your mouse; how to protect your privacy on the Web; and what to do to avoid catching a virus (a computer virus, that is!).

Terms

Before you submit a contribution to a discussion group, it is recommended that you observe or read the communications from others. This is called **lurking.**

By lurking, you can learn about the culture of a discussion group. For example, you can observe the level and style of the discussions. You may decide that a particular discussion group is not what you were looking for—in which case, unsubscribe. If the discussions are appropriate and you wish to participate, try to fit into the prevailing culture. Remember that your contributions will likely be read by hundreds of people.

For a list of some other commonly used discussion group terms, see Figure 8-12.

CONCEPT CHECK

- ✔ Give examples of the types of discussion groups you can find on the Internet.
- ✔ What is the most popular chat service on the Internet?

Electronic Commerce

Electronic commerce is buying and selling over the Internet. Web storefronts offer goods and services. Electronic payment options include check, credit card, and electronic cash.

Electronic commerce, also known as **e-commerce,** is the buying and selling of goods over the Internet. Have you ever bought anything over the Internet? If you have not, there is a very good chance that you will within the next year or two. Shopping on the Internet is growing rapidly and there seems to be no end in sight. (See Figure 8-13.)

Web Storefronts

Web storefronts are virtual stores where shoppers can go to inspect merchandise and make purchases. (See Figure 8-14.) A new type of program

ON THE WEB EXPLORATIONS

Almost all ISPs and online service providers offer e-mail service to their customers. But you can get this service for free from Hotmail, Juno Online Services, USA Net Inc., and Yahoo. To learn more about free e-mail service, visit one or more of the following sites:

http://www.hotmail.com
http://www.juno.com
http://www.usa.net
http://www.yahoo.com

On the Web Explorations

Throughout each chapter, you will notice On the Web Explorations notes that encourage you to visit well-established and informative sites to learn more about topics presented.

Concept Checks

These questions, located at the end of major sections in each chapter, encourage you to stop and assess your understanding of the concepts you have read in the preceding section. The questions are designed to be answered quickly and easily. If the questions seem difficult, you should probably review that material before continuing.

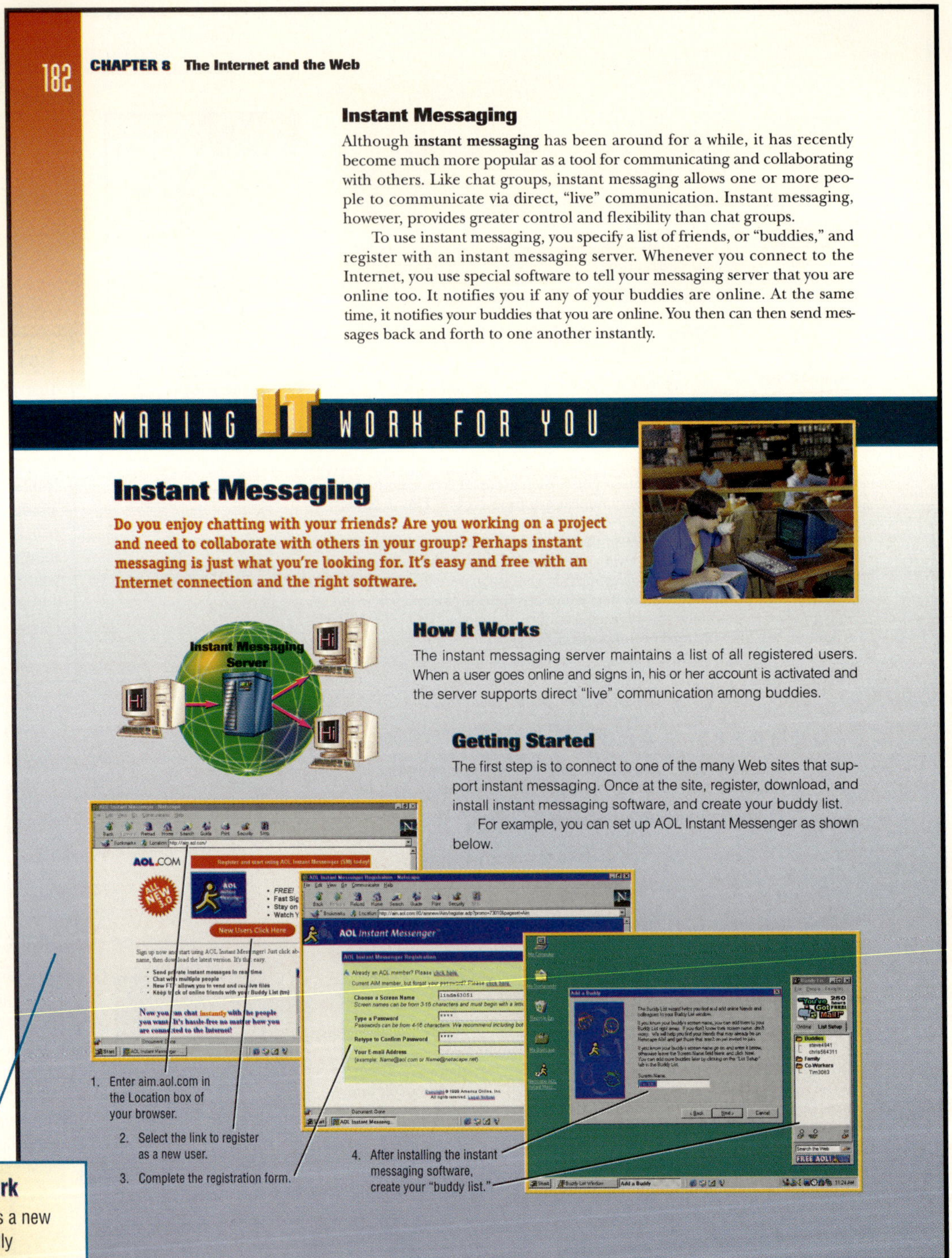

182 **CHAPTER 8 The Internet and the Web**

Instant Messaging

Although **instant messaging** has been around for a while, it has recently become much more popular as a tool for communicating and collaborating with others. Like chat groups, instant messaging allows one or more people to communicate via direct, "live" communication. Instant messaging, however, provides greater control and flexibility than chat groups.

To use instant messaging, you specify a list of friends, or "buddies," and register with an instant messaging server. Whenever you connect to the Internet, you use special software to tell your messaging server that you are online too. It notifies you if any of your buddies are online. At the same time, it notifies your buddies that you are online. You then can then send messages back and forth to one another instantly.

MAKING IT WORK FOR YOU

Instant Messaging

Do you enjoy chatting with your friends? Are you working on a project and need to collaborate with others in your group? Perhaps instant messaging is just what you're looking for. It's easy and free with an Internet connection and the right software.

How It Works

The instant messaging server maintains a list of all registered users. When a user goes online and signs in, his or her account is activated and the server supports direct "live" communication among buddies.

Getting Started

The first step is to connect to one of the many Web sites that support instant messaging. Once at the site, register, download, and install instant messaging software, and create your buddy list.

For example, you can set up AOL Instant Messenger as shown below.

1. Enter aim.aol.com in the Location box of your browser.
2. Select the link to register as a new user.
3. Complete the registration form.
4. After installing the instant messaging software, create your "buddy list."

Making IT Work

Making IT Work is a new feature that visually demonstrates how technology is used in our everyday lives. Topics covered include TV Tuner Cards; Voice Recognition Systems; Music from the Internet; Home Networking, and Instant Messaging. These "gallery" style boxes combine text and art to take you step-by-step through technological processes that are both interesting and useful.

Database Administrator

Librarians have had to be trained in the use of electronic databases so that they can help their corporate users. However, corporate databases of all sorts—not just those in the library—have become extremely important. Hence, many large organizations employ a **database administrator (DBA).** He or she helps determine the structure of the large databases and evaluates the performance of the DBMS. For shared databases, the DBA also determines which people have access to what kind of data; these are called **processing rights.** In addition, the DBA is concerned with such significant issues as security, privacy, and ethics.

CONCEPT CHECK

- ✔ What are some of the security concerns involved with databases?
- ✔ Why might an organization need a database administrator?

A Look to the Future
These boxes involve interesting discussions about future trends in information technology and their effect on our lives.

A LOOK TO THE FUTURE

The Internet on Wheels from Mercedes Benz is a leader in smart cars.

Did you see Bruce Willis's futuristic airborne taxi in *The Fifth Element*? Imagine a car that operates on its own, flies, has rocket boosters, monitors traffic conditions and weather, and entertains us as we travel. In the 21st century, smart cars may well look and act a lot like Bruce Willis's taxi . . . hopefully more sleek and efficient but just as smart.

Of course, none of today's cars can do all those things. But you can expect more cars that navigate themselves and surf the Internet in the near future. Several car makers offer global positioning systems (GPSs) that combine large databases of streets, highways, and interchanges with satellite communications. These GPSs precisely track a vehicle as it travels to its destination. You can obtain specific directions and navigational advice without ever leaving your car.

Daimler-Benz, maker of the Mercedes Benz cars, recently unveiled a concept car dubbed The Internet Multimedia on Wheels. This smart car allows occupants to access the Internet from most locations in Europe and North America. They foresee a day when you will be able to access Internet-based roadside services that will diagnose car problems remotely as well as deliver traffic advisories and headline news.

When will these smart cars be available? Don't expect to see any Internet applications in your sedan anytime soon. Most observers predict that it will be 10 years away. However, many of the other applications are already here, and more are on their way.

VISUAL SUMMARY The Internet and the Web

INTERNET APPLICATIONS

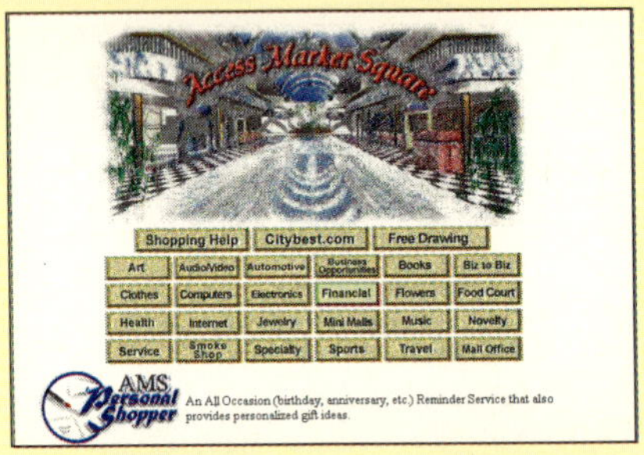

The most common Internet applications include **communicating, shopping, researching,** and **entertainment.**

ACCESS

Once connected to the Internet, your computer seemingly becomes an extension of a giant computer that branches all over the world.

Providers

The most common access is through a **provider** or **host computer.** Three widely used providers are:

- **Colleges and universities**—often offer free Internet access through their LANs.
- **Internet service providers (ISPs)**—offer access for a fee.
- **Online service providers**—offer access and a variety of other services for a fee.

Connections

To access the Internet, you need to connect to a provider. Three types of connections are **direct (dedicated), SLIP** and **PPP,** and **Terminal.**

TCP/IP

TCP/IP is a standard **protocol** of the Internet.

E-MAIL

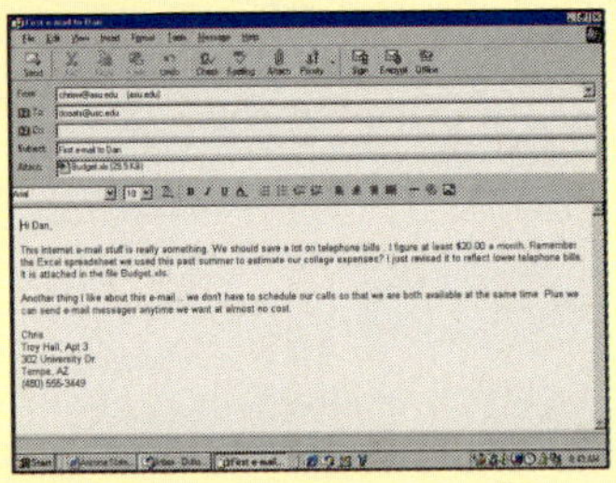

Sending and receiving **e-mail** is the most common Internet activity.

Basic Elements

E-mail messages have three basic elements:

- **Header**—contains the **subject, address,** and **attachment information.**
- **Message**—should be short and to the point.
- **Signature**—often includes sender's name, address, and telephone number.

Addresses

The Internet uses the **domain name system (DNS)** for e-mail. The first part is the **user name,** followed by the **domain name,** and then the **domain code.**

DISCUSSION GROUPS

Discussion groups support electronic communication between individuals. Three types exist:

- **Mailing lists** use e-mail **subscription addresses** to join and **list addresses** to communication to every member.
- **Newsgroups** are organized by major topic areas and use e-mail on the UseNet network to allow users to check contributions of interest.
- **Chat groups** do not use e-mail and allow direct "live" communication.

Visual Summaries

Visual Summaries incorporate text and graphics to provide you with a dynamic review of all the material presented in the chapter. The Visual Summary also serves as a useful text reference.

Chapter Review

The Chapter Review now follows a three-level format and includes exercises that reinforce a review of terms, a review of concepts, and application of concepts. This is achieved through various types of questions and exercises including matching; true/false; multiple choice; completion; short answer; concept matching; and critical thinking.

200

Chapter Review

LEVEL 1

Reviewing Facts and Terms
Matching

Match each numbered item with the most closely related lettered item. Write your answers in the spaces provided.

1. The space of electronic movement of ideas and information. ____
2. The standard protocol for the Internet. ____
3. Security system designed to protect an organization's network against external threats. ____
4. Special software used by your computer to access the Web. ____
5. Identifies a unique person or computer at the listed domain. ____
6. Programs that are automatically uploaded and operate as part

a. Applets
b. Browser
c. Cyberspace
d. DNS
e. E-commerce
f. Firewall
g. HTML
h. Hyperlinks
i. Intranet
j. Java
k. Mailing list
l. Packet

Level 1 questions and exercises help you test your recall of the basic information and terminology in the chapter.

202 CHAPTER 8 The Internet and the Web

Reviewing Concepts

LEVEL 2

Open-Ended

On a separate sheet of paper, respond to each question and statement.

1. Discuss four frequently used Internet services.
2. Describe how addresses are assigned under the domain name system.
3. What are the two types of Internet search tools? How do they differ?
4. Describe some typical Web utilities and how they can help you.
5. Discuss the similarities and differences between intranets and extranets.

Level 2 questions and exercises help you review your understanding of concepts and your ability to integrate ideas presented in different parts of the chapter.

Concept Mapping

Draw a concept map or a flow chart showing how the following terms are related. Be sure to show all relationships. Include any additional terms you can think of.

applets
browsers
chat groups
cyberspace
e-mail
end user
firewall
FTP
host computer
HTML
hyperlinks
intranets
ISP
mailing lists
plug-ins
TCP/IP
Telnet
uploading/downloading
Web site
World Wide Web

Critical Thinking Questions and Projects

LEVEL 3

Read each exercise and answer the related questions on a separate sheet of paper.

1. *Going on an Internet scavenger hunt*: Use the Internet to find information about the following topics. (Record the URLs where you found the information, and write a short description of your findings.)
   a. Hotels in London
   b. Cast members for one of your favorite television programs
   c. MTV's news for this week
   d. Employment opportunities in a career of your choice
   e. Painting as the *Mona Lisa*
   f. The weather conditions for your city (or the nearest large city)

Level 3 questions and exercises test your critical thinking skills and ability to apply the concepts you have mastered to solve problems.

On the Web Exercises 203

On the Web Exercises

1. Off-Line Browsing

Off-line browsing offers a great promise of increased productivity. What could be better than to have your computer searching the Web for you while you sleep? To learn more about off-line browsing, visit our site at http://www.mhhe.com/cit/concepts/oleary2000-2001/webex8.html to link a site that specializes in off-line browsing. Once connected, explore and learn more about off-line browsing. Print out the most informative Web page you find and write a brief paragraph summarizing the pros and cons of off-line browsing.

2. E-Cash

Several companies, including CyberCash and DigiCash, are working on different variations of e-cash. Visit our site at http://www.mhhe.com/cit/concepts/oleary2000-2001/webex8.html to link to a site that specializes in e-cash. Once connected, explore and learn more about e-cash and its alternatives. Print out the most informative Web page you find and write a brief paragraph describing how e-cash works.

3. Searching

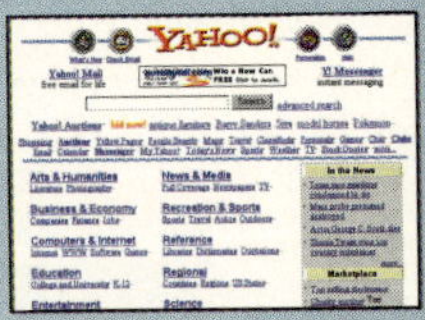

Finding relevant information quickly on the Web can be both rewarding and frustrating. Each search tool is a unique resource. Knowing which search tool to use and how to use it can save you a lot of time. To learn more about the different search tools and search techniques, visit the Yahoo site at http://www.yahoo.com and look at the subject area "Computers and Internet: Internet: Searching the Net: World Wide Web." Explore and learn more about different search tools and search techniques. Print out the Web page you find the most informative, and write a brief paragraph describing what you learned.

4. Adventure Tours

Travel to exotic places around the world without ever leaving home. To do this, visit our site at http://www.mhhe.com/cit/concepts/oleary2000-2001/webex8.html to link to a site specializing in exotic virtual travel. Once connected to the site, explore and learn more about adventure tours. Print out the Web page you find the most informative, and write a brief paragraph describing a virtual tour and discuss what you think the future is for this type of activity.

On the Web Exercises

An extension of the in-text On the Web Exercises, the On the Web Exercises present thought provoking questions that require you to access the Web and are designed to demonstrate the quantity and quality of information available on the Internet.

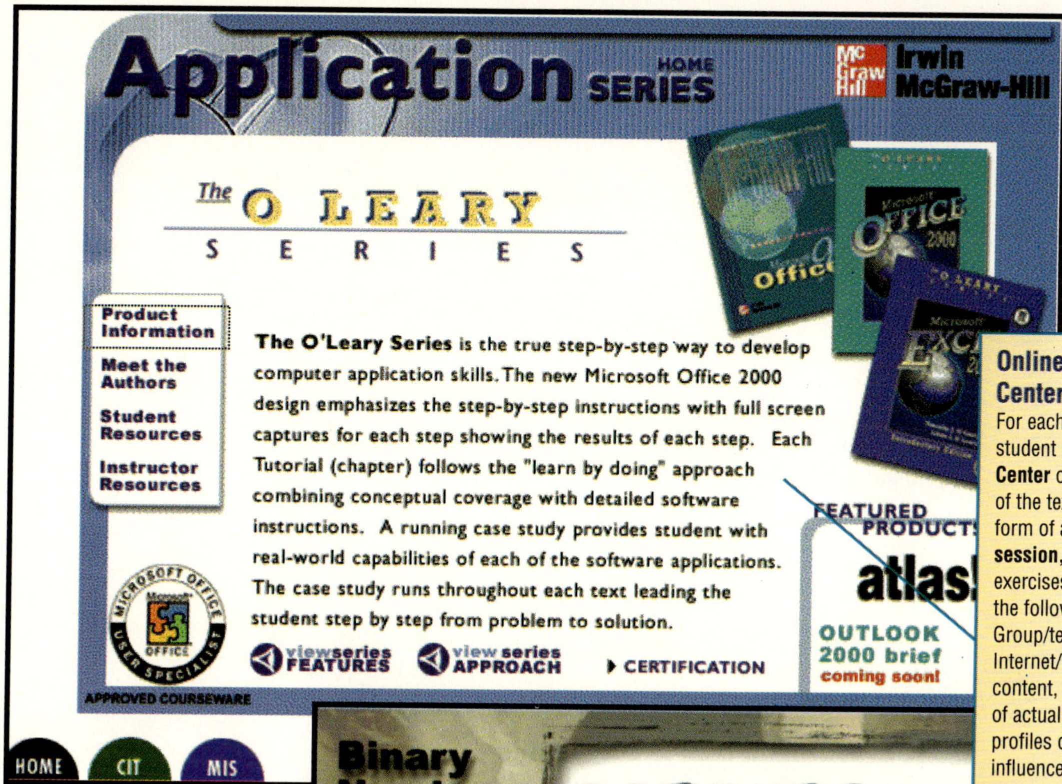

Online Learning Center

For each chapter, the student **Online Learning Center** offers both a review of the text material, in the form of an **e-learning session,** and additional exercises organized around the following themes: Group/team projects, Internet/Web-related content, mini case studies of actual companies, and profiles of careers that are influenced by information technology. The content and activities for the exercises further establish O'Leary's three-level learning approach.

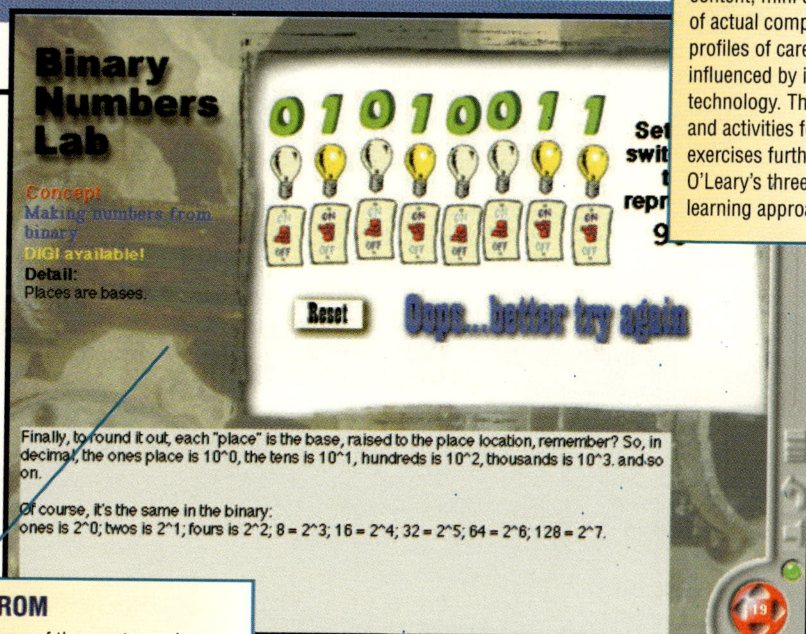

Interactive Companion CD-ROM

Use this free CD-ROM to explore some of the most popular topics in information technology. Video, interactive exercises, animation and actual 'labs" expand the reach and scope of the textbook.

Computing Essentials
2000–2001

INTRODUCTORY EDITION

CHAPTER 1

Your Future and Computer Competency

COMPETENCIES

After you have read this chapter, you should be able to:

1. **Explain the five parts of an information system: people, procedures, software, hardware, and data.**
2. **Distinguish application software from system software.**
3. **Distinguish four kinds of computers—microcomputer, minicomputer, mainframe, and supercomputer—and describe hardware devices for input, processing, storage, output, and communications.**
4. **Describe document, worksheet, database, and presentation files.**
5. **Explain computer connectivity, the Internet, and the Web.**

Computer competency: This notion may not be familiar to you, but it's easy to understand. The purpose of this book is to help you become *competent* in computer-related skills. Specifically, we want to help you walk into a job and immediately be valuable to an employer. In this chapter, we first present an overview of what makes up an information system: people, procedures, software, hardware, and data. Competent end users need to understand these basic parts and how connectivity through the Internet and the Web expands the role of information technology (IT) in our lives. In subsequent chapters, we will describe these parts of information systems in detail.

Ten years ago, most people had little to do with computers, at least directly. Of course, they filled out computerized forms, took computerized tests, and paid computerized bills. But the real work with computers was handled by specialists—

programmers, data-entry clerks, and computer operators.

Then microcomputers came along and changed everything. Now it is easy for nearly everybody to use a computer. People who use microcomputers are called end users. Today:

- Microcomputers are common tools in all areas of life. Writers write, artists draw, engineers and scientists calculate—all on microcomputers. Students and businesspeople do all this, and more.
- New forms of learning have developed. People who are homebound, who work odd hours, or who travel frequently may take courses by telephone-linked home computers. A college course need not fit within the usual time of a quarter or a semester.
- New ways to communicate, to find people with similar interests, and to buy goods are available. All kinds of people are using electronic mail, electronic commerce, and the Internet to meet and to share ideas and products.

What about you? How can microcomputers enhance *your* life?

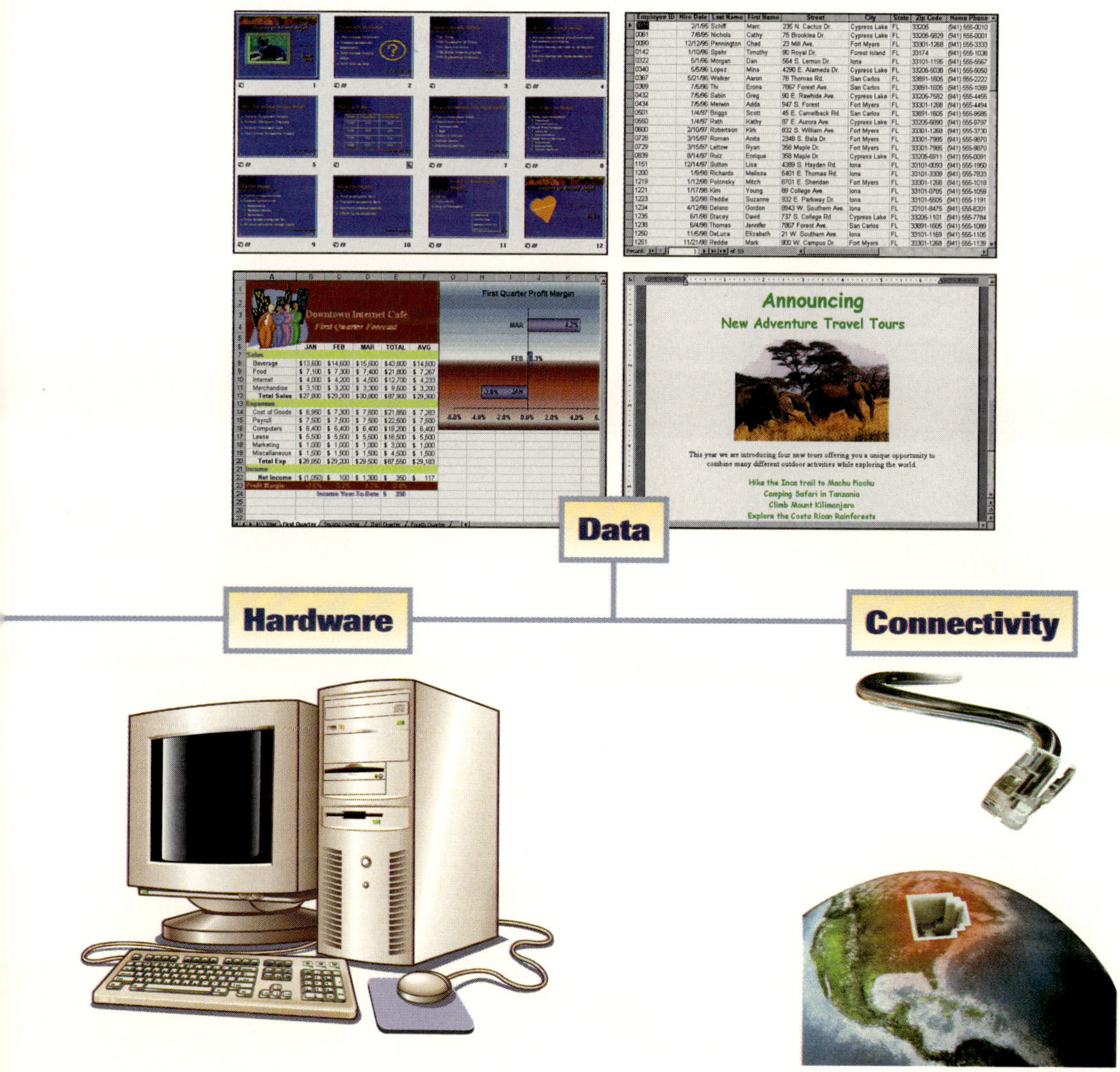

Information Systems

An information system has five parts: people, procedures, software, hardware, and data.

When you think of a microcomputer, perhaps you think of just the equipment itself. That is, you think of the monitor or the keyboard. There is more to it than that. The way to think about a microcomputer is as part of an information system. An **information system** has five parts: *people, procedures, software, hardware,* and *data.* (See Figure 1-1.)

- **People:** It is easy to overlook people as one of the five parts of a microcomputer system. Yet that is what microcomputers are all about—making **people,** end users like yourself, more productive.
- **Procedures: Procedures** are rules or guidelines for people to follow when using software, hardware, and data. Typically, these procedures are documented in manuals written by computer specialists. Software and hardware manufacturers provide manuals with their products.
- **Software: Software** is another name for a program or programs. A **program** consists of the step-by-step instructions that tell the computer how to do its work. The purpose of software is to convert *data* (unprocessed facts) into *information* (processed facts).
- **Hardware:** The **hardware** consists of the equipment: keyboard, mouse, monitor, system unit, and other devices. Hardware is controlled by software. It actually processes the data to create information.

FIGURE 1-1
The five parts of an information system

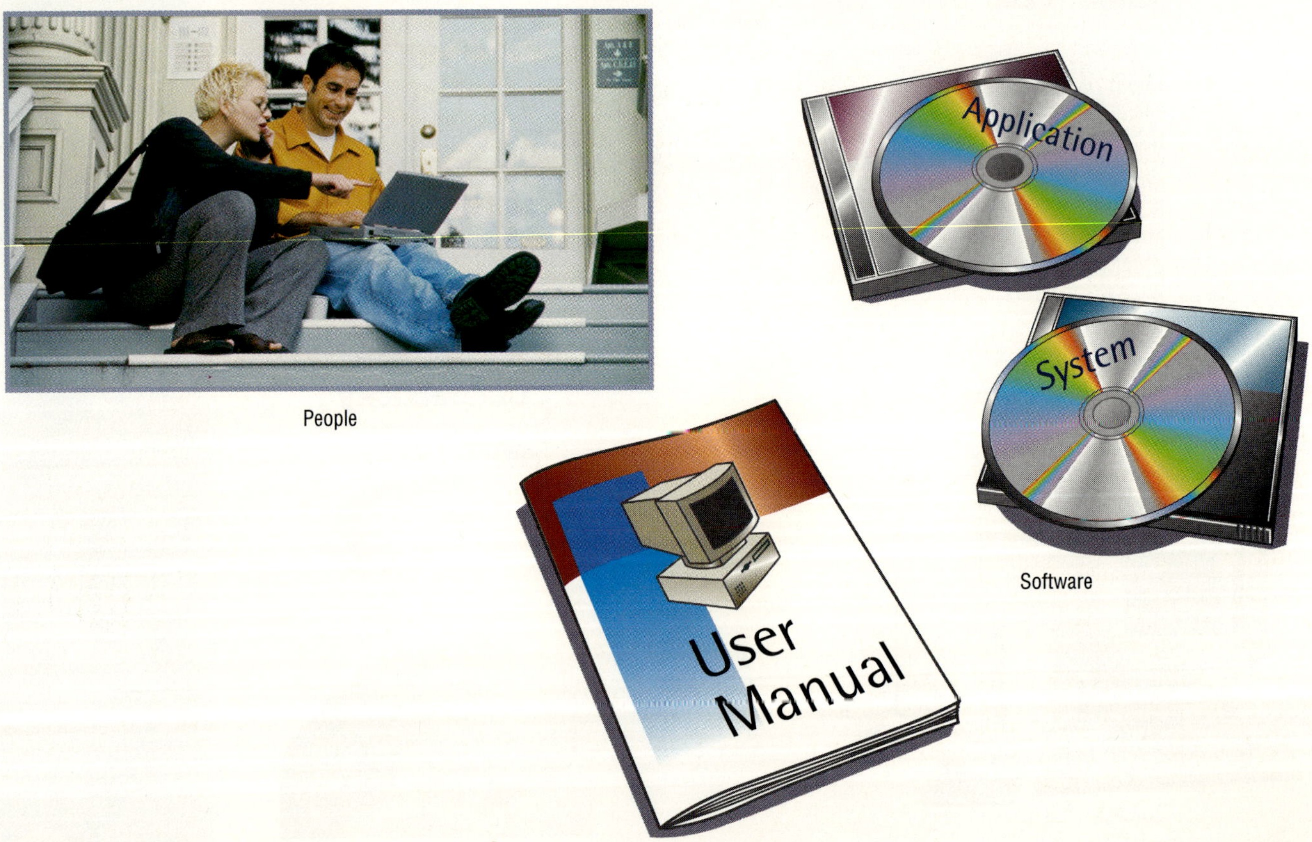

People

Software

Procedures

- **Data: Data** consists of the raw, unprocessed facts, including text, numbers, images, and sounds. Examples of raw facts are hours you worked and your pay rate. After data is processed through the computer, it is usually called **information.** An example of such information is the total wages owed you for a week's work.

In large computer systems, there are specialists who deal with writing procedures, developing software, and capturing data. In microcomputer systems, however, end users often perform these operations. To be a competent end user, you must understand the essentials of **information technology (IT),** including software, hardware, and data.

CONCEPT CHECK

✔ What are the five parts of an information system?

✔ To be a competent end user, you must understand the essentials of information technology, including ________, ________, and ________.

Data

Hardware

People

People are the most important part of an information system. Examples include people in entertainment, medicine, education, and business.

Although easy to overlook, people are surely the most important part of any information system. Our lives are touched every day by computers and information systems. Many times the contact is direct and obvious such as when we create documents using a word processing program or when we connect to the Internet.

Other times, the contact is not as obvious. Nonetheless, computers and information systems touch our lives hundreds of times every day. Consider just the following four examples. (See Figure 1-2.)

Entertainment

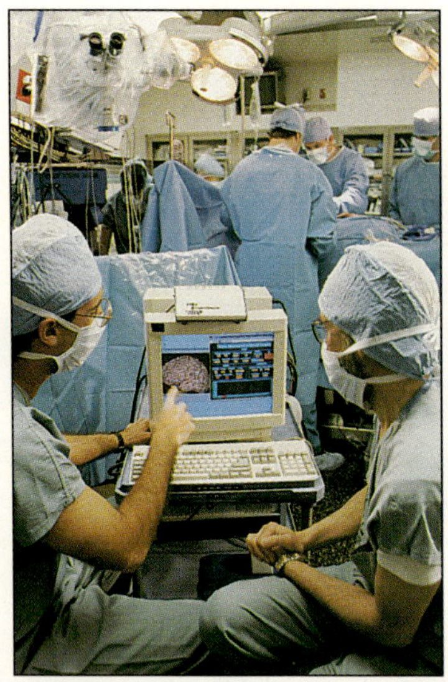

Medicine

Business

Education

FIGURE 1-2
Computers in entertainment, medicine, business, and education

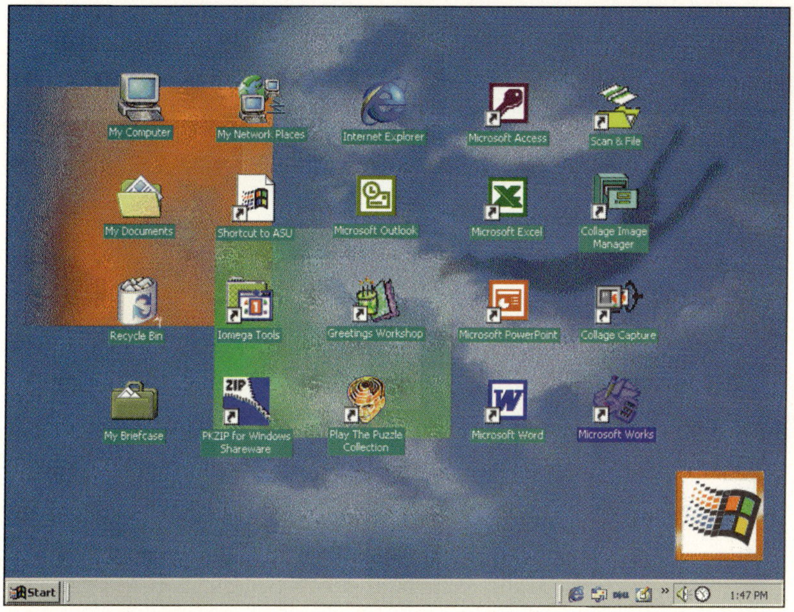

FIGURE 1-3
Windows 2000 operating system

Software

Software is of two kinds: system software and application software.

Software, as we mentioned, is another name for programs. Programs are the instructions that tell the computer how to process data into the form you want. In most cases, the words *software* and *programs* are interchangeable.

There are two major kinds of software—*system software* and *application software.* You can think of application software as the kind you use. Think of system software as the kind the computer uses.

System Software

The user interacts with application software. **System software** enables the application software to interact with the computer hardware. System software is "background" software that helps the computer manage its own internal resources.

The most important system software program is the **operating system,** which interacts with the application software and the computer. The operating system handles such details as running ("executing") programs, storing data and programs, and processing data. Windows 2000 is one of the best-known operating systems for today's microcomputer users. (See Figure 1-3.)

Application Software

Application software might be described as "end-user" software. Application software performs useful work on general-purpose tasks such as word processing and data analysis.

There are certain general-purpose programs or basic applications. These programs are widely used in nearly all career areas. They are the kind of programs you *have* to know to be considered computer competent. One of these basic applications is a browser to navigate, explore,

TIPS

Have you used the Internet? If so, then you probably already know how to use a browser. For those of you who do not, here are a few tips to get you started.

1. *Start browser.* Typically, all you need to do is double-click the browser's icon on the desktop.
2. *Enter URL.* In the browser's location box, type the URL (uniform resource locator, or address) of the Internet or Web location (site) that you want to visit.
3. *Press ENTER.* On your keyboard, press the ENTER key to connect to the site.
4. *Read and explore.* Once connected to the site, read the information displayed on your monitor. Click on underlined text to explore other locations.
5. *Close browser.* Once you are done exploring, click on your browser's CLOSE button.

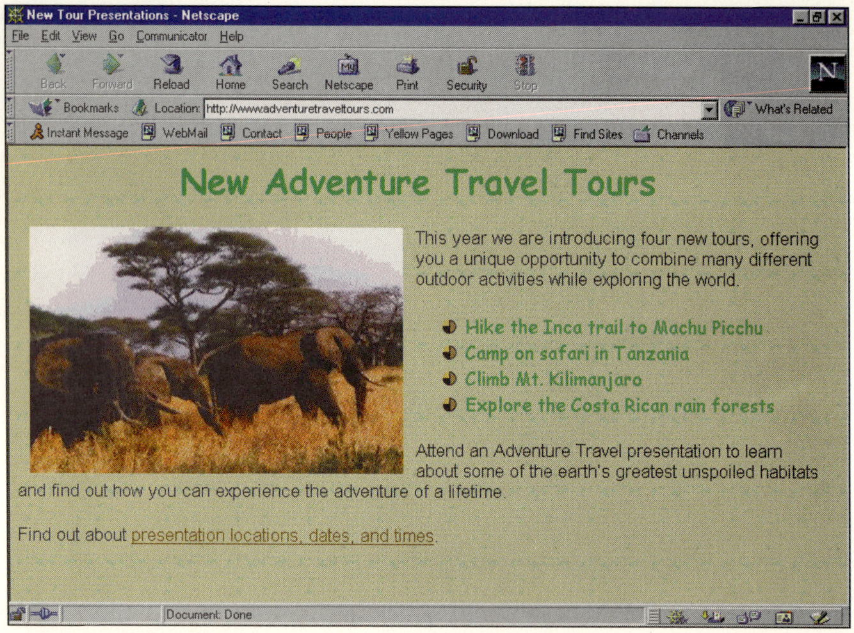

FIGURE 1-4
Browser (Netscape Navigator)

Type	Description
Word processor	Prepare written documents
Spreadsheet	Analyze and summarize numerical data
Database management system	Organize and manage data and information
Presentation graphics	Communicate a message or persuade other people
Browser	Navigate, explore, and find information on the Internet
Information manager	Maintain electronic calendars, address books, and to-do lists

FIGURE 1-5
Basic applications

and find information on the Internet. (See Figure 1-4.) The two most widely used browsers are Microsoft's Internet Explorer and Netscape's Navigator. For a summary of the basic applications, see Figure 1-5.

There are many other applications that are more specialized and widely used within certain career areas. They are the kind of programs you *should* know to be truly computer competent in the future. One of the most exciting applications is multimedia, which allows users to integrate video, music, voice, and graphics to create interactive presentations. For a summary of these specialized applications, see Figure 1-6.

CONCEPT CHECK

- ✔ Name the two major kinds of software.
- ✔ The most important system software program is the ________ ________.

Type	Description
Multimedia	Integrate video, music, voice, and graphics to create interactive presentations
Web publishers	Create interactive multimedia Web pages
Graphics programs	Create professional publications: draw, edit, and modify images
Virtual reality	Create realistic three-dimensional virtual or simulated environments
Artificial intelligence	Simulate human thought processes and actions
Project agers	Plan projects, schedule people, and control man- resources

FIGURE 1-6
Specialized applications

Hardware

Four types of computers are supercomputer, mainframe computer, minicomputer, and microcomputer. Microcomputer hardware consists of the system unit, input/output, secondary storage, and communications devices.

Computers are electronic devices that can follow instructions to accept input, process that input, and produce information. This book focuses principally on microcomputers. However, it is almost certain that you will come in contact, at least indirectly, with other types of computers.

Types of Computers

There are four types of computers: supercomputers, mainframe computers, minicomputers, and microcomputers.

- **Supercomputers:** The most powerful type of computer is the **supercomputer.** These machines are special, high-capacity computers used by very large organizations. For example, NASA uses supercomputers to track and control space explorations.
- **Mainframe computers:** These large computers occupy specially wired, air-conditioned rooms. Although not nearly as powerful as supercomputers, **mainframe computers** are capable of great processing speeds and data storage. (See Figure 1-7.) For example, insurance companies use mainframes to process information about millions of policyholders.

FIGURE 1-7
Mainframe computer (IBM ES/9000)

- **Minicomputers:** Also known as **midrange computers, minicomputers** are desk-sized machines. Medium-sized companies or departments of large companies typically use them for specific purposes. For example, production departments use minicomputers to monitor certain manufacturing processes and assembly-line operations.
- **Microcomputers:** Although the least powerful, **microcomputers** are the most widely used and fastest-growing type of computer. Apple recently introduced their iMac computers. (See Figure 1-8.) Categories of microcomputer include *desktop, notebook,* and *personal digital assistants.* **Desktop computers** are small enough to fit on top of or alongside a desk yet are too big to carry around. **Notebook computers** are portable, weigh between 4 and 10 pounds, and fit into most briefcases. (See Figure 1-9.) **Personal digital assistants (PDAs)** are also known as **palmtop computers** or **handheld computers.** They combine pen input, writing recognition, personal organizational tools, and communications capabilities in a very small package. (See Figure 1-10.)

Microcomputer Hardware

ON THE WEB EXPLORATIONS

Intel is a leading manufacturer of microprocessors. To learn more about this company, visit its Web site at
http://www.intel.com

Hardware for a microcomputer system consists of a variety of different devices. See Figure 1-11 for a typical system. This physical equipment falls into four basic categories: system unit, input/output, secondary storage, and communication devices. Because we discuss hardware in detail later in this book, we will present just a quick overview here.

- **System unit:** The **system unit** is electronic circuitry housed within the computer cabinet. (See Figure 1-12.) Two important components of the system unit are the *microprocessor* and *memory.* The **microprocessor** controls and manipulates data to produce information. **Memory,** also known as **primary storage** or **random access memory (RAM),** holds data and program instructions for processing the data. It also holds the processed information before it is output. Memory is sometimes referred to as *temporary storage* because its contents will typically be lost if the electrical power to the computer is disrupted.
- **Input/output devices: Input devices** translate data and programs that humans can understand into a form that the computer can process.

FIGURE 1-8
Colorful computers from Apple (iMac)

FIGURE 1-9
Desktop and notebook computers

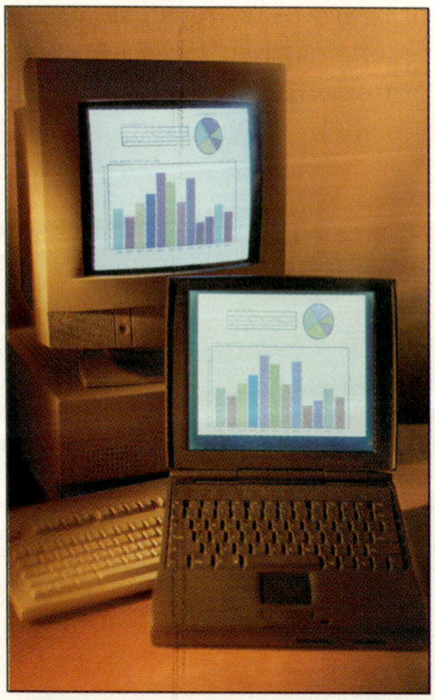

FIGURE 1-10
Personal digital assistant (Palm Pilot)

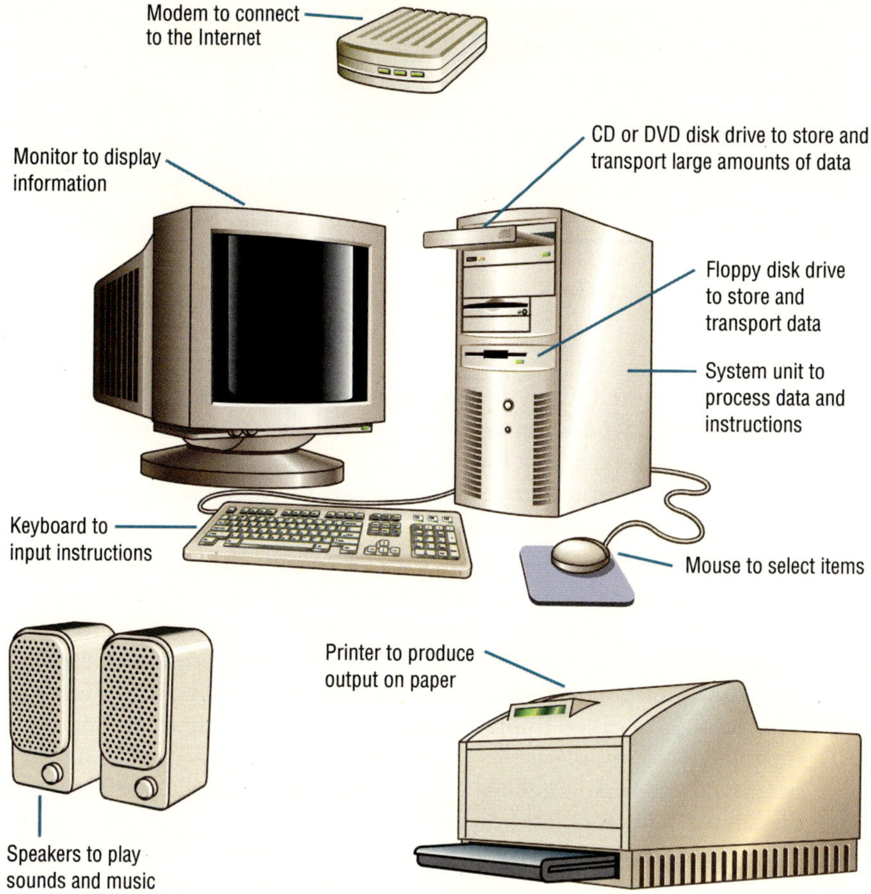

FIGURE 1-11
Microcomputer system

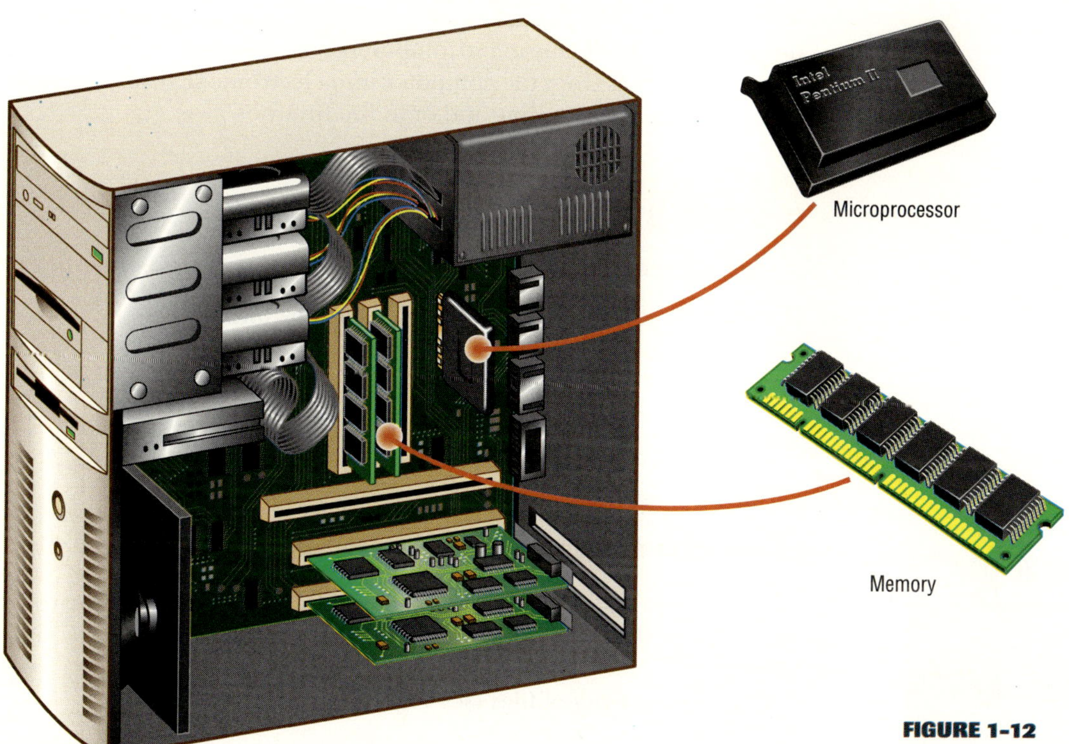

FIGURE 1-12
System unit

FIGURE 1-13
Keyboard and mouse

The most common input devices are the **keyboard** and the **mouse.** (See Figure 1-13.) **Output devices** translate the processed information from the computer into a form that humans can understand. The most common output devices are **monitors** or **video display screens** (see Figure 1-14) and **printers.**

FIGURE 1-14
Monitor

- **Secondary storage devices:** Unlike memory, **secondary storage devices** hold data and programs even after electrical power to the computer system has been turned off. The most important kinds of secondary media are *floppy, hard,* and *optical disks.* **Floppy disks** are widely used to store and transport data from one computer to another. (See Figure 1-15.) They are called floppy because data is stored on a very thin flexible, or floppy, plastic disk. **Hard disks** are typically used to store programs and very large data files. Using a rigid metallic platter, hard disks have a much greater capacity and are able to access information much faster than floppy disks. **Optical disks** use laser technology and have the greatest capacity. (See Figure 1-16.) The two basic types of optical disks are **compact discs (CDs)** and **digital versatile** (or **video) discs (DVDs).**
- **Communications devices: Communications hardware** sends and receives data and programs from one computer or secondary storage device to another. Many microcomputers use a **modem** to convert electronic signals from the computer into electronic signals that can travel over a telephone line and onto the Internet.

FIGURE 1-15
A 3½" floppy disk

FIGURE 1-16
An optical disk

CONCEPT CHECK

✔ List the four types of computers.

✔ Name the four categories of microcomputer hardware.

Data

Data is stored in document, worksheet, database, and presentation files.

Data is used to describe facts about something. When stored electronically in files, data can be used directly as input for the information system.

Four common types of files (see Figure 1-17) are:

- **Document files,** created by word processors to save documents such as memos, term papers, and letters.

ON THE WEB EXPLORATIONS

Toshiba is a leader in the development of DVD. To learn more about this company, visit its Web site at **http://www.toshiba.com**

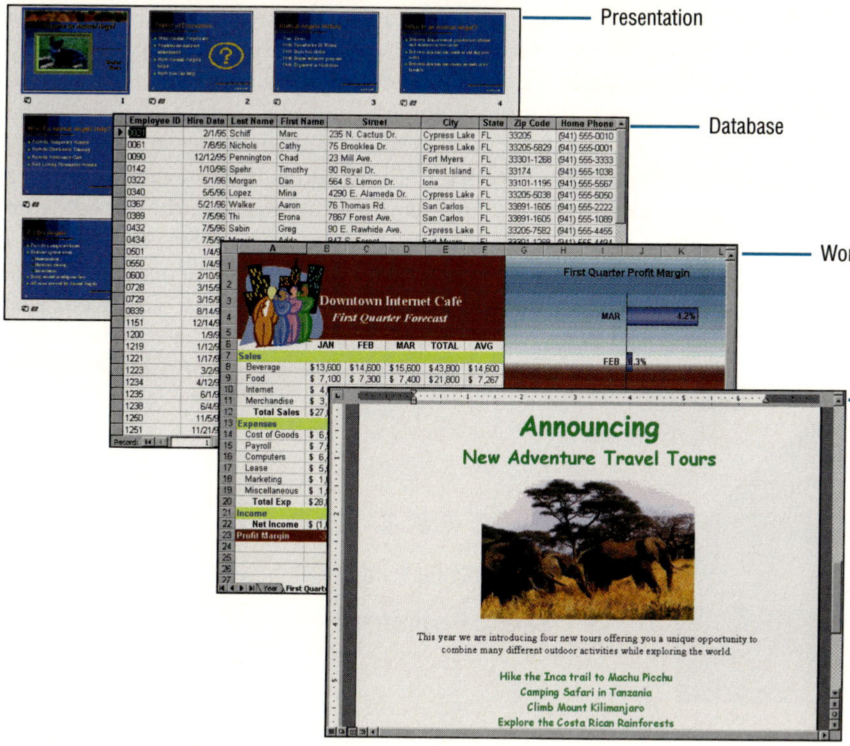

FIGURE 1-17
Four types of files: document, worksheet, database, and presentation

- **Worksheet files,** created by electronic spreadsheets to analyze things like budgets and to predict sales.
- **Database files,** typically created by database management programs to contain highly structured and organized data. For example, an employee database file might contain all the workers' names, social security numbers, job titles, and other related pieces of information.
- **Presentation files,** created by presentation graphics programs to save presentation materials. For example, a file might contain audience handouts, speaker notes, and electronic slides.

CONCEPT CHECK

✔ What is data?

✔ Name four file types in which data can be stored.

Connectivity and the Internet

Connectivity is the microcomputer's ability to communicate with other computers and information sources. The Internet is the largest network in the world.

Connectivity is the capability of your microcomputer to share information with other computers. (See Figure 1-18.) Data and information can be sent over telephone lines or cable and through the air. Thus, your microcomputer can be *connected* to other computers. It can connect you to the Internet and to many computerized data banks and other sources of information that lie well beyond your desk.

FIGURE 1-18
Computers connected together can share information

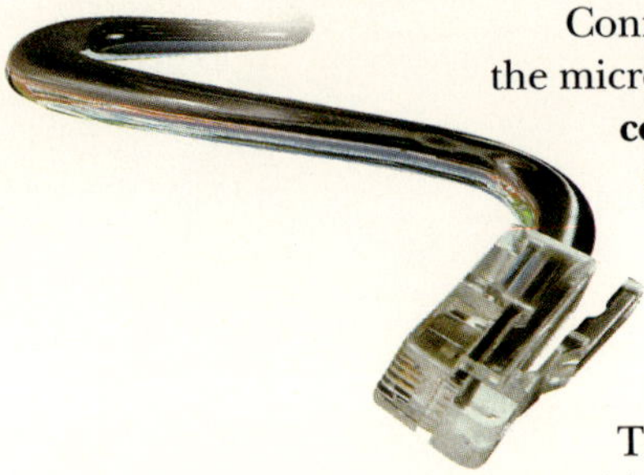

Connectivity is a very significant development, for it expands the uses of the microcomputer severalfold. Central to the concept of connectivity is the **computer network.** A network is a communications system connecting two or more computers. Networks connect people as close as the next office and as far away as halfway around the world.

The largest network in the world is the **Internet.** It is like a giant highway that connects you to millions of other people and organizations located throughout the world. (See Figure 1-19.) The Internet is a huge computer network available to nearly everyone with a microcomputer and a means to connect to it. The **Web,** also known as the **World Wide Web** or **WWW,** is an Internet service that provides a multimedia interface to numerous resources available on the Internet.

FIGURE 1-19
The Internet connects millions of people worldwide

CONCEPT CHECK

- ✔ Define connectivity.
- ✔ What is the Internet?

A LOOK TO THE FUTURE

Computer competency is understanding the rules and the power of microcomputers. Competency lets you take advantage of increasingly productive software, hardware, and the connectivity revolution that are expanding the microcomputer's capabilities.

The purpose of this book is to help you be computer competent not only in the present but also in the future. Having competency requires your having the knowledge and understanding of the rules and the power of the microcomputer. This will enable you to benefit from three important information technology developments: more powerful software, more powerful hardware, and connectivity to outside information resources. It will also help you remain computer competent and continue to learn in the future.

Powerful Software

The software now available can do an extraordinary number of tasks and help you in an endless number of ways. More and more employers are expecting the people they hire to be able to use it. Basic application software and system software are discussed in Chapters 2 and 3. More advanced application software is presented in Chapter 9.

Powerful Hardware

Microcomputers are now much more powerful than they used to be. Indeed, the newer models have the speed and power of room-size computers of only a few years ago.

continues

However, despite the rapid change of specific equipment, their essential features remain unchanged. Thus, the competent end user should focus on these features. Chapters 4 through 6 explain what you need to know about hardware: the central processing unit, input/output devices, and secondary storage. A Buyer's Guide and an Upgrader's Guide are presented at the end of this book for those considering the purchase or upgrade of a microcomputer system.

Connectivity, Internet, and Web

No longer are microcomputers and competent end users bound by the surface of the desk. Now they can reach past the desk and link with other computers to share data, programs, and information. The Internet and the Web are considered by most to be the two most important technologies for the 21st century. Accordingly, we devote Chapters 7 and 8 to discussing connectivity, communications, the Internet, and the Web.

Security and Privacy

What about people? Is there a downside to all these technological advances? Experts agree that we as a society must be careful about the potential of technology to negatively impact our personal privacy and security. Additionally, we need to be aware of potential physical and mental health risks associated with using technology. Finally, we need to be aware of negative effects on our environment caused by the manufacture of computer-related products. Thus, Chapter 10 explores each of these critical issues in detail.

Changing Times

Are the times changing any faster now than they ever have? Most people think so. Those who were alive when radios, cars, and airplanes were being introduced certainly lived through some dramatic changes. Has technology made our own times even more dynamic? Whatever the answer, it is clear we live in a fast-paced age. The Evolution of the Computer Age section presented at the end of this book tracks the major developments since computers were first introduced.

Most businesses have become aware that they must adapt to changing technology or be left behind. Many organizations are now making formal plans to keep track of technology and implement it in their competitive strategies. Nearly every corporation in the world has a presence on the Internet. Delivery services such as Federal Express and UPS provide customers with the ability to personally track the delivery of their packages. Retail stores such as JCPenney and Wal-Mart provide catalog support and sales. Banks such as Wells Fargo and Citibank support home banking and electronic commerce. You can even purchase tickets to music, theater, and sporting events on the Internet.

Clearly, such changes do away with some jobs—those of many bank tellers and cashiers, for example. However, they create opportunities for other people. New technology requires people who are truly capable of working with it. These are not the people who think every piece of equipment is so simple they can just turn it on and use it. Nor are they those who think each new machine is a potential disaster. In other words, new technology needs people who are not afraid to learn it and are able to manage it. The real issue, then, is not how to make technology better. Rather, it is how to integrate the technology with people.

After reading this book, you will be in a very favorable position compared with many other people in industry today. You will learn not only the basics of hardware, software, connectivity, the Internet, and the Web. You will also learn the most *current* technology. You will therefore be able to use these tools to your advantage—to be a winner.

VISUAL SUMMARY Your Future and Computer Competency

INFORMATION SYSTEMS

The way to think about a microcomputer is to realize that it is one part of an **information system.**

Five parts of an information system:

1. **People** are an often-overlooked part. The purpose of information systems is to make people more productive.
2. **Procedures** are rules or guidelines to follow when using software, hardware, and data.
3. **Software** (**programs**) provides step-by-step instructions to control the computer.
4. **Hardware** consists of the physical equipment.
5. **Data** consists of unprocessed facts including text, numbers, images, and sound. **Information** is processed data.

PEOPLE

People are the most important part of an information system. People are touched hundreds of times daily by computers.

Some examples:

Entertainment

Medicine

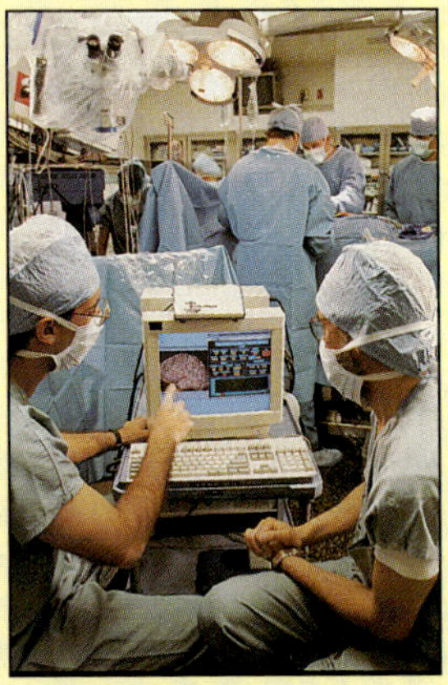

Education

Business

To prepare for your future as a competent end user, you need to understand the basic parts of an information system: people, procedures, software, hardware, and data. Also you need to understand how connectivity through the Internet and the Web expands the role of technology in our lives.

SOFTWARE

Software or **programs** consist of system and application software.

System Software

System software—*background* software that manages internal resources. An example is an operating system such as Windows 2000.

Application Software

Application software—software that performs useful work on general-purpose problems. Basic applications include:

- **Word processors** to prepare written documents.
- **Spreadsheet** to analyze and summarize numerical data.
- **Database management system** to organize and manage data.
- **Presentation graphics** to communicate or persuade.

Many other more specialized applications are used within certain career paths.

HARDWARE

Hardware is the physical equipment in an information system.

Types of Computers

There are four types of computers:

- **Supercomputers**—the most powerful.
- **Mainframe**—used by large companies.
- **Minicomputers**—also known as **midrange computers.**
- **Microcomputers**—the fastest growing. Categories include **desktop, notebook,** and **personal digital assistant.**

Microcomputer Hardware

The four categories of devices are:

- The **system unit** contains the electronic circuitry, including the CPU and memory.
- **Input/output devices** are translation units that convert human instruction into machine-readable processes.
- **Secondary storage devices** store data and programs. Typical media include **floppy, hard,** and **optical disks.**
- **Communication devices** send and receive data and programs from one computer to another. A **modem** is widely used to connect to the Internet.

DATA

Data describes something and is typically stored electronically in a file.

Common types of files are:

Document

Worksheet

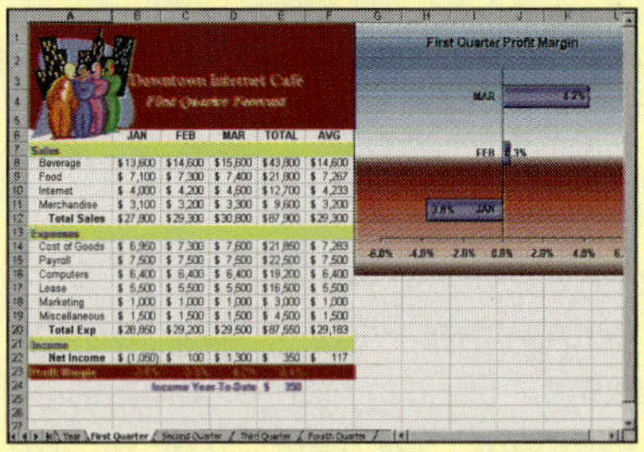

Database

Presentation

CONNECTIVITY AND THE INTERNET

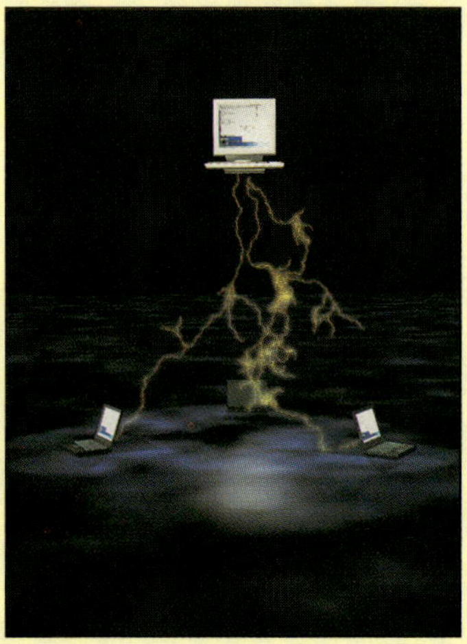

Connectivity

Connectivity is a concept describing the ability of end users to tap into resources well beyond their desktops. Computer **networks** are connected computers that share data and resources.

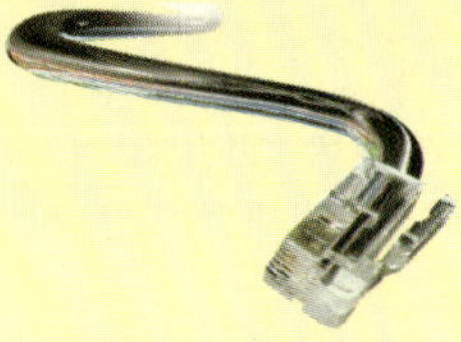

Internet

The **Internet** is the world's largest computer network. The **World Wide Web (WWW)** is an Internet service that provides a multimedia interface to resources available on the Internet.

Key Terms

application software (7)
communications hardware (12)
compact disc (CD) (12)
computer network (14)
connectivity (13)
data (5)
database file (13)
desktop computer (10)
digital versatile (or video) disc (DVD) (12)
document file (12)
floppy disk (12)
handheld computer (10)
hard disk (12)
hardware (4)
information (5)
information system (4)
information technology (IT) (5)
input device (10)
Internet (14)
keyboard (12)
mainframe computer (9)
memory (10)
microcomputer (10)
microprocessor (10)
midrange computer (10)
minicomputer (10)
modem (12)
monitor (12)
mouse (12)
notebook computer (10)
operating system (7)
optical disk (12)
output device (12)
palmtop computer (10)
people (4)
personal digital assistant (PDA) (10)
presentation file (13)
primary storage (10)
printer (12)
procedures (4)
program (4)
random access memory (RAM) (10)
secondary storage device(12)
software (4)
supercomputer (9)
system software (7)
system unit (10)
video display screen (12)
Web (14)
worksheet file (13)
World Wide Web (WWW) (14)

Chapter Review

LEVEL 1

Reviewing Facts and Terms

Matching

Match each numbered item with the most closely related lettered item. Write your answers in the spaces provided.

1. The largest network in the world. ____
2. Portable data storage made from very thin, flexible plastic. ____
3. Computers small enough to fit on top of or alongside a desk yet too large to carry around. ____
4. Used to describe facts about something. ____
5. Holds data and program instructions for processing data. ____
6. Most important system software program, interacting between the application software and the computer. ____
7. Midrange, desk-sized computers. ____
8. The capability of your microcomputer to share information with other computers. ____
9. "End-user" software used for general-purpose tasks. ____
10. Translates the processed information from the computer into a form that humans can understand. ____
11. It has five parts: people, procedures, software, hardware, and data. ____
12. Large, powerful computers capable of great processing speeds and data storage. ____

a. Application software
b. CD
c. Communications hardware
d. Computer network
e. Connectivity
f. Data
g. Desktop computer
h. Floppy disk
i. Hard disk
j. Information system
k. Input device
l. Internet
m. Mainframe
n. Memory
o. Microcomputer
p. Microprocessor
q. Minicomputer
r. Operating system
s. Optical disk
t. Output device

13. A communications system connecting two or more computers. ____
14. Secondary storage device that uses laser technology.
15. Controls and manipulates data to produce information.
16. Compact disc.
17. Translates data and programs that humans can understand into a form that the computer can process. ____
18. Sends and receives data and programs from one computer or secondary storage device to another. ____
19. Secondary storage device typically used to store programs and very large data files. ____
20. Most widely used and fastest-growing type of computer. ____

True/False

In the spaces provided, write T or F to indicate whether the statement is true or false.

1. Microcomputers are common tools in all areas of life. ____
2. Hardware consists of a monitor, a keyboard, and software. ____
3. Windows 2000 is an application program. ____
4. Memory is also known as primary storage. ____
5. A modem is used to send electronic signals over telephone lines. ____

Multiple Choice

Circle the letter of the correct answer.

1. Computers are electronic devices that accept instructions, process input, and produce:
   - **a.** information
   - **b.** prewritten programs
   - **c.** data
   - **d.** end users
   - **e.** system software
2. High-capacity computers used primarily by very large organizations or for research purposes are:
   - **a.** microcomputers
   - **b.** minicomputers
   - **c.** mainframes
   - **d.** supercomputers
   - **e.** personalcomputers
3. The microprocessor is located in the:
   - **a.** hard disk
   - **b.** system unit
   - **c.** memory
   - **d.** monitor
   - **e.** keyboard

4. Also called *temporary storage,* its contents will be lost if electrical power is disrupted or cut off:
   - **a.** secondary storage
   - **b.** basic tools
   - **c.** memory
   - **d.** operating system
   - **e.** hard disk
5. Files containing highly structured and organized data are:
   - **a.** documents
   - **b.** worksheets
   - **c.** databases
   - **d.** graphics
   - **e.** communications

Completion

Complete each statement in the spaces provided.

1. Microcomputer ________, the physical equipment, falls into four categories: the system unit, input/output, secondary storage, and communication devices.
2. Also known as midrange computers, ________ are frequently used by departments within larger organizations.
3. ________ are guidelines or rules to follow when using software, hardware, and data.
4. ________ storage devices are used to store data and programs even after electrical power has been turned off.
5. ________ are application software programs used to navigate, explore, and find information on the Internet.

Reviewing Concepts

LEVEL 2

Open-Ended

On a separate sheet of paper, respond to each question and statement.

1. Describe the five parts of an information system.
2. How would you distinguish between system software and application software?
3. Compare the four types of computers.
4. What is the difference between memory and secondary storage?
5. What are connectivity, the Internet, and the Web?

Concept Mapping

On a separate sheet of paper, draw a concept map or flowchart showing how the following terms are related. Show all relationships. Include any additional terms you can think of.

application software	desktop computer	optical disk
computer	document file	output device
computer network	floppy disk	hardware
connectivity	hard disk	information system
data	notebook	input device
database file	operating system	mainframe

memory	minicomputer	palmtop computer
microcomputer	monitor	people
microprocessor	mouse	software

Critical Thinking Questions and Projects

LEVEL 3

Read each exercise and answer the related questions on a separate sheet of paper.

1. *Your reasons for learning computing:* How are you already using computer technology? What's happened in the computer-related world in the last six months that you might have read about or seen on television? How are companies using computers to stay on the cutting edge? These are some questions you might discuss with classmates to see why computers are an exciting part of life.

   You might also consider the reasons why you want to gain computer competency. Imagine your dream career. How do you think microcomputers, from what you already know, can help you do the work you want to do? What kind of after-hours interests do you have? Assuming you could afford it, how could a microcomputer bring new skills or value to those interests?

2. *The Internet and the Web:* The Internet and Web are the most exciting connectivity developments today. If you have used the Internet or the Web, discuss your experiences by describing what you used it for, what you liked about it, and what you did not like. If you have not used the Internet or the Web, do you think you will in the near future? What would you use it for?

3. *Privacy and security:* Computer technology offers unlimited opportunities and challenges. We can do so many things faster and better. We can instantly connect to and communicate with people around the world. But have you ever thought about the other side of the coin? Will all of the changes be positive? Will everyone benefit? Discuss these issues and any others that come to mind.

On the Web Exercises

1. Virtual Shopping Malls

Like any community, the Internet community has shopping malls. Visit our Web site at http://www.mhhe.com/cit/concepts/oleary2000-2001/webex1.html to link to one of the most popular virtual malls. Browse through the mall, find a product that you are familiar with, and print out the information provided on that item. Write a paragraph describing how the prices, services, and selection of the virtual mall compare with those of a traditional mall in your community.

2. Personal Digital Assistants

PDAs are becoming more and more popular with professionals in all areas. They are widely used to store addresses, track appointments, and much more. Learn more about PDAs by connecting to the Yahoo site at http://www.yahoo.com. Look at the subject area "Computers and Internet: Hardware: PDAs" or search the key word "PDA." Print out the page of search results that you find. Follow several links to learn about the features of PDAs and then write a paragraph on the abilities of PDAs and how they differ from desktop and portable computers.

3. Virtual Libraries

It might surprise you to learn that you can visit libraries on the Web where you can browse through the stacks, research selected topics, and check out books. Several virtual libraries have *e-texts,* which are entire books on computer, that anyone can download and use. Visit our Web site at http://www.mhhe.com/cit/concepts/oleary2000-2001/webex1.html to link to one of these libraries. Find a text on a topic that interests you, print out its first page, and write a paragraph on the benefits and shortfalls of using virtual libraries as a resource for your school papers.

4. Ticket Master

Some of the hottest sites on the Web offer the latest music news, present live concerts, and provide updates on your favorite band. Visit our Web site at http://www.mhhe.com/cit/concepts/oleary2000-2001/webex1.html to link to one of the most popular music sites. Once connected to that site, check out your favorite band and print out its tour dates or information about its latest album. Write a paragraph describing how you located the information and discuss how the band could better use the Internet to promote its music.

CHAPTER 2

Application Software

COMPETENCIES

After you have read this chapter, you should be able to:

1. **Explain the features common to most types of software.**
2. **Describe word processors.**
3. **Describe spreadsheets.**
4. **Describe database management systems.**
5. **Describe presentation graphics.**
6. **Describe software suites and integrated software.**

Not long ago, trained specialists were required to perform many of the operations you can now perform with a microcomputer. Computer scientists surfed the Internet and created Web pages. Secretaries used typewriters to create professional-looking business correspondence. Market analysts used calculators to project sales. Graphic artists drew by hand. Data processing clerks created and stored files of records on large computers. Now you can do all these tasks—and many others—with a microcomputer

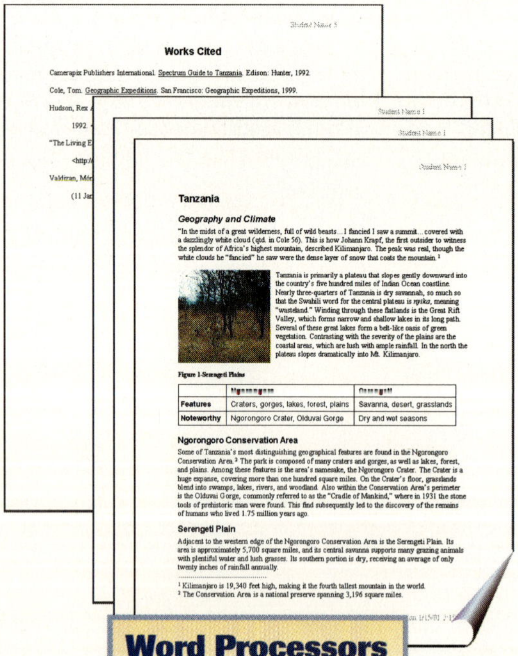

Word Processors
Create documents

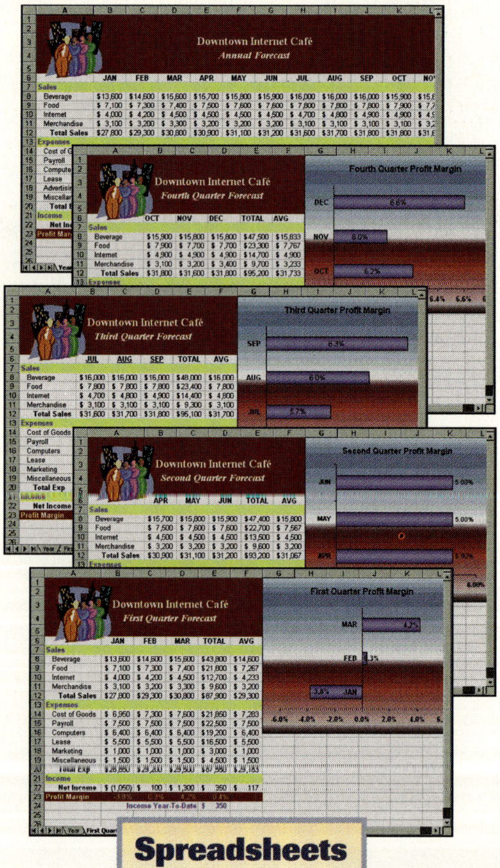

Spreadsheets
Analyze data

and the appropriate application software.

Think of the microcomputer as an *electronic* tool. You may not consider yourself very good at typing, calculating, organizing, presenting, or managing information. A microcomputer, however, can help you to do all these things—and much more. All it takes is the right kinds of software—system software and application software.

System software can be thought of as "background" software. It is a collection of programs that includes the operating system. Application software can be thought of as programs that perform "useful" work or tasks such as typing and calculating. Competent end users need to understand the capabilities of basic application software, which includes word processors, spreadsheets, database management systems, and presentation programs.

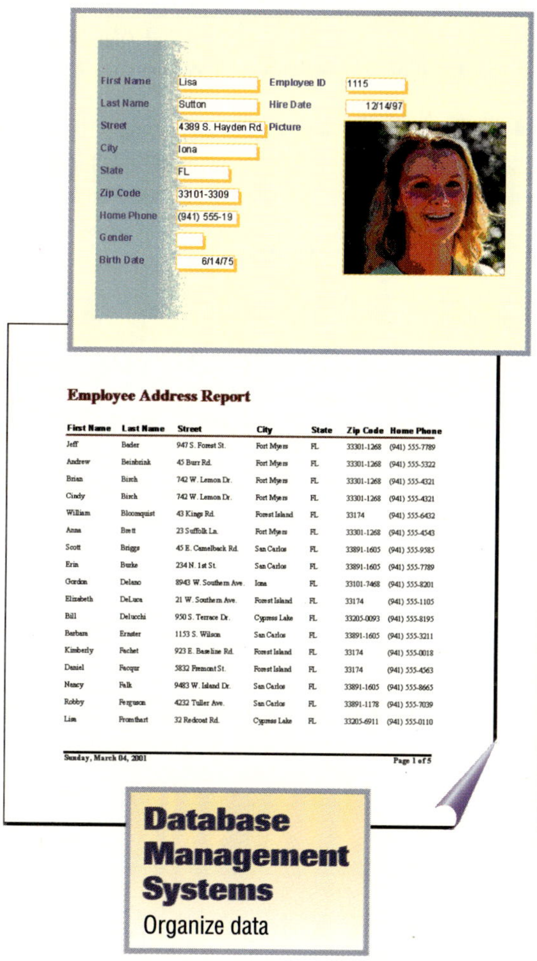

Database Management Systems
Organize data

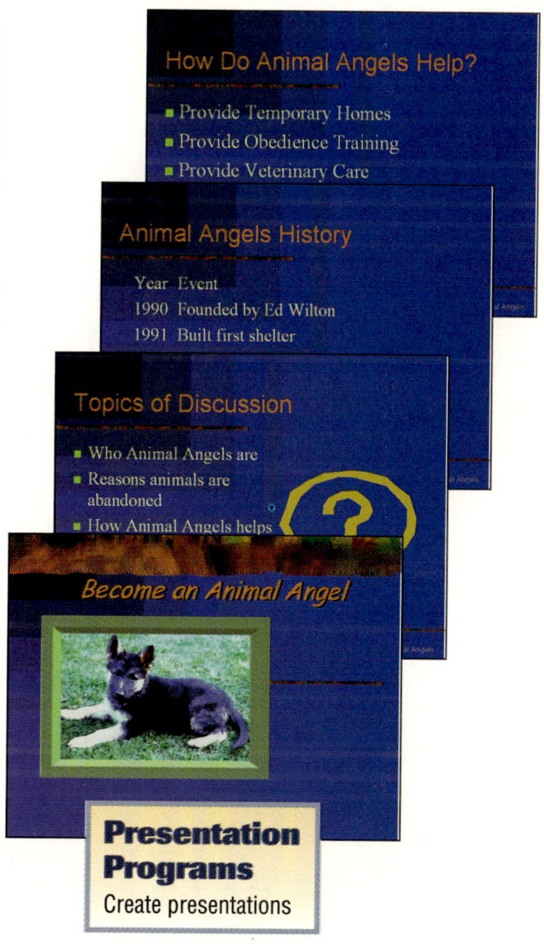

Presentation Programs
Create presentations

General-Purpose Applications

Some features are common to all kinds of applications.

Word processors, spreadsheets, database management systems, and presentation graphics are **general-purpose applications.** That is, they are designed to be used by many people to do the most common kinds of tasks. This is why they are also known as **basic applications.** These and many other types of applications and operating systems have common features. (See Figure 2-1.) The following are the most important.

FIGURE 2-1
Features

Window	Rectangular area that contains information and/or applications
Menus	Lists of commands
Toolbars	Series of buttons and menus representing various commands
Help	Source for reference information and assistance

Windows

A **window** is simply a rectangular area that can contain a document, program, or message. (Do not confuse the term *window* with the various versions of Microsoft's Windows operating systems, which are programs.) Many operating systems and application programs use windows to display information and request input. More than one window can be opened and displayed on the computer screen at one time. For example, one window might contain a browser, another a word processing program, and another a graphic image. Windows can generally be resized, moved, and closed.

Menus

Almost all software packages have **menus** to present commands. Typically, the menus are displayed in a menu bar at the top of the screen. When one of the menu items is selected, a pull-down menu appears. This is a list of commands associated with the selected menu.

Toolbars

Toolbars typically are below the menu bar. They contain buttons and menus that provide quick access to commonly used commands. The **standard toolbar** and the **formatting toolbar** are common to most applications.

Help

For most application packages, one of the commands on the menu bar is **Help.** When selected, the help options appear. These options typically include a table of contents, a search feature to locate reference information about specific commands, and access to special learning features such as tutorials and step-by-step instructions. Additionally, most applications have **context-sensitive help.** These help systems locate and display reference information directly related to the task you are performing.

To learn more about the common features of most software, study Figure 2-2.

TIPS Have you ever been working on a document when the power goes off? Your original document and all your recent changes are gone. Fortunately, most applications automatically save your work every few minutes to a temporary recovery or backup file.

Here are a few tips that might help you to quickly get back underway again.

1. *Restart your computer.*
2. *Restart the application.*
3. *Open the recovery file.* If the recovery file is not automatically opened, select the option to open it.
4. *Verify recovery file contents.* The recovery file should contain the document current up to the last automatic save. Compare the contents of the recovery file to the contents of the original file (if you have one).
5. *Save the recovery file.* If the recovery file contains the information you want, save it using the original file name or some other appropriate name.

CONCEPT CHECK

✔ What are general-purpose applications?

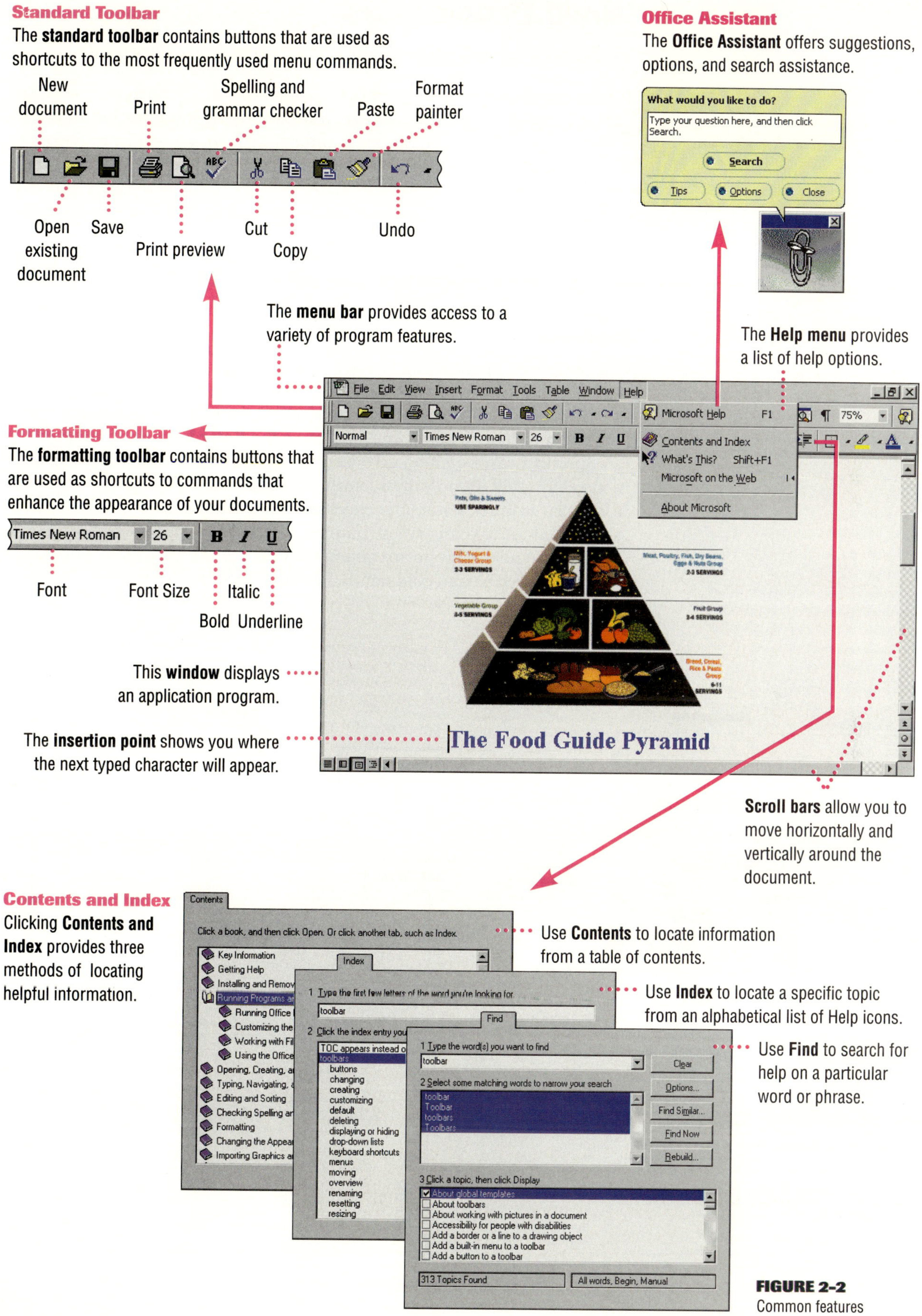

FIGURE 2-2 Common features

Word Processors

Word processing software is used to create text-based documents.

Word processing software creates text-based **documents** such as reports, letters, and memos. Word processors are one of the most flexible and widely used software tools. Students and researchers use word processors to create reports. Organizations of all types create newsletters to communicate with their members. Businesses create form letters to reach new and current customers. All types of people and organizations use word processors to create personalized Web pages.

The three most widely used word processing programs are Microsoft Word, Corel WordPerfect, and Lotus Word Pro.

Features

One basic word processing feature is **word wrap.** A word processor automatically moves the insertion point to the next line once the current line is full. As you type, the words "wrap around" to the next line. To begin a new paragraph or leave a blank line, you press the **Enter key.**

Spelling can be checked by running a **spelling checker** program. Incorrectly spelled words are identified and alternative spellings suggested. In a similar manner, a **grammar checker** will identify poor wording, excessively long sentences, and incorrect grammar.

You can quickly locate any character, word, or phrase in your document using the **search** or **find** commands. In addition, you can replace the located

Brochures

FIGURE 2-3

Letters

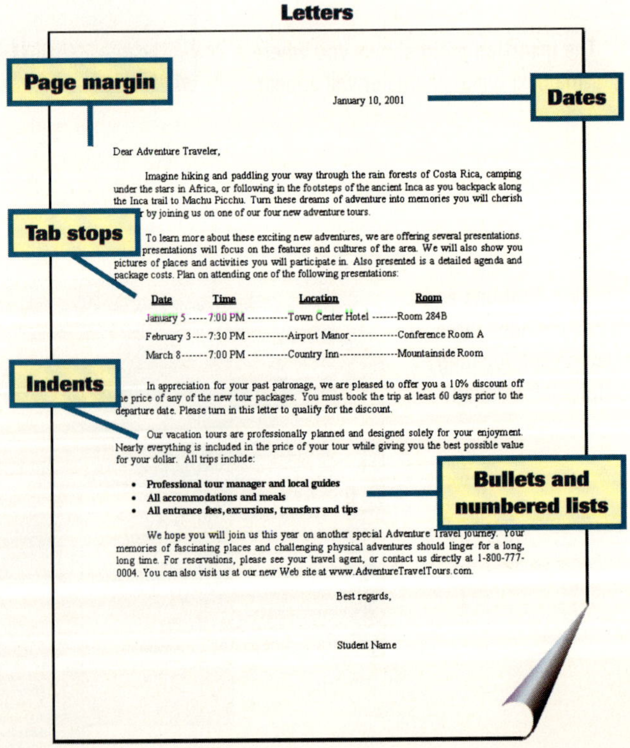

FIGURE 2-4

text with other text you specify using the **replace** command. For example, you could quickly locate each occurrence of the word *Chicago* and replace it with the word *Denver.*

Hypertext links, or **hyperlinks,** can be created to cross-reference information within the current document and between documents. Clicking on a hypertext link jumps your screen display to the specified location in the referenced document. This is most useful for viewing documents online. For example, if you cross-reference another chapter, you can add a hypertext link so the reader can jump to that chapter. Hypertext links can also reference sources on the Web.

Case

Assume that you have accepted a job as the advertising coordinator for a company called Adventure Travel. Your job is to create and coordinate the company's promotional materials, including brochures, form letters, travel reports, and the company Web page. To learn more about word processor features and how they could assist you as an advertising coordinator, see Figures 2-3 through 2-6.

CONCEPT CHECK

- ✔ What do word processors do?
- ✔ What are the three most widely used word processing programs?

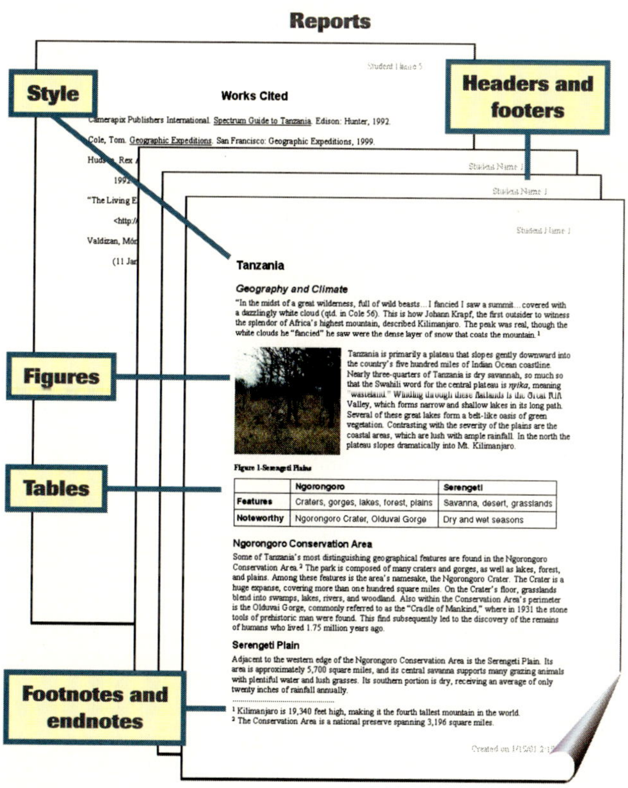

FIGURE 2-5

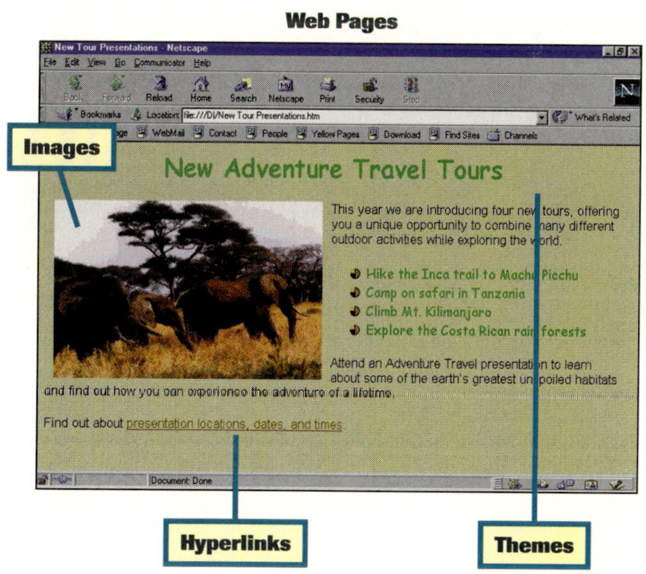

FIGURE 2-6

Spreadsheets

A spreadsheet is an electronic worksheet used to organize, manipulate, and graph data.

Spreadsheet programs organize, manipulate, and graph numeric information. Once used almost exclusively by accountants, spreadsheets are now widely used by people in nearly every profession. Teachers record students' grades. Students record their grades and calculate grade point averages. Financial analysts evaluate stock market trends. Personal trainers record the progress of their clients. Marketing professionals evaluate sales trends.

The three most widely used spreadsheet programs are Microsoft Excel, Corel Quattro Pro, and Lotus 1-2-3.

ON THE WEB EXPLORATIONS

Microsoft is one of the leaders in software development. To learn more about the company, visit its Web site at

http://www.microsoft.com

Features

Labels are often used to identify information in a worksheet. Usually a label is a word or symbol, such as a pound sign (#). A number in a cell is called a **value.** Labels and values can be displayed or formatted in different ways. For example, a label can be centered in the cell or positioned to the left or right. A value can be displayed to show decimal places, dollars, or percent (%). The number of decimal positions (if any) can be altered, and the width of columns can be changed.

Formulas are instructions for calculations. They calculate results using the number or numbers in referenced cells. For example, the formula C8 + C9 means add the value in C8 to the value in C9. **Functions** are prewritten

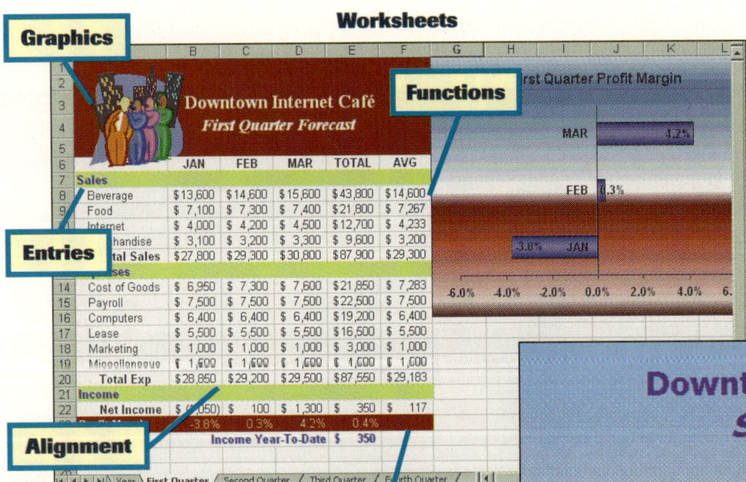

FIGURE 2-7

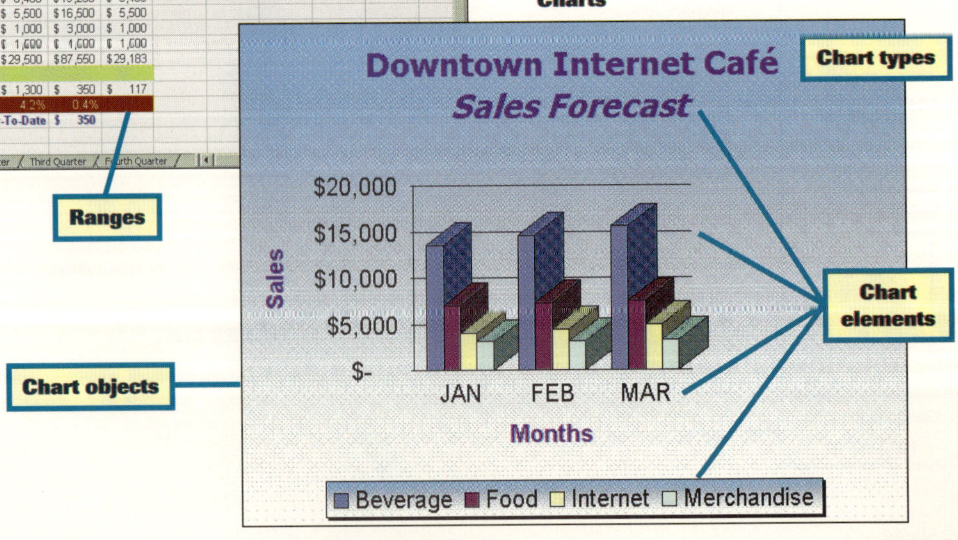

FIGURE 2-8

formulas that perform calculations automatically. For example, the function @SUM(C8:C11) adds all the values in the range of cells from C8 to C11.

If you change one or more numbers in your spreadsheet, all related formulas will recalculate automatically. Thus, you can substitute one value for another in a cell and observe the effect on other related cells in the spreadsheet. This is called **what-if analysis.**

To help visualize the data in your spreadsheets, you can create **analytical graphs** or **charts.** For example, you could display the numerical data in a worksheet as a pie chart, bar chart, or a line graph. The graphs automatically update when the data in the underlying worksheet changes.

Case

Assume that you have accepted a job as manager of the Downtown Internet Café. This café provides a variety of flavored coffees as well as Internet access. One of your responsibilities is to create a financial plan for the next year. To learn more about spreadsheet features and how they could assist you as a manager of an Internet café, see Figures 2-7 through 2-10.

CONCEPT CHECK

- ✔ What are spreadsheet programs?
- ✔ What are the three most widely used spreadsheet programs?

FIGURE 2-9

Workbook

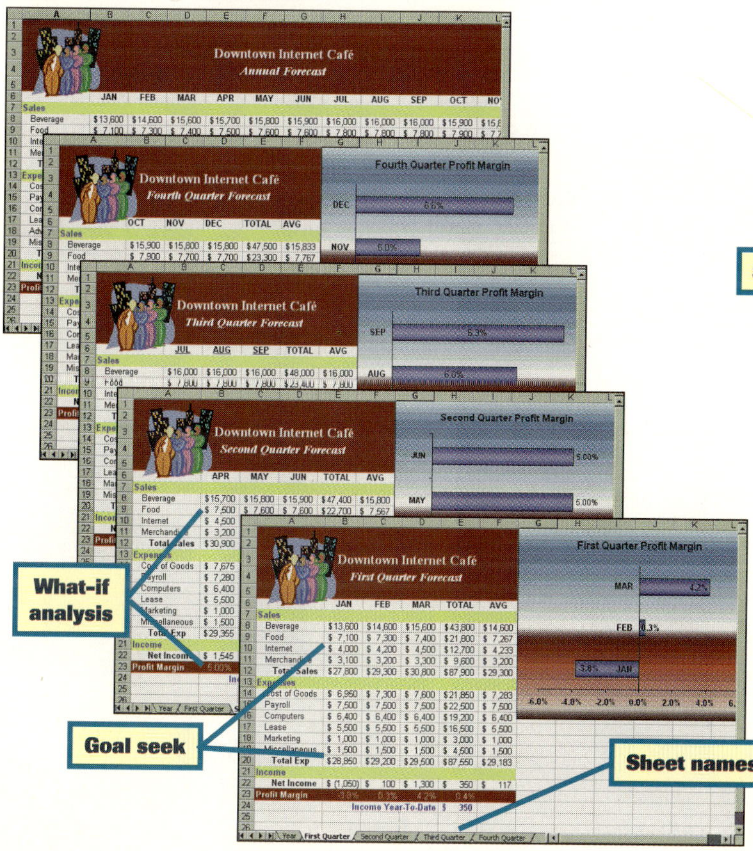

FIGURE 2-10

Working Together

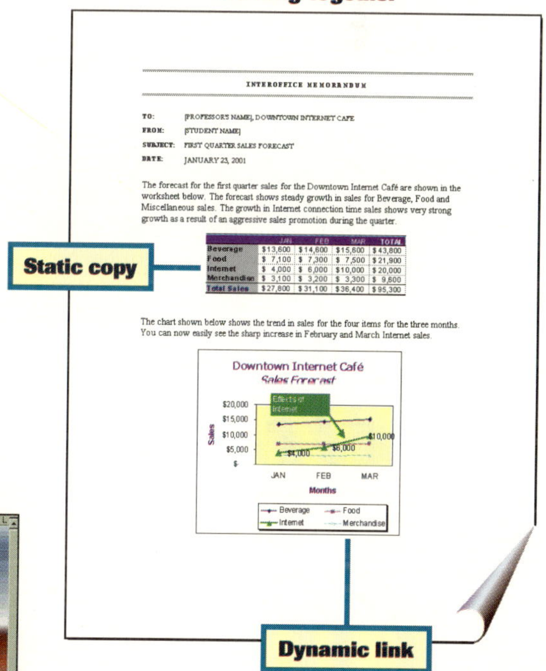

Database Management Systems

A database manager organizes a related collection of data so that information can be retrieved easily.

A *database* is a collection of related data. A **database management system (DBMS)** or **database manager** is a program that sets up, or structures, a database. It also provides tools to enter, edit, and retrieve data from the database. Database managers are used by all kinds of people, from teachers to police officers.

The **relational database** is the most widely used database structure. Data is organized into related **tables.** Each table is made up of rows called **records** and columns called **fields.** Each record contains fields of information about some specific item. For example, in an address table, a record would contain fields of information such as a person's last name, first name, and street address.

Three of the most widely used database management systems are Microsoft Access, Corel Paradox, and Lotus Approach.

ON THE WEB EXPLORATIONS

Corel is one of the leaders in software development. To learn more about the company, visit its Web site at

http://www.corel.com

Features

A basic feature of all database programs is the capability to quickly locate or find records in the database. For example, you could instruct the database manager to find and display all records in which a last name of Smith appears.

Rearranging or **sorting** is a common feature of database managers. For example, you might want to print out an entire alphabetical list of employees by last name. Built-in math formulas are used for data analysis. Using a

FIGURE 2-11

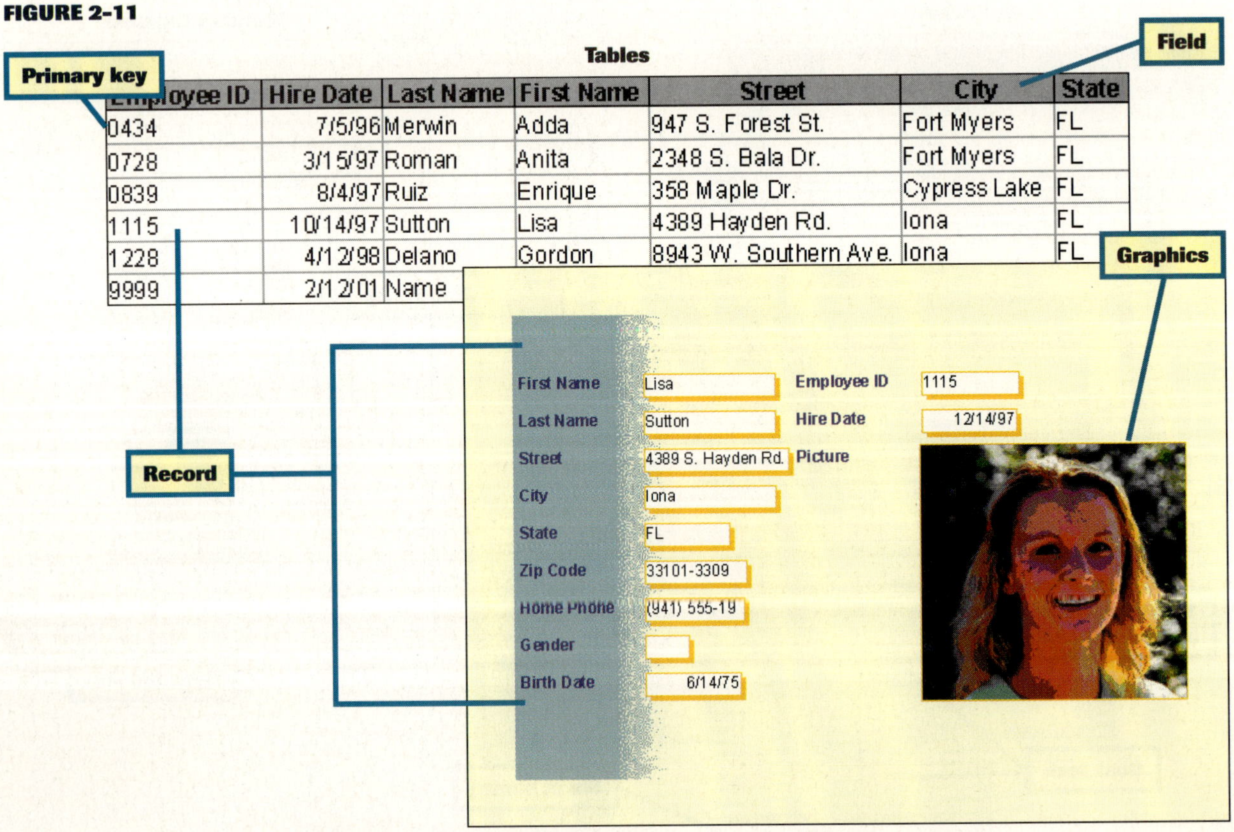

FIGURE 2-12

Forms

sales database, you could calculate the total and average commissions earned by the sales force in one part of the country.

Most database management programs include a programming control language for advanced users to create sophisticated applications. In addition, they allow direct communication to specialized mainframe databases through languages like **structured query language (SQL).**

Case

Assume that you have accepted a job as an employment administrator for the Lifestyle Fitness Club. One of your responsibilities is to create a database management system to replace the club's manual system for recording employee information. To learn more about database management system features and how they could assist you as an employee administrator at the Lifestyle Fitness Club, see Figures 2-11 through 2-14.

CONCEPT CHECK

- ✔ What is a database?
- ✔ What is a database management system (DBMS)?
- ✔ What are the three most common database management systems?

Reports

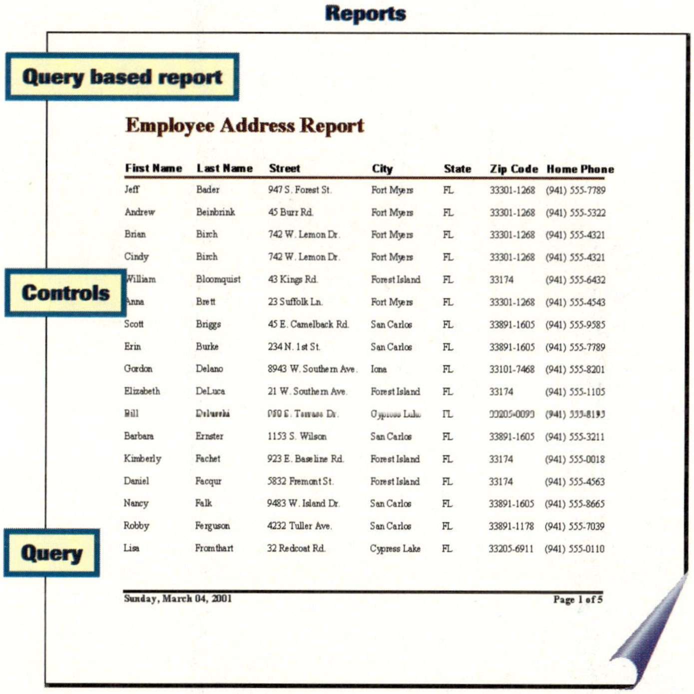

Employee Address Report

First Name	Last Name	Street	City	State	Zip Code	Home Phone
Jeff	Bader	947 S. Forest St.	Fort Myers	FL	33301-1268	(941) 555-7789
Andrew	Beinbrink	45 Burr Rd.	Fort Myers	FL	33301-1268	(941) 555-5322
Brian	Birch	742 W. Lemon Dr.	Fort Myers	FL	33301-1268	(941) 555-4321
Cindy	Birch	742 W. Lemon Dr.	Fort Myers	FL	33301-1268	(941) 555-4321
William	Bloomquist	43 Kings Rd.	Forest Island	FL	33174	(941) 555-6432
Anna	Brett	23 Suffolk Ln.	Fort Myers	FL	33301-1268	(941) 555-4543
Scott	Briggs	45 E. Camelback Rd.	San Carlos	FL	33891-1605	(941) 555-9585
Erin	Burke	234 N. 1st St.	San Carlos	FL	33891-1605	(941) 555-7789
Gordon	Delano	8943 W. Southern Ave.	Iona	FL	33101-7468	(941) 555-8201
Elizabeth	DeLuca	21 W. Southern Ave.	Forest Island	FL	33174	(941) 555-1105
Bill	[illegible]	[illegible]	[illegible]	[illegible]	[illegible]	(941) [illegible]
Barbara	Ernster	1153 S. Wilson	San Carlos	FL	33891-1605	(941) 555-3211
Kimberly	Fachet	923 E. Baseline Rd.	Forest Island	FL	33174	(941) 555-0018
Daniel	Facqur	5832 Fremont St.	Forest Island	FL	33174	(941) 555-4563
Nancy	Falk	9483 W. Island Dr.	San Carlos	FL	33891-1605	(941) 555-8665
Robby	Ferguson	4232 Tuller Ave.	San Carlos	FL	33891-1178	(941) 555-7039
Lisa	Fromthart	32 Redcoat Rd.	Cypress Lake	FL	33205-6911	(941) 555-0110

Sunday, March 04, 2001 Page 1 of 5

FIGURE 2-13

Working Together

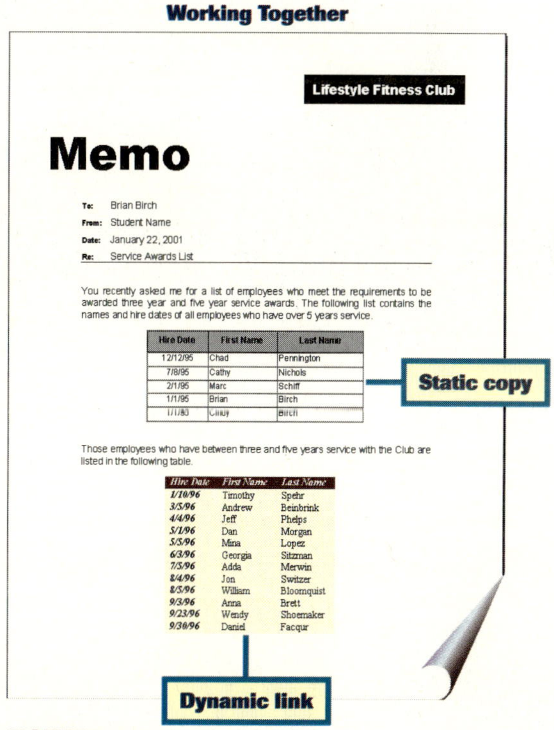

Lifestyle Fitness Club

Memo

To: Brian Birch
From: Student Name
Date: January 22, 2001
Re: Service Awards List

You recently asked me for a list of employees who meet the requirements to be awarded three year and five year service awards. The following list contains the names and hire dates of all employees who have over 5 years service.

Hire Date	First Name	Last Name
12/12/95	Chad	Pennington
7/8/95	Cathy	Nichols
2/1/95	Marc	Schiff
1/1/95	Brian	Birch
[illegible]	[illegible]	[illegible]

Those employees who have between three and five years service with the Club are listed in the following table.

Hire Date	First Name	Last Name
1/10/96	Timothy	Spehr
3/5/96	Andrew	Beinbrink
4/4/96	Jeff	Phelps
5/1/96	Dan	Morgan
5/5/96	Mina	Lopez
6/3/96	Georgia	Sitzman
7/5/96	Adda	Merwin
8/4/96	Jon	Switzer
8/5/96	William	Bloomquist
9/3/96	Anna	Brett
9/23/96	Wendy	Shoemaker
9/30/96	Daniel	Facqur

FIGURE 2-14

Presentation Graphics

Presentation graphics software helps you create professional and exciting presentations.

Research shows that people learn better when information is presented visually. A picture is indeed worth a thousand words, or numbers. **Presentation graphics** are used to combine a variety of visual objects to create attractive, visually interesting presentations.

You can use presentation graphics to create class presentations. These programs are excellent tools to communicate a message or to persuade people, such as fellow students, instructors, supervisors, or clients. Presentation graphics programs are often used by marketing or sales people as well as many others.

Three of the most widely used presentation graphics programs are Microsoft PowerPoint, Corel Presentations, and Lotus Freelance Graphics.

ON THE WEB EXPLORATIONS

Lotus is one of the leaders in developing presentation graphics. To learn more about the company, visit its Web site at **http://www.lotus.com**

Features

Most programs include features that help you organize the content of your presentation. Commonly, an outline feature is included that helps you enter

FIGURE 2-15

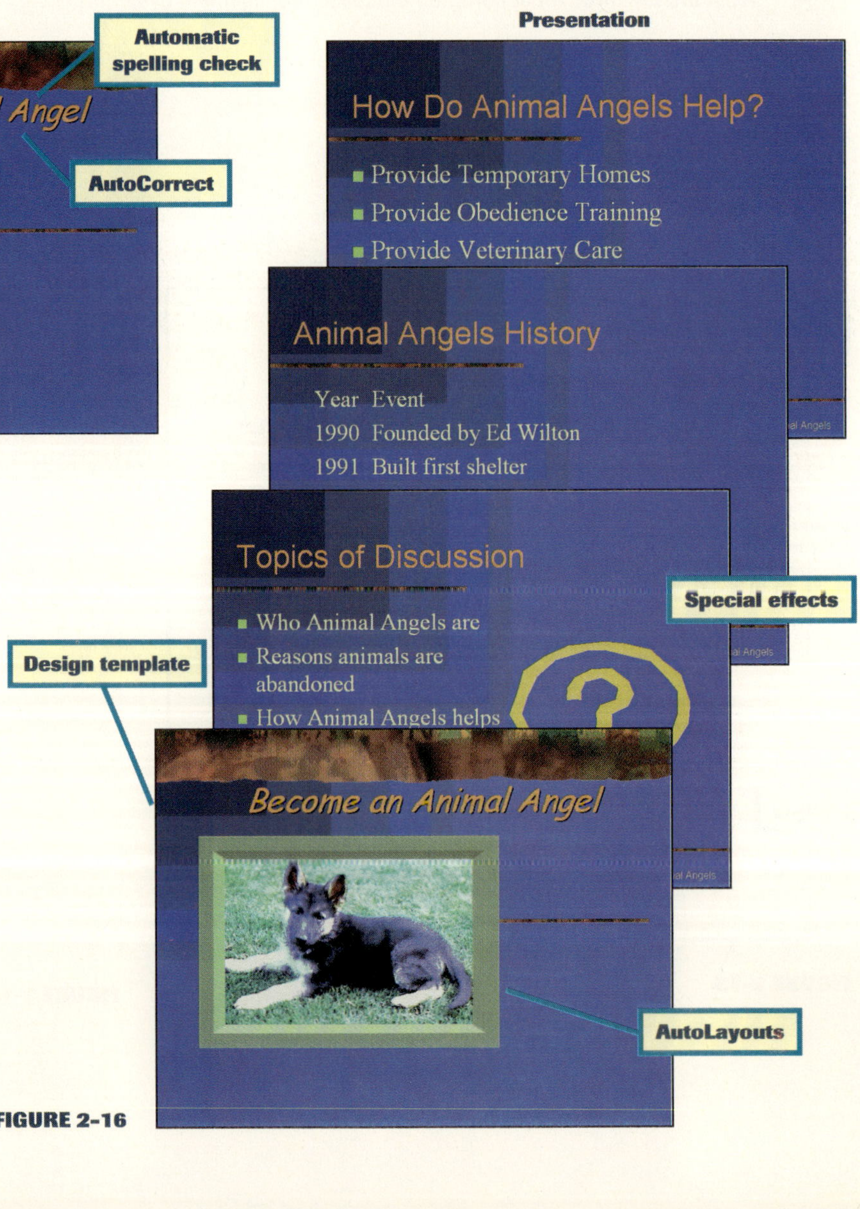

FIGURE 2-16

and organize the topics of your talk. Most programs also provide presentation **layout files** that include sample text for many different types of presentations—from selling a product to reporting on progress.

Professionally designed **templates** or model presentations are provided. These can help take the worry out of the design and layout decisions. They include selected combinations of text layouts with features such as title placement and size. Additionally, various bullet styles, background colors, patterns, borders, and other enhancements are provided.

Animations include special visual and sound effects. These effects include blinking text and transitions between topics. You can insert audio and video clips that play automatically or when selected. You can even record your own voice to provide a narration to accompany a slide show.

Case

Assume that you have volunteered to help out at a local animal shelter called Animal Angels. You have been asked to create a powerful and persuasive presentation to encourage other members from your community to volunteer. To learn more about presentation software features and how they could assist you to create a presentation for Animal Angels, see Figures 2-15 through 2-18.

> **CONCEPT CHECK**
>
> ✔ What are the three most widely used presentation graphics programs?

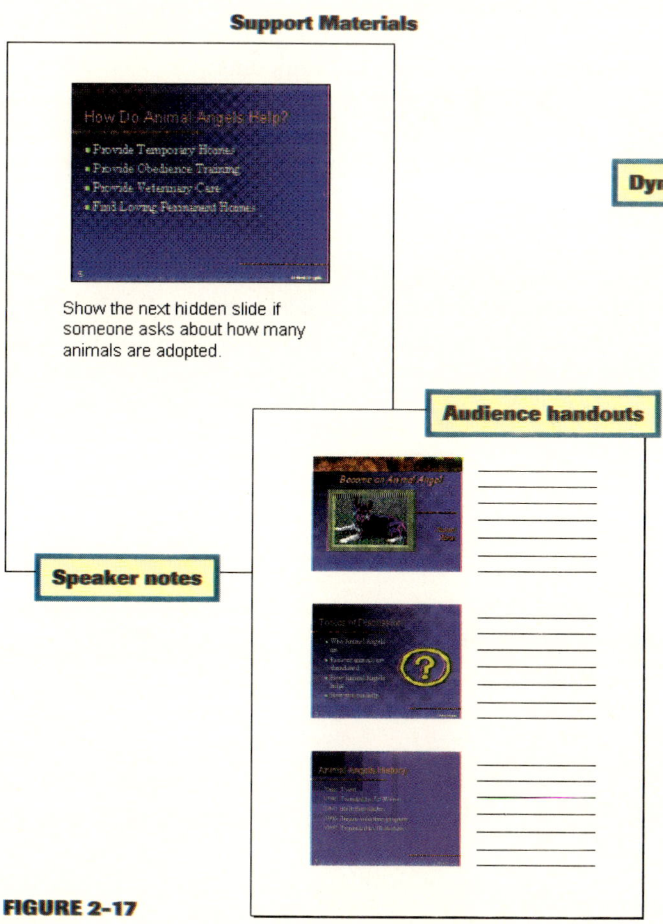

FIGURE 2-17

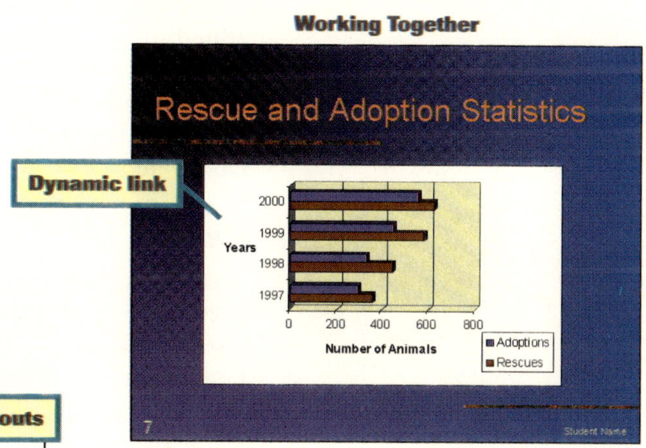

FIGURE 2-18

Software Suites

A software suite is a group of application programs. OLE allows you to share information between applications.

A **software suite** is a collection of separate applications bundled together and sold as a group. While the applications function *exactly* the same whether purchased in a suite or separately, it is significantly less expensive to buy a suite of applications than to buy each application separately.

Microsoft Office is the most popular software suite. It comes in several different versions. One of the most recent is Microsoft Office 2000 Professional Edition, which includes Word, Excel, Access, and PowerPoint. Other popular software suites are Corel WordPerfect Suite and Lotus SmartSuite.

Object Linking and Embedding

Object linking and embedding (OLE) is a powerful feature of many application programs. Using OLE, you can share information or page objects between files created in different applications. For example, you could create a chart in Excel and then use it in a Word document.

With object linking, a copy of the object from the source file is sent to the destination file along with a *link* or tie back to the source file. If the source file changes, the object in the destination file is updated automatically.

For example, if a chart created in Excel is linked to a Word document, the chart appears in the Word document. Later, if the Excel worksheet changes the chart, the Word document will be automatically updated. Object linking is useful if you want the destination document to always contain the most up-to-date information.

With object embedding, the object from the source file is *embedded* or added in the destination document. While the files are not linked, the embedded file can be run from the destination document.

For example, if a presentation created in PowerPoint is embedded in a Word document, the presentation can be run from the Word document. Object embedding is useful for providing activity and flexibility to a document.

Case

Assume that you are a marketing analyst for The Sports Company and have been working on a presentation for the annual sales meeting. You have analyzed recent sales trends using Excel and have drafted a presentation using PowerPoint. To present your work to your supervisor, you have just completed a Word document. To learn more about OLE and how you could use it, see Figure 2-19.

CONCEPT CHECK

- ✔ What is a software suite?
- ✔ What are some popular software suites?

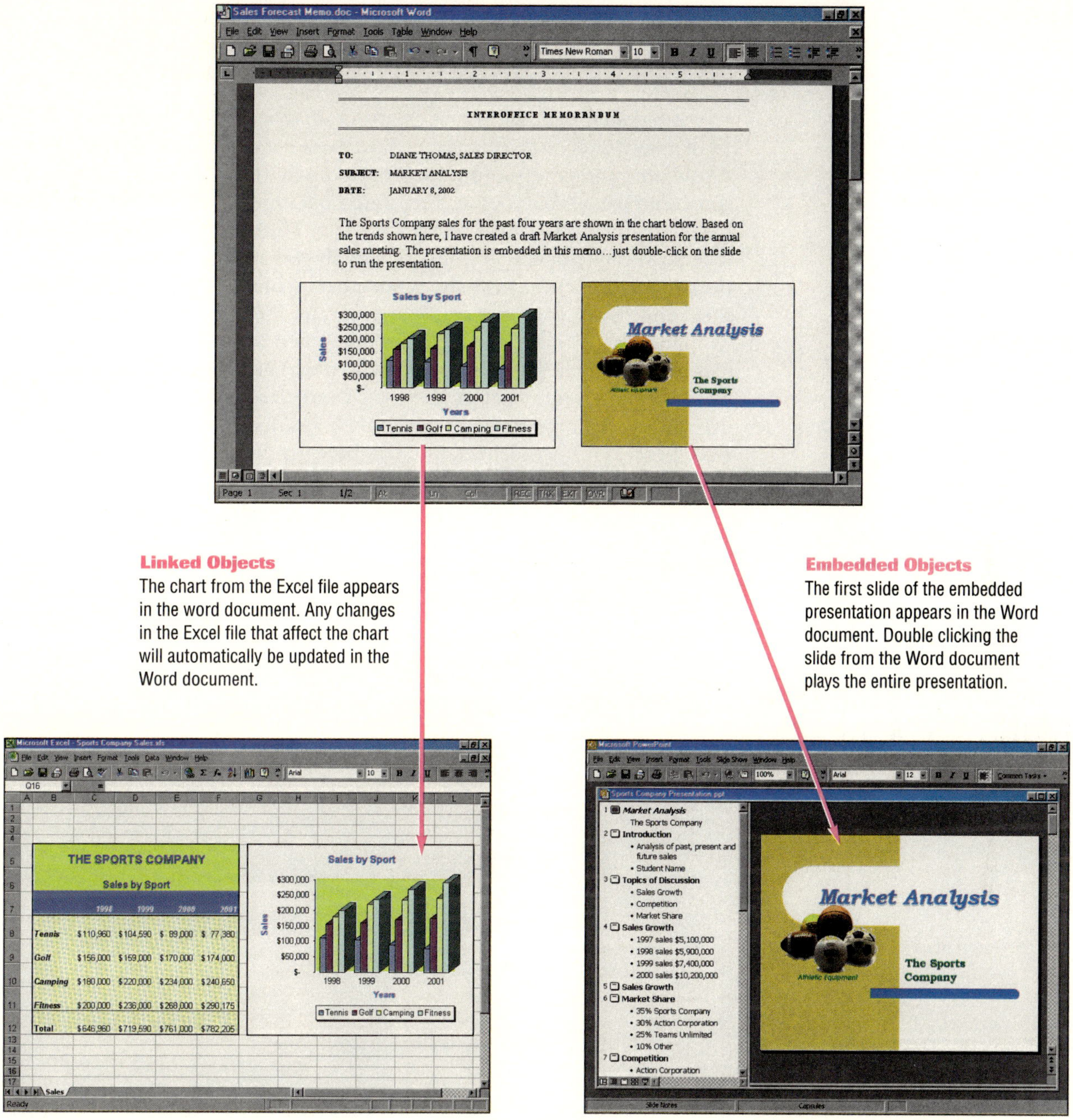

Linked objects can be charts, text, tables, slides, sounds, and video.

Embedded objects can be word processing, spreadsheet, presentation, and database files.

FIGURE 2-19
Object linking and embedding

Integrated Packages

Integrated software is an all-in-one application program.

An **integrated package** is a single program that provides the functionality of a word processor, spreadsheet, database manager, and more. For example, to create a report on the growth of sales for a sporting goods store, you could use all parts of an integrated package. You could use the database to search and retrieve yearly sales data. The spreadsheet could be used to analyze the data and graphics to visually present the data. You could use the word processor to write the report that includes tables from the spreadsheet and visuals from the graphics program. (See Figure 2-20.)

The primary disadvantage of an integrated package is that the capabilities of each function (such as word processing) are not as extensive as in the specialized programs (such as Microsoft Word). The primary advantage is that the cost of an integrated package is much less than the cost of purchasing a word processor, spreadsheet, and database manager. The most widely used integrated package is Microsoft Works.

For a summary of the basic application software, see Figure 2-21.

CONCEPT CHECK

✔ What is an integrated package?

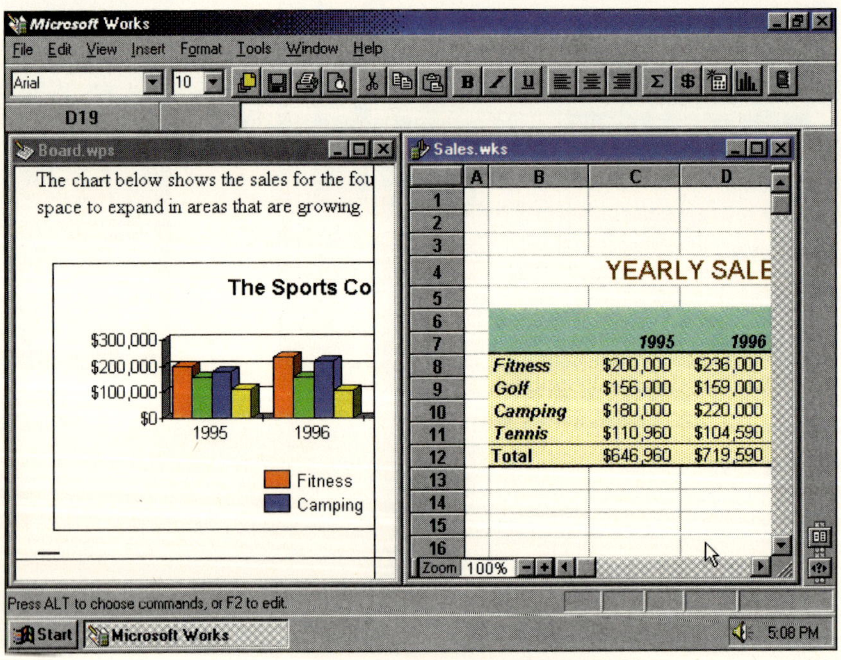

FIGURE 2-20
Integrated package (Microsoft Works for Windows 95)

Word processors	Microsoft Word, Corel WordPerfect, Lotus Word Pro
Spreadsheets	Microsoft Excel, Corel Quattro Pro, Lotus 1-2-3
Database management systems	Microsoft Access, Corel Paradox, Lotus Approach
Presentation graphics	Microsoft PowerPoint, Corel Presentations, Lotus Freelance
Software suites	Microsoft Office, Corel WordPerfect Suite, Lotus SmartSuite
Integrated packages	Microsoft Works

FIGURE 2-21
Software programs

A LOOK TO THE FUTURE

New software versions will offer more capabilities, freeing your creativity and enhancing the quality and quantity of your work.

New versions of basic application software are being released all the time. One way these programs change is in the way you interact with them. Another way is in the software's capabilities.

Interacting with them may not be as difficult as you might think. That's because almost all new software today has a similar command and menu structure. When a new version comes out, it looks and feels quite similar to the previous version. This frees you to focus on the new capabilities.

Basic applications will continue to become more and more powerful by adding breadth to their capabilities. They are no longer limited by the machines that they were designed to replace. Word processors, for example, do much more than typewriters ever could. Recent versions have added limited desktop publishing and Web page design capabilities.

What does all this mean to you? You will have access to more powerful applications, which will free your creativity and enhance the quality and quantity of your work. Additionally, you will be challenged to learn how and when to use these more powerful tools. It is for this reason that you need to know more about some of the advanced applications whose capabilities are steadily moving into basic applications.

VISUAL SUMMARY Application Software

GENERAL-PURPOSE APPLICATIONS

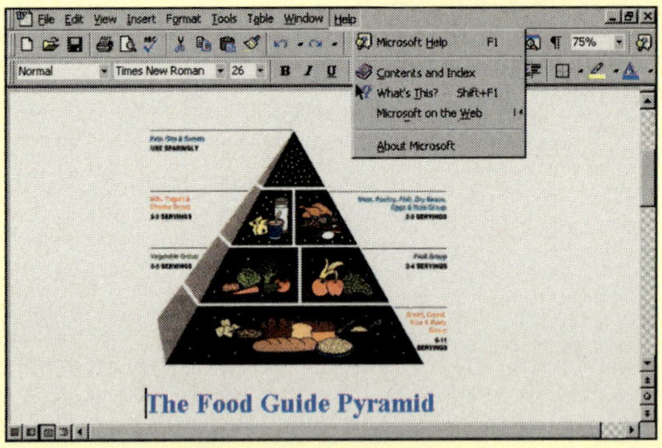

General-purpose applications are for common kinds of tasks. They include word processors, spreadsheets, database management systems, and presentation programs. Common features include the following.

Windows

Windows are rectangular areas that can contain a document, program, or message.

Menus

Menus are lists of optional commands, typically displayed in a menu bar at the top of the screen.

Toolbars

Toolbars contain buttons and menus to provide quick access to commands. Two common types are the **standard toolbar** and the **formatting toolbar.**

Help

Help typically includes a table of contents, a search feature, and access to special learning features. **Context-sensitive help** systems locate and display reference information related to the task currently being performed.

WORD PROCESSORS

Word processors allow you to create, edit, save, and print text-based **documents** including brochures, letters, and reports. They are also used to create Web pages.

Features

Principal word processing features include the following:

- **Word wrap**—automatically moves the insertions pointer to the next line.
- **Enter key**—inserts a new line.
- **Spelling checkers**—identify incorrectly spelled words and present alternative spellings.
- **Grammar checkers**—identify poor wording, faulty grammar, and long sentences.
- **Search**—quickly locates characters, words, or phrases.
- **Replace**—replaces the located text with new text.
- **Hypertext links**—provide a connection to cross-referenced information within a document to other documents.

To be a competent end user, you need to know the functionality of systems and application software. Additionally, you need to understand the capabilities of general purpose applications including word processors, spreadsheets, database management systems, and presentation programs.

SPREADSHEETS

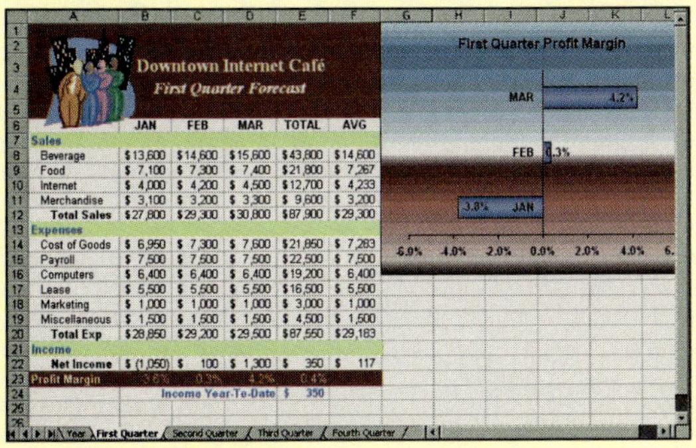

Spreadsheets are used to organize, manipulate, and graph numeric information. Also known as a **worksheet,** a spreadsheet consists of **rows** and **columns** forming **cells.** Individual cells are identified by their **cell address.** A block of adjacent cells is called a **range.**

Features

Principal spreadsheet features include the following:

- **Rows** and **columns** form **cells** in worksheet.
- **Labels** typically identify information in the spreadsheet.
- **Values** include numbers.
- **Formulas** are instructions for calculations.
- **Functions** are prewritten formulas.
- **What-if analysis** is the result of changing one or more values and observing the effect on related cells in the spreadsheet.
- **Analytical** graphs or charts are used to help visualize data in a spreadsheet.

DATABASE MANAGEMENT SYSTEMS

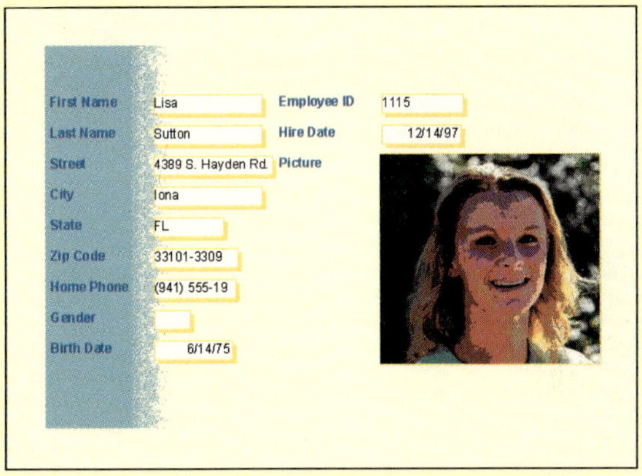

Database management systems are used to create and use databases. A **relational database** organizes data into related **tables** that are linked by **key fields.** In the tables, rows are called **records** and columns are called **fields.**

Features

Principal database management system features include the following:

- **Locate and display**—finding and displaying records.
- **Sort and analyze**—rearranging records in a database. Built-in math formulas may be used to manipulate and analyze data.
- **Program control languages**—like SQL (Structured Query Language) are programming languages for advanced users to create sophisticated database applications.

PRESENTATION GRAPHICS

Presentation graphics are used to create professional and exciting presentations.

Features

Principal presentation graphics features include the following:

- **Content development assistance**—Most provide organizational assistance using an outline feature. **Layout files** are provided to offer content assistance. These files include sample text for a variety of different types of presentations.
- **Professional design**—Sample **templates** or model presentations are provided. They include selected combinations of text layouts, bullet styles, background colors, patterns, borders, and other enhancements.
- **Animations** include special visual and sound effects including blinking text and transitions between topics. Additionally, audio and video clips can be inserted. These features add interest and keep audience attention.

SOFTWARE SUITES

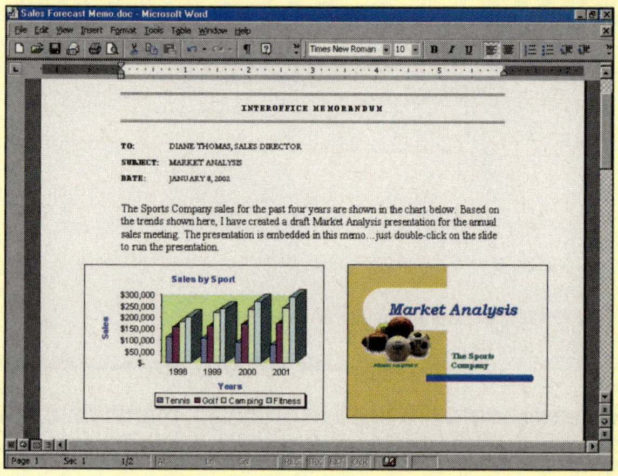

A **software suite** is a collection of individual application packages sold together. While functionally identical, application packages purchased in a suite are significantly less expensive than those purchased separately.

OLE

OLE, or **object linking and embedding,** allows sharing of information (objects) between applications.

- Object linking—linked objects are automatically updated whenever a change in the source file is changed.
- Embedded linking—the object from the source is embedded or added and can be run from the destination file.

INTEGRATED PACKAGES

An **integrated package** is a single program providing the functionality of a word processor, spreadsheet, database manager, and more. Although not as powerful, integrated packages are much less expensive than individual packages.

Key Terms

analytical graphs or charts (31)
animation (35)
basic applications (26)
context-sensitive help (26)
database management system (DBMS) (32)
database manager (32)
documents (28)
Enter key (28)
field (32)
find (28)
formatting toolbar (26)
formula (30)
function (30)
general-purpose applications (26)
grammar checker (28)
Help (26)
hyperlinks (29)
hypertext link (29)
integrated package (38)
label (30)
layout files (34)
menu (26)
object linking and embedding (OLE) (36)
presentation graphics (34)
record (32)
relational database (32)
replace (29)
search (28)
software suite (36)
sorting (32)
spelling checker (28)
spreadsheet (30)
standard toolbar (26)
structured query language (SQL) (33)
table (in database) (32)
templates (35)
toolbar (26)
value (30)
what-if analysis (31)
window (26)
word processing (28)
word wrap (28)

Chapter Review

LEVEL 1

Reviewing Facts and Terms

Matching

Match each numbered item with the most closely related lettered item. Write your answers in the spaces provided.

1. A rectangular area that can contain a document, program, or message. ____
2. Programs that organize, manipulate, and graph numeric information. ____
3. Prewritten formulas that perform calculations automatically. ____
4. Separate software application programs sold as a group. ____
5. Common feature of database managers that allows you to rearrange information. ____
6. A feature that contains buttons and menus to provide access to commonly used commands. ____
7. Software that creates text-based documents such as reports, letters, and memos. ____
8. Program that sets up, or structures, a database. ____
9. A single program that provides the functionality of a word processor, spreadsheet, database manager, and more. ____
10. Command that allows you to quickly locate any character, word, or phrase in your document. ____
11. In a database, the columns are called ____.
12. Most widely used database structure. ____
13. Word processors, spreadsheets, database management systems, and presentation graphics. ____
14. Software used to combine a variety of visual objects to create attractive, visually interesting presentations. ____

a. Word wrap
b. Integrated package
c. Relational database
d. DBMS
e. Help
f. Toolbar
g. General-purpose applications
h. Hypertext link
i. Fields
j. Menu
k. Functions
l. Presentation graphics
m. Search
n. Software suites
o. Sorting
p. Spreadsheets
q. Grammar checker
r. SQL
s. Window
t. Word processor

15. Can be created to cross-reference information within the current document and between documents. ____
16. Basic feature of a word processor that causes the words to "wrap around" to the next line as you type. ____
17. The word processing feature that identifies poor wording. ____
18. A feature common to most general-purpose applications for displaying commands. ____
19. A language that allows direct communication to specialized mainframe databases. ____
20. A command on the menu bar of most application packages that provides options such as access to special learning features. ____

True/False

In the spaces provided, write T or F to indicate whether the statement is true or false.

1. The term *window* is short way of referring to Microsoft's Windows operating systems. ____
2. Microsoft, Lotus, and Corel are applications. ____
3. Quattro Pro is a widely used word processor. ____
4. Spreadsheet programs are typically used to store and retrieve records quickly. ____
5. Presentation graphics programs provide you with professionally designed templates to simplify design and layout issues. ____

Multiple Choice

Circle the letter of the correct answer.

1. The following would not be considered a general-purpose application:
   - **a.** word processor
   - **b.** spreadsheet
   - **c.** presentation graphics program
   - **d.** music interface program
   - **e.** database management system
2. The word processing feature that identifies excessively long sentences is a:
   - **a.** spell checker
   - **b.** paste
   - **c.** copy
   - **d.** merge
   - **e.** grammar checker
3. In spreadsheets, the feature that specifies instructions for calculation is:
   - **a.** formulas
   - **b.** format
   - **c.** recalculation
   - **d.** consolidation
   - **e.** value
4. A tool used frequently by marketing people to communicate a message or to persuade clients:
   - **a.** word processors
   - **b.** spreadsheets
   - **c.** browser
   - **d.** database managers
   - **e.** presentation graphics

5. A collection of separate Windows applications sold as a group:
   - a. combined
   - b. suite
   - c. browser
   - d. integrated
   - e. spreadsheet

Completion

Complete each statement in the spaces provided.

1. A ________ is a rectangular area that can contain a document, program, or message.
2. The ________ is an electronic worksheet.
3. ________ ________ are used to create professional and exciting presentations.
4. ________ ________ software is used to create newsletters.
5. A basic feature of all database programs is the capability to quickly ________ records in the database.

Reviewing Concepts

LEVEL 2

Open-Ended

On a separate sheet of paper, respond to each question and statement.

1. What is context-sensitive help?
2. Describe the concept of what-if analysis.
3. Explain the purpose of presentation graphics.
4. Name three well-known spreadsheet packages.
5. What is the difference between an integrated package and a software suite? What are the advantages and disadvantages to each?

Concept Mapping

On a separate sheet of paper, draw a concept map or a flowchart showing how the following terms are related. Show all relationships. Include any additional terms you can think of.

database management system
database manager
documents
field
formula
function
general-purpose applications
hypertext link
integrated package
analytical graphs
column
context-sensitive help
key field
label
layout files
menu
presentation graphics
range
record
row
search
software suite
spreadsheet
structured query language
toolbar
value
what-if analysis
window
word processing
worksheet

Critical Thinking Questions and Projects

LEVEL 3

Read each exercise and answer the related questions on a separate sheet of paper.

1. *New versions and releases*: Software companies seem to be offering new versions and releases of their application packages all the time.
   - **a.** Take one application package (like Microsoft Word, Excel, or PowerPoint) and find out how many variations have been released in the past three years.
   - **b.** If you own one variation of an application package and a new one is released, does yours become obsolete? Discuss and defend your position.
   - **c.** If you own one variation of a software package and a new version is released, should you upgrade to the newer version? What factors should be considered? If you decide to upgrade, how would you go about doing it?
   - **d.** Why do you suppose software manufacturers offer new variations of their software?
2. *Three ways to acquire application software*: The following exercise can be extremely useful. Concentrate on a category of software of personal interest to you—say, word processing or spreadsheets. Go to the library or use the Web to find information on the following three methods of acquiring software. Which route seems to be the best for you? Why?
   - **a.** *Public domain software* is software you can get for free. Someone writes a program and offers to share it with everyone without charge. Generally, you find these programs by belonging to a microcomputer users group. Or, you find them by accessing an electronic bulletin board using your telephone-linked computer. Be aware that the quality of the software can vary widely. Some programs may be excellent and some may be poor.
   - **b.** *Shareware* is inexpensive. It is distributed free, in the same way as public domain software. After you have used it for a while and decide you like it, you're supposed to pay the author for it. Again, the quality varies. Some shareware is excellent.
   - **c.** *Commercial software* consists of brand-name packages, such as those we mentioned in this chapter. Prices and features vary. Fortunately, there are several periodicals that provide ratings and guides. *PC World* polls its readers to find out the best software brands in various categories. The magazine releases the results in its October issue. Other periodicals (for example, *PC* magazine, *MacWorld*, *Infoworld*) also have surveys, reviews, and ratings.
3. *Ethics*: In addition to the three recommended ways to acquire software listed in question 2, two other ways are (1) to copy programs from a friend and (2) to purchase unauthorized copies of programs.
   - **a.** Have you ever had a friend ask to copy one of your programs? Or have you asked someone to make a copy of one of his or her programs? Do you think there is anything wrong with sharing programs in this manner? Identify and discuss the key issues.
   - **b.** Have you ever purchased a bootleg copy of a music CD? As you likely know, bootleg copies are much less expensive and often nearly as good as the originals. Have you ever purchased a bootleg copy of an application program? Do you think there is anything wrong with purchasing unauthorized copies of programs? Identify and discuss the key issues.

On the Web Exercises

1. Corel Office 2000 Suites

Microsoft's major competitor in the office suite market is Corel. To learn more about Corel and their products, visit the Corel Web site at http://www.corel.com. Once connected to that site, explore and learn more about the Corel's office suites. Print out the most informative Web page and write a paragraph describing the different versions of Corel office suites.

2. Learning Applications

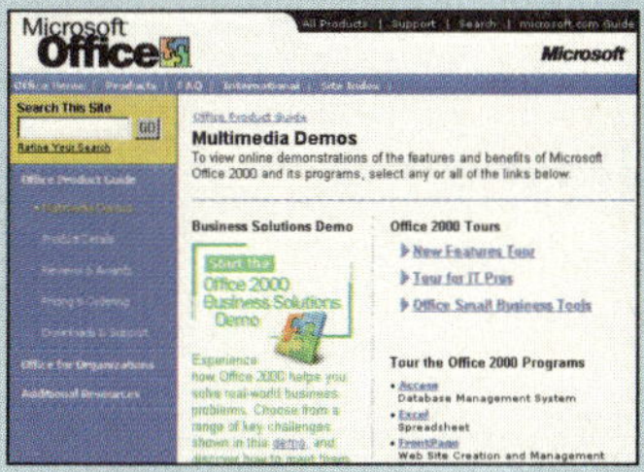

With so many different types of applications available, it can be difficult to know where to begin learning. Visit our site at http://www.mhhe.com/cit/concepts/oleary2000-2001/webex2.html for a link to a site providing some suggestions. At this site you will find descriptions and tutorials for some of the most widely used basic applications. Select one, read about it, and run its tutorial. Write a paragraph describing the application and the tutorial and what you learned from it.

3. Presentation Software

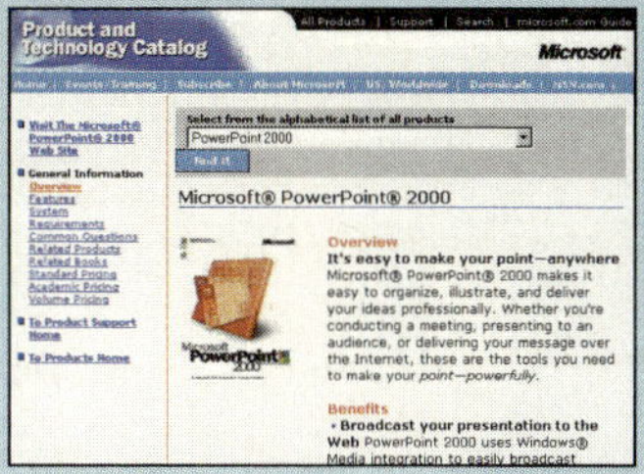

Microsoft's PowerPoint can help you create effective and professional-looking presentations. Learn more about this basic application by visiting our site at http://www.mhhe.com/cit/concepts/oleary2000-2001/webex2.html, which provides a link to Microsoft's Web site. Once at the site, read about PowerPoint's capabilities and uses. Write a paragraph summarizing some of PowerPoint's most powerful features, and describe how you could use this program to effectively convey ideas to an audience.

4. Computer Games

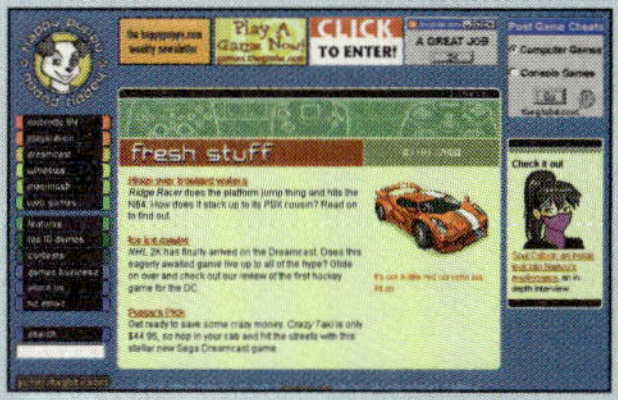

Computers are not all work and no fun. Learn more about computer games by visiting our site at http://www.mhhe.com/cit/concepts/oleary2000-2001/webex2.html, where you'll find a link to a Web site that describes some of the newest and best games. Check out the demos, or go to the pressroom to read reviews on the latest in computer entertainment. Choose a game, and print out the information presented. Write a summary of the game, describe who will likely use the game, and define the system requirements needed to run the game.

CHAPTER 3

Browsers, Personal Information Managers, Operating Systems, and Utilities

COMPETENCIES

After you have read this chapter, you should be able to:

1. **Describe how browsers are used to navigate, find information, and communicate.**
2. **Discuss the functionality of personal information managers.**
3. **Describe the four kinds of system software.**
4. **Describe the most widely used microcomputer operating systems.**
5. **Describe the five essential utility programs.**

Time—it's a precious thing. Some say it is the most precious of all commodities. Do you have enough of it? Are you balancing school, work, friends, and family? Almost all of us are looking for ways to become more efficient—to do more in less time. We want to meet all of our responsibilities and still have *some* time left for ourselves. That's where this chapter comes in.

With the right kinds of software, you can use a microcomputer as a personal productivity tool. In the previous chapter, we discussed some

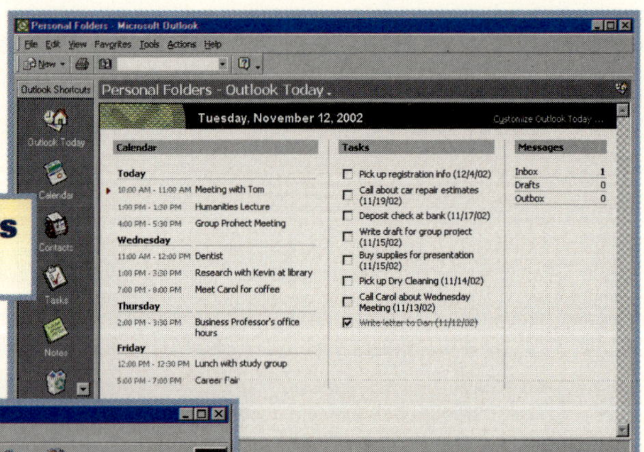

Information Managers
Help you get and stay organized

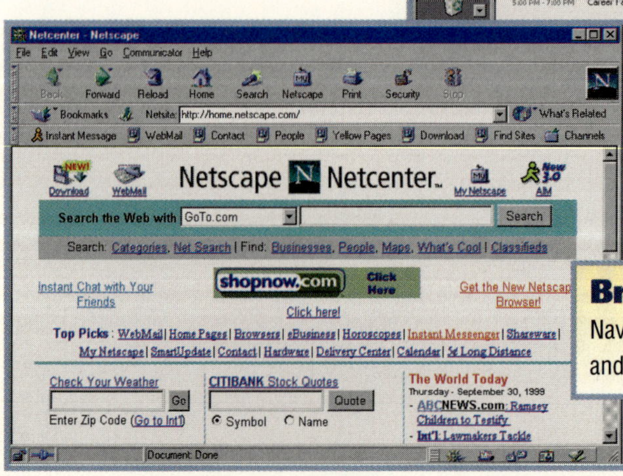

Browsers
Navigate, search for information, and communicate using the Web

of these programs. Word processors, spreadsheets, database managers, and presentation programs are general-purpose tools that can improve your efficiency and productivity. In this chapter we'll discuss some more specialized tools.

You can surf the Web, locate information, and communicate with friends and family using browser software. You can use personal information management software to maintain electronic organizers with calendars, address books, and to-do lists. System software programs help control many of the behind-the-scenes computer operations. In particular, operating systems and utility programs provide tools you can use to maximize your computer's efficiency.

To manage time effectively, competent end users need to understand the functionality and the capabilities of browsers, personal information managers, and system software, including operating systems and utilities.

Browsers

Browsers connect to the Web, allowing navigation, searching for information, and communicating with others.

Browsers are used to connect you to remote computers, open and transfer files, display text and images, and provide in one tool an uncomplicated interface to the Internet and the Web. At one time, browsers were considered specialized programs used primarily by computer professionals. Now, browsers are widely used by almost everyone who uses a computer.

The two most widely used browsers are Microsoft's Internet Explorer and Netscape's Navigator. (See Figure 3-1.)

The things you can do on the Internet and the Web are almost endless. The most common activities include navigating or surfing the Web, finding or searching for information, and communicating with others. (A thorough and detailed discussion of the Internet and the Web is presented in Chapter 8.)

ON THE WEB EXPLORATIONS

Netscape is one of the leaders in developing browser software. To learn more about the company, visit its Web site at

http://www.netscape.com

Navigating the Web

Navigating the Web means to move from one Web site to another. Often called **surfing** or **browsing** the Web, this activity is like reading a magazine and jumping not only from one article to another within the magazine but also from the magazine to different magazines, books, movies, and so on. There are millions of different Web sites. See Figure 3-2 for a short list of some popular sites.

There are a number of different ways to navigate from one site or one Web page to another. One of the most common ways is to directly enter a Web site address. Another common way is to use connections provided on a Web page. These connections are called **hypertext links** and are typically represented by colored and underlined text.

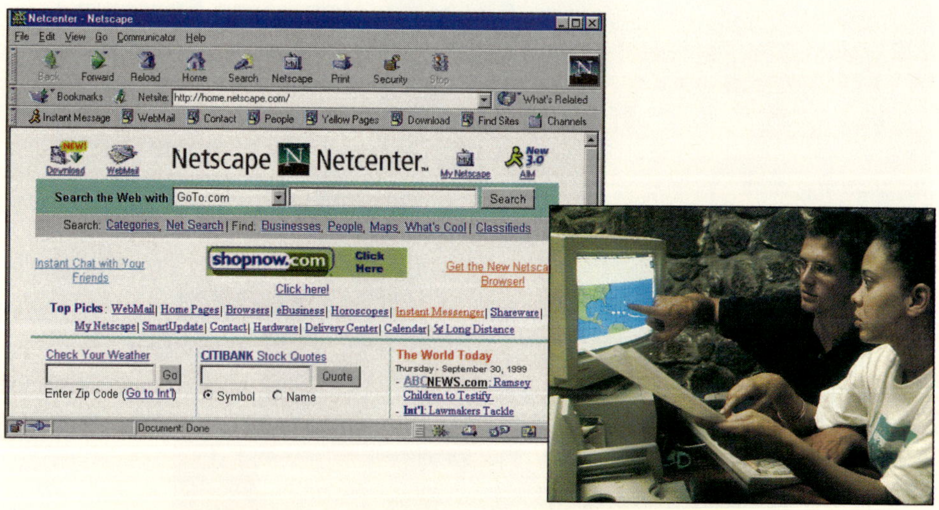

FIGURE 3-1
Netscape Navigator

Description	Site
NBC programming	www.nbc.com
New and used car sales	www.autobytel.com
Medical information	www.mayohealth.org
Active vacations	www.adventurequest.com

FIGURE 3-2
Popular Web sites

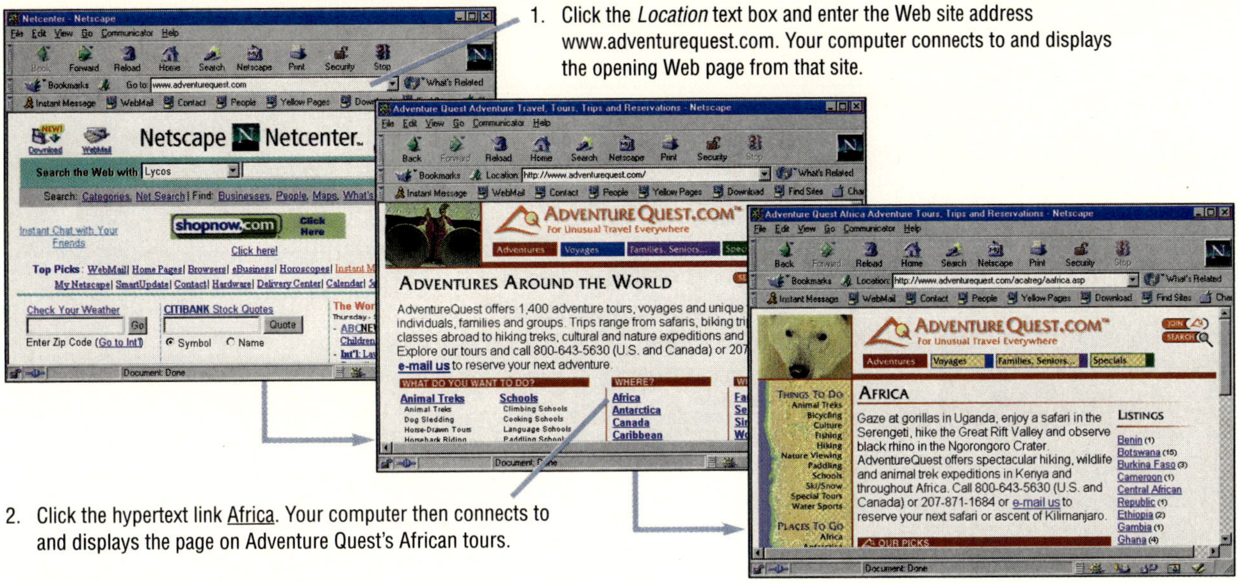

FIGURE 3-3
Navigating the Web

For example, you could use Netscape to connect to the Adventure Quest Web site and then to find information on Adventure Quest's African tours by taking the steps shown in Figure 3-3.

Finding Information

Do you want to catch up on your favorite television program? Are you buying a new or used car? Planning on doing some research for a school paper? You can do all of these things and much more on the Web. The challenge is finding or searching for the information you want.

Most browsers include a search facility that connects you to Web sites that specialize in finding information. For example, to find information about aerobic exercise, you could use Netscape by following the steps shown in Figure 3-4.

Communicating

Communicating is the most popular Internet activity. Using a browser, you can send and receive messages to and from friends and family located almost anywhere in the world. These messages are called **e-mail.**

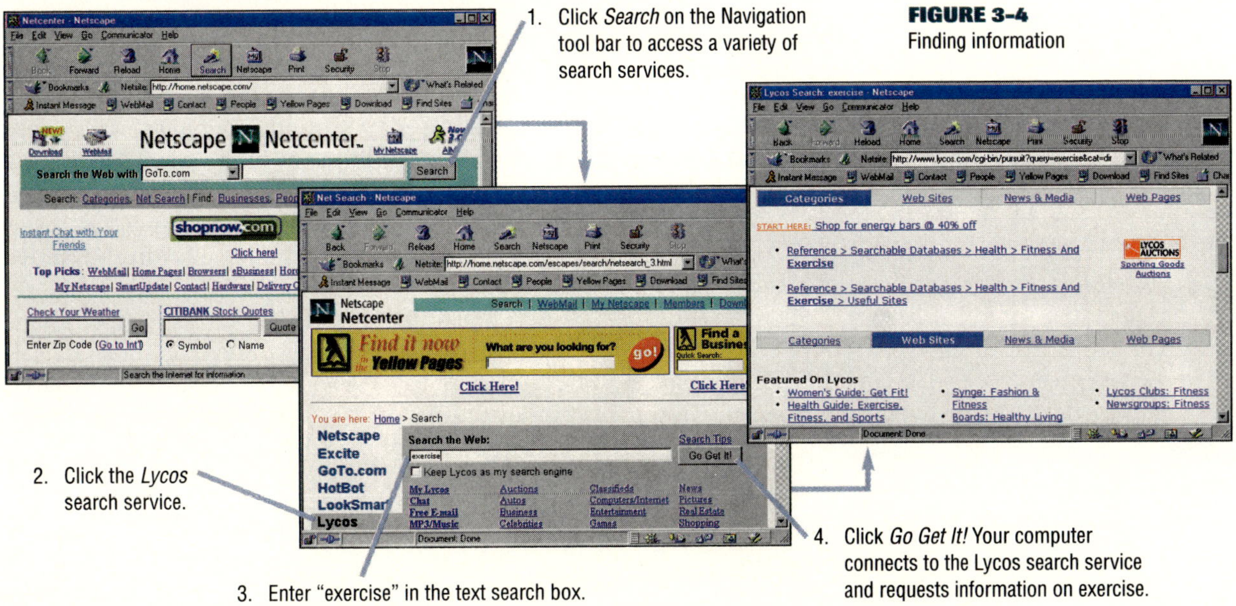

FIGURE 3-4
Finding information

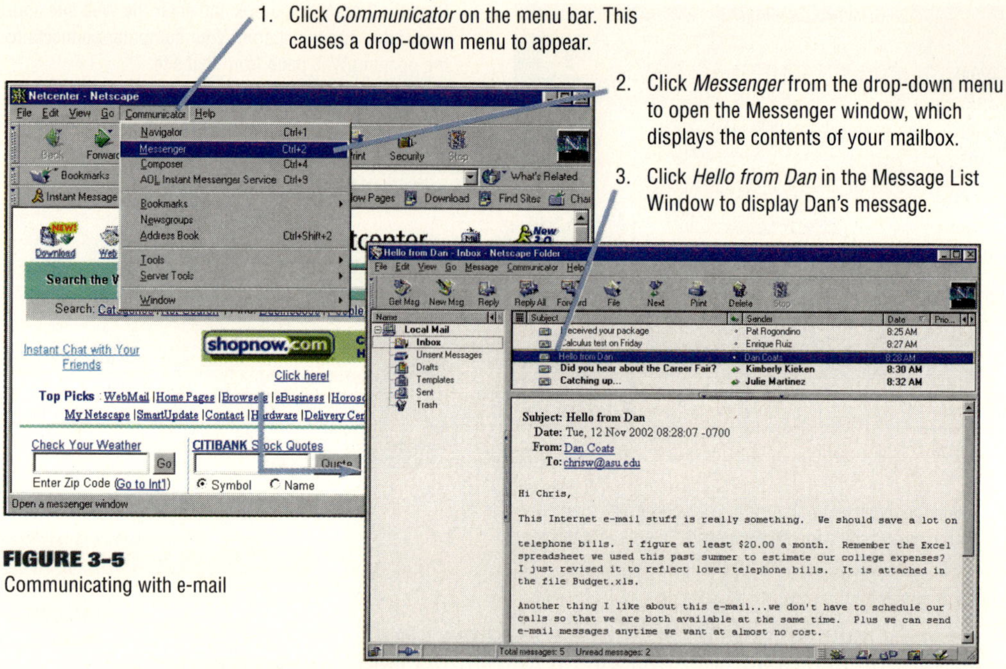

FIGURE 3-5
Communicating with e-mail

For example, you could use Netscape to receive a message from Dan, a friend attending the University of Southern California by taking the steps shown in Figure 3-5.

CONCEPT CHECK

- ✔ What is the function of a browser?
- ✔ What is meant by "navigating" or "surfing" the Web?
- ✔ Name the two most widely used browsers.

Personal Information Managers

A personal information manager is a program that helps you get organized and stay organized. It also helps you communicate with others.

Stop and think for a minute about what you do in a typical day, week, month, and year. Professionals in all kinds of jobs do similar things. They schedule meetings, make to-do lists, and record important names, addresses, and telephone numbers. They jot down notes, make future plans, and record important dates like anniversaries and birthdays.

You may use some of the same tools that many professionals use to keep track of all these things. Such tools include calendars, Rolodex files, address books, index cards, wall charts, notepads, binders, and Post-it notes. **Personal information managers (PIMs),** also known as **desktop managers,** are programs that provide electronic alternatives for these tools.

Two widely used PIMs are Microsoft Outlook and Lotus Organizer. (See Figure 3-6.)

FIGURE 3-6
Personal folder—Outlook Today

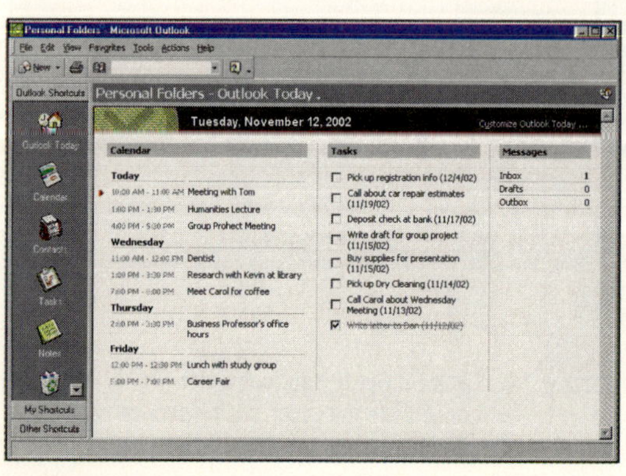

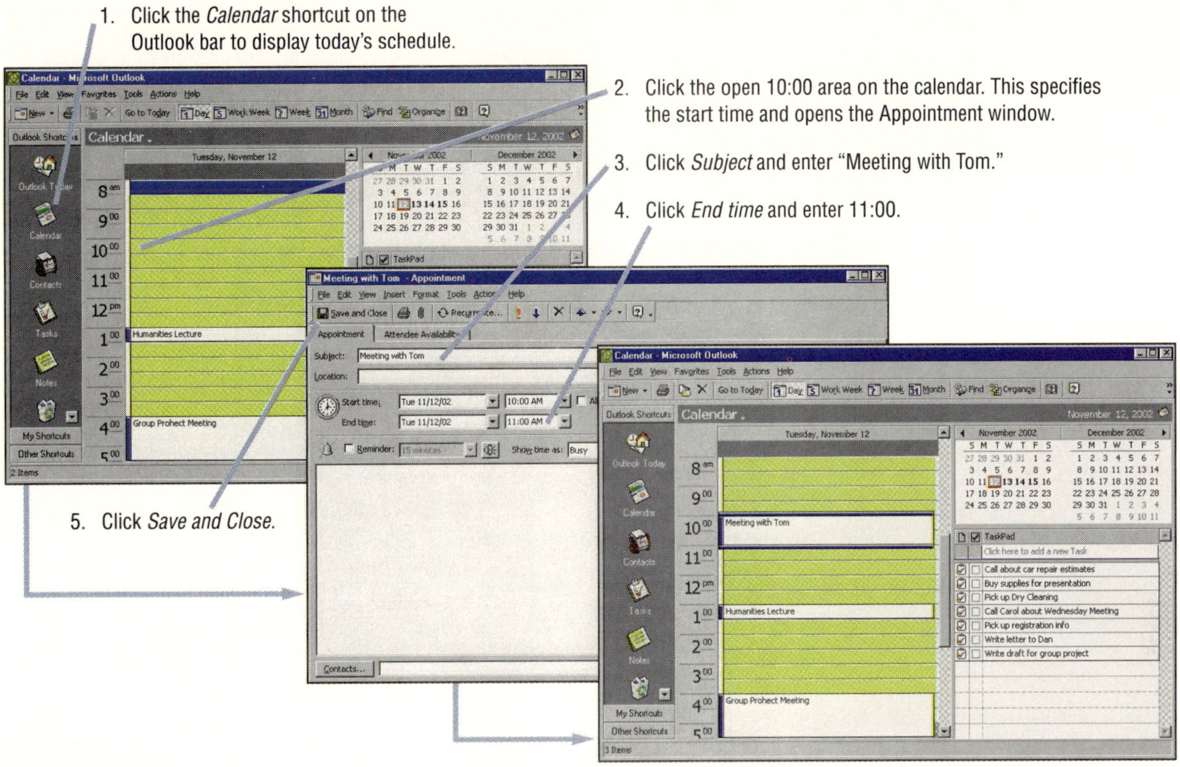

FIGURE 3-7
Using the calendar

Calendar

One of the most important features is the calendar. It operates like an electronic appointment book that keeps track of events, holidays, assignments, and project schedules. Additionally, most calendars provide assistance in scheduling meetings and organizing projects.

For example, you could use Outlook to schedule a meeting with Tom for November 12 that starts at 10:00 and ends at 11:00, as shown in Figure 3-7.

Contacts

Electronic contacts or address books are an essential feature for all PIMs. Like a traditional address book, they are used to record names, addresses, and telephone numbers. In addition, electronic address books are linked to the other parts of a PIM to save you time and energy.

For example, you could use Outlook to locate Dan Coats's postal and e-mail addresses by taking the steps shown in Figure 3-8.

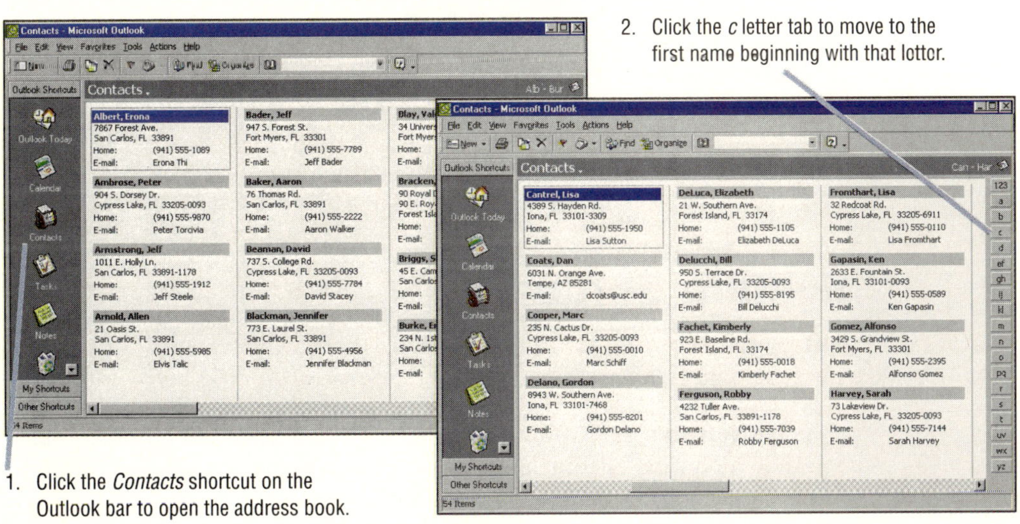

FIGURE 3-8
Using contacts

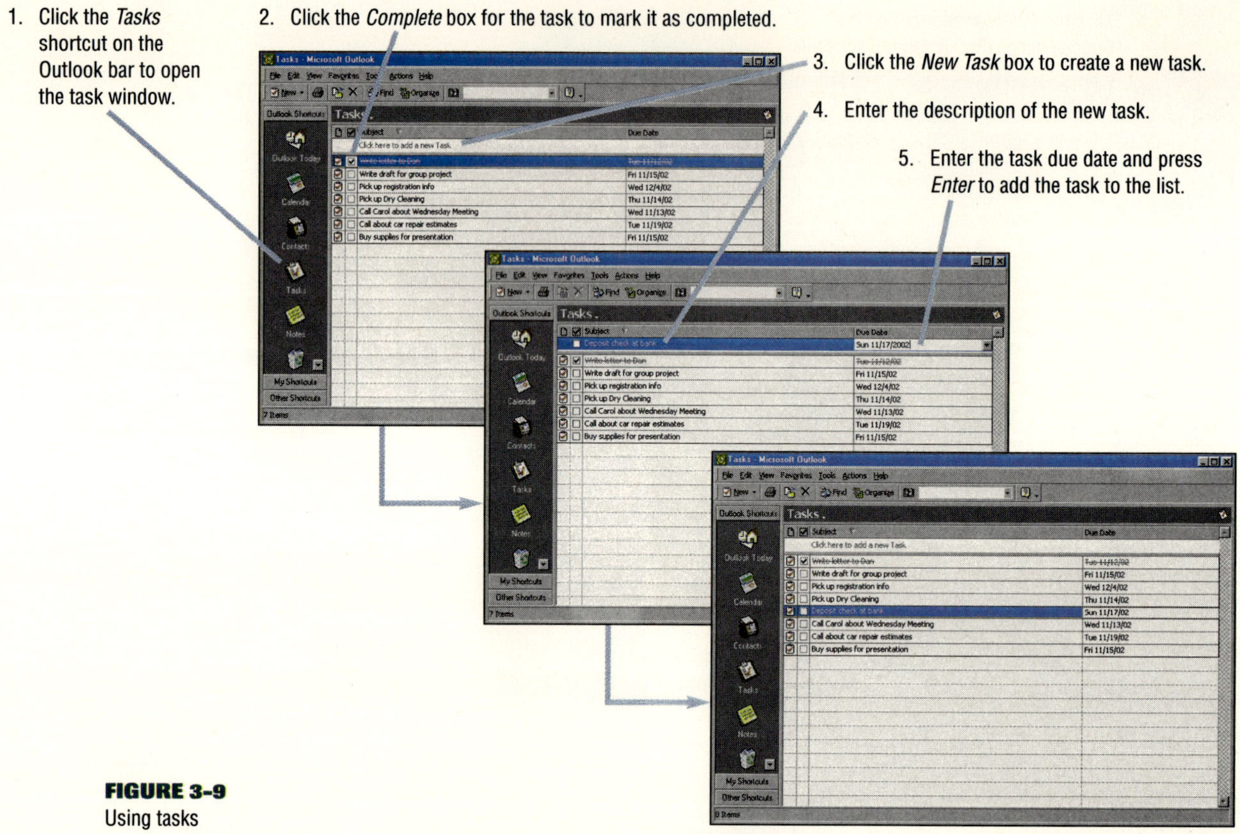

FIGURE 3-9
Using tasks

Tasks

For busy people, organization is often the key to success. A basic feature of all PIMs is a task organizer, or to-do list. It provides two basic functions. First, it records, displays, and reminds you of tasks you need to complete. For example, a task might be a weekly meeting with a project group. Second, it works to record, display, coordinate, and communicate tasks assigned to a group.

You could use Outlook to update your daily task list. For example, you have just completed one of your tasks, writing a letter to Dan. Additionally, you need to add a new task to remind you to deposit a check at the bank. You can update your task list by taking the steps shown in Figure 3-9.

CONCEPT CHECK

- ✔ What is a personal information manager (PIM)?
- ✔ What are some features of a typical PIM?

System Software

System software consists of operating systems, utilities, device drivers, and language translators.

System software deals with the physical complexities of computer hardware. It consists of four kinds of programs: operating systems, utilities, device drivers, and language translators.

- **Operating systems** are programs that operate your microcomputer. They coordinate computer resources, provide an interface between users and the computer, and run applications.
- **Utilities,** also known as **service programs,** perform specific tasks related to managing computer resources or files. They include programs to help users identify hardware problems, locate lost files, and back up data.
- **Device drivers** are specialized programs designed to allow particular input or output devices to communicate with the rest of the computer system.
- **Language translators** convert the programming instructions written by programmers into a language that computers understand and process.

CONCEPT CHECK

✔ What is system software?

✔ What kinds of programs can be found in system software?

Operating Systems

Operating systems manage resources, provide a user interface, and run applications. Windows, Mac OS, and Unix are widely used operating systems.

Every computer has an operating system and every operating system performs three basic functions: managing resources, providing a user interface, and running applications.

- **Resources:** These programs coordinate all the computer's **resources** including keyboard, mouse, printer, monitor, storage devices, and memory.
- **User interface:** Users interact with application programs and computer hardware through a **user interface.** Almost all operating systems today provide a windows-like **graphical user interface** (**GUI**) in which graphic objects called **icons** are used to represent commonly used features.
- **Applications:** These programs load and run **applications** such as word processors and spreadsheets. Most operating systems support **multitasking,** or the ability to run more than one application at a time.

For end users, the most important operating systems are those for microcomputers. These include Windows, Mac OS, and Unix.

Windows

By far the most popular microcomputer operating system today is Microsoft's **Windows** with over 90 percent of the market. Windows is designed to run with Intel and Intel-compatible microprocessors such as the Pentium III. It comes in a variety of different versions including Windows 95, Windows 98, and Windows 2000.

Windows gets its name from its use of rectangular boxes called windows. These boxes are extensively used to display information and run programs. Multiple windows can be open at the same time, making it easy to multitask, or work with different programs simultaneously.

Classic view

Web-style view

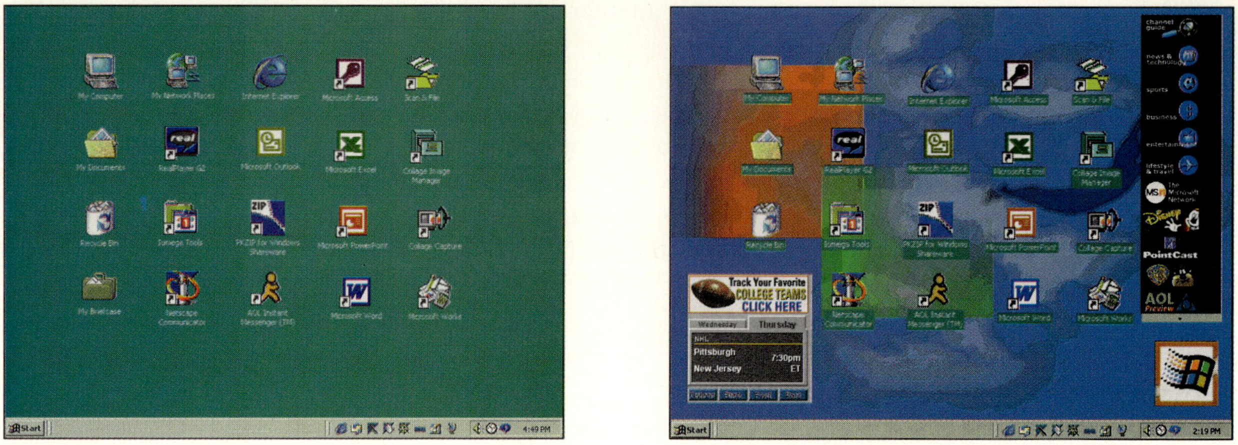

FIGURE 3-10
Desktop views

Windows provides a user interface called the **desktop.** This desktop has two basic views: *classic* and *Web-style.* (See Figure 3-10.) The Web-style view gives Windows a look and feel of the Internet Explorer browser. In the Web-style view, you can use Microsoft's **Active Desktop** to display "active content" from Web pages on your desktop. For example, you could have constantly updating news, weather, sports, and stock prices.

One of the most common ways for users to interact with the Windows operating system is by selecting icons. For example, you could use icons to list the contents of your *My Documents* folder by taking the steps shown in Figure 3-11.

The **Start menu** displays a list of commands that can be used to gain access to information, change hardware settings, find information, get online help, run programs, log off a network, and shut down your computer system. For example, you could use the Start menu to run the Netscape Navigator program as shown in Figure 3-12.

Mac OS

The **Mac OS** is designed to run on Macintosh computers. While its market share is much less than that of Windows, it is a very powerful and easy-to-use operating system. It comes in a variety of different versions. Mac OS 8.5 includes **Sherlock,** an innovative search feature for locating information on the Web or on your hard drive. (See Figure 3-13.)

FIGURE 3-11
Using icons

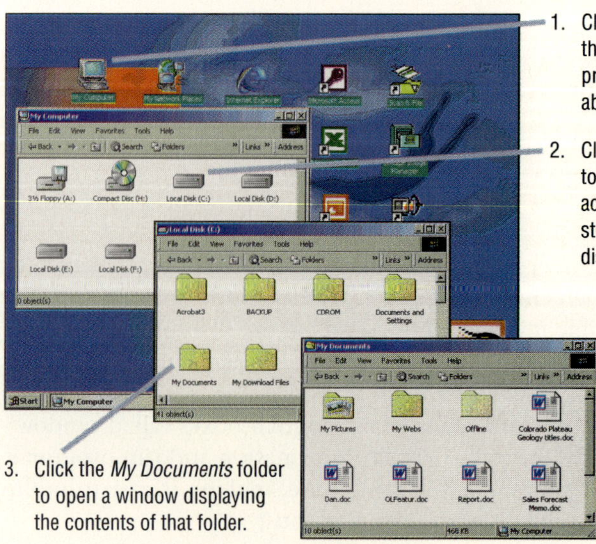

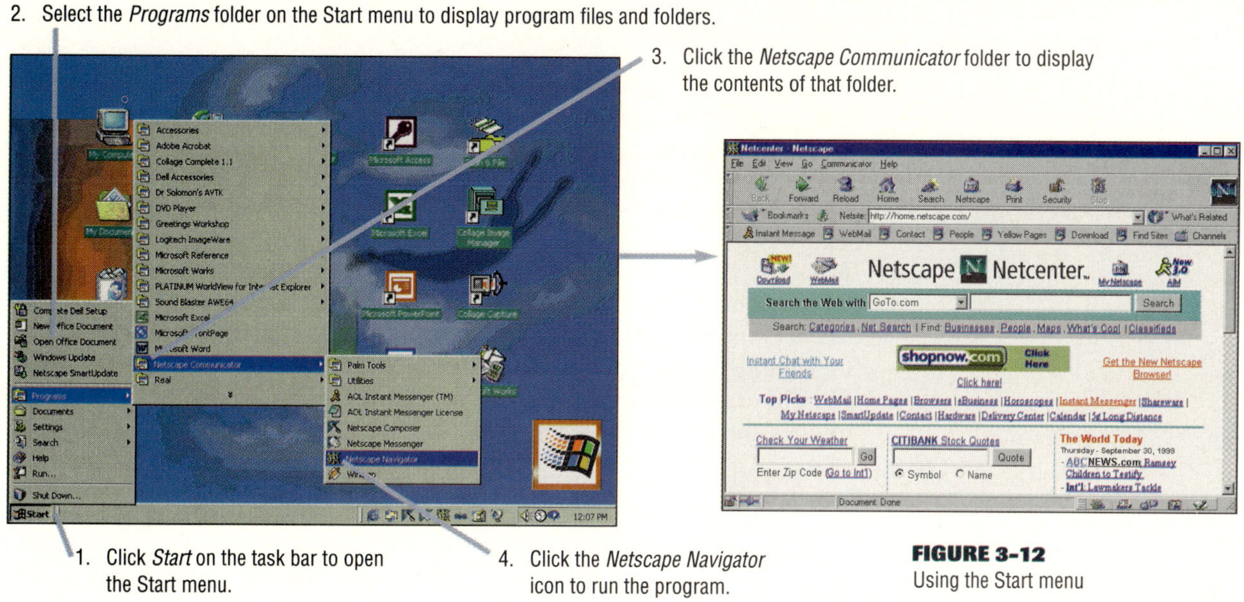

FIGURE 3-12
Using the Start menu

Unix

The **Unix** operating system was originally designed to run on minicomputers in network environments. Now, it is also used by powerful microcomputers and by servers on the Web. There are a large number of different versions of Unix. One receiving a great deal of attention today is **Linux**.

While Windows and the Mac OS are proprietary operating systems (that is, they are owned and licensed by a company), Linux is not. As a graduate student at the University of Helsinki, Linus Torvalds developed Linux in 1991. He has provided the operating system free to others and has encouraged further development. (See Figure 3-14.)

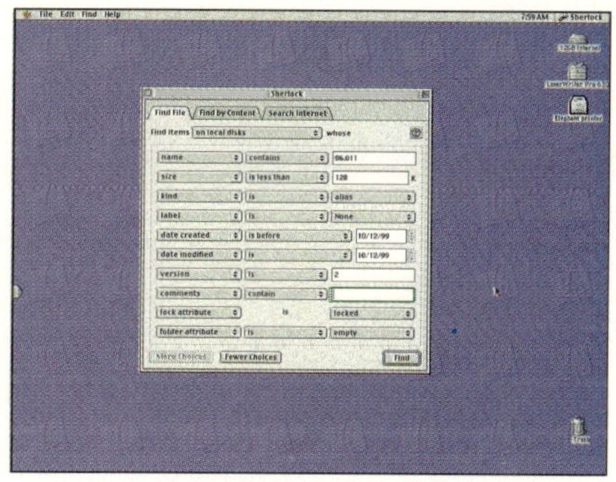

FIGURE 3-13
Mac OS

CONCEPT CHECK

- ✔ List the three basic functions of an operating system.
- ✔ Name some common operating systems for microcomputers.

FIGURE 3-14
Recent version of Linux and Linus Torvalds, the founder of Linux

Utilities

Utilities are programs that make computing easier. Operating systems often include utility programs. Norton SystemWorks and McAfee Office are utility suites.

Ideally, microcomputers should run and run and run without problems. However, that simply is not the case. All kinds of things can happen—internal hard disks can crash, destructive programs called viruses can invade a system, computers can freeze up, operations can slow down, and so on. These events can make computing very frustrating. That's where utilities come in. Utilities are specialized programs designed to make computing easier.

There are hundreds of different utility programs. The five most essential utilities are:

- **Troubleshooting programs** that recognize and correct problems, ideally before they become serious problems.
- **Antivirus programs** that guard your computer system against viruses or other damaging programs that can invade your computer system.
- **Uninstall programs** that allow you to safely and completely remove unneeded programs and related files from your hard disk.
- **Backup programs** that make copies of files to be used in case the originals are lost or damaged.
- **File compression programs** that reduce the size of files so they require less storage space and can be sent more efficiently over the Internet.

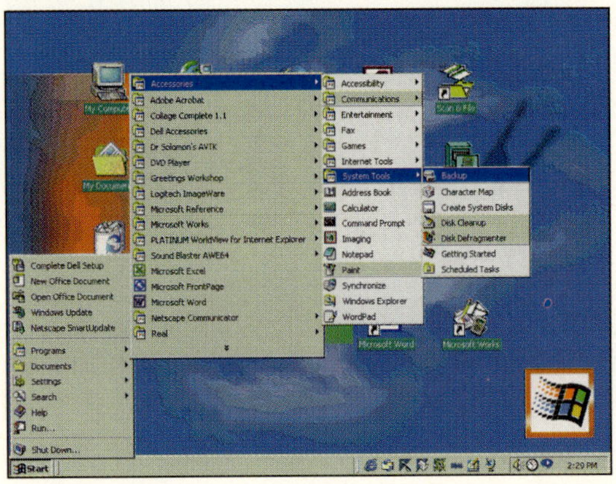

FIGURE 3-15
Windows utilities

Most operating system programs provide some utility programs. Even more powerful utility programs can be purchased separately or in utility suites.

Windows Utilities

The Windows operating systems are accompanied with several utility programs, including Backup, Disk Cleanup, and Disk Defragmenter. These utilities can be accessed from the Systems Tools menu. (See Figure 3-15.)

For example by selecting *Backup* from the Windows 2000 System Tools menu, you can create a backup for your hard disk as shown in Figure 3-16.

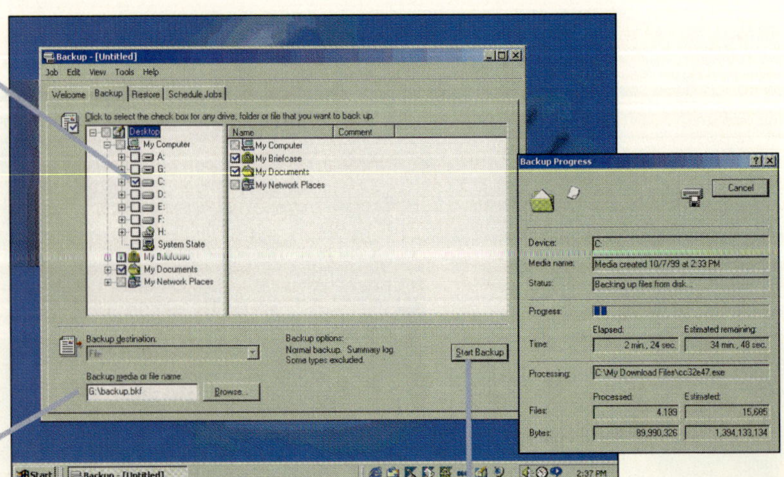

FIGURE 3-16
Backup utility

FIGURE 3-17
Disk cleanup utility

When you surf the Web a variety of programs and files are saved on your hard disk. Many of these and other files are not essential. **Disk Cleanup** is a trouble shooting utility that identifies and eliminates nonessential files. This frees up valuable disk space and improves system performance.

For example, by selecting Disk Cleanup from the Windows 2000 System Tools menu, you can eliminate unneeded files on your hard disk as shown in Figure 3-17.

Typically, after a hard disk has been used for a period of time, a large file cannot be stored in one location. Rather, the file has to be broken up, or *fragmented,* into small parts and the parts are stored wherever space is available. After a period of time, the hard disk becomes highly fragmented, slowing operations.

Disk Defragmenter is a utility program that locates and eliminates unnecessary fragments, rearranges files and unused disk space to optimize operations. For example, by selecting Disk Defragmenter form the Windows 2000 Systems Tool menu, you can defrag your hard disk as shown in Figure 3-18.

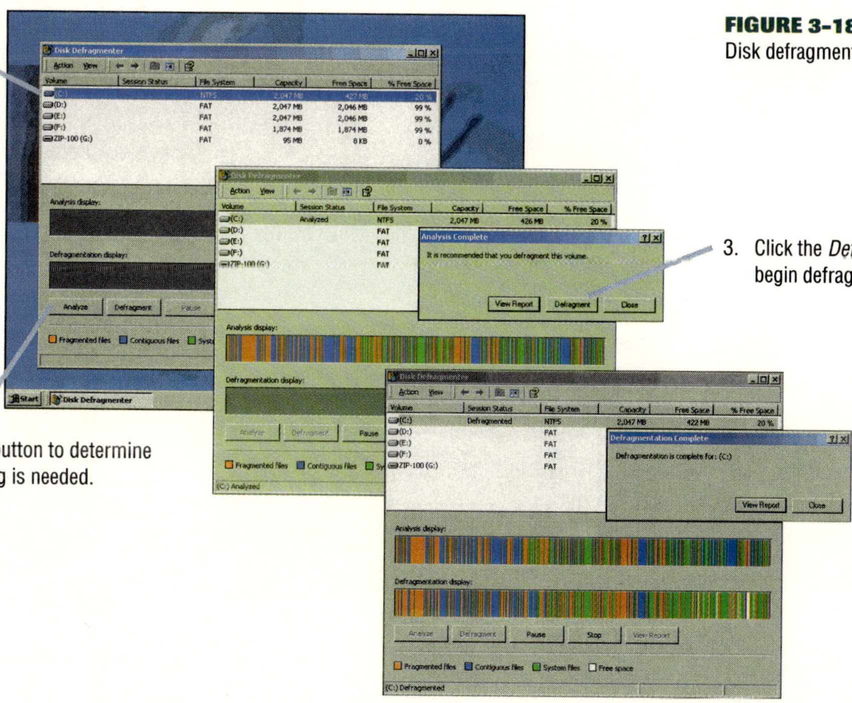

FIGURE 3-18
Disk defragmenter utility

ON THE WEB EXPLORATIONS

Norton is one of the leaders in developing utility software. To learn more about this company, visit its Web site at **http://www.norton.com**

While these and other utility programs included with Windows are effective, specialty programs offer a wider variety and higher level of support. These programs can be purchased separately or in suites.

Utility Suites

Like application software suites, utility suites combine several programs into one package. Buying the package is less expensive than buying the programs separately. The two best-known utility suites are McAfee Office and Norton SystemWorks. (See Figure 3-19.)

Norton SystemWorks includes a suite of four separate program groups. Each group can be purchased separately or as part of the suite.

- **Norton Utilities** is a collection of 17 separate troubleshooting utilities. These programs can be used to find and fix problems, improve system performance, prevent problems from occurring, and troubleshoot a variety of other problems.
    - **Norton AntiVirus** is a collection of antivirus programs that can protect your system from over 21,000 different viruses, quarantine or delete existing viruses, and automatically update its virus list to check for the newest viruses. (See Figure 3-20.)
    - **Norton CleanSweep** is a collection of programs that guide you through the process of safely removing programs and files you no longer need. (See Figure 3-21.) Additionally, they will archive, move, and make backup of programs as well as clean up your hard disk. They can also protect your existing files from damage when you install new programs.
    - **Norton CrashGuard** is a collection of troubleshooting utilities. These programs can automatically protect you against programs that crash or freeze the display screen. Before an event causes your system to crash or freeze, CrashGuard intervenes, providing you with options to recover your current work.
- **Norton Web Services** monitors your system for out-of-date software and notifies you of available software updates that can be installed automatically from the Internet.

FIGURE 3-19
Norton SystemWorks

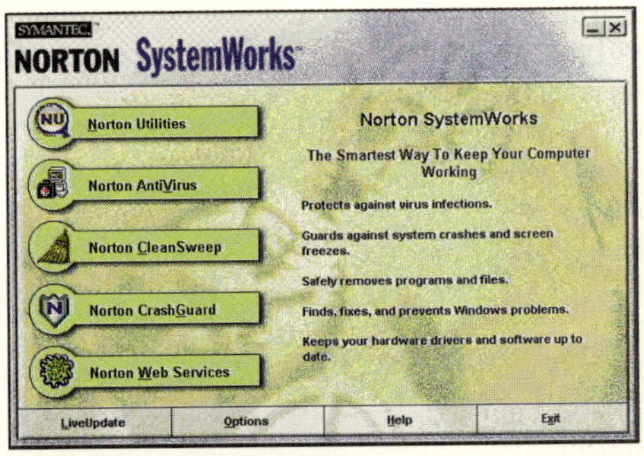

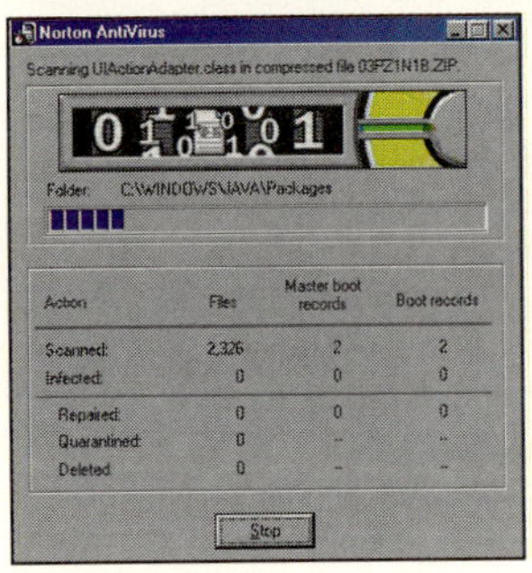

FIGURE 3-20
Norton AntiVirus

CONCEPT CHECK

- ✔ What are utilities?
- ✔ List some common utilities.
- ✔ Name some of the utility suites currently available.

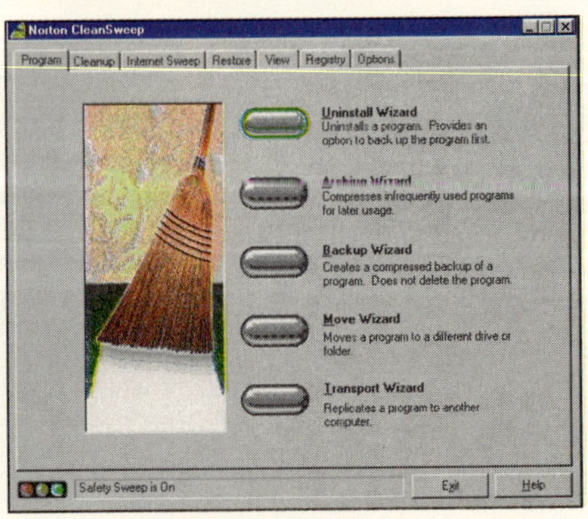

FIGURE 3-21
Norton CleanSweep

A LOOK TO THE FUTURE

New versions of operating systems are being released all the time. While Microsoft's Windows is by far the dominant operating system for today's microcomputers, others are trying to narrow the gap. All are striving toward better hardware support, simpler installations, and greater ease of use.

The next generation of Windows promises to provide a variety of enhanced hardware capabilities, including support for home networks. Using special programs such as Internet Connection Sharing, multiple users on different computers will be able to connect to a home network at the same time and surf the Web sharing a single telephone line and Internet connection. Moreover, home networking will be taken to a new level of connectivity. Future Windows versions will support microcomputer interaction and control over smart appliances, including refrigerators, stereos, and heating and cooling systems.

Expect greater challenges to Windows' dominance. Apple will continue to offer newer and more powerful versions of its Macintosh operating system. New versions of Linux will provide user interfaces to match Windows, and new applications written specifically for Linux will enhance its appeal. Finally, BeOS, (pronounced "bee-O-S") is a young operating system gaining popularity with multimedia developers and programmers. It handles complex 3D graphics and animations better than the competitors and could become a serious operating system contender.

In the near future, operating systems will likely retain their current look and feel. Behind the scenes, however, they will continue to become more powerful, more intuitive, and require less user interaction. Increasing competition promises to accelerate this trend.

VISUAL SUMMARY Browsers, Personal Information Managers, Operating Systems, and Utilities

BROWSERS

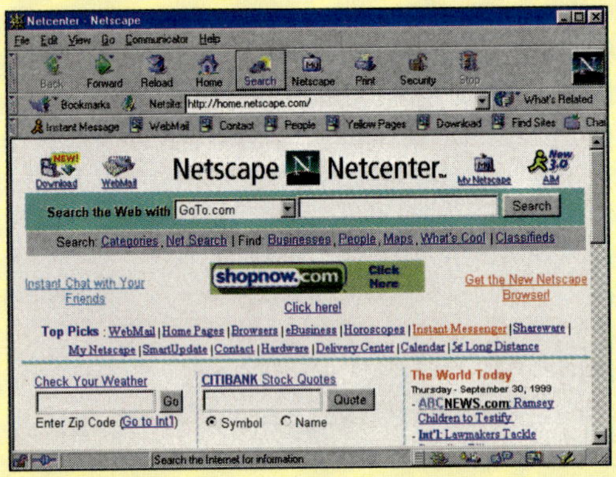

Browsers are programs that connect to remote computers, open and transfer files, display text and images, and provide an uncomplicated interface to the Internet and the Web.

Common activities on the Internet and Web are: *navigating* or *surfing* the Web, *finding* or *searching for information*, and *communicating* with others.

Navigating the Web

Navigating the Web (also known as **surfing** or **browsing**) means to move from one Web site to another. Two common ways to navigate:

- Enter Web address in the Location box.
- Use **hyperlinks** or connections between related Web pages.

Finding Information

With so much information available on the Web, the challenge is finding or locating what you want. Most browsers contain search facilities that connect you to Web sites that specialize in finding information.

Communicating

Communicating is the most popular Internet activity. You can communicate with friends and family using **e-mail.**

PERSONAL INFORMATION MANAGERS

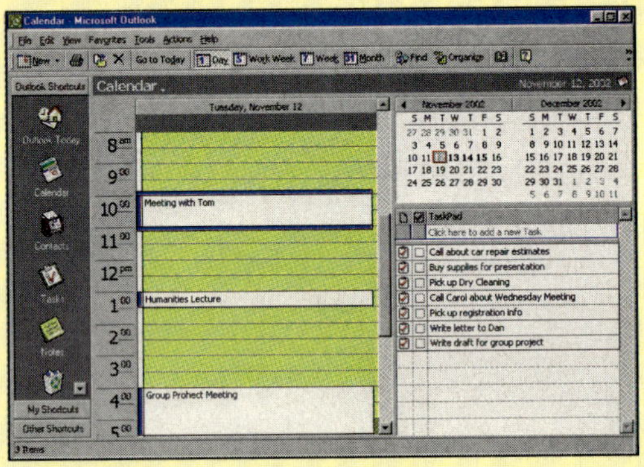

Personal information mangers (also known as **PIMs** and **desktop managers**) are electronic organizers designed to help you get organized and stay organized. PIMs contain a variety of features, including maintaining *calendars, contacts,* and *tasks.*

Calendar

The **calendar** is one of the most important features. Like an electronic appointment book, it tracks events, holidays, assignments, and project schedules.

Contacts

Electronic **contacts** or address books are an essential part of all PIMs. Like a traditional address book, they record names, addresses, and telephone numbers. Linked to other PIM activities, the contacts lists save time and energy.

Tasks

A basic feature of all PIMs is a **task** organizer, or to-do list. It provides two basic functions: (1) recording, displaying, and reminding you of tasks you need to complete and (2) recording, displaying, coordinating, and communicating tasks assigned to a group.

To manage time effectively, competent end users need to understand the functionality and the capabilities of browsers, personal information managers, and system software, including operating systems and utilities.

OPERATING SYSTEMS

Operating systems perform three basic functions: manage resources, provide a user interface, and run programs. Windows, Mac OS, and Unix are popular operating systems for microcomputers.

Windows

Windows is the most widely used operating system today. The name Windows comes from the rectangular boxes (windows) used to display information and run applications.

Multiple windows can be open to **multitask,** or work with different programs simultaneously. The **desktop** is the user interface provided by Windows. **Icons** are often used to interact with the Windows operating system. Another common way is to use the **Start menu.**

Mac OS

The **Mac OS** runs on Macintosh computers. Although not as widely used as Windows, it is very powerful and easy to use. Mac OS 8.5 includes **Sherlock,** an innovative search feature for locating information on the Web or on your hard drive.

Unix

The **Unix** operating system was originally designed to run on minicomputers in network environments. **Linux** is one version of Unix that is receiving a great deal of attention.

UTILITIES

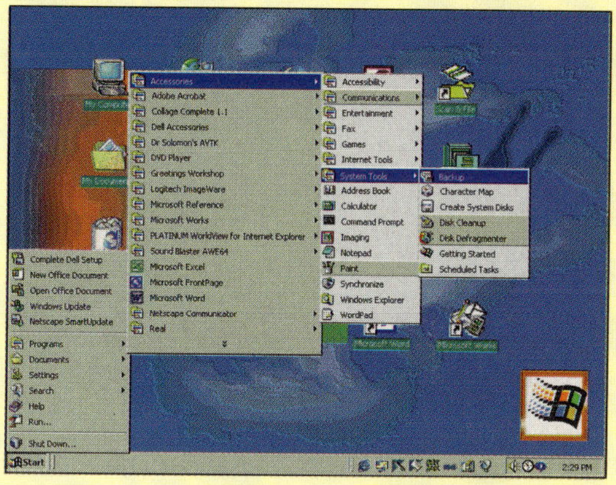

Utilities are specialized programs designed to make computing easier. While there are hundreds of different utility programs, the most essential are: **troubleshooting, antivirus, uninstall, backup,** and **file compression programs.**

Windows Utilities

The Windows operating systems come with several utility programs. These utilities can be accessed from the Systems Tools menu. Three such utilities are *Backup*, *Disk Cleanup*, and *Disk Defragmenter*.

- **Backup**—to back up your hard disk.
- **Disk Cleanup**—a troubleshooting utility for monitoring storage capacity.
- **Disk Defragmenter**—to locate and eliminate unnecessary fragments, rearranges files and unused disk space.

Utility Suites

Utility suites combine several programs into one package. McAfee Office and Norton SystemWorks are the best-known.

Key Terms

Active Desktop (56)
antivirus programs (58)
applications (55)
backup programs (58)
browser (50)
browsing (50)
desktop (56)
desktop managers (52)
device drivers (55)
Disk Cleanup (59)
Disk Defragmenter (59)
e-mail (51)
file compression programs (58)
graphical user interface (GUI) (55)
hypertext links (50)
icons (55)
language translators (55)
Linux (57)
Mac OS (56)
multitasking (55)
navigating (50)
Norton AntiVirus (60)
Norton CleanSweep (60)
Norton CrashGuard (60)
Norton Utilities (60)
Norton Web Services (60)
operating systems (55)
personal information managers (PIMs) (52)
resources (55)
service programs (55)
Sherlock (56)
Start menu (56)
surfing (50)
system software (54)
troubleshooting programs (58)
uninstall programs (58)
Unix (57)
user interface (55)
utilities (55)
Windows (55)

Chapter Review

LEVEL 1

Reviewing Facts and Terms

Matching

Match each numbered item with the most closely related lettered item. Write your answers in the spaces provided.

1. One term for moving between different Web sites. ____
2. Connections within one Web page that take you to a related Web page. ____
3. Program that helps you get organized and stay organized. ____
4. Perform specific tasks related to managing computer resources or files. ____
5. Allow particular input or output devices to communicate with the rest of the computer system. ____
6. Operating system originally designed to run on minicomputers in network environments. ____
7. Through this, users interact with application programs and computer hardware. ____
8. Programs such as word processors and spreadsheets. ____
9. Deals with the physical complexities of computer hardware. ____
10. Programs that operate your computer. ____
11. Allow you to safely and completely remove unneeded programs and related files from your hard disk. ____
12. User interface in Windows. ____
13. Operating system designed to run only on Macintosh computers. ____
14. Convert the programming instructions written by programmers into a language that computers understand and process. ____

a. Applications
b. Backup programs
c. Browsing
d. Desktop
e. Device drivers
f. Disk Cleanup
g. File compression programs
h. Hypertext links
i. Language translators
j. Linux
k. Mac OS
l. Operating systems
m. PIMs
n. System software
o. Troubleshooting programs
p. Uninstall programs
q. Unix
r. User interface
s. Utilities
t. Windows

15. One popular, and free, version of the Unix operating system. ____
16. Recognize and correct problems. ____
17. Operating system that gets its name from its use of rectangular boxes called windows. ____
18. Make copies of files to be used in case originals are lost or damaged. ____
19. Reduce the size of files so they require less storage space. ____
20. Troubleshooting utility for monitoring storage capacity. ____

True/False

In the spaces provided, write T or F to indicate whether the statement is true or false.

1. A connection on one Web page that directs you to a related Web page is called a Web portal. ____
2. A basic feature of all PIMs is word processing. ____
3. System software deals with the physical complexities of computer hardware. ____
4. The Mac OS is designed to run on Macintosh computers. ____
5. Disk Defragmenter is a utility program that rearranges files and unused disk space to optimize operations. ____

Multiple Choice

Circle the letter of the correct answer.

1. An operating system provides a:
   - **a.** user interface
   - **b.** window
   - **c.** database
   - **d.** sort box
   - **e.** grammar checker
2. System software consists of all of the following except:
   - **a.** utilities
   - **b.** device drivers
   - **c.** language translators
   - **d.** operating systems
   - **e.** browsers
3. Moving from one Web site to another is called:
   - **a.** navigating
   - **b.** Web hopping
   - **c.** Web cruising
   - **d.** window shopping
   - **e.** multitasking
4. Programs that help you get organized and communicate with others are:
   - **a.** operating systems
   - **b.** browsers
   - **c.** personal information managers
   - **d.** utilities
   - **e.** desktop organizers
5. Designed to repair or prevent certain frustrating problems, these specialized programs perform specific tasks related to managing computer resources or files:
   - **a.** presentation graphics programs
   - **b.** spreadsheets
   - **c.** utilities
   - **d.** browsers
   - **e.** PIMs

Completion

Complete each statement in the spaces provided.

1. ________ connect to the Web and create Web pages.
2. Windows provides a user interface called the ________.

3. ________ is the ability that most operating systems have to run more than one application at a time.
4. ________ ________ are specialized programs designed to allow particular input or output devices to communicate with the rest of the computer system.
5. Programs that coordinate computer resources, provide an interface between users and the computer, and run applications are called ________ ________.

Reviewing Concepts

LEVEL 2

Open-Ended

On a separate sheet of paper, respond to each question and statement.

1. Describe some of the different ways to navigate from one Web site to another.
2. Compare the three most common microcomputing operating systems. Where are you likely to find each one being used?
3. Explain how you might go about finding information on the Web about the health benefits of vitamins.
4. Outline the features that PIMs typically provide.
5. Describe the five most essential utilities.

Concept Mapping

On a separate sheet of paper, draw a concept map or a flowchart showing how the following terms are related. Show all relationships. Include any additional terms you can think of.

Active Desktop
applications
browser
desktop
desktop managers
device drivers
disk cleanup
disk defragmenter
file compression programs
graphical user interface
hypertext links
Linux
Mac OS
multitasking
navigating
Norton Utilities
operating systems
PIMs
resources
system software
Unix
user interface
Windows

Critical Thinking Questions and Projects

LEVEL 3

Read each exercise and answer the related questions on a separate sheet of paper.

1. *Wealth of information on the Internet:* Have you ever tried to define a computer term you're expected to know, but don't? If, after looking through manuals and other reference books, you still can't find the term, you can try the Web site www.whatis.com, which might just have what you're looking for. It contains an extensive database of computer technology terms and their meaning, as well as links to related sites and current technology topics. This is a very useful site to remember!

   Take a look at whatis.com. Either type "compression" into their search feature or find it in their alphabetical listing of terms. Read through the information they provide about file compression and click all the hyperlinks (colored text) to find out about related topics. When you're done, write a summary about file compression based on what you've learned from whatis.com.
2. *Future of the Internet:* More and more people have access to high-speed Internet connections at home, school computer labs, place of employment, and so on. High-speed Internet connections include cable modems, DSL connections, ISDN lines, and some others. Cable modems, for instance, take only seconds to download files that might take

a 56K modem several minutes to download. These high-speed connections make it more time-effective, and certainly more enjoyable, to download large files such as music and video files, animations, or complex Web pages.

As more people gain high-speed Internet access, how will this shape the future of the Internet? Knowing that you will need to keep the attention of a worldwide audience who will be able download large pieces of information quickly, what kind of Internet services can you imagine developing?

3. *Operating systems and competition:* Operating systems control the basic functions of your computer—how your CPU communicates with all other hardware devices and how applications are run—and give the user an interface with the computer. There are currently several operating systems available, depending on the computer platform (Windows, Mac OS, UNIX). Each of these comes in several versions, with different versions usually representing an evolved form of a previous version: Windows 98, Windows 2000, Mac OS 8, Mac OS 9, UNIX, LINUS, Solaris, Free BSD, and so on.

   New operating systems seem to come out every one to two years, depending on platform. The average user may not notice many changes from one operating system to the next. Yet they keep coming out. Is this necessary, or is it just a cash cow for computer companies? Can you stay with an older operating system and still remain compatible as others change? Is LINUX (an operating system easily found for free) a real threat to Windows, especially in light of the antitrust legal proceedings with Microsoft?

On the Web Exercises

1. Microsoft's Windows

Microsoft created the famous Windows operating system. To learn more about Microsoft's most recent operating systems, visit their Web site at http://www.microsoft.com. Once connected to that site, explore and learn more about the newest operating system from Microsoft. Print out the most informative Web page and write a paragraph describing the most important features of this new operating system.

2. Linux

Unix is a powerful, versatile operating system used by many computer professionals. Some observers believe that the Linux version will become popular for home users and computer novices. To learn about Linux visit our Web site at http://www.mhhe.com/cit/concepts/oleary2000-2001/webex3.html for a link to a related site. Once connected to that site, explore and learn more about Linux. Print out the Web page you find most interesting. Write a paragraph or two discussing the strengths and weaknesses of Linux in comparison to Microsoft Windows and identifying applications that are better suited for Windows and those that are better suited for Linux.

3. Virus Protection

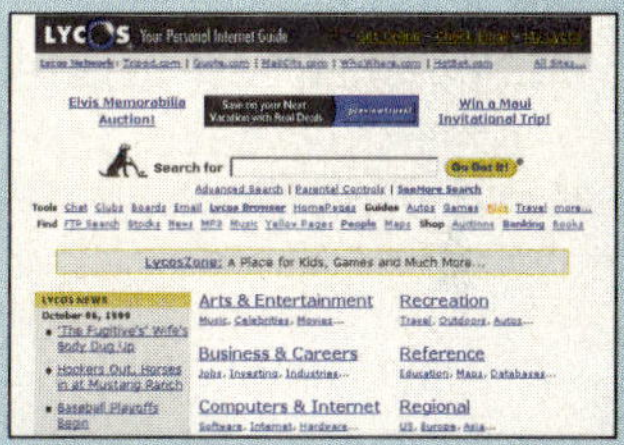

Computer viruses are a serious and well-researched topic on the Web. Viruses have been used to cripple a dictator in the Gulf War and to humiliate Fortune 500 companies. To learn more about viruses, search using the www.lycos.com Web site. Visit several Web sites and print out the Web page you find most interesting. Select two virus protection programs and write a paragraph or two comparing their strengths and weaknesses.

4. Online PIMs

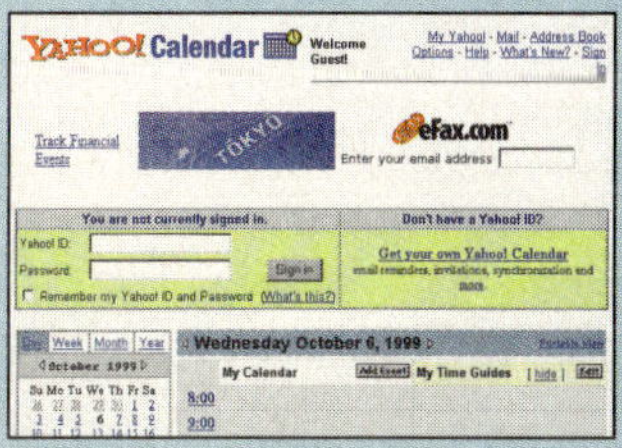

A recent trend in the Internet is online PIMs. These PIMs are popular because they are generally free, easy to use, and accessible from anywhere you can access the Internet. Go to www.calendar.yahoo.com and sign up for a free PIM account. Experiment with it by adding yourself and some of your classmates or friends to the address book. Use the calendar to record your class times and set a meeting for your next class period. Invite a classmate or friend to this meeting via e-mail using the Invitations option of the PIM. Print out your schedule and write a paragraph discussing whether or not a PIM would be useful to you. Provide specific examples.

The System Unit

CHAPTER 4

COMPETENCIES

After you have read this chapter, you should be able to:

1. **Describe how a computer uses binary codes to represent data in electrical form.**
2. **Discuss each of the major system unit components.**
3. **Explain the differences among the three types of memory.**
4. **Discuss the three principal types of bus lines.**
5. **Discuss five types of ports.**

How are application programs executed? That is the subject of this chapter. Why are some microcomputers more powerful than others? The answer lies in three words: *speed, capacity,* and *flexibility.* After reading this chapter, you will be able to judge how fast, powerful, and versatile a particular microcomputer is. As you might expect, this knowledge is valuable if you are planning to buy a new microcomputer system or to upgrade an existing system. (The buyer's guide and the upgrader's guide at the end of this book provide additional information.) It will also help

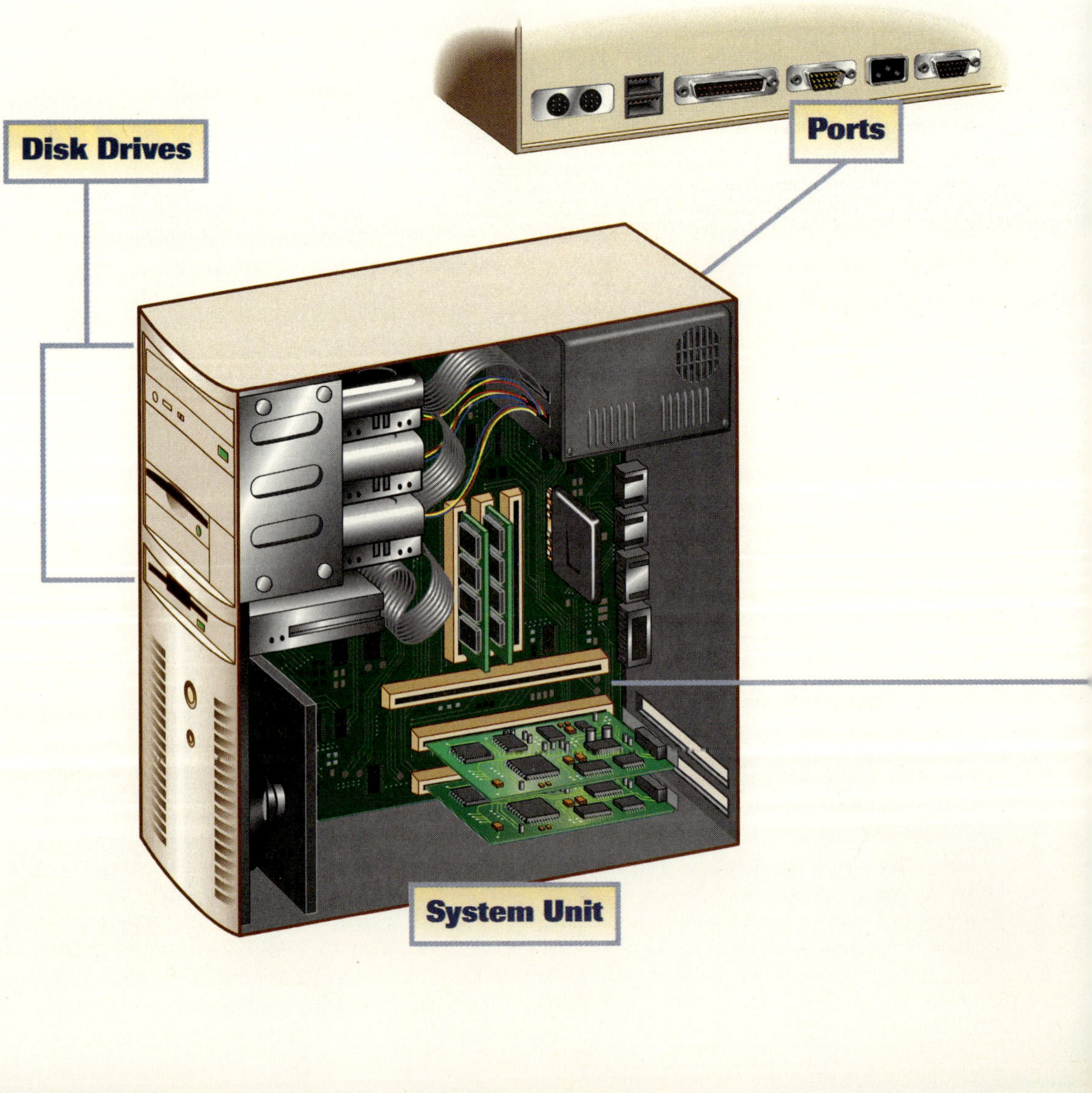

you to evaluate whether or not an existing microcomputer system is powerful enough for today's new and exciting applications.

Sometime you may get the chance to watch when a technician opens up a microcomputer to fix it. You will see that it is basically a collection of electronic circuitry. There is no need for you to understand how all these components work. However, it is important to understand the principles. Once you do, you will then be able to determine how powerful a particular microcomputer is. This will help you judge whether it can run particular kinds of programs and can meet your needs as a user.

Competent end users need to understand the functionality of the basic components in the system unit, including the system board, microprocessor, memory, system clock, expansion slots and cards, bus lines, ports, and cables.

Electronic Data and Instructions

Data and instructions are represented electronically with a binary, or two-state, numbering system. The three principal binary coding schemes are ASCII, EBCDIC, and Unicode.

People follow instructions and process data using letters, numbers, and special characters. For example, if we wanted someone to add the numbers 3 and 5 together and record the answer, we might say "please add 3 and 5 and write the sum on a piece of paper." The system unit, however, is electronic circuitry and cannot directly process such a request. Before anything can occur within the system unit, a conversion must occur from what we understand to what the system unit can electronically process.

What is the most fundamental statement you can make about electricity? It is simply this: It can be either *on* or *off.* Indeed, there are many forms of technology that can make use of this two-state on/off, yes/no, present/absent arrangement. For instance, a light switch may be on or off, or an electric circuit open or closed. A magnetized spot on a tape or disk may have a positive charge or a negative charge. This is the reason, then, that the binary system is used to represent data and instructions.

The decimal system that we are all familiar with has 10 digits (0, 1, 2, 3, 4, 5, 6, 7, 8, 9). The **binary system,** however, consists of only two digits—0 and 1. Each 0 or 1 is called a **bit**—short for *bi*nary digi*t.* In the system unit, the 0 can be represented by electricity being off, and the 1 by electricity being on. In order to represent numbers, letters, and special characters, bits are combined into groups of eight bits called **bytes.** Each byte typically represents one character.

Binary Coding Schemes

Now let us consider an important question. How are characters represented as 0s and 1s ("off" and "on" electrical states) in the computer? The answer is in the use of *binary coding schemes.* (See Figure 4-1.)

Code	Uses
ASCII	Microcomputers
EBCDIC	Larger computers
Unicode	International languages

FIGURE 4-1
Binary codes

Two of the most popular binary coding schemes use eight bits to form each byte. These two codes are *ASCII* and *EBCDIC.* (See Figure 4-2.) A recently developed code, *Unicode,* uses sixteen bits.

- **ASCII,** pronounced "*as*-key," stands for *A*merican *S*tandard *C*ode for *I*nformation *I*nterchange. This is the most widely used binary code for microcomputers.
- **EBCDIC,** pronounced "*eb*-see-dick," stands for *E*xtended *B*inary *C*oded *D*ecimal *I*nterchange *C*ode. It was developed by IBM and is used primarily for large computers.
- **Unicode** is a 16-bit code designed to support international languages like Chinese and Japanese. These languages have too many characters to be represented by the eight-bit ASCII and EBCDIC codes. Unicode was developed by Unicode, Inc., with support from Apple, IBM, and Microsoft.

Symbol	ASCII	EBCDIC
A	0100 0001	1100 0001
B	0100 0010	1100 0010
C	0100 0011	1100 0011
D	0100 0100	1100 0100
E	0100 0101	1100 0101
F	0100 0110	1100 0110
G	0100 0111	1100 0111
H	0100 1000	1100 1000
I	0100 1001	1100 1001
J	0100 1010	1101 0001
K	0100 1011	1101 0010
L	0100 1100	1101 0011
M	0100 1101	1101 0100
N	0100 1110	1101 0101
O	0100 1111	1101 0110
P	0101 0000	1101 0111
Q	0101 0001	1101 1000
R	0101 0010	1101 1001
S	0101 0011	1110 0010
T	0101 0100	1110 0011
U	0101 0101	1110 0100
V	0101 0110	1110 0101
W	0101 0111	1110 0110
X	0101 1000	1110 0111
Y	0101 1001	1110 1000
Z	0101 1010	1110 1001

Symbol	ASCII	EBCDIC
!	0010 0001	0101 1010
"	0010 0010	0111 1111
#	0010 0011	0111 1011
$	0010 0100	0101 1011
%	0010 0101	0110 1100
&	0010 0110	0101 0000
(	0010 1000	0100 1101
)	0010 1001	0101 1101
*	0010 1010	0101 1100
+	0010 1011	0100 1110
0	0011 0000	1111 0000
1	0011 0001	1111 0001
2	0011 0010	1111 0010
3	0011 0011	1111 0011
4	0011 0100	1111 0100
5	0011 0101	1111 0101
6	0011 0110	1111 0110
7	0011 0111	1111 0111
8	0011 1000	1111 1000
9	0011 1001	1111 1001

FIGURE 4-2
ASCII and EBCDIC binary coding schemes

When you press a key on the keyboard, a character is automatically converted into a series of electronic pulses that the system can recognize. For example, pressing the letter *A* on a keyboard causes an electronic signal to be sent to the microcomputer's system unit. The system unit then converts it to the ASCII code of 0100 0001. (See Figure 4-3.)

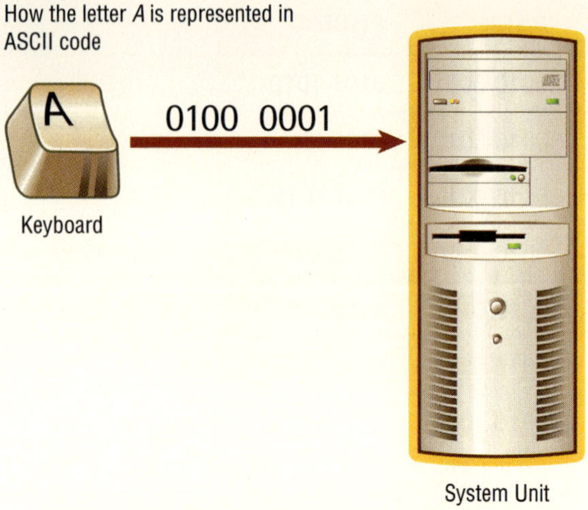

FIGURE 4-3
How the letter *A* is represented in ASCII code

All instructions and data have to be converted into binary data before they can be executed. For example, the instructions 3 + 5 requires 24 bits using the ASCII coding scheme. (See Figure 4-4.)

Why are coding schemes important? Whenever files are used or shared by different computers or applications, the same coding scheme must be used. Generally, this is not a problem if both computers are microcomputers since both would most likely use ASCII code. And most microcomputer applications store files using this code. However, problems occur when files are shared between microcomputers and larger computers that use EBCDIC code. The files must be translated from one coding scheme to the other before processing can begin. Fortunately, special conversion programs are available to help with this translation.

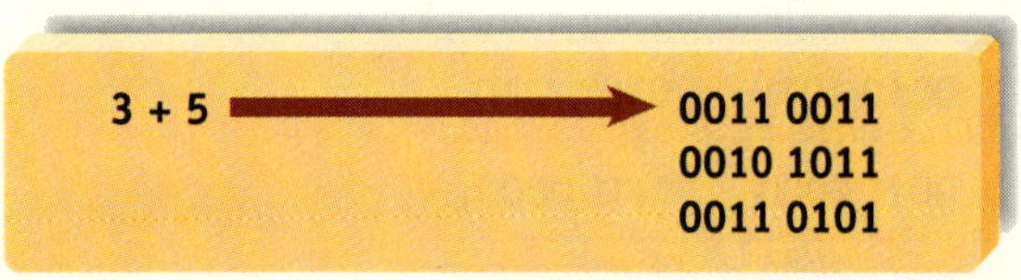

FIGURE 4-4
ASCII code for 3 + 5

CONCEPT CHECK

- ✔ The ________ system is used to represent data and instructions.
- ✔ Name the three binary coding schemes.
- ✔ All instructions and data must be converted into ________ ________ before they can be executed.

System Board

The system board connects all system components and allows input and output devices to communicate with the system unit.

FIGURE 4-5
System board

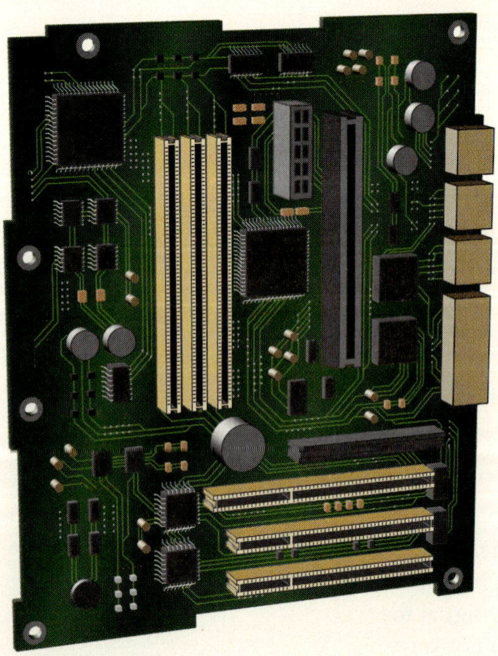

The **system board** is also known as the **main board** or **motherboard.** (See Figure 4-5.) The system board is the communications web for the entire computer system. Every component of the system unit connects directly to the system board. It acts as a data path allowing the various components to communicate with one another. External devices such as keyboard, mouse, and monitor could not communicate with the system unit without the system board.

On a desktop computer, the system board is located at the bottom of the systems unit. On a tower unit, the system board is located on one of the sides. It is a large flat circuit board covered with sockets and other electronic parts, including a variety of chips. A **chip** consists of a tiny circuit board etched on a postage-stamp-sized square of sandlike material called silicon. (See Figure 4-6.) A chip is also called a **silicon chip, semiconductor,** or **integrated circuit.** Chips are mounted on carrier packages, which then plug into sockets on the system board.

Microprocessor

The CPU is located on the microprocessor chip and has two components—the control unit and the arithmetic-logic unit. RISC and CISC are two types of microprocessors.

FIGURE 4-6
Chip

In a microcomputer system, the **central processing unit (CPU)** or **processor** is contained on a single chip called the microprocessor. Typically, this microprocessor is contained within a cartridge that plugs in to the system board. (See Figure 4-7.) The microprocessor is the "brains" of the system. It has two basic components: the control unit and the arithmetic-logic unit.

Control Unit

The **control unit** tells the rest of the computer system how to carry out a program's instructions. It directs the movement of electronic signals between memory—which temporarily holds data, instructions, and processed information—and the arithmetic-logic unit. It also directs these control signals between the CPU and input and output devices.

FIGURE 4-7
Microprocessor cartridge

Arithmetic-Logic Unit

The **arithmetic-logic unit,** usually called the **ALU,** performs two types of operations—arithmetic and logical. *Arithmetic* operations are, as you might expect, the fundamental math operations: addition, subtraction, multiplication, and division. *Logical* operations consist of comparisons. That is, two pieces of data are compared to see whether one is equal to (=), less than (<), or greater than (>) the other.

Microprocessor Chips

Chip capacities are often expressed in word sizes. A **word** is the number of bits (such as 16, 32, or 64) that can be accessed at one time by the CPU. The more bits in a word, the more powerful—and the faster—the computer is. A 32-bit-word computer can access 4 bytes at a time. A 64-bit-word computer can access 8 bytes at a time. Therefore, the 64-bit computer is faster.

Microcomputers process data and instructions in millionths of a second, or **microseconds.** Supercomputers, by contrast, operate at speeds measured in nanoseconds and even picoseconds—1,000 to 1 million times as fast as microcomputers. (See Figure 4-8.)

There are two types of microprocessor chips.

- **CISC chips:** The most common type of microprocessor is the **complex instruction set computer (CISC)** chip. This design was popularized by Intel and is the basis for their line of microprocessors. It is the most widely used chip design with thousands of programs written specifically for it. Intel's Pentium II and Pentium III are recent CISC chips. Two other manufacturers of CISC chips are AMD and Cyrix.

ON THE WEB EXPLORATIONS

Motorola is a leader in RISC research and development. To learn more about the company, visit its Web site at **http://www.motorola.com**

Unit	Speed
Millisecond	Thousandth of a second
Microsecond	Millionth of a second
Nanosecond	Billionth of a second
Picosecond	Trillionth of a second

FIGURE 4-8
Processing speeds

Microprocessor	Type	Typical Use
Pentium	CISC	Microcomputers
PowerPC	RISC	Apple Computers
ALPHA	RISC	Supercomputers, workstations
MIPS	RISC	Workstations, video games

FIGURE 4-9
Popular microprocessors

- **RISC chips: reduced instruction set computer (RISC)** chips use fewer instructions. This design is simpler and less costly than CISC chips. A recent Motorola chip developed with IBM and Apple is the PowerPC chip. Two other recent RISC chips are Digital Equipment Corporation's (DEC) Alpha chip and Silicon Graph's MIPS chip. These chips are used in many of today's most powerful microcomputers. See Figure 4-9 for a table of popular microprocessors.

Some specialized processor chips are available. One example is the tiny built-in microprocessor used in **smart cards.** Smart cards are about the size of a credit card. They can be used to hold health insurance information, frequent flier records, or driver's license information, and so on. While this technology has been around for some time, it has received more attention lately. The federal government has suggested a National Health Security smart card for all individuals. This card would be used for a number of applications, including monitoring federal financial assistance programs.

CONCEPT CHECK

- ✔ What role does the system board play in a computer?
- ✔ Which two basic components make up the CPU?
- ✔ Name two types of microprocessor chips.

Memory

Three types of memory are RAM, ROM, and CMOS.

There are three well-known types of memory chips: random-access memory (RAM), read-only memory (ROM), and complementary metal-oxide semiconductor (CMOS).

RAM

Random-access memory (RAM) chips hold the program and data that the CPU is presently processing. (See Figure 4-10.) That is, it is *temporary* or volatile storage. (Secondary storage, which we shall describe in Chapter 6, is *permanent* storage, such as the data stored on diskettes. Data from this kind of storage must be loaded into RAM before it can be used.)

RAM is called temporary because as soon as the microcomputer is turned off, everything in RAM is lost. It is also lost if there is a power failure that

FIGURE 4-10
RAM chips

disrupts the electric current going to the microcomputer. For this reason, as we mentioned earlier, it is a good idea to save your work in progress. That is, if you are working on a document or a spreadsheet, every few minutes you should save, or store, the material.

There is a relatively new type of RAM, however, that is not temporary. **Flash RAM** or **flash memory** chips can retain data even if power is disrupted. This type of memory is more expensive than RAM and used primarily in high-end portable computers.

Knowing the amount of RAM is important! Some software programs may require more memory capacity than a particular microcomputer offers. For instance, Excel 2000 requires 20MB of RAM. Additional RAM is needed to hold any data or other applications. However, many microcomputers—particularly older ones—may not have enough memory to hold the program, much less work with it. The capacity or amount of RAM is expressed in bytes. There are four commonly used units of measurement to describe memory capacity. (See Figure 4-11.)

Even if your computer does not have enough RAM to hold a program, it probably can run the program using **virtual memory.** Most of today's operating systems support virtual memory. With virtual memory, large programs are divided into parts and the parts stored on a secondary device, usually a hard disk. Each part is then read into RAM only when needed. In this way, computer systems are able to run very large programs.

Unit	Capacity
Kilobyte (KB)	1,000 bytes
Megabyte (MB)	1 million bytes
Gigabyte (GB)	1 billion bytes
Terabyte (TB)	1 trillion bytes

FIGURE 4-11
Memory capacity

TIPS Does your computer seem to be getting slower and slower? Perhaps it's so slow you are thinking about buying a new one. Before doing that, consider the following suggestions that might add a little zip to your current system.

1. *Uninstall programs you no longer need.* Explore the contents of your hard disk and identify programs that you no longer need. If you have Windows 95 or Windows 98, use Start/Settings/Control Panel/Add/Remove Programs to access the Uninstall feature.
2. *Remove unneeded fonts.* If you have Windows 95 or 98, use Start/Settings/Control Panel/Fonts to determine the different font types stored on your system. To see a sample of any font type, double-click it. Review the fonts and delete those you will not need.
3. *Empty the Recycle Bin.* If you have Windows 95 or Windows 98, files are not removed from your hard disk when you delete them. Rather, they are moved to the Recycle Bin. To empty or remove files from the Recycle Bin, open the Recycle Bin and use File/Empty Recycle Bin.

Another term you are apt to hear about in conjunction with RAM is **cache memory** or **RAM cache.** Cache (pronounced "cash") memory is used to store the most frequently accessed information stored in RAM. The cache acts as a temporary high-speed holding area between the memory and the CPU. In a computer with a cache (not all machines have one), the computer detects which information in RAM is most frequently used. It then copies that information into the cache. When needed, the CPU can quickly access the information from the cache. Most newer microprocessors have cache memory built in.

ROM

Read-only memory (ROM) chips have programs built into them at the factory. Unlike RAM chips, ROM chips are not volatile and cannot be changed by the user. "Read only" means that the CPU can read, or retrieve, the programs written on the ROM chip. However, the computer cannot write—encode or change—the information or instructions in ROM.

ROM chips typically contain special instructions for detailed computer operations. For example, ROM instructions may start the computer, give keyboard keys their special control capabilities, and put characters on the screen. ROMs are also called **firmware.**

CMOS

A **complementary metal-oxide semiconductor (CMOS)** chip provides flexibility and expandability for a computer system. It contains essential information that is required every time the computer system is turned on. The chip supplies such information as the amount of RAM, type of keyboard, mouse, monitor, and disk drives. Unlike RAM, it is powered by a battery and does not lose its contents when the power is turned off. Unlike ROM, its contents can be changed to reflect changes in the computer system such as increased RAM and new hardware devices.

See Figure 4-12 for a summary of the three types of memory.

CONCEPT CHECK

- ✔ Name three well-known types of memory chips.
- ✔ What makes RAM different from ROM?

Type	Use
RAM	Programs and data
ROM	Fixed start-up instructions
CMOS	Flexible start-up instructions

FIGURE 4-12
Memory

System Clock

Speed of computer operations is measured in megahertz, or millionths of a second.

The **system clock** controls the speed of operations within a computer. This speed is expressed in **megahertz** (abbreviated **MHz**). One megahertz equals 1 million cycles (beats) per second. The faster the clock speed, the faster the computer can process information.

Expansion Slots and Cards

Expansion slots provide an open architecture. Expansion cards provide network connections, TV tuner cards, and more.

Computers are known for having different kinds of "architectures." Machines that have **closed architecture** are manufactured in such a way that users cannot easily add new devices. Most microcomputers have **open architecture.** They allow users to expand their systems by providing **slots** on the system board. Users can insert optional devices known as **expansion cards** into these slots. (See Figure 4-13.) Expansion cards are also called **plug-in boards, controller cards, adapter cards,** and **interface cards.**

Expansion cards plug into slots inside the system unit. Ports on the cards allow cables to be connected from the expansion cards to devices outside the system unit. Among the kinds of expansion cards available are:

- **Network adapter cards:** These cards are used to connect a computer to one or more other computers. This forms a communication network whereby users can share data, programs, and hardware. The **network adapter card** typically connects the system unit to a cable that connects to the other devices on the network. The network adapter card plugs into a slot inside the system unit.
- **Small computer system interface (SCSI—pronounced "scuzzy") card:** Most computers have only a limited number of expansion slots. A **SCSI card** uses only one slot and can connect as many as seven devices to the system unit. These cards are used to connect such devices as printers, hard-disk drives, and CD-ROM drives to the system unit.

FIGURE 4-13
Expansion card

FIGURE 4-14
TV tuner card

- **TV tuner cards:** Now you can watch television and surf the Internet at the same time. **Television boards** contain a TV tuner and a video converter that changes the TV signal into one that can be displayed on your monitor. (See Figure 4-14.) This **PC/TV** combination has become increasingly popular and has led to specialized large-screen systems with high-quality audio called **home PCs.**
- **PC cards:** To meet the size and constraints of portable computers, credit card–sized expansion boards have been developed. These cards can be easily inserted and replaced from the outside of a portable computer. They are called **PC cards** or **Personal Computer Memory Card International Association (PCMCIA) cards.** (See Figure 4-15.) These cards can be used for a variety of purposes, including increasing memory and connecting to other computers.

MAKING IT WORK FOR YOU

TV Tuner Cards and Video Clips

Want to watch your favorite television program while you work? Perhaps you would like to include a video clip from television and include it in a class presentation. It's easy using a video TV card.

How It Works

A video capture card converts signals from a television or VCR into signals that your computer can process. Once the card has been installed, you can view, capture, and use television video clips in a variety of ways.

Viewing

You can be running an application such as PowerPoint and view your favorite TV shows, by taking the steps shown in Figure A.

FIGURE A

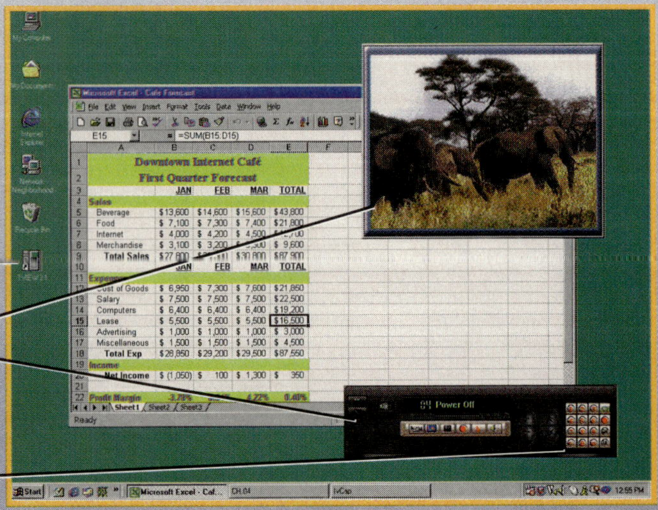

1. Click the TV icon on the desktop.
2. Size and move the television window and control box window.
3. Select the channel.

A wide variety of other expansion boards exist. Some of the most widely used are the following: Video adapter cards are used to adapt a variety of color video display monitors to a computer. CD-ROM cards connect optical disk drives (which we discuss in Chapter 6), and sound boards can record and play back digital sound.

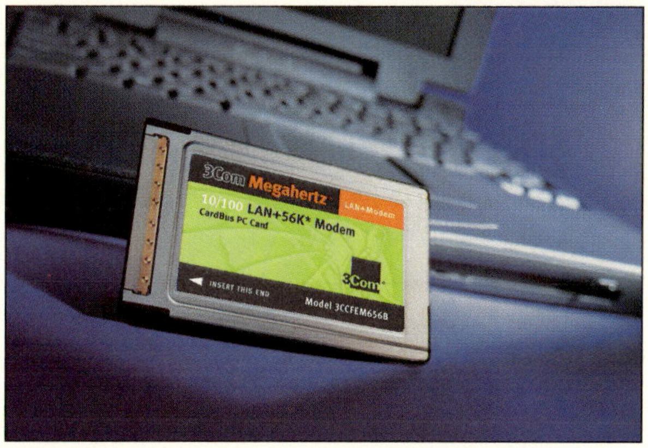

FIGURE 4-15
A PC card

Capturing

You can capture the video playing in the TV window into a file by taking the steps shown in Figure B.

FIGURE B

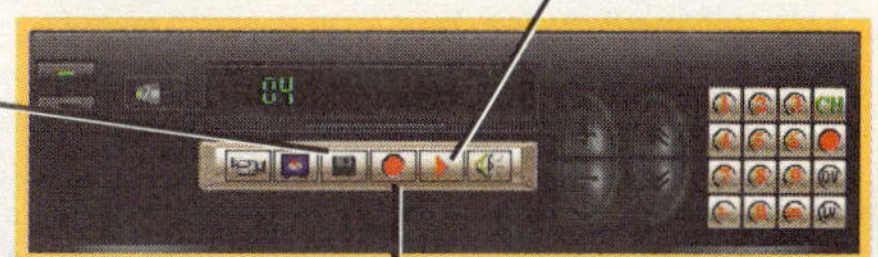

Using

Once captured in a file, a video can be used in any number of ways. It can be added to a Web page, attached to an e-mail, or added to a class presentation.

For example, you could include a video clip into a PowerPoint presentation by taking the steps shown in Figure C.

FIGURE C

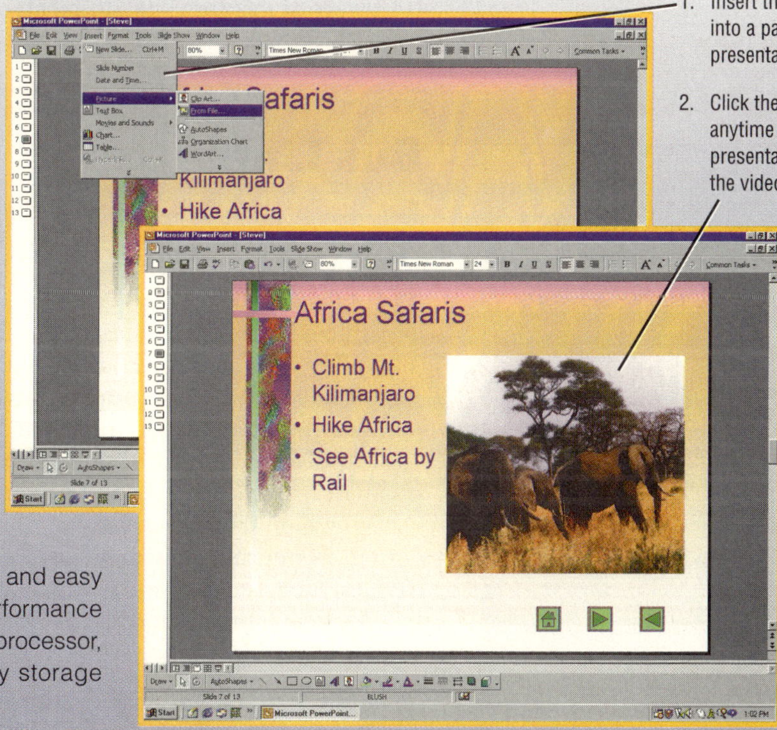

TV tuner cards are relatively inexpensive and easy to install. Some factors limiting their performance on your computer are the speed of your processor, the amount of memory, and secondary storage capacity.

TIPS Having problems or want to upgrade your system and would like professional help? Here are a few suggestions.

1. *Select a reputable computer store.* Consider local as well as national chain stores. Check them out with the Better Business Bureau.
2. *Visit the store with your computer.* Ideally, have a knowledgeable friend accompany you. Describe the problem and get a written estimate. Ask about the company's warranty.
4. *Tag your system.* If you leave the system, attach a tag with your name, address, and telephone number.
5. *Pay by credit card.* If a dispute occurs, many credit card companies will intervene on your side.

To access the capabilities of an expansion board, the board must be inserted into a slot in the system unit and the system reconfigured to recognize the new board. Reconfiguration may require setting special switches on the expansion board and creating special configuration files. This can be a complex and difficult task. A recent development known as **Plug and Play** promises to eliminate this task.

Plug and Play is a set of hardware and software standards recently developed by Intel, Microsoft, and others. It is an effort by hardware and software vendors to create operating systems, processing units, and expansion boards, as well as other devices, that are able to configure themselves. Ideally, to install a new expansion board all you have to do is insert the board and turn on the computer. As the computer starts up, it will search for these Plug and Play devices and automatically configure the devices and the computer system.

Plug and Play is an evolving capability. A limited number of completely Plug and Play–ready systems exist today. However, observers predict that within the next few years this will become a widely adopted standard, and adding expansion boards will be a simple task.

CONCEPT CHECK

- ✔ What is the difference between a closed architecture and an open architecture?
- ✔ There are several kinds of expansion cards available. In general, these cards allow users to do what for their system?
- ✔ What role does a SCSI card play in expansion?

Bus Lines

Bus lines provide data pathways that connect various system components.

FIGURE 4-16
Bus lines

A **bus line**—also known as **data bus** or simply **bus**—connects the parts of the CPU to each other. It also links the CPU to various other components on the system board. A bus is a data roadway along which bits travel. (See Figure 4-16.) Such data pathways resemble a multilane highway. The more lanes there are, the faster traffic can go through. Similarly, the greater the capacity of a bus, the more powerful and faster the operation. A 64-bit bus has greater capacity than a 32-bit bus, for example.

Why should you even have to care about what a bus line is? The answer is that, as microprocessor chips have changed, so have bus lines. Many devices, such as expansion boards, will work with only one type of bus line.

A system unit has more than one type of bus line. The three principal bus lines (or "architectures") are:

- **Industry Standard Architecture (ISA)** was developed for the IBM Personal Computer. First it was an 8-bit-wide data path; then it was 16 bits wide. Although too slow for many of today's applications, the ISA bus is still widely used.

- **Peripheral Component Interconnect (PCI)** was originally developed to meet the video demands of graphical user interfaces. PCI is a high-speed 32-bit or 64-bit bus that is over 20 times faster than ISA buses. The PCI is expected to replace the ISA bus in the near future. PCI buses are widely used to connect the CPU, memory, and expansion boards.
- **Accelerated Graphics Port (AGP)** is the newest bus and over twice as fast as the PCI bus. While the PCI bus is used for a variety of purposes, the AGP bus is dedicated to the acceleration of graphics performance. Widely used for graphics and 3-D animations, the AGP is replacing the PCI bus for the transfer of video data.

CONCEPT CHECK

✔ What is a bus?

✔ What is the function of a bus line?

✔ List the three principal bus lines. Which is fastest?

Ports and Cables

Ports are connecting sockets. Cables connect input and output devices to ports.

A **port** is a connecting socket on the outside of the system unit. (See Figure 4-17.) Some ports, like the mouse and keyboard ports, are for specific devices. Others, like those listed below, can be used for a variety of different devices.

- **Serial ports** are used for a wide variety of purposes. They are used to connect a mouse, keyboard, modem, and many other devices to the system unit. Serial ports send data one bit at a time and are very good for sending information over a long distance.
- **Parallel ports** are used to connect external devices that need to send or receive a lot of data over a short distance. These ports typically send eight bits of data simultaneously across eight parallel wires. Parallel ports are mostly used to connect printers to the system unit.

FIGURE 4-17
Ports

ON THE WEB EXPLORATIONS

Micron Inc. is one of the largest manufacturers of system unit components. To learn more about the company, visit its Web site at

http://www.micron.com

- **Accelerated graphics ports (AGPs)** are used to connect monitors. They are able to support high-speed graphics and other video input.
- **Universal serial bus (USB) ports** are expected to gradually replace serial and parallel ports. They are faster, and one USB port can be used to connect several devices to the system unit.
- **FireWire ports** are the newest type. They are even faster than USB ports and are used to connect high-speed printers and even video cameras to the system unit.

Cables are used to connect input and output devices to the system unit via the ports. See Figure 4-18 for some of the most common types of cables.

For a summary of the major system unit components, see Figure 4-19.

CONCEPT CHECK

- ✔ There are several different kinds of ports. What is the general function of a port?
- ✔ Cables connect ________ and ________ devices to the system unit via the ports.

Cable	Port	Devices
	Mouse	Mouse
	Keyboard	Keyboard
	Serial	Mouse, modem, keyboard
	Parallel	Printer, CD-ROM drive, Zip drive
	AGP Video	Monitor
	USB	Modem, joy stick, scanner
	FireWire	Video camera

FIGURE 4-18
Cables

Component	Function
System board	Holds the various other system components
Microprocessor	Contains the CPU on a single chip
Memory	Holds programs and instructions
System clock	Controls the speed of computer operations
Expansion slots and boards	Connect to system board to allow expansion of system capabilities
Bus lines	Connect various internal system components
Ports	Connect outside devices to system unit

FIGURE 4-19
Major components of a system unit

A LOOK TO THE FUTURE

Intel's Mobil Module and Xircom's PC cards could lead the way to desktop computing power in notebook computers.

Wouldn't it be nice if you could conveniently carry one of today's most powerful microcomputers? One that was light, compact, and would run on batteries? You could take it to class, to a group project meeting, or even to the beach.

Of course that's what notebook computers are all about. Unfortunately, the power of today's notebook microprocessors lags behind their desktop counterparts. Additionally, notebooks are priced higher than desktops with comparable performance. But all that may change in the next few years.

Intel, a leader in microprocessor technology, has recently taken steps to reduce the performance lag between notebooks and desktops. One step is the recent development of the Intel Mobil Module. This module combines multiple functions including the microprocessor onto a single circuit board. It will allow notebook manufacturers to readily switch to newer processors as they become available. Another step is Intel's purchase of 12.5 percent of Xircom, a maker of PC cards used to connect notebooks to corporate networks. Observers note that future Xircom products will likely encourage managers to replace their corporate desktop systems with notebooks.

Will your next computer be a notebook? There is a clear trend. Today more than one in four microcomputer buyers purchase a notebook computer and that number is expected to increase in the next few years.

VISUAL SUMMARY The System Unit

ELECTRONIC REPRESENTATION

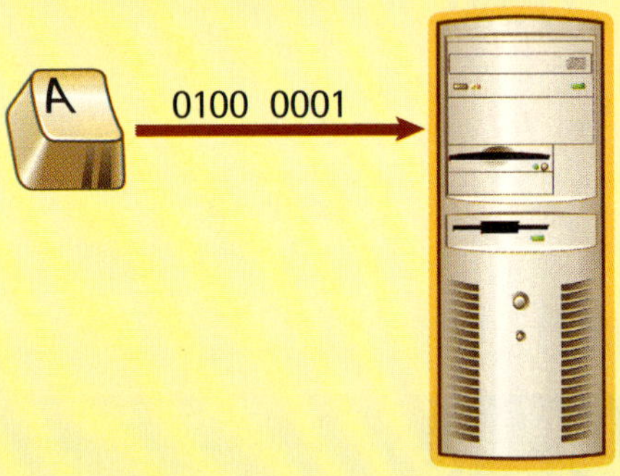

Data and instructions are represented **electronically** with a two-state **binary system** of numbers (0 and 1). Each 0 or 1 is called a **bit**. A **byte** consists of eight bits and represents one character.

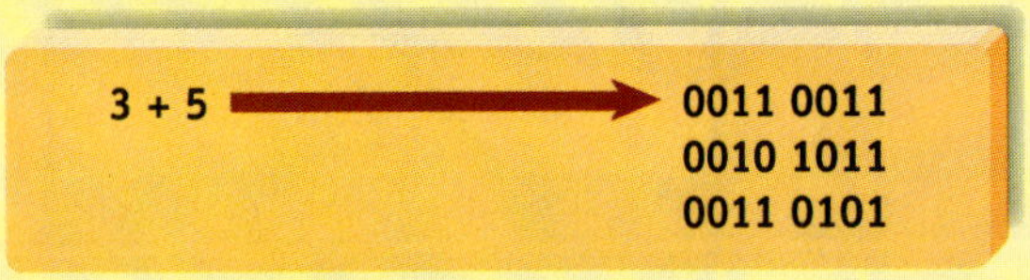

Binary Coding Schemes

Binary coding schemes convert binary data into characters. Three such schemes are:

- **ASCII**—the most widely used for microcomputers
- **EBCDIC**—developed by IBM and used primarily by large computers
- **Unicode**—16-bit code to support international languages like Chinese and Japanese.

SYSTEM BOARD

The **system board**, also known as the **main board** or the **motherboard**, connects all system components. It is a flat circuit board covered with sockets and other electronic parts, including a variety of chips.

A **chip**, also known as a **silicon chip**, **semiconductor**, or **integrated circuit**, is a postage-stamp-sized circuit board.

To be a competent end user, you need to understand how data and programs are represented electronically. Additionally, you need to understand the functionality of the basic components in the system unit: system board, microprocessor, memory, system clock, expansion slots and cards, bus lines, and ports and cables.

MICROPROCESSOR

Unit	Speed
Millisecond	Thousandth of a second
Microsecond	Millionth of a second
Nanosecond	Billionth of a second
Picosecond	Trillionth of a second

The **microprocessor** plugs into the system board, contains the **CPU,** and is the "brains" of the system unit. Two basic components of the microprocessor are the *control unit* and the *arithmetic-logic* unit.

Control Unit

The **control unit** executes programs by directing the other system components. It directs electronic signals between memory, the arithmetic-logic unit, and input/output devices.

Arithmetic-Logic Unit

The **arithmetic-logic unit,** commonly referred to as the **ALU,** performs arithmetic (math) and logical (comparisons) operations.

Microprocessor Chips

A **word** is the number of bits (such as 16, 32, or 64) that can be accessed by the microprocessor at one time. The more bits in a word, the more powerful the microprocessor.

Two types of microprocessor chips are:

- **Complex instruction set computer (CISC)** chips are the basis for Intel's Pentium II and Pentium III microprocessors.
- **Reduced instruction set computer (RISC)** chips use fewer instructions. They are the basis for IBM and Motorola's PowerPC microprocessor.

Smart cards contain built-in microprocessor chips.

MEMORY

There are three types of **memory** chips: RAM, ROM, and CMOS.

RAM

RAM chips are called **temporary** or **volatile** because their contents are lost if power is disrupted.

- **Flash RAM** or **flash memory** is a special type of RAM that does not lose its contents when power is disrupted.
- **Virtual memory** uses the hard disk to run large programs on systems with limited memory.
- **Memory cache** or **RAM cache** is a high-speed holding area for frequently used data and information.

ROM

ROM chips are permanent and control essential system operations.

CMOS

CMOS chips provide flexibility and expandability to computer systems.

Unit	Capacity
Kilobyte (KB)	1,000 bytes
Megabyte (MB)	1 million bytes
Gigabyte (GB)	1 billion bytes
Terabyte (TB)	1 trillion bytes

SYSTEM CLOCK

The **system clock** controls the speed of computer operations. It is measured in **megahertz (MHz).**

EXPANSION SLOTS AND CARDS

Expansion slots and **cards** allow additional devices to be added to a computer system.

Expansion Slots

Expansion slots connect the system board to expansion cards.

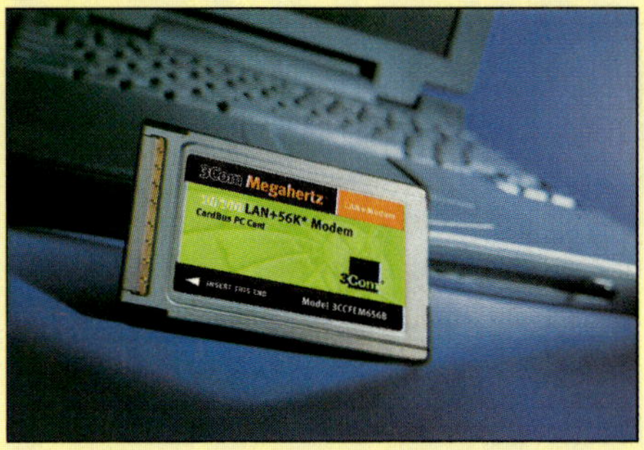

Expansion Cards

Expansion cards provide network connections, SCSI connections, PC/TV or combined computer and TV operations, PC cards for expanding portable computer capabilities, and more.

Plug and Play is an evolving set of hardware and software designed to assist the installation of expansion cards.

BUS LINES

Bus lines provide data pathways that connect various system components. Three principal types are:

- **ISA**—older and slower but still widely used.
- **PCI**—high-speed; used to connect CPU, memory, and expansion boards.
- **AGP**—fastest; used for video data.

PORTS AND CABLES

Ports and **cables** allow external devices to connect to the system unit.

Ports

Ports are connecting sockets on the outside of the system unit. They are used to connect keyboards, mouse, monitors, modems, and printers. The five most common types are **serial, parallel, AGP, USB,** and **FireWire.**

Cables

Cables are used to connect external devices to the system unit via ports.

Key Terms

accelerated graphics port (AGP) (81)
adapter card (77)
arithmetic-logic unit (ALU) (73)
ASCII (70)
binary system (70)
bit (70)
bus (80)
bus line (80)
byte (70)
cable (81)
cache memory (76)
central processing unit (CPU) (73)
chip (72)
closed architecture (77)
complementary metal-oxide semiconductor (CMOS) (76)
complex instruction set computer (CISC) (73)
control unit (73)
controller card (77)
data bus (80)
EBCDIC (70)
expansion card (77)
FireWire ports (81)
firmware (76)
flash memory (75)
flash RAM (75)
home PC (78)
Industry Standard Architecture (ISA) (80)
integrated circuit (72)
interface card (77)
main board (72)
megahertz (MHz) (77)
microseconds (73)
motherboard (72)
network adapter card (77)
open architecture (77)
parallel port (81)
PC card (78)
PC/TV (78)
Peripheral Component Interconnect (PCI) (81)
Personal Computer Memory Card International Association (PCMCIA) card (78)
Plug and Play (80)
plug-in board (77)
port (81)
processor (73)
RAM cache (76)
random-access memory (RAM) (74)
read-only memory (ROM) (76)
reduced instruction set computer (RISC) (74)
semiconductor (72)
serial port (81)
silicon chip (72)
slots (77)
small computer system interface (SCSI) card (77)
smart card (74)
system board (72)
system clock (77)
television board (78)
Unicode (70)
universal serial bus (USB) port (82)
virtual memory (75)
word (73)

Chapter Review

LEVEL 1

Reviewing Facts and Terms

Matching

Match each numbered item with the most closely related lettered item. Write your answers in the spaces provided.

1. This system consists of only two digits—0 and 1. ____
2. This is the number of bits that can be accessed at one time by the CPU. ____
3. This feature allows your computer to run a large program even if there is not enough RAM to hold the program. ____
4. Cards with built-in, specialized microprocessors that can hold information such as health insurance or frequent flier records. ____
5. A CPU can only read, or retrieve, programs written on this type of memory chip. ____
6. With reduced instruction sets, these chips are used in many of today's most powerful microcomputers. ____
7. This type of memory is volatile, and all data stored in this fashion are lost when the computer is turned off. ____
8. Credit card–sized expansion boards that can be used for a variety of functions, including increasing memory and connecting to other computers. ____

a. AGP
b. ALU
c. Binary system
d. Bus
e. Byte
f. Cache memory
g. CISC
h. Closed architecture
i. CMOS
j. Control unit
k. CPU
l. EBCDIC
m. Expansion card
n. Flash RAM
o. Megahertz (MHz)

9. Used to connect external devices that need to send or receive a lot of data over a short distance. ____
10. Most microcomputers have this kind of design that allows users to expand their system via slots on the system board. ____
11. Another name for the system board—the part that connects all system components and allows input and output devices to communicate with the system unit. ____
12. The speed of operations within a computer is measured in these units. ____
13. Type of memory that can retain data even if power is disrupted. ____

p. Motherboard
q. Open architecture
r. Parallel port
s. PCMCIA
t. RAM
u. RISC
v. ROM
w. Smart card
x. Virtual memory
y. Word

14. These plug into slots inside the system unit and allow the user to expand the computer's capabilities. ____
15. Binary coding scheme used primarily for large computers. ____
16. The "brains" of the system, it contains the control unit and the arithmetic-logic unit. ____
17. Tells the rest of the computer how to carry out a program's instructions. ____
18. Contains essential information that is required every time the computer system is turned on. ____
19. Computers with this design are manufactured in such a way that users cannot easily add new devices. ____
20. The most common type of microprocessor. ____
21. Memory used to store the most frequently accessed information stored in RAM. ____
22. A group of eight bits. ____
23. A data roadway between various system components along which bits travel. ____
24. The newest bus, more than twice as fast as the PCI bus, dedicated to the acceleration of graphics performance. ____
25. Performs two types of operations—arithmetic and logical. ____

True/False

In the space provided, write T or F to indicate whether the statement is true or false.

1. In a microcomputer, the CPU is located on a single chip called the microprocessor. ____
2. A grouping of eight bytes is called a bit. ____
3. Another name for the system board is the processor board. ____
4. CISC chips use fewer instructions than RISC chips. ____
5. A SCSI card can be used to connect several different devices to the system unit. ____
6. ROM is volatile memory that cannot be changed by the user. ____

Multiple Choice

Circle the letter of the correct answer.

1. The ALU performs arithmetic operations and:
   - **a.** stores data
   - **b.** logical operations
   - **c.** binary calculations
   - **d.** reduced instruction calculations
   - **e.** parity checks

2. The binary code that is widely used with microcomputers is:
   a. ASCII
   b. EBCDIC
   c. BCD
   d. DEC/MVS
   e. Unicode
3. The number of bits that can be processed at one time is a:
   a. register
   b. cycle
   c. byte
   d. word
   e. PROM
4. Three types of memory chips are RAM, ROM, and:
   a. RISC
   b. main
   c. MCA
   d. CD-ROM
   e. CMOS
5. The bus originally designed to meet video demands is:
   a. EISA
   b. ISA
   c. PCI
   d. MCA
   e. PCMCIA

Completion

Complete each statement in the spaces provided.

1. Bit is short for ________ ________.
2. The most common type of microprocessor chip is ________.
3. ________ memory allows computers with limited memory to run large programs.
4. ________ memory chips retain data even if the power is disrupted.
5. Data and instructions move along the system board using ________ lines.

Reviewing Concepts

LEVEL 2

Open-Ended

On a separate sheet of paper, respond to each question and statement.

1. Describe two basic components of the CPU.
2. What are the four commonly used units of measurements to describe memory capacity? Define each.
3. What is the difference between RISC and CISC chips?
4. Name four expansion cards and describe the function of each.
5. Name the three most common bus lines and describe their differences.
6. Name and describe describe five ports.

Concept Mapping

On a separate sheet of paper, draw a concept map or a flowchart showing how the following terms are related. Show all relationships. Include any additional terms you can think of.

arithmetic-logic unit	CPU	RAM
ASCII	EBCDIC	RAM cache
binary system	expansion card	RISC
bus	flash RAM	ROM
byte	ISA	SCSI
cache memory	motherboard	semiconductor
CISC	open architecture	serial port
closed architecture	parallel port	system board
CMOS	PC card	system clock
control unit	PCMCIA	virtual memory

Critical Thinking Questions and Projects

LEVEL 3

Read each exercise and answer the related questions on a separate sheet of paper.

1. *An inexpensive microcomputer system:* The prices of microcomputer systems have been decreasing for some time. You can buy them from computer stores, pay to have one built for you, or purchase them via mail order or the Internet. Look through print and Web sources to find three low-priced systems. Read each advertisement, make a list of all the computer terms used, and write down their definitions. Prepare a table comparing the three systems. Some factors to include in your table are price, memory capacity, storage capacity, processor type, display type, expansion capability, and software included. If you were to purchase one of these systems, which would you select, and why?

2. *The mobile office:* The mobile office does not have a fixed location, but like the traditional office it has support facilities such as computers, printers, and fax and copy machines. The central piece of equipment in a mobile office is the notebook computer. Since many jobs now require frequent travel, a functional mobile office is essential.

   Many hotels now offer specially equipped hotel rooms and business centers. For example, many Hyatt Hotels have the Hyatt Business Plan, which provides guest rooms with microcomputers, modems, and fax machines. Additionally, a 24-hour business center provides printer, photocopy, and office supply support.

   Suppose you have a job that requires a mobile office. Before making any hotel reservations, you should ensure that essential support facilities are available. Contact a major hotel chain to determine its support for mobile computing. Specifically, find out the following:

   a. Are in-room microcomputers and fax machines available? What are the charges?

   b. Is there a business center on site? What support is provided? What are the hours? What are the charges?

   c. If a business center is not available, will the front desk provide basic services such as faxing, copying, and printing? What are the charges?

3. *Security:* Expensive equipment has a way of getting lost. Most organizations report that theft of their computer equipment is an ever-increasing problem. Police report that one of the most common items taken in home burglaries is computer hardware. People who use and travel with notebook computers need to be particularly careful.

   a. What security measures are in place at your school or business to ensure against theft of keyboards, mice, printers, and entire systems? Can you suggest additional safeguards?

b. Do you have any insurance policies that cover theft of a computer system from your home, your dorm, or your car? Do you have coverage for loss of a notebook computer at school or on a trip? How much coverage, if any, do you have?

c. In the recent past, the FBI issued a warning to travelers who use notebook computers. The warning described a popular scam that involves a team of three members and takes place at typical airport security checkpoints with a conveyor belt and a walk-through metal detector. Can you figure out how this scam might work and what you can do to avoid being a victim?

On the Web Exercises

1. Microprocessors

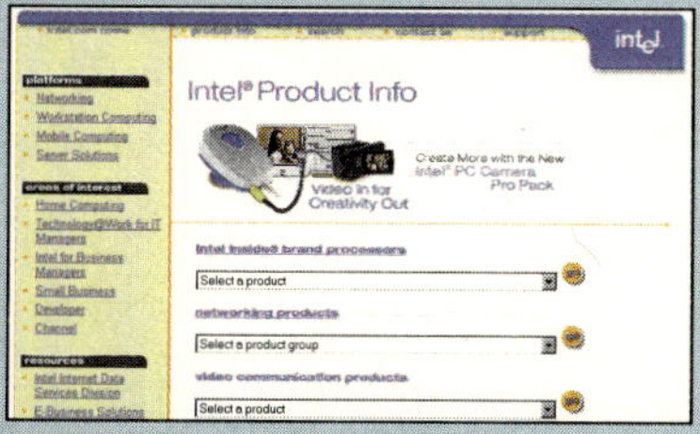

The Intel Corporation is one of the leaders in microprocessor design. To learn more about their most recent microprocessors, visit our Web site at http://www.mhhe.com/cit/concepts/oleary2000-2001/webex4.html to link to Intel's Web site. Once connected to that site, select two current microprocessors. Print out the pages that best describe each microprocessor. Write a paragraph comparing the two.

2. Desktops and Notebooks

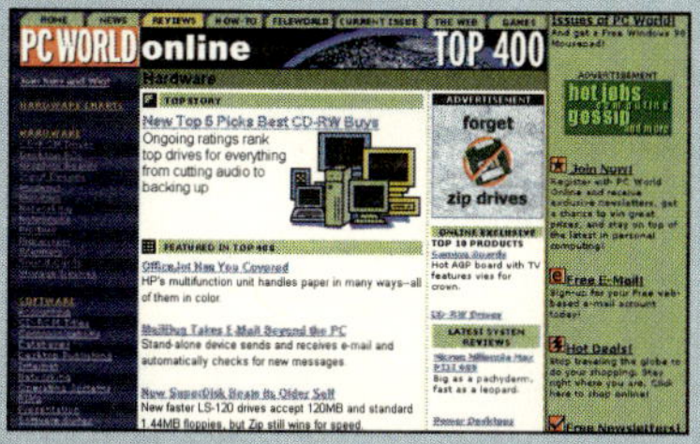

There are several sites on the Web from which you can learn more about the newest desktops and notebooks on the market today. Visit our Web site at http://www.mhhe.com/cit/concepts/oleary2000-2001/webex4.html to link to one of these sites. Once connected to that site, check out the different models and select the one that best meets your needs. Print out the specifications for your chosen computer and write a paragraph describing how this computer best suits your needs.

3. Universal Serial Bus

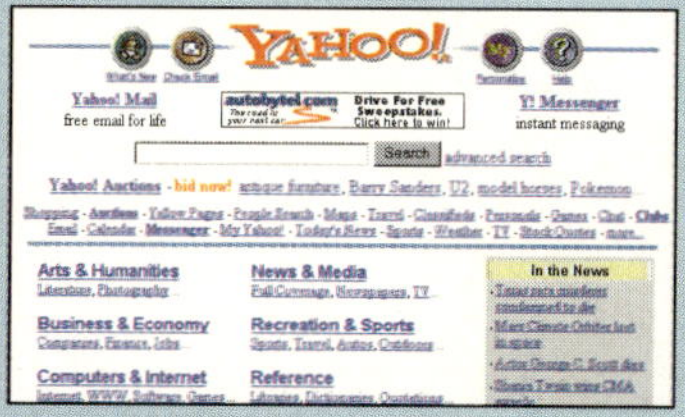

The Universal serial bus (USB) is the next evolution of computer ports. It was developed through the collaboration of seven leading-edge companies. To learn more about this technology, visit the Yahoo site at http://www.yahoo.com and search using the keywords "USB" and "universal serial bus". Follow several of the links to learn more and print the Web page you find the most informative. Write a brief summary of what you learned about USB.

4. Wired

Several magazines now publish their works on the Internet. One of the leading ones is the techno savvy magazine, *Wired*. Visit our Web site at http://www.mhhe.com/cit/concepts/oleary2000-2001/webex4.html to link to the *Wired* site. Once connected, select an article of interest to you. Print out the article and write a paragraph summarizing the article and explaining why you selected it.

CHAPTER 5

Input and Output

COMPETENCIES

After you have read this chapter, you should be able to:

1. **Explain the difference between keyboard and direct-entry input devices.**
2. **Describe the features of keyboards and the four types of terminals.**
3. **Describe direct-entry devices used with microcomputers.**
4. **Discuss voice recognition systems.**
5. **Describe monitors and monitor standards.**
6. **Describe printers (ink-jet, laser, thermal) and plotters (pen, ink-jet, electrostatic, and direct-imaging).**
7. **Describe voice-output devices.**

How do you get data to the CPU? How do you get information out? Here we describe the two most important places where the computer interfaces with people. The first half of the chapter covers input devices; the second half covers output devices.

People understand language, which is constructed of letters, numbers, and punctuation marks. However, computers can understand only the binary machine language of 0s and 1s. Input and output devices are essentially translators. Input devices translate symbols that people

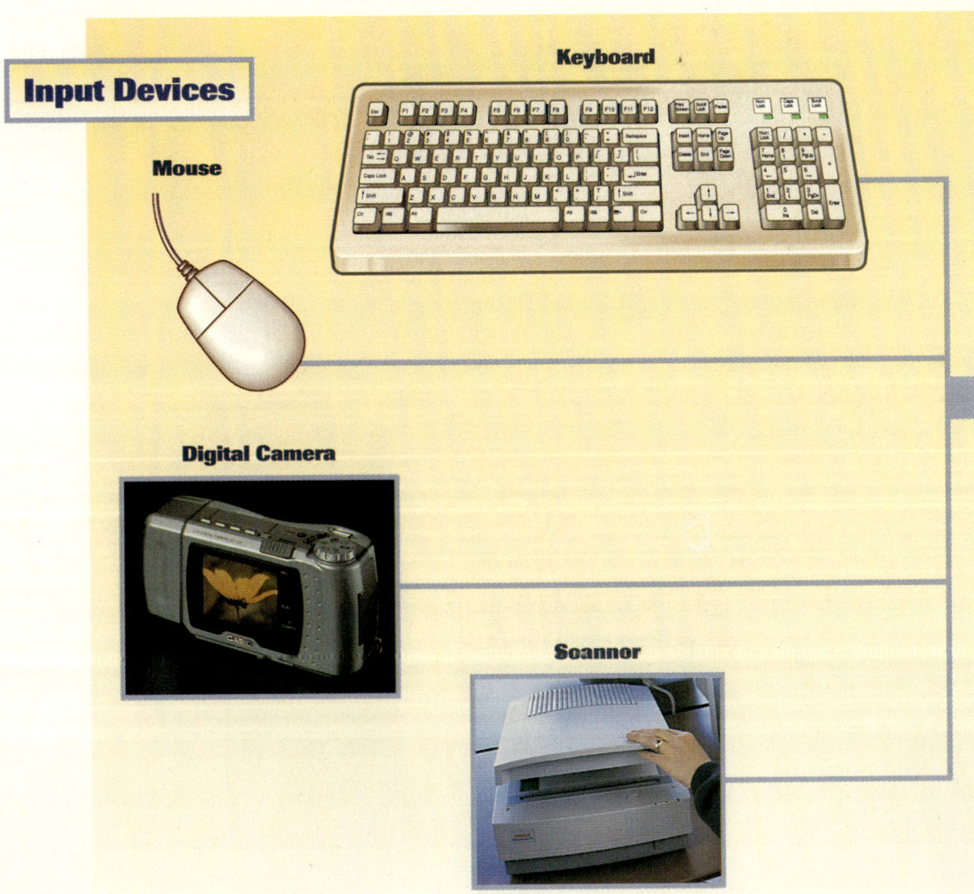

understand into symbols that computers can process. Output devices do the reverse: They translate machine output to output people can comprehend.

Competent end users need to know about the most commonly used input devices, including keyboards, mice, digital cameras, and scanners. Additionally, they need to know about the most commonly used output devices, including monitors, printers, plotters, and speakers.

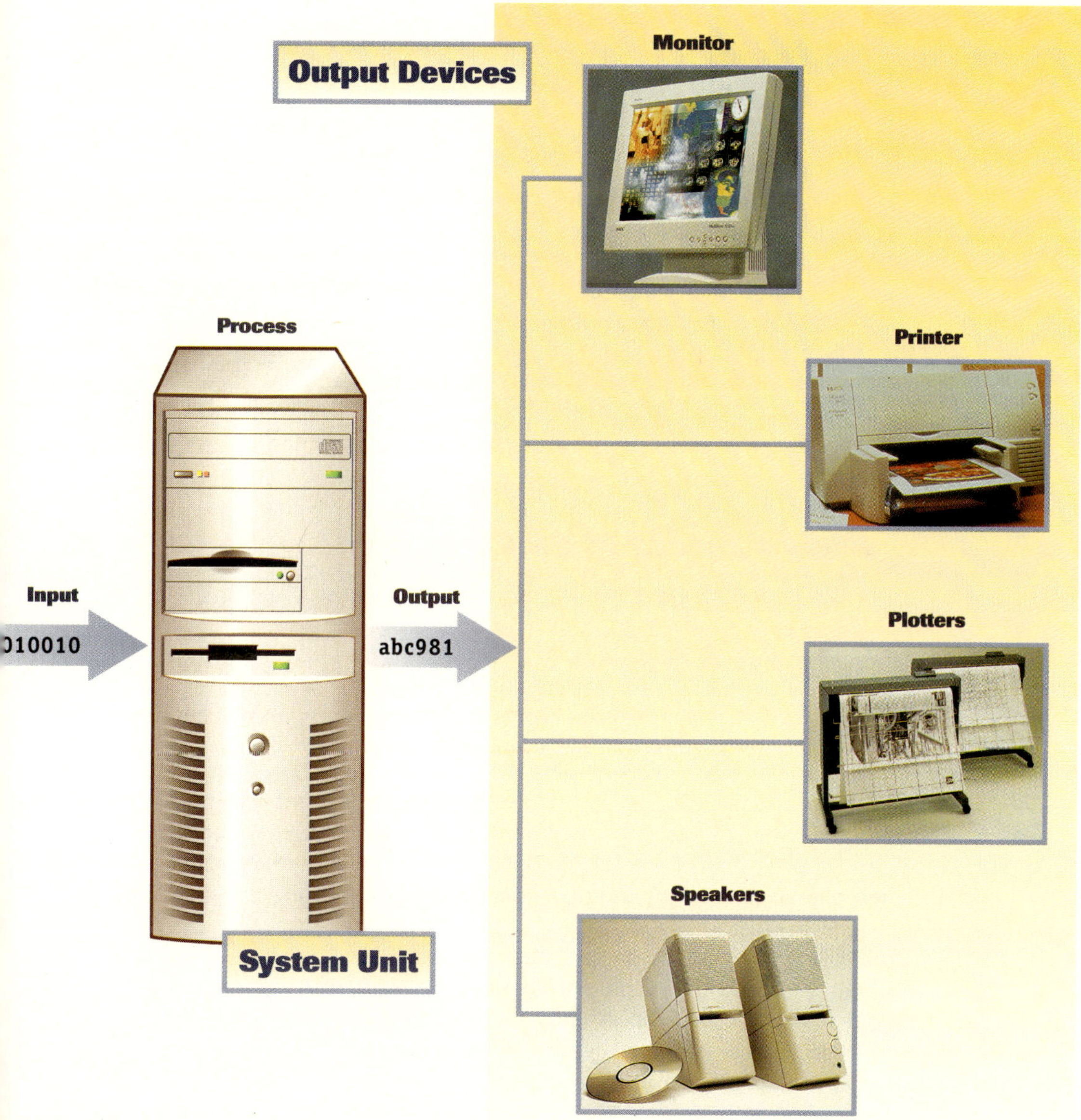

Input: Keyboard versus Direct Entry

Input devices convert people-readable data into machine-readable form. Input may be by keyboard or direct entry.

Input devices take data and programs people can read or understand and convert them to a form the computer can process. This form consists of machine-readable electronic signals of 0s and 1s that we described in Chapter 4. Input devices are of two kinds: keyboard entry and direct entry.

FIGURE 5-1
A point-of-sale terminal

- **Keyboard entry:** Data is input to the computer through a *keyboard* that looks like a typewriter keyboard but has additional keys. In this method, the user typically reads from an original document called the **source document.** The user enters that document by typing on the keyboard.
- **Direct entry:** Data is made into machine-readable form as it is entered into the computer; no keyboard is used.

An example of an input device that uses both keyboard and direct entry is a **point-of-sale (POS) terminal.** This is the sort of electronic cash register you see in many stores. (See Figure 5-1.) When clerks sell a can of paint, for example, they can record the sale by typing in the information (product code, purchase amount, tax) on the keyboard. Or they can use a handheld **wand reader** or **platform scanner** to read special characters on price tags as direct entry. The wand reflects light on the characters. The reflection is then changed by photoelectric cells to machine-readable code. Whether by keyboard entry or direct entry, the results will appear on the POS terminal's digital display.

CONCEPT CHECK

✔ What are input devices?

✔ How does keyboard entry differ from direct entry?

Keyboard Entry

In keyboard entry, people type input. There are four types of terminals: dumb, intelligent, network, and Internet.

Probably the most common way in which you will input data, at least at the beginning, is by using a keyboard. Keyboards convert numbers, letters, and special characters that people understand into electrical signals. These signals are sent to and processed by the system unit.

Keyboards

A computer keyboard combines a typewriter keyboard with a numeric keypad. Additionally, it has many special-purpose keys. Some keys such as the *Caps Lock* key are **toggle keys.** These keys turn a feature on or off. Others such as the *Ctrl* key are **combination keys** that perform an action when held down in combination with another key. To learn more about keyboard features, see Figure 5-2.

FIGURE 5-2
Traditional keyboard

There are two basic keyboard designs. The traditional design or straight design is shown in Figure 5-2. The contour design splits and slopes the keyboard. (See Figure 5-3.) Many people prefer the contour design because it is more natural and comfortable.

FIGURE 5-3
Microsoft's Natural keyboard

Terminals

A **terminal** is a form of input (and output) device that connects you to a mainframe or other type of computer called a *host computer* or *server.* There are four kinds of terminals:

- A **dumb terminal** can be used to input and receive data, but it cannot process data independently. It is used only to gain access to information from a computer. Such a terminal may be used by an airline reservations clerk to access a mainframe computer for flight information.
- An **intelligent terminal** includes a processing unit, memory, and secondary storage such as a magnetic disk. Essentially, an intelligent terminal is a microcomputer with communications software and a telephone hookup (modem) or other communications link. These connect the terminal to the larger computer or to the Internet. An increasingly popular type is the **Net PC,** also known as the **Net Personal Computer.** These low-cost and limited microcomputers typically have only one type of secondary storage (an internal hard disk drive), a sealed system unit, and no expansion slots.
- A **network terminal,** also known as a **thin client** or **network computer,** is a low-cost alternative to an intelligent terminal. Most network terminals do not have a hard-disk drive and must rely on a host computer or server for application and system software. These devices are becoming increasingly popular in many organizations.

TIPS Is your keyboard looking tired and dirty? Are the keys sticking? Then it may be time to clean your keyboard. Follow the guidelines below to make it shine again.

1. *Disconnect.* Turn off the computer and disconnect the keyboard.
2. *Vacuum.* Use a vacuum or a blow-dryer to remove dust and particles from the keyboard.
3. *Clean keys.* Using a soft cloth moistened with 90 percent isopropyl alcohol, gently clean the key surfaces. Carefully dry with another soft cloth.
4. *Clean case.* Using a soft cloth moistened with liquid cleaning solution, clean the keyboard case. Dry with another soft cloth.
5. *Reconnect.* When the keys and case are completely dry, plug in the keyboard and turn on the computer.

FIGURE 5-4
Internet terminal

- An **Internet terminal,** also known as a **Web terminal,** provides access to the Internet and displays Web pages on a standard television set. (See Figure 5-4.) These special-purpose terminals offer Internet access without a microcomputer. Unlike the other types of terminals, Internet terminals are used almost exclusively in the home.

CONCEPT CHECK

✔ Keyboards convert numbers, letters, and special characters into _______ _______ to be processed by the system unit.

✔ List the four types of keyboard entry terminals.

Direct Entry

Direct entry creates machine-readable data that can go directly to the CPU. Direct entry includes pointing, scanning, and voice-input devices.

Direct entry is a form of input that does not require data to be keyed by someone sitting at a keyboard. Direct-entry devices create machine-readable data on paper or magnetic media, or feed it directly into the computer's CPU. This reduces the possibility of human error being introduced (as often happens when data is being entered through a keyboard). It is also an economical means of data entry. Direct-entry devices may be categorized in three ways: pointing devices, scanning devices, and voice-input devices.

Pointing Devices

Pointing, of course, is one of the most natural of all human gestures. There are a number of devices that use this method as a form of direct-entry input:

- **Mouse:** A **mouse** controls a **pointer** that is displayed on the monitor. The pointer usually appears in the shape of an arrow. It frequently, however, changes shape depending on the application. The standard mouse has a ball on the bottom and is attached with a cord to the system unit. (See Figure 5-5.) The standard mouse has evolved over time with many predecessors. (See Figure 5-6.)

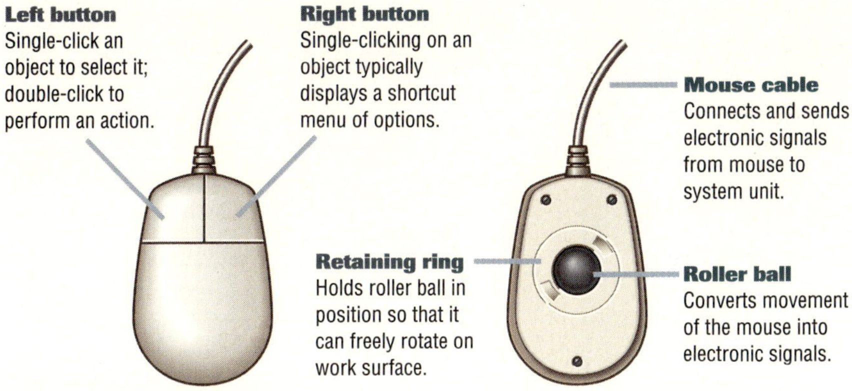

FIGURE 5-5
Standard mouse

FIGURE 5-6
The evolving mouse

Three devices similar to a mouse are trackballs, touch surfaces, and pointing sticks. You can use the **trackball,** also known as the **roller ball,** to control the pointer by rotating a ball with your thumb. You can use **touch surfaces** to control the pointer by moving and tapping your finger on the surface of a pad. (See Figure 5-7.) You can use a **pointing stick,** located in the middle of the keyboard, to control the pointer by directing the stick with your finger. (See Figure 5-8.)

- **Joystick:** The **joystick** is the most popular input device for computer games. You control game actions by varying the pressure, speed, and direction of the joystick. Additional controls such as buttons and triggers are used to specify commands or initiate specific actions. (See Figure 5-9.)
- **Touch screen:** A **touch screen** is a particular kind of monitor screen covered with a plastic layer. (See Figure 5-10.) Behind this layer are crisscrossed invisible beams of infrared light. This arrangement enables someone to select actions or commands by touching the screen with a finger. Touch screens are easy to use, especially when people need information quickly. They are commonly used at automated teller machines (ATMs), information centers, restaurants, and department stores.

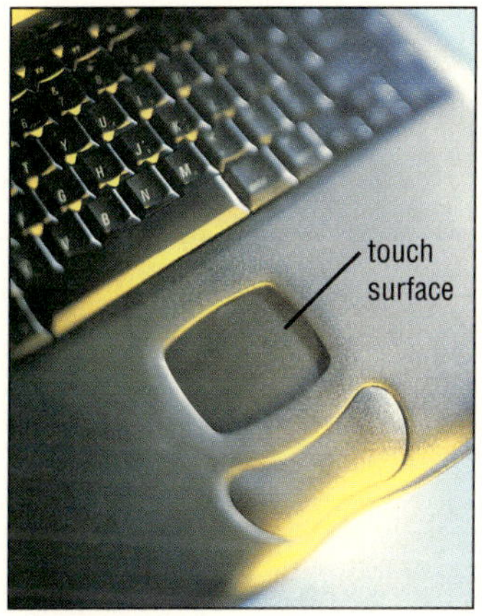

FIGURE 5-7
A touch surface: typically part of a portable computer

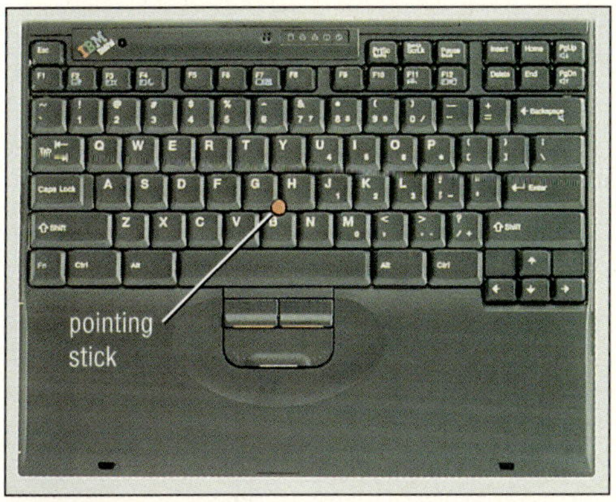

FIGURE 5-8
A pointing stick: typically part of a portable computer

FIGURE 5-9
A joystick: used for computer games

FIGURE 5-10
A touch screen: a consumer application

TIPS Does your mouse pointer move smoothly across your screen? Or does it jerk, start, and stop occasionally? If it does, then it may be time for a cleaning. To clean a standard mouse, follow these steps:

1. *Disconnect.* Turn off the computer and disconnect the mouse from the computer.
2. *Take out ball.* Turn the mouse upside down, gently unscrew the cover to the compartment containing the mouse ball with your thumbs, and allow the ball to drop into your hand.
3. *Clean ball.* Clean the ball with a mild detergent or alcohol and a soft cloth; then dry it with a clean, lint-free cloth.
4. *Clean compartment.* Blow into the ball compartment to remove any dust or lint from the inside. Remove any oil on the rollers in the compartment by cleaning with a cotton swab and tape-head cleaner.
5. *Reassemble.* Put the ball back into the compartment and replace the cover.
6. *Reconnect.* Connect the mouse and you're ready to go.

If you do not have a standard mouse, consult the manufacturer's Web page for cleaning instructions.

- **Light pen:** A **light pen** is a light-sensitive penlike device. (See Figure 5-11.) The light pen is placed against the monitor. This closes a photoelectric circuit and identifies the spot for entering or modifying data. Light pens are used by engineers, for example, in designing anything from microprocessor chips to airplane parts.
- **Digitizer:** A **digitizer** is a device that can be used to trace or copy a drawing or photograph. The item to be copied is placed on a flat **digitizing tablet.** A special **stylus** connected to a computer is then used to trace the item. (See Figure 5-12.) As the stylus moves from one position to another, the computer records its position on the digitizing tablet. After the item has been traced, its image can be displayed on the screen, printed out on paper, or stored on the computer system for later use. Digitizers are often used by designers, architects, and engineers.
- **Digital camera: Digital cameras** are similar to traditional cameras except that images are recorded digitally on a disk or in the camera's memory rather than on film. (See Figure 5-13.) You can take a picture, view it immediately, and even place it on your own Web page, within minutes. Although faster than traditional photography, digital camera prices are typically higher, and image quality is not quite as good. Digital cameras are particularly popular with real estate agents, who use them to capture images of homes to be displayed on their Web pages.

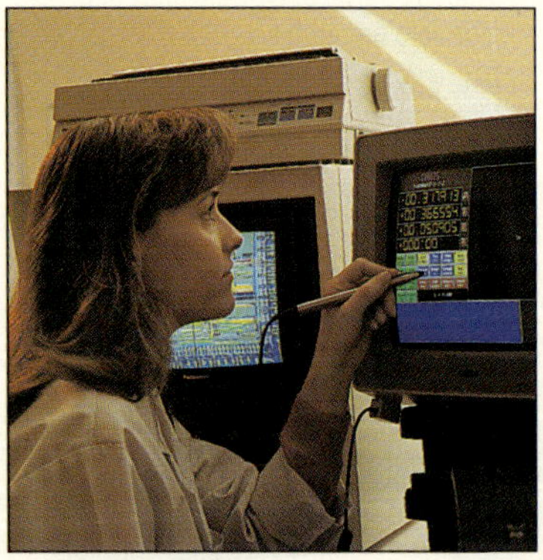

FIGURE 5-11
A light pen: a hospital application

FIGURE 5-12
A digitizer: an engineering application

FIGURE 5-13
A digital camera: viewing a captured image

- **Digital video cameras:** Unlike traditional video cameras, **digital video cameras** record motion digitally on a disk or in the camera's memory. Compared to traditional video cameras, the image quality is better and the price is higher. A digital video camera can also double as a digital camera by capturing still digital images. With their costs declining, digital video cameras are becoming more and more popular with businesses and home users.
- **Digital notebook:** Taking class notes may never be the same again. **Digital notebooks** use a regular notepad on top of an electronic pad. (See Figure 5-14.) Whenever you move a special pen across the notepad, a signal tracing your movements is sent to and stored in the electronic pad. These notebooks can store up to 50 pages of notes before they reach their capacity. The notes are transferred to a microcomputer where they can be viewed, organized, and edited as needed.

ON THE WEB EXPLORATIONS

The Cross Pen Computing Group is a leader in developing digital notebooks. To learn more about the company, visit its Web site at

http://www.cross-pcg.com

Scanning Devices

Direct-entry scanning devices record images of text, drawings, or special symbols. The images are converted to digital data that can be processed by a computer or displayed on a monitor. Scanning devices include the following:

- **Image scanner:** An **image scanner,** also known simply as a **scanner,** copies or reproduces images. There are two basic types. One, the

FIGURE 5-14
A digital notebook: a student application

FIGURE 5-15
An image scanner: reproducing color images

flatbed scanner, is much like a copy machine. (See Figure 5-15.) The image to be scanned is placed on a glass surface and the scanner records the image from below. The other type, the **portable scanner,** is typically a handheld device that slides across the image, making direct contact. (See Figure 5-16.) With both devices, the light and dark areas as well as color of the image are recorded as points or dots. After the image has been scanned, it can be displayed on the screen, printed on paper, or stored on the computer system for later use. Image scanners are becoming widely used input devices. They are commonly used in desktop publishing to scan graphic images that can then be placed in a page of text.

- **Fax machine: Facsimile transmission machines,** commonly called **fax machines,** scan the image of a document to be sent. The light and dark areas of the image are converted into a format that can be sent

FIGURE 5-16
Portable scanner: capturing text and graphics

electronically over telephone lines. The receiving fax machine converts the signals back to an image and recreates it on paper.

Although dedicated fax machines are popular, many people use their microcomputers with a **fax/modem board** that provides the independent capabilities of a fax and a modem.

- **Bar-code readers:** You are probably familiar with **bar-code readers** from grocery stores. (See Figure 5-17.) Bar-code readers are photoelectric scanners that read the **bar codes,** or vertical zebra-striped marks, printed on product containers. Supermarkets use a bar-code system called the Universal Product Code (UPC). The bar code identifies the product to the supermarket's computer, which has a description and the latest price for the product. The computer automatically tells the POS terminal what the price is. And it prints the price and the product name on the customer's receipt.
- **Character and mark recognition devices:** There are three kinds of scanning devices—formerly used only with mainframes—now found in connection with the more powerful microcomputers.

  Magnetic-ink character recognition (MICR) is a direct-entry method used in banks. This technology is used to automatically read those futuristic-looking numbers on the bottom of checks. A special-purpose machine known as a **reader/sorter** reads characters made of ink containing magnetized particles.

  Optical-character recognition (OCR) uses special preprinted characters, such as those printed on utility and telephone bills. They can be read by a light source and changed into machine-readable code. A common OCR device is the handheld *wand reader* discussed earlier in this chapter. (See Figure 5-18.) These are used in department stores to read retail price tags by reflecting light on the printed characters.

  Optical-mark recognition (OMR) is also called **mark sensing.** An OMR device senses the presence or absence of a mark, such as a pencil mark. OMR is often used to score multiple-choice tests such as the College Board's Scholastic Aptitude Test and the Graduate Record Examination.

FIGURE 5-17
A bar-code reader: recording product codes

FIGURE 5-18
A wand reader: recording product codes

Voice-Input Devices

Voice-input devices convert a person's speech into a digital code. By far the most widely used voice-input device is the microphone. This input device, when combined with a sound card and appropriate software, forms a **voice recognition system.** (See Figure 5-19.) These systems enable users to operate microcomputers and to create documents using voice commands. Recently, portable voice recognition systems have been introduced. (See Figure 5-20.) These units typically are able to record for up to one hour. They can also connect to a computer system through the system unit's serial port to save files and print documents.

Most voice recognition systems must be "trained" to the particular user's voice. This is done by matching the user's spoken words to patterns previously stored in the computer. More advanced systems that can recognize the same

MAKING IT WORK FOR YOU

Voice Recognition Systems and Dictating a Paper

Tired of using your keyboard to type term papers and to control programs? Perhaps voice recognition is just what you're looking for. It's easy with the right software and hardware.

How It Works

A voice recognition system consists of a combination of standard hardware components and some specialized software like NaturallySpeaking from Dragon Systems, Inc. Once the software has been trained, you can dictate papers and surf the Web using only voice commands.

Training the Software

The first step is to train your system to recognize your voice. For example, you can train NaturallySpeaking as shown in Figure A.

1. Create your personal user profile, which will store your speech patterns.
2. Read prearranged standard text to teach the software your unique speech patterns.
3. Refine your profile to include specialized vocabulary.

FIGURE A

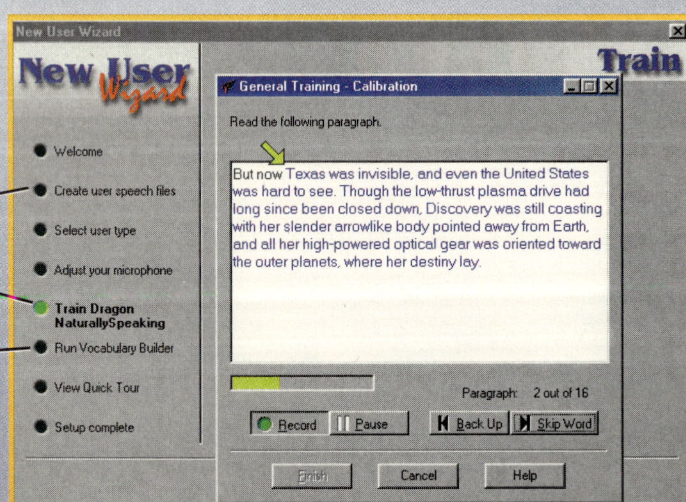

Dictating

Once your system has been trained, you can use it to interact with a variety of applications.

For example, you can create a text document using voice recognition software and Word. As you speak into the microphone, your words will appear on your monitor and in the word processing document. (See Figure B.)

FIGURE B

1. Using a microphone, dictate the text you want to appear in the Word document.
2. As you speak, the voice recognition system interprets your spoken words.
3. Once interpreted, text is inserted into the Word document.

FIGURE C

1. Instruct your computer to load your browser.

2. Instruct your computer to go to the location box, dictate the Web address and instruct your computer to connect to that Web address.
3. Surf by selecting and connecting to hypertext links.

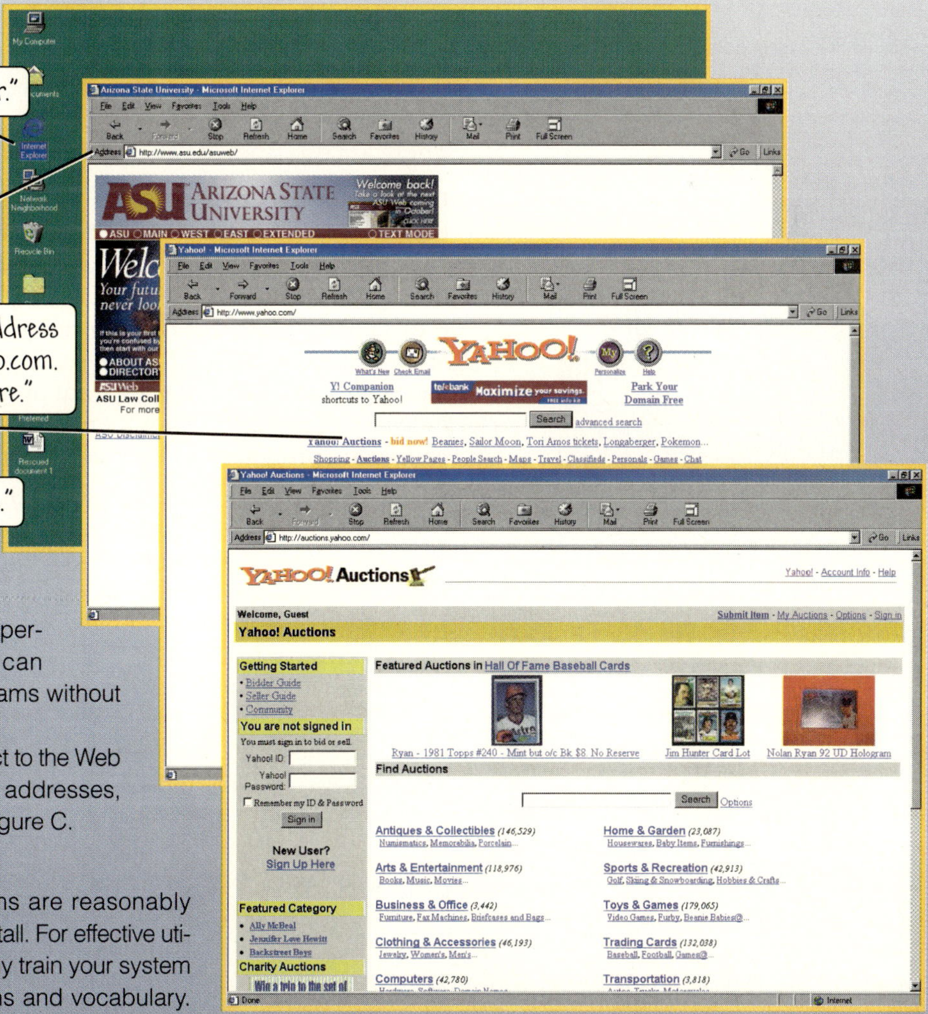

Surfing

You can control many computer operations with just your voice. You can load, run, and interact with programs without using your mouse or keyboard.

For example, you could connect to the Web through your browser, enter Web addresses, and use hyperlinks as shown in Figure C.

Many voice recognition programs are reasonably priced and are relatively easy to install. For effective utilization, however, you must carefully train your system to recognize your speech patterns and vocabulary.

FIGURE 5-19
Voice recognition system

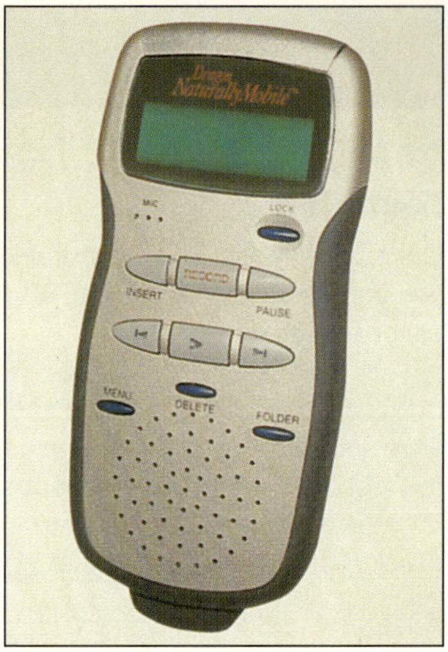

FIGURE 5-20
Portable voice recognition system

word spoken by many different people have been developed. However, until recently the list of words has been limited. One voice recognition system, the Dragon Dictate, identifies over 30,000 words and adapts to individual voices. There are even systems that will translate from one language to another, such as from English to Japanese.

There are two types of voice recognition systems:

- **Discrete speech:** A common activity in business is preparing memos and other written documents. **Discrete-speech recognition systems** have been widely used in the legal, medical, and other professions to directly convert the spoken word into printed material. Users dictate into a microphone that is connected to a microcomputer. The microcomputer takes the audio signal, converts it to a digital signal, and then analyzes it using a special program. The program recognizes individual words and stores them in a file. Using a standard word processing program, the file can be retrieved, edited, and printed out.
- **Continuous speech: Continuous-speech recognition systems** are considered to be one of the key technologies for the 21st century. They are more natural and conversational than discrete word systems. Continuous-speech systems are able to recognize individual words and phrases in context. For example, continuous-speech recognition systems are able to distinguish between same-sounding words like *there*, *their*, and *they're*. These systems are able to accept dictation as well as spoken commands to operate many of today's applications including Word and Excel. Two well-known systems are NaturallySpeaking from Dragon Systems and ViaVoice from IBM.

ON THE WEB EXPLORATIONS

Dragon Systems Inc. is a leader in developing continuous-speech systems. To learn more about the company, visit its Web site at

http://www.naturalspeech.com

CONCEPT CHECK

✔ Define direct entry.

✔ Three devices similar to a mouse are ________, ________, and ________.

✔ What are two basic types of image scanners?

✔ What do voice-input devices do?

Output: Monitors, Printers, Plotters, Voice

Output devices convert machine-readable information into people-readable form.

Data that is input to and then processed by the computer remains in machine-readable form until output devices make it people-readable. The output devices we shall describe for microcomputers are monitors, printers, plotters, and voice-output.

Monitors

Monitor standards indicate screen quality. Some monitors are used on the desktop; others are portable.

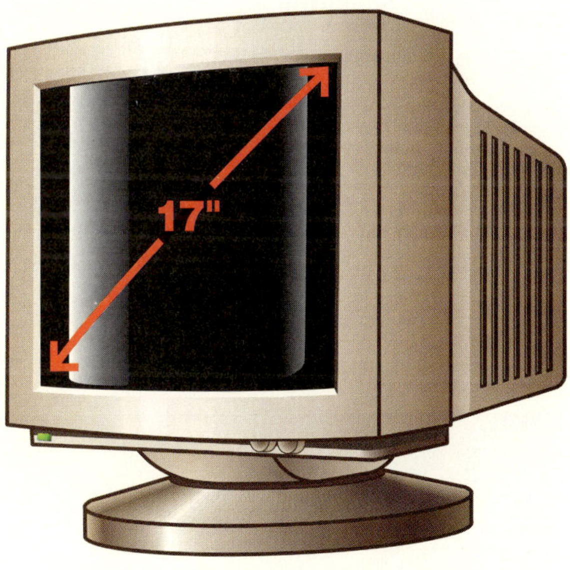

FIGURE 5-21
A 17-inch monitor

The most frequently used output device is the **monitor.** Two important characteristics of monitors are *size* and *clarity*. A monitor's size is indicated by the diagonal length of its viewing area. (See Figure 5-21.) Common sizes are 15, 17, 19, and 21 inches. Larger monitors have the advantage of displaying more information at one time; however, they are more expensive.

A monitor's clarity is indicated by its **resolution,** which is measured in pixels. **Pixels** are individual dots or "picture elements" that form images on a monitor. For a given size monitor, the greater the resolution (the more pixels), the better the clarity of the image. For a given level of clarity, larger monitors require a higher resolution (more pixels).

Standards

To indicate a monitor's resolution capabilities, several standards have evolved. The four most common today are SVGA, XGA, SXGA, and UXGA. (See Figure 5-22.)

- **SVGA** stands for *S*uper *V*ideo *G*raphics *A*rray. It has a minimum resolution of 800 by 600 pixels. A few years ago, SVGA was the most popular standard. Today, it is used primarily with 15-inch monitors.
- **XGA** stands for *E*xtended *G*raphics *A*rray. It has a resolution of up to 1,024 by 768 pixels. It is a popular standard today, especially with 17- and 19-inch monitors.
- **SXGA** stand for *S*uper *E*xtended *G*raphics *A*rray. This standard has a resolution of 1,280 by 1,024 pixels. It is popular with 19- and 21-inch monitors.

Standard	Pixels
SVGA	800 × 600
XGA	1,024 × 768
SXGA	1,280 × 1,024
UXGA	1,600 × 1,200

FIGURE 5-22
Resolution standards

TIPS Are there a few layers of dust on your monitor? Can you see fingerprints? Then it may be time to clean your monitor. Here are a few cleaning suggestions.

1. *Disconnect.* Turn off the monitor and unplug the electricity.
2. *Clean screen.* If the screen is really dirty, use an antistatic CRT cleaner. Otherwise, use a dry static-free cloth to dust off the screen.
3. *Clean cabinet.* Clean the cabinet with a soft cloth dampened with cleaning solution (never use benzene, paint thinner, or other volatile substance). Dry with a soft cloth.
4. *Reconnect.* Reconnect the electricity and turn on the monitor.

- **UXGA** stands for *U*ltra *E*xtended *G*raphics *A*rray. UXGA is the newest and highest standard. Although not as widely used as the XGA and SXGA monitors, its popularity is expected to increase dramatically as 21-inch monitors become more widely used. UXGA monitors are primarily used for high-end engineering design and graphic arts.

Cathode-Ray Tubes

The most common type of monitor for the office and the home is the **cathode-ray tube (CRT).** (See Figure 5-23.) These monitors are typically placed directly on the system unit or on the desktop. CRTs are similar in size and technology to televisions. Compared to other types of monitors, their primary advantages are low cost and excellent resolution. Their primary disadvantage is size.

Flat-Panel Monitors

ON THE WEB EXPLORATIONS

NEC Technologies is a leader in developing flat-panel monitors. To learn more about the company, visit its Web site at

http://www.nec.com

Because CRTs are too bulky to be transported, portable monitors (see Figure 5-24) known as **flat-panel monitors** or **liquid crystal display (LCD) monitors** were developed. Unlike the technology used in CRTs, the technology for portable monitors involves liquid crystals. Flat-panel monitors are much thinner than CRTs. Once used exclusively for portable computers, flat-panel monitors are now starting to be used for desktop systems as well.

There are two basic types of flat-panel monitors: *passive-matrix* and *active-matrix.* **Passive-matrix** or **dual-scan monitors** create images by scanning the entire screen. This type requires very little power, but the clarity of the images is not as sharp. **Active-matrix** or **thin film transistor (TFT) monitors** do not scan down the screen; instead, each pixel is independently activated. More colors with better clarity can be displayed. Active-matrix monitors are more expensive and require more power.

FIGURE 5-23
CRT monitors

FIGURE 5-24
A flat-panel monitor

As we mentioned in Chapter 4, an exciting recent development is the merger of microcomputers and television called **PC/TV.** This is becoming possible through the establishment of all-digital **high-definition television (HDTV).** HDTV delivers a much clearer and more detailed wide-screen picture than regular television. Additionally, because the output is digital, it enables users to readily freeze video sequences to create still images. These images can then be digitized and output as artwork or stored on disks for later use. This technology is very useful to graphic artists, publishers, and educators.

CONCEPT CHECK

- ✔ What do output devices do?
- ✔ __________, measured in pixels, indicates a monitor's clarity.
- ✔ List the four standards of monitor resolution.

Printers

There are three types of printers: ink-jet, laser, and thermal.

The images output on a monitor are often referred to as **soft copy.** Information output on paper—whether by a printer or by a plotter—is called **hard copy.** Three popular kinds of printers used with microcomputers are ink-jet, laser, and thermal.

FIGURE 5-25
An ink-jet printer

Ink-Jet Printer

An **ink-jet printer** sprays small droplets of ink at high speed onto the surface of the paper. This process not only produces a letter-quality image but also permits printing to be done in a variety of colors. (See Figure 5-25.) Ink-jet printers are the most widely used printer. They are reliable, quiet, and inexpensive. Ink-jet printers are used wherever color and appearance are important, as in advertising and public relations.

Laser Printer

The **laser printer** uses a technology similar to that used in a photocopying machine. (See Figure 5-26.) It uses a laser beam to produce images with excellent letter and graphics quality. More expensive than ink-jet printers, laser printers are used in applications requiring high-quality output.

There are two categories of laser printers. **Personal laser printers** are inexpensive and used by many single users. They typically can print four to six pages a minute. **Shared laser printers** are more expensive and are used (shared) by a group of users. Shared laser printers typically print over 30 pages a minute.

TIPS Is your ink-jet printer producing smeared pages? Are the characters looking blurry? Then it could be time to give it a cleaning. Here are a few cleaning suggestions:

1. *Disconnect.* Turn off the printer and unplug the electricity.
2. *Open.* Open the printer and locate the spray nozzles.
3. *Clean.* Wipe the nozzles with a dry lint-free cloth or a swab moistened with distilled water.
4. *Reconnect.* When completely dry, plug in the printer and turn it on.

To prevent clogging in the future, always allow your printer to finish printing the current page and to return the print head to its resting position before removing the page or turning off the power.

FIGURE 5-26
A laser printer

Printer	Characteristics	Typical Use
Ink-jet	High color quality; inexpensive; sprays drops of ink on paper	Internal and external communications, advertising pieces
Laser	Very high quality; uses photo-copying process	Desktop publishing, external documents
Thermal	Very high quality; uses heat elements on special paper	Art and design work

FIGURE 5-27
Three types of printers

Thermal Printer

A **thermal printer** uses heat elements to produce images on heat-sensitive paper. Originally these printers were used in scientific labs to record data. More recently, color thermal printers have been widely used to produce very high quality color artwork and text.

Color thermal printers are not as popular because of their cost and the requirement of specially treated paper. They are a more special-use printer that produces near-photographic output. They are widely used in professional art and design work where very high quality color is essential.

Some of the important characteristics of the three most widely used microcomputer printers are summarized in Figure 5-27.

ON THE WEB EXPLORATIONS

Hewlett-Packard is a leading manufacturer of printers and of multifunction devices that combine a printer, copier, scanner, and fax into one product. To learn more about the company, visit its Web site at

http://www.hp.com

Other Printers

There are several other types of printers. Two are the dot-matrix printer and the chain printer. Dot-matrix printers form characters or images using a series of small pins on a print head. Once the most widely used microcomputer printer, dot-matrix printers are inexpensive and reliable but quite noisy. In general, they are used for tasks where a high-quality image is not essential. Thus, they are often used for documents that are circulated within an organization rather than shown to clients and the public. Their sales have declined dramatically in the past few years.

You probably won't find a chain printer standing alone on a desk next to a microcomputer. This is because a chain printer is an expensive, high-speed machine originally designed to serve minicomputers and mainframes. However, you may see one in organizations that link several microcomputers together by a communications network.

CONCEPT CHECK

- ✔ What are the three printer types commonly used with microcomputers?
- ✔ What type of printer is typically used for art and design work?

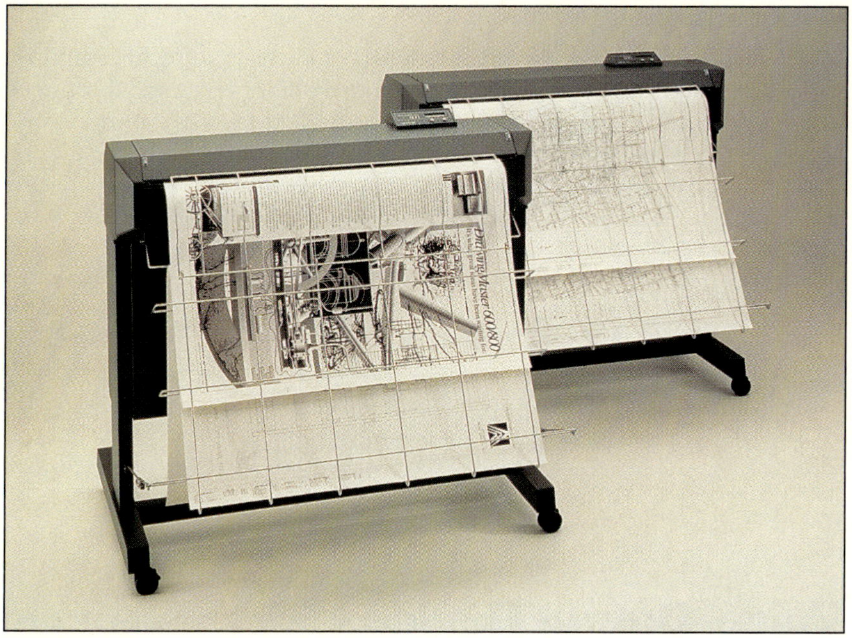

FIGURE 5-28
A pen plotter

Plotters

Plotters are special-purpose drawing devices.

Plotters are special-purpose output devices for producing bar charts, maps, architectural drawings, and even three-dimensional illustrations. Plotters can produce high-quality multicolor documents and also documents that are larger than most printers can handle. There are four types of plotters: pen, ink-jet, electrostatic, and direct imaging.

Pen Plotter

Pen plotters (see Figure 5-28) create plots by moving a pen or pencil over drafting paper. (With some pen plotters, the paper moves and the pen remains stationary.) Pen plotters are the least expensive plotters and the easiest to maintain. Their major limitations are slower speed and an inability to produce solid fills and shading. Nevertheless, they have been the most popular type of plotter.

Ink-Jet Plotter

Ink-jet plotters create line drawings and solid-color output by spraying droplets of ink onto paper. Their best features are their speed, high-quality output, and quiet operation. The major disadvantage of ink-jet plotters is that the spray jets can become clogged and thus require more maintenance. Ink-jet plotters are used by a wide variety of workers, including engineers and automotive designers.

FIGURE 5-29
An electrostatic plotter

Electrostatic Plotter

Whereas pen plotters use pens, **electrostatic plotters** use electrostatic charges to create images made up of tiny dots on specially treated paper. (See Figure 5-29.) The image is produced when the paper is run through a developer. Electrostatic plotters produce high-resolution images and are much faster than either pen or ink-jet plotters. These plotters, unfortunately, use expensive chemicals that are considered hazardous. Electrostatic plotters are used for applications that require high-volume and high-quality outputs such as in advertising and graphic arts design.

Direct-Imaging Plotter

Direct-imaging plotters or **thermal plotters** create images using heat-sensitive paper and electrically heated pins. This type of plotter is comparably priced with electrostatic plotters, quite reliable, and good for high-volume work. However, direct-imaging plotters require expensive paper and typically create only two-color output. These plotters are typically used for very specific applications such as creating maps.

CONCEPT CHECK

- ✔ What are plotters?
- ✔ When might you need a plotter instead of a printer?

Voice-Output Devices

Voice-output devices vocalize prerecorded sounds.

FIGURE 5-30
Stereo speakers

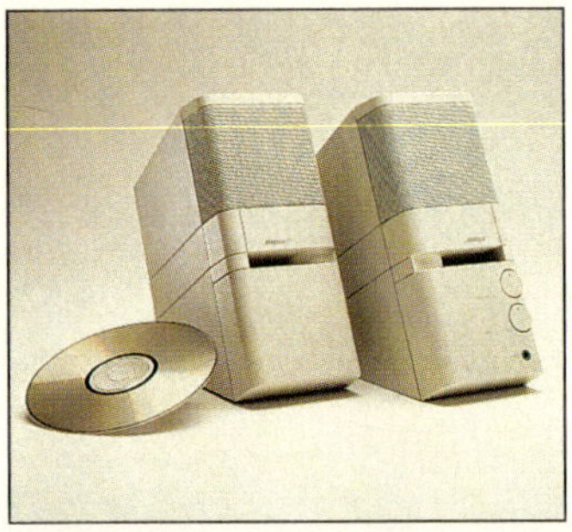

Voice-output devices make sounds that resemble human speech but actually are prerecorded vocalized sounds. With one Macintosh program, the computer speaks the synthesized words "We'll be right back" if you type in certain letters and numbers. (The characters are *Wiyl biy ray5t bae5k*—the numbers elongate the sounds.) Voice output is not anywhere near as difficult to create as voice input. In fact, there are many occasions when you will hear synthesized speech being used. Examples are found in soft-drink machines, on the telephone, and in cars.

The most widely used voice-output devices are stereo speakers and headphones. (See Figures 5-30 and 5-31.) These devices are connected to a sound card in the system unit. The sound card is used to capture as well as play back recorded sounds.

Voice output is used as a reinforcement tool for learning, such as to help students study a foreign language. It is also used in many supermarkets at the checkout counter to confirm purchases. One of its most powerful capabilities is to assist the physically challenged. Some Web sites use so-called **chatterbots,** or virtual characters, that allow you to ask questions and get answers. (See Figure 5-32.)

FIGURE 5-31
Flat panel speakers

CONCEPT CHECK

- ✔ What do voice-output devices do?
- ✔ List some examples of where you might encounter voice-output.

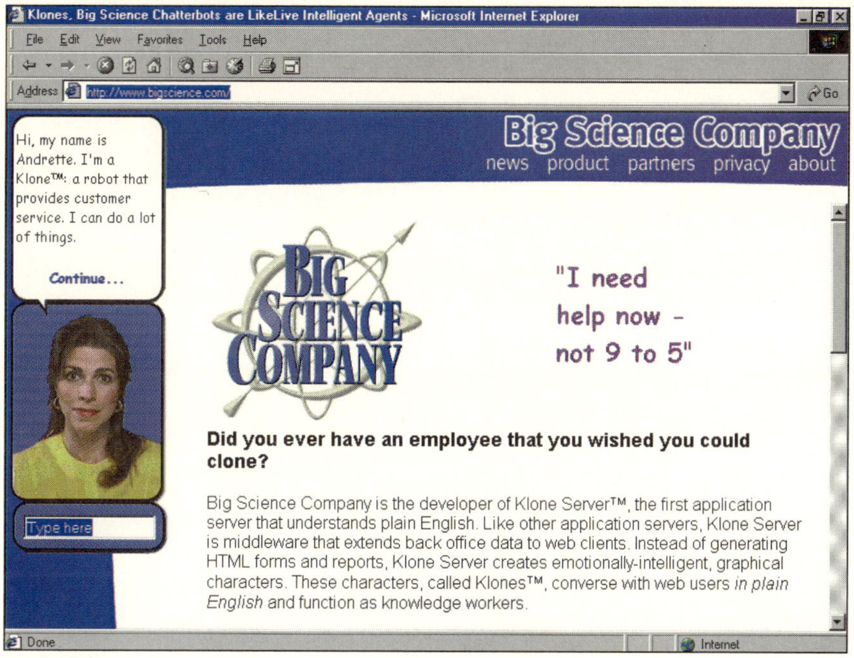

FIGURE 5-32
Chatterbot

A LOOK TO THE FUTURE

Microsoft's Investment in WebTV and introduction of Broadcast Technology could lead the way to the merger of all digital television and microcomputers.

Have you been hearing a lot about digital TV? It promises to combine the power and flexibility of a microcomputer with the entertainment capabilities of a large-screen TV. You and a whole group of friends could play computer games, interact with life-sized figures, surf the Web, capture video, edit it, and paste into electronic presentations.

Of course, that's what PC/TV is all about. These systems contain special devices that convert analog signals required for today's television sets to digital signals required for microcomputers. Unfortunately, this conversion greatly constrains the speed, flexibility, and quality of these systems. But all that's going to change in the next few years.

All-digital television broadcasting is just getting started and promise greater image and sound quality. The Federal Communications Commission is leading the way. Every major network is required to offer digital signals to their top 30 markets this year.

Microsoft, a leader in software technology, has recently taken steps to position itself for this change. One step has been the recent investment of nearly a half billion dollars in WebTV, a company that manufactures Internet terminals for television sets. Another step is the introduction of Broadcast Technology in Microsoft's Windows operating systems. This technology presents a cable TV interface that lets you choose content on screen from the Internet, local TV, cable TV, and other sources.

Will your current television set become useless? It will not be able to display the new digital signals; by the year 2006, all analog broadcasts are expected to be eliminated. However, the transition to digital will occur gradually over the next few years.

VISUAL SUMMARY Input and Output

KEYBOARD ENTRY

Input devices translate data and programs that people understand into a form that a computer can process. Two kinds of input are *keyboard* and *direct entry.*

Keyboard entry can be categorized as *keyboards* and *terminals.*

Keyboards

Both traditional and natural **keyboards** have various types of keys including **toggle keys**, and **combination keys**.

Terminals

Terminals connect to the host computer or server. Four kinds of terminals are:

- **Dumb**—sends and receives only; no processing.
- **Intelligent**—sends, receives, and processes; popular type is **Net PC.**
- **Network**—provides low-cost alternative to intelligent terminal.
- **Internet**—accesses Internet and displays on a television set; does not require microcomputer.

DIRECT ENTRY

Direct entry devices can be categorized as *pointing, scanning*, or *voice-input.*

Pointing

Pointing devices allow users to directly use their hand(s) to input data. Most common is the **mouse.**

Three devices similar to the mouse are **trackballs, touch surfaces,** and **pointing sticks.**

Other pointing devices include:

- **Joysticks**—control game action by varying pressure, speed, and direction.
- **Touch screens**—touching finger to screen to control operations.
- **Light pens**—directed at screen to control operations.
- **Digitizers**—convert images to digital data using **stylus** and **digitizing tablet.**
- **Digital cameras**—record still-image photos on disk and in memory.
- **Digital video cameras**—record motion digitally on tape, on disk, or in memory.
- **Digital notebooks**—electronic pads record handwriting as digital data.

To be a competent end user you need to be aware of the most commonly used input and output devices. These devices are translators for information into and out of the system unit. Two kinds of input are keyboard and direct entry. Output devices include monitors, printers, plotters, and voice-output.

DIRECT ENTRY

Scanning

Scanners convert images to digital data. There are two basic types of scanners:

- **Flatbed scanners** are like copy machines.
- **Portable scanners** are handheld devices.

Widely used scanning devices include **image scanners, fax machines, bar-code readers, MIRC, OCR,** and **OMR** devices.

Voice-Input Devices

These devices convert a person's spoken words into digital data. **Voice recognition systems** are a combination of hardware and software that allows users to control operations and create documents using voice commands.

Two types of voice recognition systems:

- **Discrete-speech recognition systems** recognize only individual words.
- **Continuous-speech recognition systems** recognize individual words and phrases in context; key technology for the 21st century.

MONITORS

Output devices translate machine output to output that people can understand. Output devices include *monitors, printers, plotters,* and *voice-output.*

Monitor size is indicated by diagonal length of viewing area. Monitor clarity is indicated by **resolution,** measured in **pixels.**

Standards

Monitor standards indicate resolution capabilities.

Standard	Pixels
SVGA	800 × 600
XGA	1,024 × 768
SXGA	1,280 × 1,024
UXGA	1,600 × 1,200

Cathode-Ray Tubes

CRTs are similar to televisions in size and technology. They are typically placed on a system unit or directly on a desk. Their primary advantages are low cost and high resolution.

Flat-Panel Monitors

Flat-panel monitors are used for portable computers and becoming more popular for desktop systems. Two basic types are:

- **Passive-matrix (dual-scan)**—requires little power but image is not as sharp.
- **Active matrix** or **thin film transistor (TFT)**—requires more power, is more expensive, but produces sharper images.

PRINTERS

Output from monitors is called **soft copy.** Output from a **printer** is called a **hard copy.**

Three widely used types are: *ink-jet, laser,* and *thermal.*

Ink-Jet

Ink-jet printers spray ink onto the surface of the paper. They are reliable, quiet, and inexpensive.

Laser

Laser printers use technology similar to that used in copy machines. They are more expensive than ink-jet printers. Produce excellent quality letter and graphics quality.

Personal lasers are for single users. **Shared lasers** are faster, more expensive and powerful. They are designed for multiple users.

Thermal

Thermal printers use heat elements to produce images on heat-sensitive paper. Thermal printers are the most expensive and produce the highest quality color images.

Other Types

Other types of printers include *dot-matrix printers* and *chain printers.*

PLOTTERS

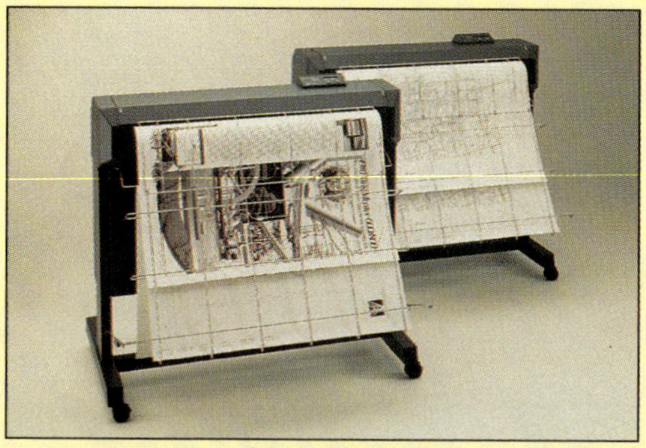

Plotters produce multicolor bar charts, maps, architectural drawings, and three-dimensional illustrations. Four types are as follows.

Pen

Pen plotters create a drawing by moving a pen or pencil over drafting paper. They are the most popular and least expensive.

Ink-Jet

Ink-jet plotters are fast, quiet, and very good at producing solid-color output. The jets, however, can become clogged and require maintenance.

Electrostatic

These plotters use **electrostatic** charges to create high-quality and high-volume output on specially treated paper. Costly chemicals considered dangerous to the environment, however, are required for the development process.

Direct-Imaging

Direct-imaging plotters use electrically heated pins to create two-color output on special heat-sensitive paper. Due to expensive requirements and limited color output, these plotters are specialty devices.

VOICE-OUTPUT DEVICES

Voice-output devices make sounds resembling human speech. The most widely used devices are stereo speakers and headphones.

Key Terms

active-matrix monitor (106)
bar codes (101)
bar-code reader (101)
cathode-ray tube (CRT) (106)
chatterbots (110)
combination key (94)
continuous-speech recognition system (104)
digital camera (98)
digital notebook (99)
digital video camera (99)
digitizer (98)
digitizing tablet (98)
direct entry (96)
direct-imaging plotter (110)
discrete-speech recognition systems (104)
dual-scan monitor (106)
dumb terminal (95)
electrostatic plotter (109)
facsimile transmission (fax) machine (100)
fax/modem board (101)
flatbed scanner (100)
flat-panel monitor (106)
hard copy (107)
high-definition television (HDTV) (107)
image scanner (99)
ink-jet plotter (109)
ink-jet printer (107)
intelligent terminal (95)
Internet terminal (96)
joystick (97)
keyboard entry (94)
laser printer (107)
light pen (98)
liquid crystal display (LCD) monitor (106)
magnetic-ink character recognition (MICR) (101)
mark sensing (101)
monitor (105)
mouse (96)
Net Personal Computer (Net PC) (95)
network computer (95)
network terminal (95)
optical-character recognition (OCR) (101)
optical-mark recognition (OMR) (101)
passive-matrix monitor (106)
PC/TV (107)
pen plotter (109)
personal laser printer (107)
pixels (105)
platform scanner (94)
plotters (109)
pointer (96)
pointing stick (97)
point-of-sale (POS) terminal (94)
portable scanner (100)
reader/sorter (101)
resolution (105)
roller ball (97)
scanner (99)
shared laser printer (107)
soft copy (107)
source document (94)
stylus (98)
SVGA (105)
SXGA (105)
terminal (95)
thermal plotter (108)
thermal printer (108)
thin client (95)
thin film transistor (TFT) monitor (106)
toggle key (94)
touch screen (97)
touch surface (97)
trackball (97)
UXGA (105)
voice-input device (102)
voice-output device (110)
voice recognition systems (102)
wand reader (94)
Web terminal (96)
XGA (105)

Chapter Review

LEVEL 1

Reviewing Facts and Terms

Matching

Match each numbered item with the most closely related lettered item. Write your answers in the spaces provided.

1. Vocalizes prerecorded sounds. ____
2. Controls a pointer that is displayed on the monitor. ____
3. Inexpensive laser printers used by many single users. ____
4. Considered to be one of the key technologies for the 21st century. ____
5. All-digital, this delivers a much clearer and more detailed wide-screen picture. ____
6. Special-purpose output device that creates line drawings and solid-color output by spraying droplets of ink onto paper. ____
7. Flat-panel monitor where each pixel is independently activated, allowing more colors and better clarity to be displayed. ____

a. Active-matrix monitor
b. Bar-code reader
c. Continuous-speech recognition system
d. Direct entry
e. Dumb terminal
f. Electrostatic plotter
g. HDTV

8. Input that does not require data to be keyed—machine-readable data can go directly to the CPU. ____
9. Can be used to input and receive data, but it cannot process data independently. ____
10. Uses electrostatic charges to create images made up of tiny dots on specially treated paper. ____
11. Printer that sprays small droplets of ink at high speed onto the surface of the paper. ____
12. Scanning device that uses special preprinted characters. ____
13. Special-purpose drawing devices. ____
14. Describes a monitor's clarity, measured in pixels. ____
15. A specialized pointing device, connected to a computer, used to trace an item placed on a digitizing tablet. ____
16. Photoelectric scanners that read bar codes. ____
17. Low-cost and limited microcomputers that typically have only one type of secondary storage, a sealed system unit, and no expansion slots. ____
18. Usually appears in the shape of an arrow on the monitor. ____
19. Super Extended Graphics Array. ____
20. Input device that uses both keyboard and direct entry—a sort of electronic cash register. ____

h. Ink-jet plotter
i. Ink-jet printer
j. Mouse
k. Net PC
l. OCR
m. Personal laser printer
n. Plotters
o. Pointer
p. POS terminal
q. Resolution
r. Stylus
s. SXGA
t. Voice-output device

True/False

In the spaces provided, write T or F to indicate whether the statement is true or false.

1. Input devices translate symbols that people understand into symbols that computers can process. ____
2. A plotter is a device that can be used to trace or copy a drawing or photograph. ____
3. Banks use a method called magnetic-ink character recognition (MICR) to automatically read and sort checks. ____
4. Laser printers are highly reliable, but the quality of their output limits their use to rough drafts and in-house communications. ____
5. Plotters are special-purpose drawing devices. ____
6. The most common type of home or office monitor is an UXGA. ____

Multiple Choice

Circle the letter of the correct answer.

1. The *Caps Lock* key is a __________ key.
   a. function
   b. numeric
   c. toggle
   d. cursor control
   e. combination

2. A device that converts images on a page to electronic signals that can be stored in a computer:
   a. monitor
   b. scanner
   c. plotter
   d. MICR
   e. POS
3. The type of intelligent terminal that typically has only one type of secondary storage, a sealed system unit, and no expansion slots:
   a. PC/TV
   b. Web terminal
   c. digital modem
   d. Net PC
   e. network device
4. The printer that can produce very high quality images using heat elements on heat-sensitive paper:
   a. dot-matrix
   b. laser
   c. ink-jet
   d. plotter
   e. thermal
5. The plotter that creates images using heat-sensitive paper and electrically heated pins:
   a. pen
   b. ink-jet
   c. direct-imaging
   d. scanner
   e. electrostatic
6. Which of the following is NOT a scanning device:
   a. bar-code reader
   b. digitizing tablet
   c. fax machine
   d. optical-mark recognition
   e. portable scanner

Completion

Complete each statement in the spaces provided.

1. A device similar to a mouse that controls the pointer by rotating a ball controlled with the thumb is __________.
2. __________ machines are popular office machines that scan the image of a document to be sent.
3. __________ is a monitor standard used primarily with 15-inch monitors.
4. The __________ printer is the most widely used.
5. __________ devices make sounds that resemble human speech.
6. __________ __________ control the pointer by moving and tapping your finger on the surface of a pad.

Reviewing Concepts

LEVEL 2

Open-Ended

On a separate sheet of paper, respond to each question and statement.

1. What are the differences between keyboard entry and direct entry?
2. What is a POS terminal? Describe the processing capabilities of a POS terminal and examples of where you might find POS terminals in use.
3. Distinguish among the four kinds of terminals: dumb, intelligent, network, and Internet.
4. What are pixels? What do they have to do with screen resolution?
5. Compare the various kinds of direct-entry devices. For the ones you have never used personally, give an example of where you might encounter them.
6. Distinguish between discrete-speech and continuous-speech recognition systems.

Concept Mapping

On a separate sheet of paper, draw a concept map or a flowchart showing how the following terms are related. Show all relationships. Include any additional terms you can think of.

active-matrix monitor
bar codes
bar-code reader
digital camera
digital notebook
digitizer
direct entry
dual-scan monitor
electrostatic plotter
fax machine
ink-jet plotter
ink-jet printer
Internet terminal
joy stick
laser printer
LCD monitor
monitor
mouse
network computer
optical-character recognition
passive-matrix monitor
pen plotter
plotters
pointer
POS terminal
resolution
scanner
portable scanner
stylus
SVGA
SXGA
terminal
thermal printer
touch screen
UXGA
video display
voice recognition systems
voice-input/output device
wand reader
XGA

Critical Thinking Questions and Projects

LEVEL 3

Read each exercise and answer the related questions on a separate sheet of paper.

1. *Multifunction devices*: Multifunction devices are also known as information appliances. These all-in-one devices provide a variety of input and output capabilities in one piece of equipment. Most offer scanning, faxing, copying, and printing capabilities. To learn more about them, visit a local computer store and/or use the Web. Determine what advantages and disadvantages they offer compared to purchasing separate, more specialized devices.
2. *Security and privacy*: Security cameras are becoming more widely used by retail stores to monitor customers as they select items, as well as to monitor parking structures, elevators, dressing rooms, and restrooms. Many homes have security monitors for the front door and for a child's room. Computer-enhanced videotapes from security cameras have been successfully used to catch and prosecute shoplifters and abusive care providers.
   a. Does your school, home, or place of work use security cameras? If it does, describe where and why they are used.

b. Some people would point out that while security devices may be effective for security, they represent a threat to personal privacy. Discuss your position on this potential trade-off.

c. Do you think the use of security cameras should be controlled? If so, how and under what conditions?

On the Web Exercises

1. SoundBlaster

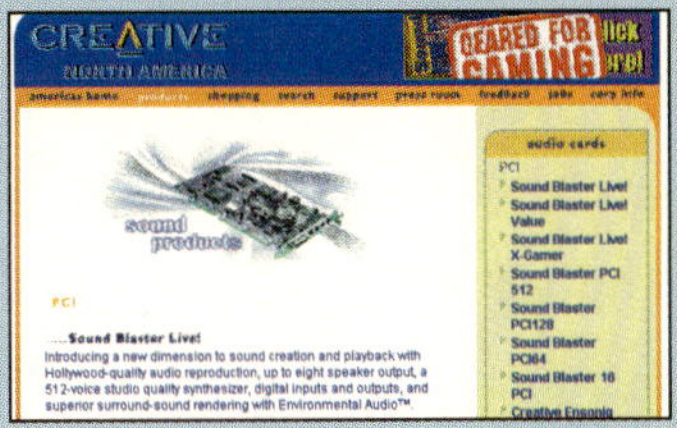

Creative Lab is one of the pioneers in sound input and output technologies. Its SoundBlaster family of sound cards is an industry standard for affordability, quality, and reliability. Visit our Web site at http://www.mhhe.com/cit/concepts/oleary2000-2001/webex5.html to link to the SoundBlaster site. Once connected to that site, check out the newest sound card. Print out the Web page describing the specifications of this card and write a paragraph comparing the card to its predecessors.

2. WebTV

In order to provide Internet access to a wider audience, the company WebTV Networks, Inc. has eliminated the need for a traditional computer when surfing the Web. Using a Web terminal connected to a TV set, anyone can access the Internet without the expense of a computer. To learn more about WebTV's Web terminal, visit our Web site at http://www.mhhe.com/cit/concepts/oleary2000-2001/webex5.html to link to WebTV's site. Once connected to that site, learn how to use your TV to access the Web. Print out the Web page you find most informative. Write a paragraph discussing the relative advantages and disadvantages of TV versus computer access to the Internet.

3. Speech Recognition

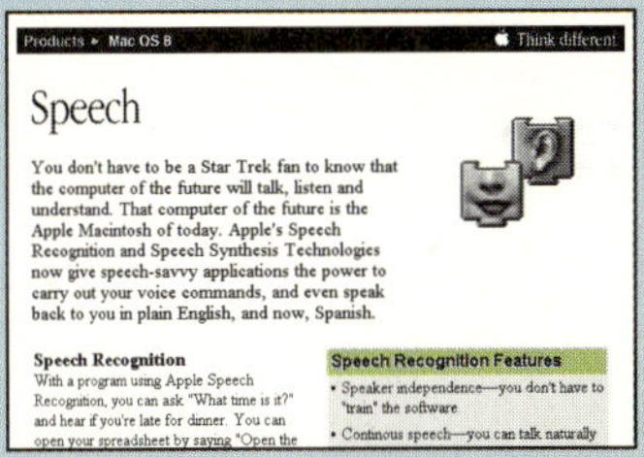

Apple Computer is one of the leaders in speech recognition technology. Visit our Web site at http://www.mhhe.com/cit/concepts/oleary2000-2001/webex5.html to link to Apple's speech recognition and speech synthesis home page. Once connected to the Apple site, investigate the latest in speech recognition and speech synthesis software. Print out the Web page you found to be the most informative. Write a paragraph describing why these new developments will or will not be useful in real-world business applications.

4. Movie Magic

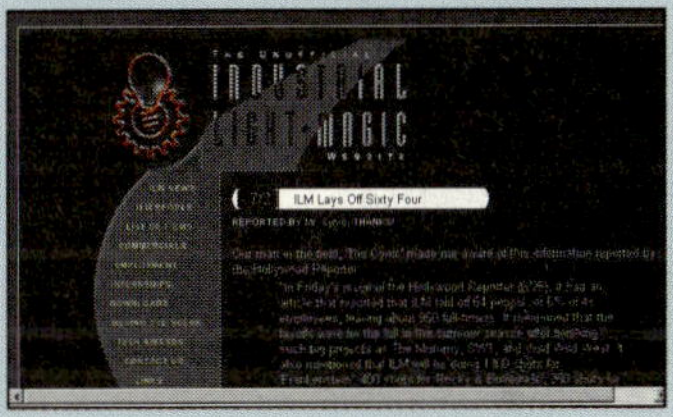

A variety of input and output devices have been used to create dramatic special effects in movies. To learn how these devices are used to create movie magic, visit our Web site at http://www.mhhe.com/cit/concepts/oleary2000-2001/webex5.html to link to a Web site on special effects. Once connected to that site, print out the Web page that you find most interesting. Write a brief paragraph on one movie magic technique that most interests you and how you found it on the Web site.

CHAPTER 6

Secondary Storage

COMPETENCIES

After you have read this chapter, you should be able to:

1. **Describe today's standard floppy disk and compare it to Zip, SuperDisks, and HiFD disks.**
2. **Describe the following kinds of disks: internal hard disks, hard-disk cartridges, and hard-disk packs.**
3. **Describe ways to improve hard-disk operations: disk caching, redundant arrays of inexpensive disks, and data compression.**
4. **Compare the CD and DVD formats.**
5. **Describe the different types of optical disks.**
6. **Describe magnetic tape streamers and magnetic tape reels.**

An essential feature of every computer is the ability to save—that is, store—information. Computers can save information permanently, after you turn them off. This way, you can save your work for future use, share information with others, or modify information already available. Secondary storage holds information external from the CPU. Secondary storage allows you to store programs, such as Word and Excel. It also allows you to store the data processed by

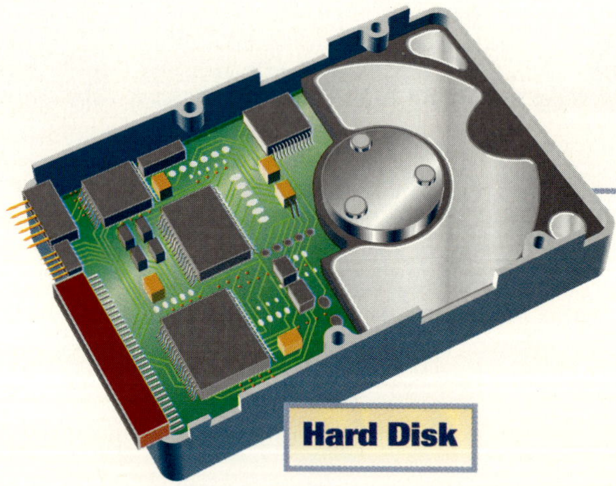

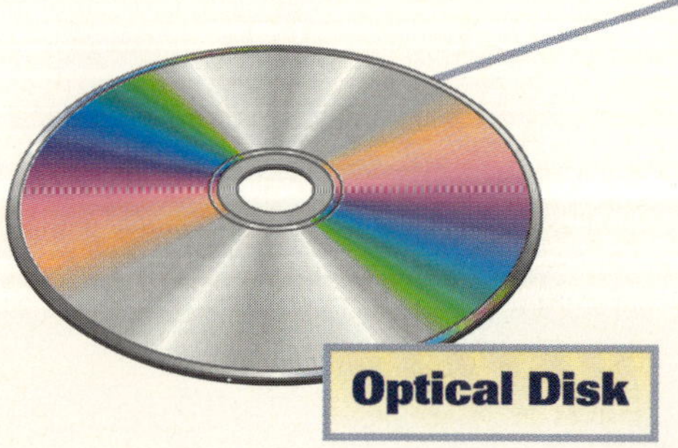

programs, such as text or the numbers in a spreadsheet.

We described random-access memory (RAM) in Chapter 4. This is the *internal* and *temporary* storage of data and programs in the computer's memory. Once the power is turned off or interrupted, everything in internal storage disappears. Such storage is therefore said to be **volatile storage.** Thus, we need *external, more permanent,* or **nonvolatile storage** for data and programs. We also need external storage because users need much more capacity than is possessed by a computer's primary memory.

Competent end users need to be aware of the different types of secondary storage. They need to know the capabilities, limitations, and uses of floppy disks, hard disks, optical disks, and magnetic tapes.

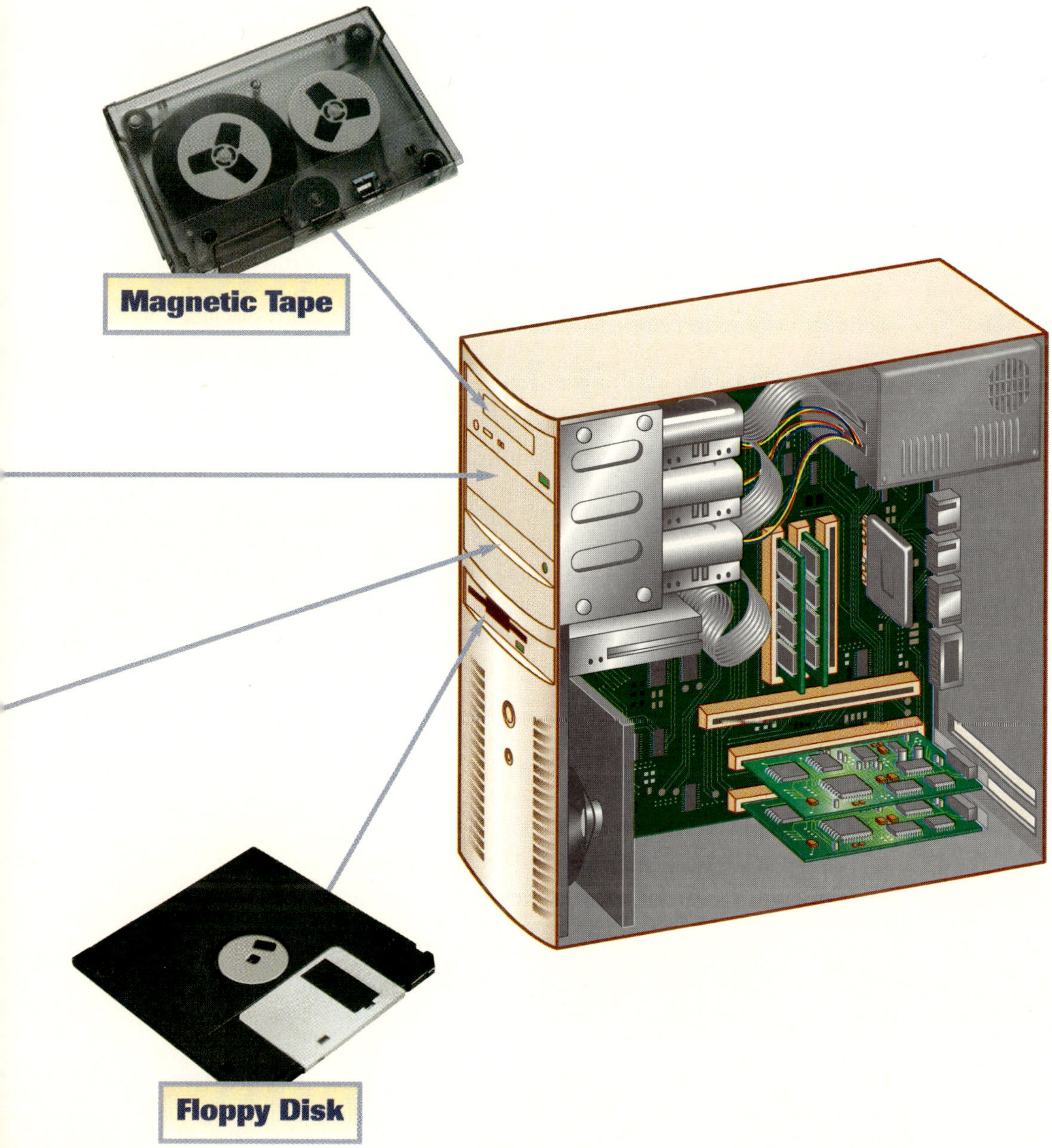

Floppy Disks

Floppy disks are removable storage media. Today's standard is 1.44 MB. Tomorrow's might be a Zip, SuperDisk, or HiFD. Data is recorded on tracks and sectors.

Floppy disks, often called **diskettes** or simply **disks,** are a portable or removable storage media. They are used to store and to transport word processing, spreadsheet, and other types of files. They use flat circular pieces of Mylar plastic that rotate within a jacket. Data is stored as electromagnetic charges on a metal oxide film coating the Mylar plastic. Data and programs are represented by the presence or absence of these charges, using the ASCII or EBCDIC data representation codes.

ON THE WEB EXPLORATIONS

Iomega and Imation are leaders in developing high-capacity floppy disks. To learn more about the companies, visit their Web sites at

http://www.iomega.com
http://www.superdisk.com

Floppy disks are also called **flexible disks,** and **floppies.** This is because the plastic disk inside the diskette covers is flexible, not rigid. Although there are several different types of floppy disks, there is just one standard and several others that are competing to become the next standard.

Today's Standard

The most widely used floppy disk is the **1.44 MB 3½-inch disk.** (See Figure 6-1.) These disks are typically labeled **2HD,** which means "two-sided, high-density." This disk can store 1.44 megabytes—the equivalent of 400 typewritten pages. It has a thin exterior jacket made of hard plastic to protect the flexible disk inside. When the disk is inserted into a floppy disk drive, the shutter slides open to expose the 3½-inch flexible disk. A read-write head from the disk drive moves across the exposed disk to store and retrieve data.

FIGURE 6-1
A 3½-inch floppy disk

These disks also have a **write-protect notch.** When the notch is open, data cannot be added on the disk. This is to provide protection against accidentally writing over information on the disk that you want to keep.

Tomorrow's Standard Floppy Disk

Today's standard floppy disk is very reliable and widely used to store data. Its major limitation is its capacity. While 1.44 MB is fine for many text and spreadsheet files, it is not sufficient to hold larger files. For example, many presentations far exceed 1.44 MB. Most multimedia applications require greater capacity.

Several other floppy disks, known as **floppy-disk cartridges,** are competing to become the next higher capacity floppy disk standard. These contenders are also 3½-inch; however, they are thicker and require special disk drives. The three best known are Zip disks, SuperDisks, and HiFD disks.

FIGURE 6-2
Zip disk

- **Zip disks** are produced by Iomega and typically have a 100 MB or 250 MB capacity—over 170 times as much as today's standard floppy disk. Zip drives are a standard feature on many of today's system units. They are widely used to store multimedia, database, large text, and spreadsheet files. Many observers predict that Zip disks will become the next floppy disk standard. (See Figure 6-2.)
- **SuperDisks** are produced by Imation and have a 120 MB capacity. They have one major advantage over Zip disks. SuperDisk drives are able to read and store data on today's 1.44 MB standard disk. Zip disk drives cannot. For this reason, SuperDisks are popular for use with notebook computers.
- **HiFD disks** from the Sony Corporation are the newest challenger. They have a capacity of 200 MB, and, like SuperDisk drives, HiFD disk drives are able to use today's 1.44 MB standard disks.

Description	Capacity
2HD	1.44 MB
Zip	100 MB/250 MB
SuperDisk	120 MB
HiFD	200 MB

FIGURE 6-3
Typical floppy-disk capacities

Each of these will likely improve its capacity and speed in the near future. Will one of them become the next standard floppy disk? While most observers believe one *will* become the next standard, they are less certain *when* this will occur. For a summary of floppy disks, see Figure 6-3.

TIPS Are you concerned about losing the data stored on your floppy disks? Actually, floppy disks are quite durable, and taking care of them boils down to just a few basic rules.

1. *Don't bend.* Don't bend, flex, or put heavy weights on them.
2. *Don't touch.* Don't touch anything visible through the protective jacket.
3. *Avoid extreme conditions.* Keep disks away from strong magnetic fields, extreme heat, and any chemicals such as alcohol and other solvents.
4. *Use storage boxes.* Store disks in a sturdy plastic storage box.

Of course the best protection is to make a backup or duplicate copy of your disk.

The Parts of a Floppy Disk

Data is recorded on a disk in rings called **tracks.** (See Figure 6-4.) These tracks are closed concentric circles, not a single spiral as on a phonograph record. Unlike a phonograph record, these tracks have no visible grooves. Looking at an exposed floppy disk, you would see just a smooth surface. Each track is divided into invisible wedge-shaped sections known as **sectors.**

Some disks are manufactured without tracks and sectors in place. They must be adapted to the type of microcomputer and disk drive you are using. You do this using a process called *formatting,* or *initializing.*

CONCEPT CHECK

- ✔ How do floppy disks store information?
- ✔ What is today's standard floppy disk?
- ✔ What are likely to be tomorrow's standard floppy disks?

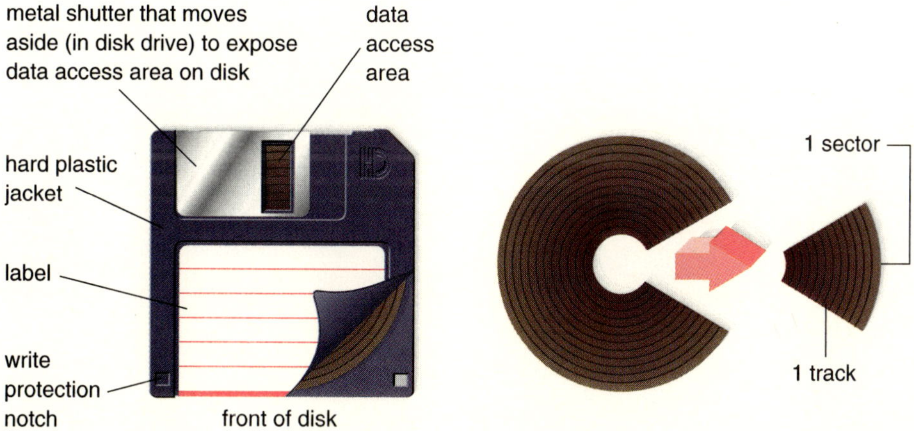

FIGURE 6-4
The parts of a 3½-inch floppy disk

Hard Disks

Hard disks are of three types: internal hard disk, hard-disk cartridge, and hard-disk pack.

While floppy disks use thin flexible plastic disks, **hard disks** use thicker, ridged metallic platters. (See Figure 6-5.) Hard disks are able to store and retrieve information much faster and have a greater capacity. They are sensitive instruments. The read-write head rides on a cushion of air about 0.000001 inch thick. It is so thin that a smoke particle, fingerprint, dust, or human hair could cause what is known as a head crash. (See Figure 6-6.)

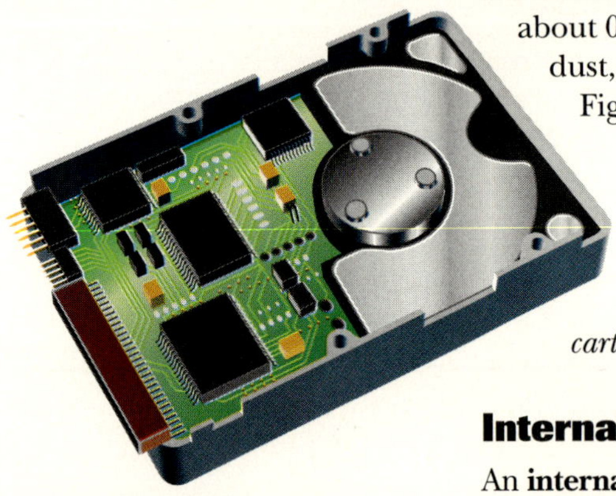

FIGURE 6-5
Hard disk

A **head crash** happens when the surface of the read-write head or particles on its surface contact the magnetic disk surface. A head crash is a disaster for a hard disk. It means that some or all of the data on the disk is destroyed.

There are three types of hard disks: *internal hard disk, hard-disk cartridge,* and *hard-disk pack.*

Internal Hard Disk

An **internal hard disk** is also known as a **fixed disk** because it is located inside the system unit. It is used to store programs and large data files. For example, nearly every microcomputer uses its internal hard disk to store its operating system and major applications like Word and Excel.

An internal hard disk consists of one or more metallic platters sealed inside a container. The container includes the motor for rotating the disks. It also contains an access arm and read-write heads for writing data to and reading data from the disks. From the outside of a microcomputer, an internal hard disk looks like part of a front panel on the system cabinet. Typically, inside are four 3½-inch metallic platters with access arms that move back and forth. (See Figure 6-7.)

Internal hard disks have two advantages over floppy disks: capacity and speed. A 10-gigabyte internal hard disk, for instance, can hold almost as much information as 7,000 standard floppy disks. Moreover, access is faster. For these reasons, almost all of today's powerful applications are designed to be stored on and run from an internal hard disk. Adequate capacity or size of a microcomputer's internal hard disk is essential.

ON THE WEB EXPLORATIONS

Seagate is one of the leaders in developing high-capacity internal hard disks. To learn more about the company, visit its Web site at

http://www.seagate.com

FIGURE 6-6
Materials that can cause a head crash

Hard-Disk Cartridges

While internal hard disks provide fast access, they have a fixed amount of storage and cannot be easily removed. **Hard-disk cartridges** are as easy to remove as a cassette from a videocassette recorder. The amount of storage available to a computer system is limited only by the number of cartridges.

Hard disk cartridges are used primarily to complement an internal hard disk. Because the cartridges are easily removed, they are particularly useful to protect or secure sensitive information. For example, personnel administrators need to have access to highly confidential employee information. When information is stored on a hard-disk cartridge, it is readily available, yet can be easily locked up when not in use. Other uses for hard-disk cartridges include backing up the contents of the internal hard disk and providing additional hard disk capacity.

The typical capacity for a hard-disk cartridge is 2 gigabytes. Two well-known hard-disk cartridges are Jaz from Iomega and SparQ from SyQuest. (See Figure 6-8.)

TIPS Does your internal hard-disk drive run a lot and seem slow? Are you having problems with lost or corrupted files? The problem could be with fragmented files—files that when saved were broken into pieces (fragments) and stored in different locations on your hard disk. To clean up the disk and speed up access, consider defragging. If you are using Windows 95, 98, or 2000:

1. *Start Disk Defragmenter.* Use Start/Programs/Accessories/System Tools/Disk Defragmenter to start defragmenting your disk. Defragging rearranges the file parts so that they are stored in adjacent locations.
2. *Keep working.* You can continue running other applications while your disk is being defragmented. Unfortunately, your computer operates more slowly, and Disk Defragmenter takes longer to finish.

It is recommended that you defrag your disk on a regular basis. If you have Windows 98 or 2000, you can schedule this task to be done automatically for you—use Start/Programs/Accessories/System tools/Scheduled tasks.

Hard-Disk Packs

Hard-disk packs are removable storage devices used to store massive amounts of information. (See Figure 6-9.) Their capacity far exceeds the other types of hard disks. Although you may never have seen one, it is almost certain that you have used them. Microcomputers that have access to the Internet, minicomputers, or mainframes often have access to external hard-disk packs through communication lines. Banks and credit card companies use them to record financial information.

FIGURE 6-7
Inside of an internal hard-disk drive

FIGURE 6-8
Removable hard-disk cartridge

FIGURE 6-9
Hard-disk packs

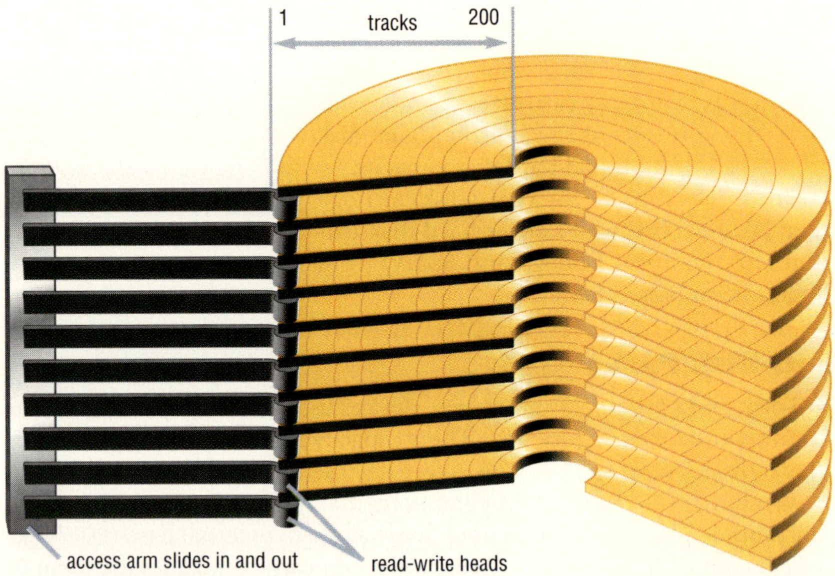

FIGURE 6-10
How a hard-disk pack works

Hard-disk packs consist of several platters aligned one above the other. They resemble a stack of phonograph records. The difference is that there is space between the disks to allow the access arms to move in and out. (See Figure 6-10.) Each access arm has two read-write heads. One reads the disk surface above it; the other reads the disk surface below it. A disk pack with 11 disks provides 20 recording surfaces. This is because the top and bottom outside surfaces of the pack are not used.

All the access arms move in and out together. However, only one of the read-write heads is activated at a given moment. **Access time** is the time between the computer's request for data from secondary storage and the completion of the data transfer.

You may well use your microcomputer to gain access to information over a telephone or other communications line. (We show this in the next chapter.) Such information is apt to be stored on disk packs. For example, one large information service, named Dialog, has over 300 databases. These databases cover all areas of science, technology, business, medicine, social science, current affairs, and humanities. All of these are available through a telephone link with your desktop computer. There are more than 100 million items of information, including references to books, patents, directories, journals, and newspaper articles. Such an information resource may be of great value to you in your work.

For a summary of the different types of hard disks, see Figure 6-11.

Type	Description
Internal	Fast access to applications, fixed
Cartridge	Complement to internal hard disk, removable
Disk pack	Massive storage capacity, removable

FIGURE 6-11
Types of hard disks

Performance Enhancements

Three ways to improve the performance of hard disks are disk caching, redundant arrays of inexpensive disks, and file compression/decompression.

Disk caching improves hard-disk performance by anticipating data needs. It requires a combination of hardware and software. During idle processing time, frequently used data is read from the hard disk into memory (cache). When needed, the data is then accessed directly from memory. The transfer rate from memory is much faster than from hard disk. As a result, overall system performance is often increased by as much as 30 percent.

Redundant arrays of inexpensive disks (RAIDs) improve performance by expanding external storage. Groups of inexpensive hard-disk drives are related or grouped together using networks and special software. These grouped disks are treated as a single large-capacity hard disk. They can outperform single disks of comparable capacities.

File compression and **file decompression** increase storage capacity by reducing the amount of space required to store data and programs. File compression is not limited to hard-disk systems. It is frequently used to compress files on floppy disks as well. File compression also helps to speed up transmission of files from one computer system to another. Sending and receiving compressed files across the Internet is a common activity.

Special file compression programs scan files for ways to reduce the amount of required storage. One way is to search for repeating patterns. The repeating patterns are replaced with a token, leaving enough so that the original can be rebuilt or decompressed.

File compression programs typically can shrink files to a quarter of their original size. Two well-known file compression programs are WinZip from Nico Mak Computing and PKZip from PKWare.

TIPS Are you running short of hard-disk storage space? Want to send a large file or several files at once over the Internet? You can save both space and valuable connection time by compressing the files first. Here's how, using WinZip, a popular compression program:

1. *Start.* Start the WinZip program.
2. *Create file.* Click the *New* button on the toolbar to create and name a zip file.
3. *Select.* Locate and select the file(s) you want to compress.
4. *Compress.* Click the *Add* button to compress and add the selected file(s) to the zip file.

You can now replace the selected file(s) with the much smaller zip file. To access the original files at any time, use the *WinZip Extract* button.

CONCEPT CHECK

- ✔ What are the three types of hard disks?
- ✔ Internal hard disks have two advantages over floppy disks: ________ and ________.
- ✔ ________-________ ________ are removable storage devices used to store massive amounts of information.
- ✔ List three ways to improve the performance of hard disks.

FIGURE 6-12
Optical disk

Optical Disks

Optical disks use laser technology. CD and DVD are optical disk formats.

Today's optical disks can hold over 4.7 gigabytes of data. (See Figure 6-12.) That is the equivalent of over 1 million typewritten pages or a medium-sized library all on a single disk. Optical disks are having a great impact on storage today, but we are probably only beginning to see their effects.

In optical-disk technology, a laser beam alters the surface of a plastic or metallic disk to represent data. Unlike floppy and hard disks, which use magnetic charges to represent 1s and 0s, optical disks use reflected light. The 1s and 0s are represented by flat areas called **lands** and bumpy areas called **pits** on the disk surface. The disk is read by a laser that projects a tiny beam of light on these areas. The amount of reflected light determines whether the area represents a 1 or a 0. (See Figure 6-13.)

Optical disks come in many different sizes including 3½, 4¾, 5¼, 8, 12, and 14 inches. The most common size is 4¾-inch. Data is stored on these disks in different ways or different formats. The two most common are CD and DVD.

TIPS Do you like to listen to music while working on your computer? If you have a CD-ROM drive you can use it to play your favorite CDs while you work. Just follow these simple steps:

1. *Insert headphones.* Insert your headphone jack (commonly located on the front of the CD-ROM drive or on the back of your computer) or turn on your speakers.
2. *Insert CD.* Insert the music CD into the drive.
3. *Start player.* If the CD does not play automatically and you use either Windows 95, 98, or 2000, choose Start/Programs/Accessories/Entertainment/CD Player to start the Windows CD player.
4. *Adjust volume.* Adjust the volume by clicking the speaker icon on the taskbar.

Although you can use the CD-ROM drive on your computer to play music CDs, do not use your audio CD player to play CDs intended for computers—this could damage your audio CD player's speakers.

Compact Disc

Compact disc, or as it is better known, **CD,** format is the most widely used today. (See Figure 6-14.) CD drives are standard on many microcomputer systems. Typically, CD drives can store 650 megabytes of data on one side of a CD. One important characteristic of CD drives is their speed. The rotational speed is important because it determines how fast data can be transferred from the CD. For example, a 24X or 24-speed CD drive can transfer 3.6 MB per second, while

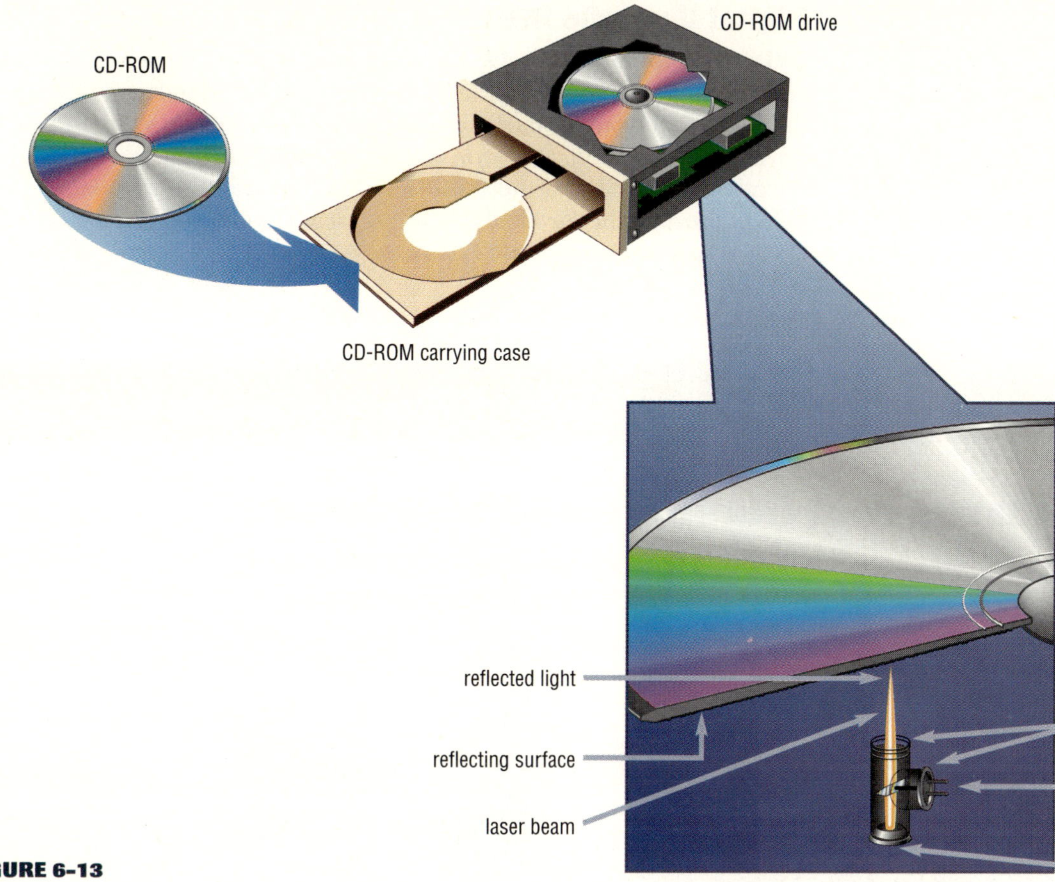

FIGURE 6-13
How a CD-ROM works

a 32X drive can transfer 4.8 MB per second. The faster the drive, the faster data can be read from the CD and used by the computer system.

There are three basic types of CDs: CD-ROM, CD-R, and CD-RW:

- **CD-ROM,** which stands for *compact disc–read only memory,* is similar to a commercial music CD. *Read-only* means it cannot be written on or erased by the user. Thus, you as a user have access only to the data imprinted by the publisher. CD-ROMs are used to distribute large databases and references. They are also used to distribute large software application packages. For example, Microsoft Office is available on a single CD-ROM or on 38 floppy disks. One advantage of the CD-ROM version is that installation from one CD-ROM to the internal hard disk is much faster and easier.
- **CD-R** stands for *CD-recordable.* Also known as **WORM,** or *write once, read many,* CD-Rs can be written to once. After that they can be read many times without deterioration but cannot be written on or erased. CD-Rs are used to archive or to permanently store large amounts of important information.
- **CD-RW** stands for *compact disc rewritable.* Also known as **erasable optical disks,** these disks are very similar to other CD-Rs except that the disk surface is not permanently altered when data is recorded. Because they can be changed, CD-RWs are often used to create and edit multimedia presentations.

FIGURE 6-14
CD in drive

Digital Versatile Disc

DVD stands for *digital versatile disc* or *digital video disc*. This is a relatively new and evolving format. DVD and DVD drives are very similar to CDs except that more data can be packed into the same amount of space. The DVD drives can store 4.7 gigabytes on one side of a DVD—more than seven times the capacity of a CD. Furthermore, many DVD drives can store data on both sides of the disk, thereby doubling the capacity. Soon-to-be-released DVDs are likely to have a 17-gigabyte capacity.

MAKING IT WORK FOR YOU

CD-R Drives and Music from the Internet

Did you know that you can use the Internet to locate music, download it to your computer, and create your own compact discs? All it takes is the right software, hardware, and a connection to the Internet.

How It Works

Music is available on the Internet in special compressed music files called MP3s. You can download these music files to your system via your Internet connection. Using your system and some specialized software, you can store and play these files. You can even create a custom CD using a CD-R drive.

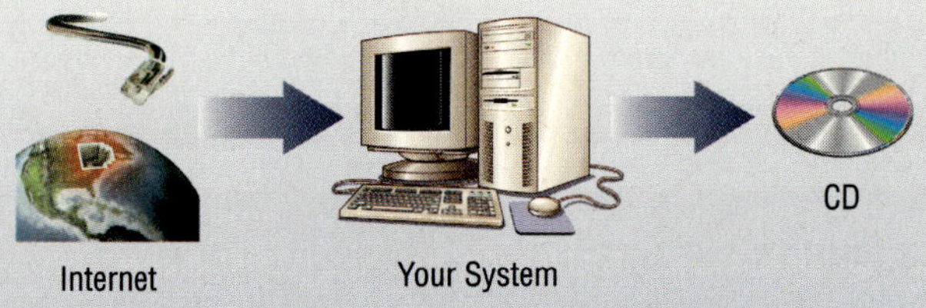

Downloading Music

There are several sites on the Web that offer free music that you can download to your system. Some Web sites are set up to offer a convenient way to browse and select these files, such as www.mp3.com.

For example, you can download files to your system as shown in Figure A.

FIGURE A

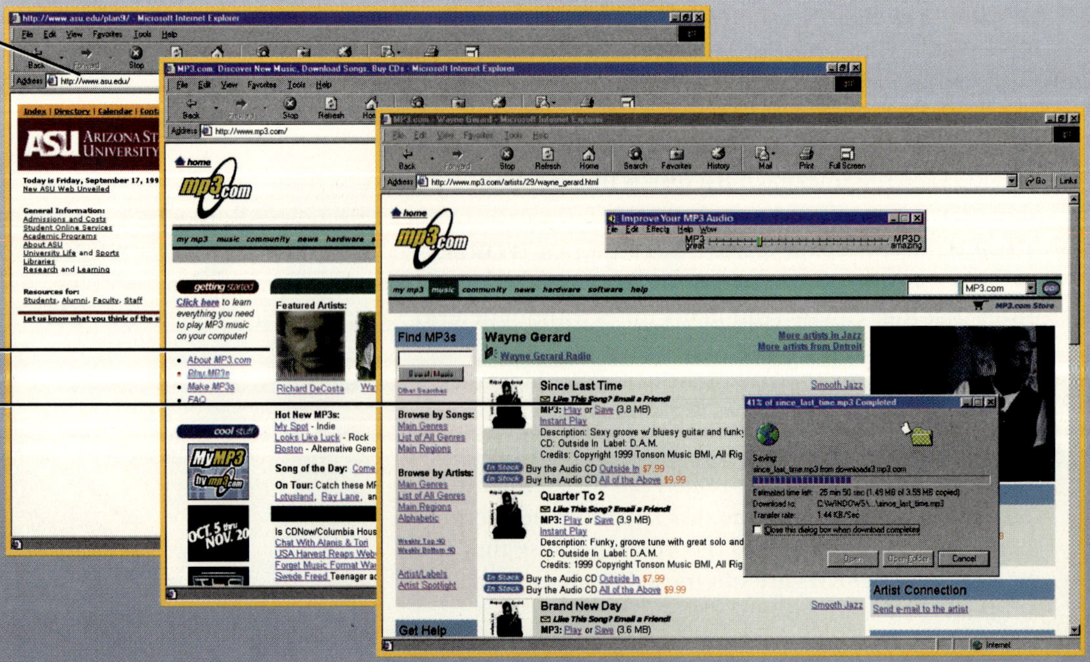

While CDs may be the standard optical disk format today, most observers predict that DVDs will soon replace them. Many of today's more powerful microcomputer systems come with DVD drives. Like CDs, there are three basic types of DVDs:

- **DVD-ROM** stands for *digital versatile disc–read only memory.* DVD-ROMs are having a major impact on the video market. While CD-ROMs can store just over an hour of fair-quality video, DVD-ROMs can provide over two hours of very high quality video and sound comparable to that found in motion picture theaters.

Playing Music

To arrange and play downloaded music files, you need specialized software called a player. WinAmp from Nullsoft (www.winamp.com) is one of the best known.

For example, using WinAmp, you can play music files as shown in Figure B.

FIGURE B

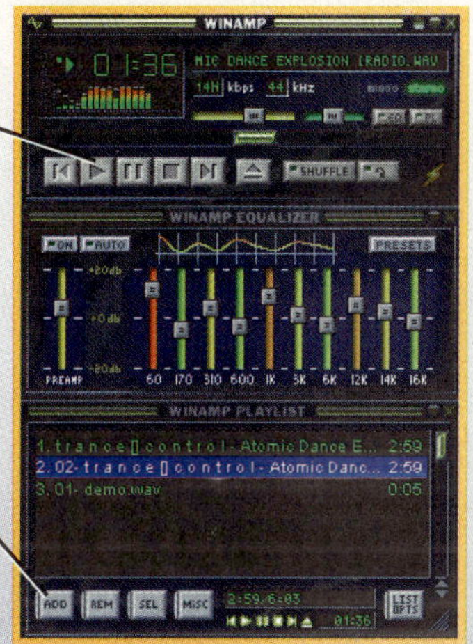

2. Click the *Play* button to play the music.

1. Click the *Add* button to select the music files to play from your hard-disk drive.

Creating a Custom CD

If your computer is equipped with a CD-R or CD-RW drive, you can create your own music CDs. You'll need a blank recordable compact disc and special CD-creation software, such as Easy CD Creator by Adaptec. You use this software to organize and save the music files onto your CD.

For example, using Easy CD Creator, you can create a custom CD as shown in Figure C.

FIGURE C

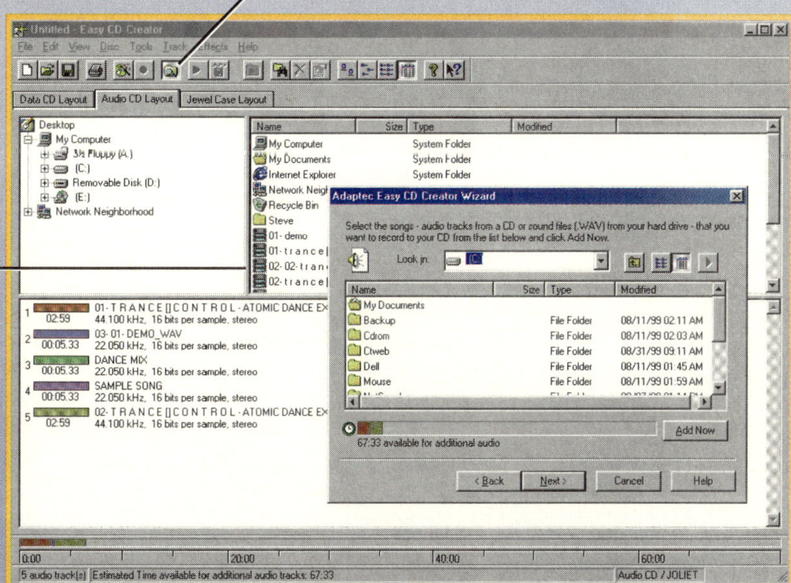

2. Click the *Create CD* button to start the process of recording the CD.

1. Select the music files from your hard drive.

Not all MP3 files can be legally copied. To protect yourself, only download music files from reputable sites.

Format	Type	Typical Capacity	Description
CD	CD-ROM	650MB	Fixed content, used to distribute databases, reference books, and software
	CD-R	650 MB	Written-to one time only, used to archive large amounts of data
	CD-RW	650 MB	Reusable, used to create and edit large multimedia presentations
DVD	DVD-ROM	4.7 GB	Fixed content, distribute theater-quality video and sound presentations
	DVD-R	4.7 GB	Written-to one time only, used to archive very large amounts of data
	DVD-RAM (DVD-RW)	2.6 to 5.2 GB	Reusable, used to create and edit large-scale multimedia presentations

FIGURE 6-15
Types of optical disks

- **DVD-R** stands for *DVD-recordable.* DVD-Rs and DVD-R drives are starting to be used to create permanent archives for large amounts of data. Currently, they are not as widely used as CD-Rs because of their higher costs. This is expected to change as the costs for DVD-R become lower.
- **DVD-RAM** (*DVD–random-access memory*) and **DVD-RW** (*DVD-rewritable*) have recently been introduced. They are two different types of reusable DVD disks. Like CD-RW, they can be used over and over again. They will be used for a wide variety of applications including the creation and editing of large-scale multimedia presentations.

For a summary of optical disk storage capacities, see Figure 6-15.

CONCEPT CHECK

- ✔ Optical disks can hold over ________ gigabytes of data.
- ✔ How much data can be stored on one side of a CD?
- ✔ How much data can DVD drives store on one side of a DVD?

Magnetic Tape

Magnetic tape streamers and magnetic tape reels are used primarily for backup purposes.

To find a particular song on an audiotape, you may have to play several inches of tape. Finding a song on an audio compact disc, in contrast, can be much faster. You select the song, and the disc player moves directly to it. That, in brief, represents the two different approaches to external storage. The two approaches are called *direct access* and *sequential access.*

Disks provide fast, direct access. Tapes provide sequential access. With tape, information is stored in sequence, such as alphabetically. You may have to search a tape past all the information from *A* to *P,* say, before you get to *Q.*

FIGURE 6-16
Magnetic tape

This may involve searching several inches or feet, which takes time. (See Figure 6-16.)

Although tape may be slow to access specific information, it is an effective way of making a *backup,* or duplicate, copy of your programs and data. Today, magnetic tape is used almost exclusively for that purpose.

There are two forms of tape storage. These are *magnetic tape streamers,* for use with microcomputers, and *magnetic tape reels,* for use with minicomputers and mainframes.

Magnetic Tape Streamers

Many microcomputer users with hard disks use a device called a **magnetic tape streamer** or a **backup tape cartridge unit.** (See Figure 6-17.) This enables you to duplicate or make a backup of the data on your hard disk onto a tape cartridge. Typical capacities of such tape cartridges are 10 to 20 gigabytes. Advanced forms of backup technology known as **digital audiotape (DAT) drives,** which use 2-inch by 3-inch cassettes, store 4 gigabytes or more. If your internal hard disk fails, you can have it repaired (or get another hard disk). You can restore all your lost data and programs in a matter of minutes from the backup tapes.

Magnetic Tape Reels

The cassette tapes you get for an audiotape recorder are only about 200 feet long. They record 200 characters to the inch. A reel of magnetic tape used with minicomputer and mainframe systems, by contrast, is ½-inch wide and

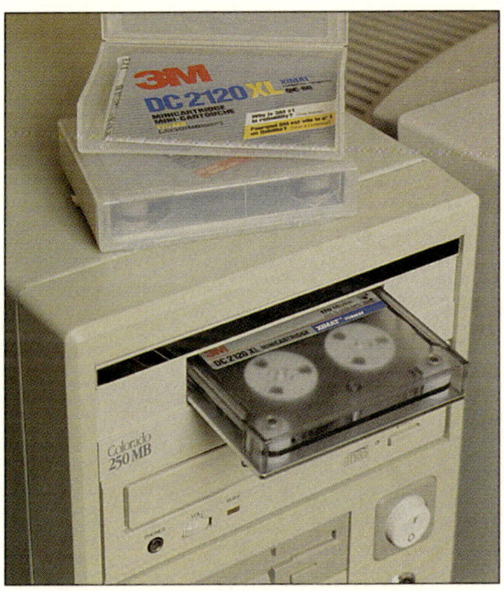

FIGURE 6-17
Magnetic tape streamer

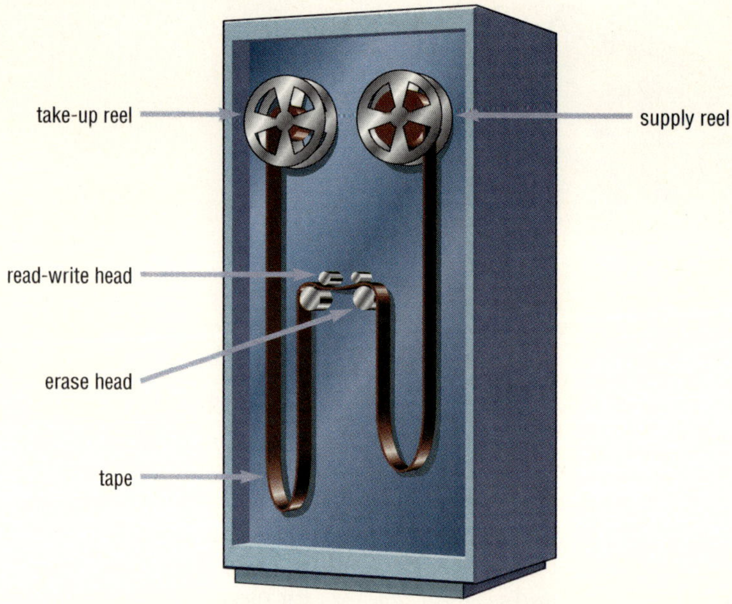

FIGURE 6-18
Tape reels for recording data on magnetic tape

½-mile long. It stores 1,600 to 6,400 characters to the inch. Such tapes are run on **magnetic tape drives** or **magnetic tape units.** (See Figure 6-18.) You may never actually see these devices yourself. However, as a microcomputer user sharing storage devices with others, you may have access to them through a minicomputer or mainframe.

For the typical microcomputer user, the four storage options—floppy disk, hard disk, optical disk, and magnetic tape—are complementary, not competing. Almost all microcomputers today have at least one floppy-disk drive and one hard-disk drive. For those users who need access to vast amounts of data, an optical drive is added. Those who need to back up lots of data and programs may add magnetic tape drives.

A LOOK TO THE FUTURE

Near-field recording devices use lasers and solid immersion lens. Holographic storage systems use three-dimensional holograms.

Have you ever wondered why we need such large-capacity secondary storage devices? As we mentioned earlier, DVD-RWs with a 17-gigabyte capacity are expected. When will this trend of increasing capacity end? Probably not in the near future.

As we use more graphical interfaces like Windows 2000, store images from the Web, and work with more advanced applications like multimedia and virtual reality, the demand for larger and faster secondary storage devices will continue to grow. Fortunately, several new technologies promise to meet this demand.

One is called near-field recording. These devices use a revolutionary new drive head that utilizes lasers and a special focusing lens called a solid immersion lens. This lens precisely directs the laser's path, thereby allowing more information to be stored on a disk. Near-field recording devices are expected to cost the same as today's hard disk systems yet provide ten times more storage capacity.

A bit further on the horizon is holographic storage. Holograms, as you may know, are those shimmering, three-dimensional images often seen on credit cards. Holographic systems can store data equivalent to thousands of books inside a container the size of a sugar cube.

When will we be able to purchase systems using these new technologies? Prototypes have been created and we can expect to see near-field recording devices and holographic systems in the next few years.

VISUAL SUMMARY Secondary Storage

FLOPPY DISKS

Floppy disks are also known as **diskettes** or simply as **disks.** They are inexpensive, removable storage media. Floppy disks are primarily used to save and transport documents.

Today's Standard

Today's standard floppy disk is the **1.44 MB 3½-inch disk,** or **2HD.** It is by far the most widely used floppy disk today. Due to its relatively low storage capacity, however, it is expected to be replaced by higher capacity floppy disks.

Tomorrow's Standard

Three types of **floppy-disk cartridges** are competing to become the next standard:

- **Zip disks**—considered by many to be the leading contender to replace today's standard; storage capacity 100 MB and 250 MB.
- **SuperDisks**—120 MB capacity; SuperDisk drives are able to read today's standard disks.
- **HiFD**—200 MB capacity; like SuperDisk drives, HiFD drives are able to read today's standard disks.

Parts of a Floppy Disk

Data is recorded in rings called **tracks.** Each track is divided into wedge-shaped sections known as **sectors.** The process of preparing a disk with tracks and sectors is called **formatting** or **initializing.**

HARD DISKS

Compared to floppy disks, **hard disks** are much faster and provide much greater storage. They are used to store programs and large amounts of data. Three types are *internal, hard disk cartridge,* and *hard-disk pack.*

Internal Hard Disk

An **internal hard disk** or **fixed disk** is located inside the system unit.

Hard-Disk Cartridge

Unlike internal hard disks, **hard-disk cartridges** are removable and only the number of cartridges limits the amount of storage capacity.

Hard-Disk Pack

Hard-disk packs consist of several platters and have a capacity that greatly exceeds both internal and hard-disk cartridges. Hard-disk packs are used primarily by minicomputer and mainframe computer systems.

Performance Enhancements

Three ways to improve hard disk performance are:

- **Disk caching**—reduces time to access data by anticipating data needs.
- **RAIDs**—expand storage capacity by grouping inexpensive hard disk drives.
- **File compression and decompression**—increases storage capacity by reducing the space required to store data and programs.

To be a competent end user you need to be aware of the different types of secondary storage. You need to know their capabilities, limitations, and uses. There are four basic types: floppy disk, hard disk, optical disk, and magnetic tape.

OPTICAL DISKS

While floppy and hard disks use magnetic charges to represent data and programs, optical storage uses reflected light. Two types are **compact discs** and **digital versatile discs.**

Compact Disc

Compact discs or **CDs** are the most widely used optical disks today. With a typical capacity of 650 MB, there are three basic types:

- **CD-ROM**—used to distribute large databases, references, and application packages.
- **CD-R**—also known as **WORM,** used to archive data.
- **CD-RW**—reusable; used to create and edit large multimedia presentations.

Digital Versatile Disc

Digital versatile discs or digital video discs or **DVDs** are similar to CDs with far greater capacity. Three basic types are:

- **DVD-ROM**—used to distribute full length feature films with theater-quality video and sound.
- **DVD-R**—expected to replace CD-R as prices decline.
- **DVD-RAM** and **DVD-RW**—two recently introduced standards for reusable DVDs; used to develop very large scale multimedia projects.

MAGNETIC TAPE

Magnetic tape is a sequential-access storage medium. It is used primarily to back up or duplicate data and programs. Two types are *tape streamers* and *tape reels.*

Magnetic Tape Streamers

Magnetic tape streamers are also known as **backup tape cartridge units.** Used almost exclusively with microcomputers, these units use tape cartridges to back up hard disks. **Digital audiotape (DAT)** is a high capacity, advanced technology for magnetic tape.

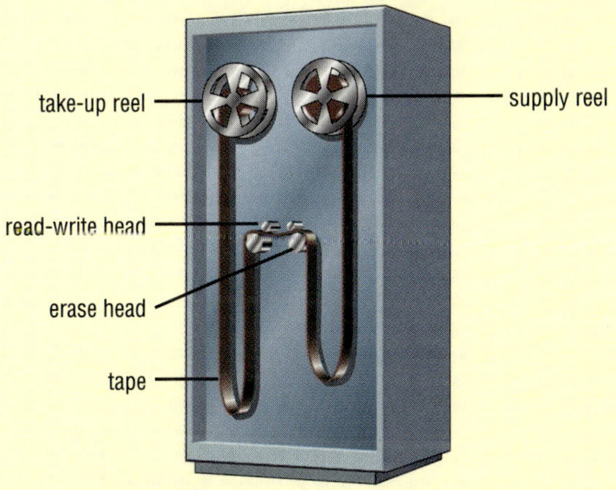

Magnetic Tape Reels

Magnetic tape reels are used to back up minicomputer and mainframe storage devices. The tape is run on **magnetic drives** or **magnetic tape units.**

Key Terms

access time (126)
backup tape cartridge unit (133)
CD (compact disc) (128)
CD-R (129)
CD-ROM (129)
CD-RW (129)
digital audiotape (DAT) drive (133)
disk (122)
disk caching (127)
diskette (122)
DVD (digital versatile, or video, disc) (130)
DVD-R (DVD-recordable) (132)
DVD-RAM (DVD–random-access memory) (132)
DVD-ROM (digital versatile disc–read only memory) (131)
DVD-RW (DVD-rewritable) (132)
erasable optical disk (129)
file compression (127)
file decompression (127)
fixed disk (124)
flexible disk (122)
floppies (122)
floppy disk (122)
floppy-disk cartridge (122)
hard disk (124)
hard-disk cartridge (125)
hard-disk pack (125)
head crash (124)
HiFD disk (122)
internal hard disk (124)
lands (128)
magnetic tape drive (134)
magnetic tape streamer (133)
magnetic tape unit (134)
nonvolatile storage (121)
1.44 MB 3½-inch disk (122)
pits (128)
redundant arrays of inexpensive disks (RAIDs) (127)
sector (123)
SuperDisk (122)
track (123)
2HD (122)
volatile storage (121)
WORM (129)
write-protect notch (122)
Zip disk (122)

Chapter Review

LEVEL 1

Reviewing Facts and Terms

Matching

Match each numbered item with the most closely related lettered item. Write your answers in the spaces provided.

1. Write once, read many. ____
2. Optical disk that can store up to 4.7 gigabytes per side. ____
3. Time between the computer's request for data from secondary storage and the completion of the data transfer. ____
4. Helps increase storage capacity by reducing the amount of space required to store data and programs. ____
5. Erasable optical disks. ____
6. Happens when the surface of the read-write head or particles on its surface contact the magnetic disk surface. ____
7. Invisible wedge-shaped sections on a floppy disk. ____
8. Also known as diskettes, or simply as disks. ____
9. Bumpy areas on the surface of an optical disk that represent portions of data. ____
10. A device that allows you to duplicate or make a backup of the data on your hard disk on a tape cartridge.
11. Magnetic tape drives that use 2-inch by 3-inch cassettes capable of storing 4 gigabytes or more. ____
12. Improves hard-disk performance by anticipating data needs. ____
13. Recordable DVDs. ____
14. Data is recorded on a disk in rings. ____

a. Access time
b. CD
c. CD-RW
d. DAT drive
e. Disk caching
f. DVD
g. DVD-R
h. File compression
i. Floppy disk
j. Hard disk
k. Head crash
l. Magnetic tape streamer
m. Pits
n. Sector
o. Track
p. WORM
r. Zip disk

15. Ridged metallic platter used to store and retrieve information. ____

16. Floppy-disk cartridge that typically stores either 100 MB or 250 MB. ____

17. Optical disk that can store up to 650 megabytes per side. ____

True/False

In the spaces provided, write T or F to indicate whether the statement is true or false.

1. Secondary storage holds information within the CPU. ____
2. Floppy disks are also known as flexible disks and as floppies. ____
3. Sectors are wedge-shaped sections on a disk. ____
4. CD-Rs can be erased and used over and over again. ____
5. Laser beams are used to record data on optical disks. ____
6. An internal hard disk consists of one or more metallic platters sealed inside a container. ____

Multiple Choice

Circle the letter of the correct answer.

1. Which of the following is exclusively a sequential-access storage media?
   a. floppy disk
   b. hard disk
   c. magnetic tape
   d. CD-ROM
   e. WORM
2. Data is stored on concentric circles called:
   a. platters
   b. tracks
   c. ovals
   d. wedges
   e. sectors
3. The disk with the greatest capacity is:
   a. Zip
   b. 3½-inch two-sided, double-density
   c. SuperDisk
   d. CD-ROM
   e. DVD-ROM
4. The hard-disk type that has several platters aligned one above the other is the:
   a. Zip disk
   b. hard-disk pack
   c. floppy-disk array
   d. hard-disk cartridge
   e. disk cache
5. The method of improving hard-disk performance by anticipating data needs is:
   a. disk compression
   b. disk caching
   c. disk decompression
   d. RAIDs
   e. virtual processing

Completion

Complete each statement in the spaces provided.

1. A __________ disk is read by a laser projecting a beam of light.
2. Data is recorded on a disk in rings called __________.
3. Internal hard disks have two advantages over floppy disks: __________ and speed.
4. __________ __________ are removable storage devices with massive capacity.
5. The two forms of tape storage are magnetic tape streamers and magnetic tape __________.

6. Hard disks are typically used to store __________ and __________.
7. The process of preparing a disk with tracks and sectors is called __________.

Reviewing Concepts

LEVEL 2

Open-Ended

On a separate sheet of paper, respond to each question and statement.

1. Explain the difference between direct-access storage and sequential-access storage. Which is more apt to be identified with magnetic disk and which with magnetic tape?
2. What are three contenders to become the next floppy-disk standard? Define their storage capacities.
3. What are the three types of hard disks? What are their relative advantages and disadvantages?
4. What is so disastrous about a head crash?
5. What are the two types of optical disks? Discuss their differences and similarities.
6. Describe one important function that magnetic tape storage can provide.

Concept Mapping

On a separate sheet of paper, draw a concept map or a flowchart showing how the following terms are related. Show all relationships. Include any additional terms you can think of.

access time	DVD-R	head crash
backup tape cartridge unit	DVD-RAM	internal hard disk
CD	DVD-ROM	magnetic tape drive
CD-R	DVD-RW	pits
CD-ROM	file compression	RAIDs
CD-RW	file decompression	sector
DAT drive	floppy disk	track
disk	floppy disk cartridge	volatile storage
disk caching	hard disk	WORM
diskette	hard disk cartridge	write-protect notch
DVD	hard-disk pack	Zip disk

Critical Thinking Questions and Projects

LEVEL 3

Read each exercise and answer the related questions on a separate sheet of paper.

1. *Obtaining a DVD-ROM drive:* Suppose you have a microcomputer system that does not have a DVD-ROM drive, and you would like to have one. You have three options: (1) purchase an external DVD-ROM drive that connects to one of the ports in the back of your system unit; (2) purchase and install an internal DVD-ROM directly into your system unit; or (3) purchase a new microcomputer system that has a DVD-ROM drive.

   Research each of the three options and prepare a set of written guidelines that could be used to make the best choice.
2. *Privacy:* By the end of the year 2000, sales for DVD-ROM drives are expected to be well over four times those for CD-ROM drives. Some experts believe the shift to DVD technology will have a dramatic and rapid impact. They point out that individuals will be able to own and access the contents of an entire library from a single disk. Of course, other types of information will be available as well.

Do you foresee any new businesses developing? What about the collection and distribution of information? Do you foresee any personal privacy concerns?

3. *Ethics and security:* The software industry has long faced the problem of software piracy, which is the illegal copying and distribution of programs. Some individuals purchase one copy of a program such as Excel and use special software to illegally make and sell copies. Now with current full-length motion pictures being sold on DVDs, the motion picture industry is facing a similar problem. Some individuals purchase one copy and use special software and computers equipped with DVD-ROM and/or DVD-RW drives to make additional copies for resale.
   - **a.** Do you think illegal copying of motion pictures from DVDs is currently a serious problem for the motion picture industry? Why or why not?
   - **b.** Do you think the problem will become more serious in the future? Why or why not?
   - **c.** Do you think this illegal copying and distribution of motion pictures can be controlled? Why or why not?

On the Web Exercises

1. DVD Entertainment Systems

The DVD home entertainment system is more than just a new entertainment standard. It is also a new standard for DVD-ROMs. To learn more about DVD home entertainment systems, visit our Web site at http://www.mhhe.com/cit/concepts/oleary2000-2001/webex6.html to link to a site that specializes in DVD. Once at the site, explore and learn more about DVD. Be sure to check out the Frequently Asked Questions (FAQ) page. Print out the Web page that you find most informative. Write a paragraph addressing the following questions: What is DVD? How do DVDs compare to compact discs (CDs)?

2. JAZ Drives

The ever-increasing demands on hard-disk space has led to Iomega's innovations in high-capacity removable disk drives. For example, the Jaz drive can store 1 gigabyte on a single disk. To learn more about these drives, visit our Web site at http://www.mhhe.com/cit/concepts/oleary2000-2001/webex6.html to link to Iomega's Web site. Once connected to that site, check out the available drives. Choose a drive that would be helpful to you in your career and print out its specifications. Write a paragraph discussing how this drive would help you and how it is superior to the other drives available.

3. Advances in Storage Technology

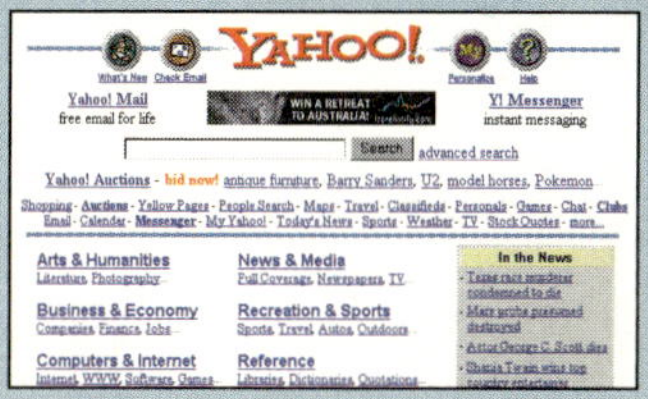

Secondary storage technology is changing fast. One way to keep informed on the latest innovations is to search the many magazines that publish articles on the Web. Visit the Yahoo site at http://www.yahoo.com and look under the subcategory of "Computers and Internet: Magazines: Personal Computers: PC Compatibles." Find an article of interest, print it out, and write a brief paragraph summarizing the article.

4. Buying a Car?

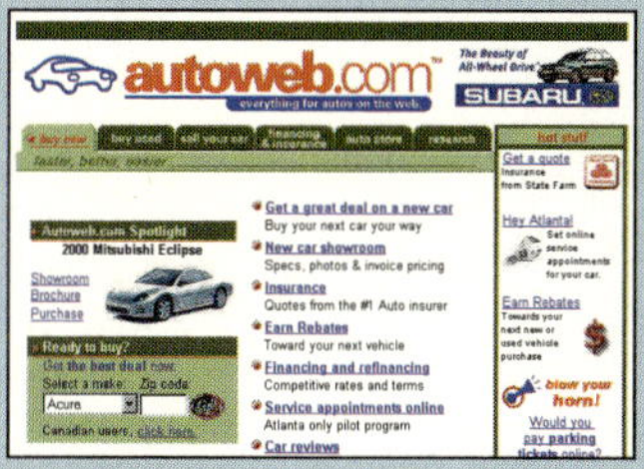

Looking for a new or used car? Interested in the Kelly blue book trade-in price on your current car? Visit our Web site at http://www.mhhe.com/cit/concepts/oleary2000-2001/webex6.html to link to a site that will answer many of your car-buying questions. Once at the site, find the best deal possible on a new or used car of your choice. Print out the information and write a brief paragraph on how you found it.

CHAPTER 7

Communications and Connectivity

COMPETENCIES

After you have read this chapter, you should be able to:

1. **Describe connectivity options: fax machines, e-mail, voice-messaging systems, videoconferencing systems, shared resources, and online services.**
2. **Describe conventional modems, T1, ISDN, DSL, cable modem, and satellite connections.**
3. **Describe the cable and air communications channels—telephone, coaxial, fiber-optic, microwave, and satellite.**
4. **Discuss bandwidth, serial versus parallel transmission, direction and modes of data transmission, and protocols.**
5. **Explain network architecture—configurations and strategies.**
6. **Describe local area, metropolitan area, and wide area networks.**

A familiar instrument—the telephone—has extended our uses for the microcomputer enormously. With the telephone or other kinds of communications equipment, you can connect your microcomputer to the microcomputers of other people, to the Internet, and to other, larger computers located throughout the world. As we've mentioned earlier, this *connectivity* puts incredible power on your desk. The result is increased productivity—for you as an individual and for the groups and organizations of which you are a member. Connectivity has become

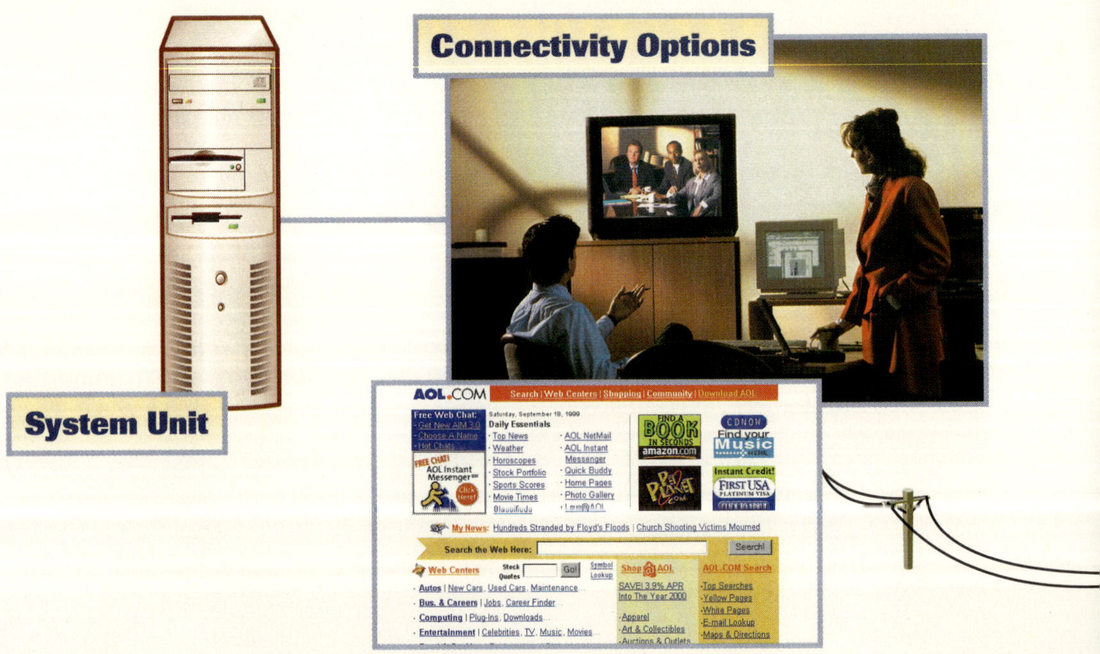

particularly important in business, where individuals now find themselves connected in networks to other individuals and departments.

Data communications systems are the electronic systems that transmit data over communications lines from one location to another. You might use data communications through your microcomputer to send information to a friend using another computer. You might work for an organization whose computer system is spread throughout a building, or even throughout the country or world. That is, all the parts—input and output units, processor, and storage devices—are in different places and linked together. Or you might use *telecommunications* lines—telephone lines—to tap into information located in an outside data bank. You could then transmit it to your microcomputer for your own reworking and analysis.

Competent end users need to understand the concept of connectivity and the various connectivity options. Additionally, they need to know the essential parts of communications technology, including connections, channels, transmission, network architectures, and network types.

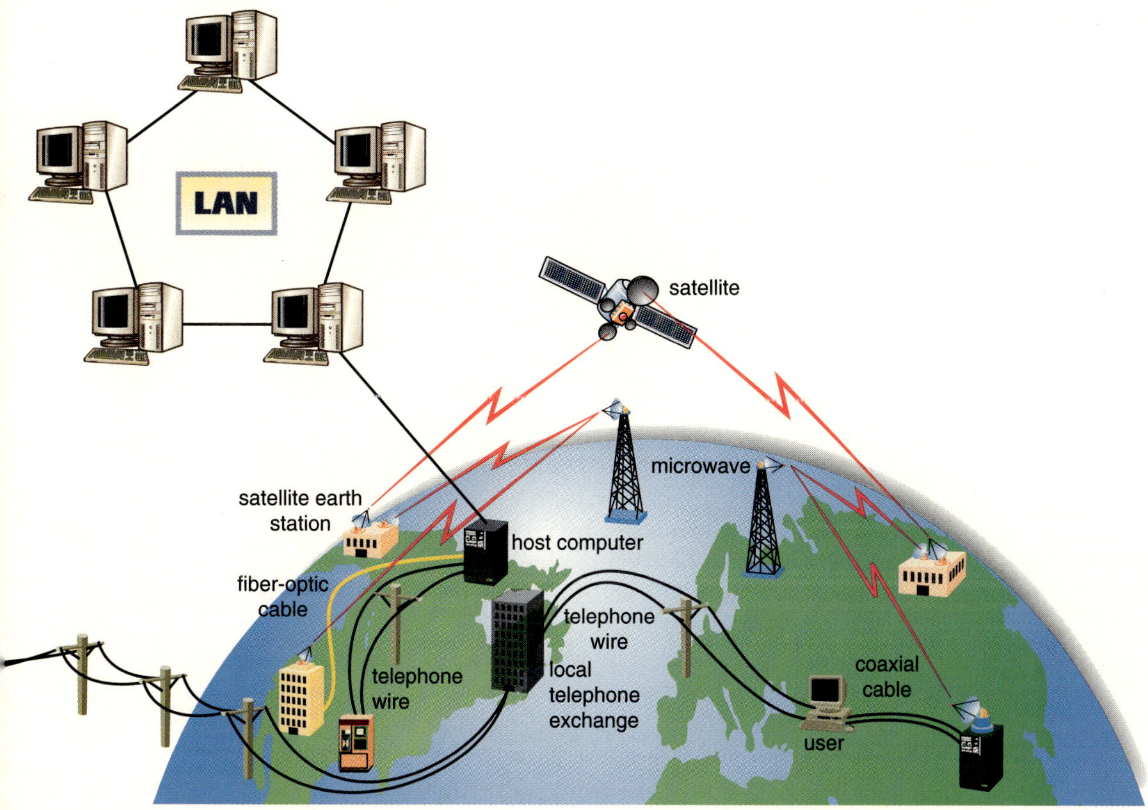

Communications and Connectivity

With communications capability, microcomputer users can transmit and receive data and gain access to electronic information resources.

You may have a desktop microcomputer next to a telephone. You may (or may someday) have a portable computer and a cellular phone in your car. Or you may have a microcomputer that is directly connected to other computers without telephone lines at all. (See Figure 7-1.) Whatever the case, communications systems present many opportunities for transmitting and receiving information, giving you access to many resources. This brings up the important revolution discussed in this chapter, that of connectivity.

FIGURE 7-1
Communications

Connectivity means you can connect your microcomputer by telephone or other telecommunications links to other computers and information sources almost anywhere. (See Figure 7-2.) With this connection, you are linked to the world of larger computers. This includes minicomputers and mainframes and their large storage devices, such as disk packs, and their enormous volumes of information. Thus, computer competence becomes a matter of knowing not only about microcomputers but also about larger computer systems and their information resources.

Let us consider the options that connectivity makes available to you. These include *fax machines, e-mail, voice-messaging systems, videoconferencing systems, shared resources,* and *online services.*

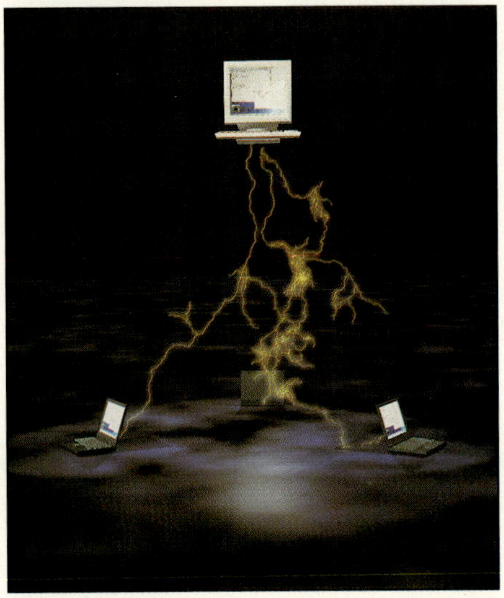

FIGURE 7-2
Connectivity: electricity between computers

Fax Machines

Fax machines—facsimile transmission machines—have become essential machines in almost all offices. (See Figure 7-3.) As we mentioned in Chapter 6, these devices scan the image of a document. They convert the image to signals that can be sent over a telephone line to a receiving machine. This machine prints the image out on paper. Microcomputers, using fax/modem circuit boards, can be used to send and receive fax messages.

If you are in the business of meeting deadlines—as most people are—a fax machine is invaluable. Construction engineers can get cost estimates to major contractors. Advertising people can get prospective ad layouts to their clients. Just as important, because people often respond better to pictures than to text, fax can get a picture to them quickly. Rather than giving a friend detailed directions to your house, you could simply fax a map.

FIGURE 7-3
A fax machine

E-Mail

E-mail, also known as **electronic mail,** is a way of sending an electronic letter or message between individuals or computers. It is like an answering machine in that you can receive messages even when you are not home. Unlike an answering machine, e-mail can contain text, graphics, and images as well as sound. E-mail can also be used to communicate with more than one person at a time, to conveniently schedule meetings, to keep current on important events, and much more.

At one time, e-mail was used only by large organizations. Now, it is widely used by just about everyone. Students use it to communicate with their instructors and fellow students. (See Figure 7-4.) Parents use it to contact their children's teachers, and grandparents use e-mail to communicate with their grandchildren. Procedures for sending and receiving e-mail will be discussed in detail in Chapter 8.

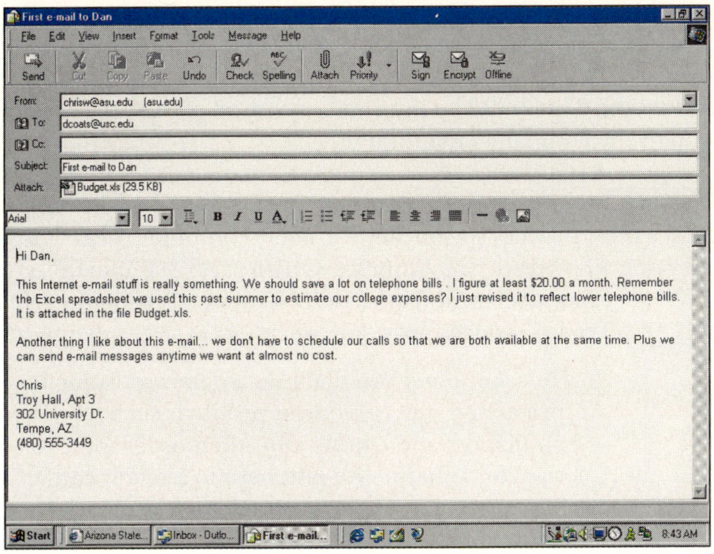

FIGURE 7-4
E-mail

Voice-Messaging Systems

Voice-messaging systems are computer systems linked to telephones that convert the human voice into digital bits. They resemble conventional answering machines and electronic-mail systems. However, they can receive large numbers of incoming calls and route them to the appropriate "voice mailboxes." They can deliver the same message to many people. These systems allow callers to leave "voice mail"—recorded voice messages. They can forward calls to your home or hotel, if you wish. When you check for your messages, you can speed through them or slow them down. You can dictate replies into the phone, and the system will send them out.

Videoconferencing Systems

Videoconferencing systems are computer systems that allow people located at various geographic locations to have in-person meetings. Many corporations have long used specially equipped videoconferencing rooms to hold large group meetings. Top-level executives scattered across the country and the world can meet periodically. Moreover, they can meet at a moment's notice to address emergency situations. Although very expensive, videoconferencing saves considerable travel time and costs.

Today, inexpensive desktop videoconferencing systems are widely used. These systems use microcomputers equipped with inexpensive video cameras and microphones that sit atop the computer monitor. Now, two or more people located in different cities or countries can conveniently and inexpensively meet face-to-face. (See Figure 7-5.)

FIGURE 7-5
Videoconferencing

Shared Resources

An important aspect of connectivity is that it lets microcomputer users share expensive hardware. We have mentioned many of these: laser printers, chain printers, disk packs, and magnetic tape storage. Only in rare instances would a single microcomputer user need the use of, say, a disk pack. However, several microcomputers linked in a network make this option not only feasible but in many cases even essential.

Another important aspect of connectivity is the ability to share data. You may have a personal database that only you use. However, it may also be data you share with others. The data might be stored on your microcomputer's hard disk. Or it might be located somewhere else. That is, you might use a shared database, like one a company might provide its employees so they can share information. This could be information stored on disk packs and accessible through the company's mainframe.

Online Services

Several businesses offer services specifically for microcomputer users. Four well-known service providers are America Online, AT&T WorldNet, CompuServe, and Microsoft Network. (See Figure 7-6.) Typical services provided are:

FIGURE 7-6
America Online

- **Teleshopping:** You dial into a database listing prices and descriptions of products such as appliances and clothes. You then order what you want and charge the purchase to a credit card. The merchandise is delivered later by a package delivery service.
- **Home banking:** If you arrange it with your bank, you may be able to use your microcomputer to pay some bills. Such bills include those owed to big department stores and utility companies. You can also make loan payments and transfer money between accounts.
- **Investing:** You can get access to current prices of stocks and bonds and enter buy and sell orders.
- **Travel reservations:** Just like a travel agent, you can get information on airline schedules and fares. You can also order tickets, charging the purchase to your credit card. (See Figure 7-7.)
- **Internet access:** The most-used service from any of the providers is access to the Internet. Chapter 8 is dedicated to the Internet and the Web.

See Figure 7-8 for a summary of the many connectivity options.

ON THE WEB EXPLORATIONS

America Online is one of the leading national online service providers. To learn more about the company, visit its Web site at

http://www.aol.com

CONCEPT CHECK

✔ What are some ways that people can be "connected"?

FIGURE 7-7
Travel-reservation Web site

Option	Function
Fax machines	Convert images to signals and send them over telephone lines to receiving fax machines
E-mail	Electronic letter or message sent between individuals or computers
Voice-mail messaging	Convert a voice message to digital bits and distribute to many locations over telephone lines
Videoconferencing systems	Systems allowing in-person electronic meeting between individuals or groups located in different places
Shared resources	Microcomputer users may share expensive hardware, data, and information
Online services	Provide wide range of activities including teleshopping, banking, investments, and travel reservations services

FIGURE 7-8
Summary of connectivity options

User Connection

Conventional modems convert analog and digital signals. Other user connections are T1, ISDN, DSL, and cable modems.

A great deal of computer communications takes place over telephone lines. However, because the telephone was originally designed for voice transmission, telephones typically send and receive **analog signals.** (See Figure 7-9.) Computers, in contrast, send and receive **digital signals.** These represent the presence or absence of an electronic pulse—the on/off binary signals we mentioned in Chapter 4. To convert the digital signals of your microcomputer to analog and vice versa, you need a modem.

Modems

The word *modem* is short for "*mo*dulator-*dem*odulator." **Modulation** is the name of the process of converting from digital to analog. **Demodulation** is the process of converting from analog to digital. The modem enables digital microcomputers to communicate across analog telephone lines. Both voice communications and data communications can be carried over the same telephone line.

The speed with which modems transmit data varies. Communications speed is typically measured in *bits per second (bps).* (See Figure 7-10.) The higher the speed, the faster you can send and receive information. For example, transferring an image like Figure 7-9, might take 75 seconds with a 33.6 kbps modem and only 45 seconds with a 56 kbps modem.

FIGURE 7-9
Analog versus digital signals

Unit	Speed
bps	bit per second
kbps	thousand bits per second
mbps	million bits per second
gbps	billion bits per second

FIGURE 7-10
Communication speeds

FIGURE 7-11
Internal modem

Types of Modems

There are three types of conventional modems: external, internal, and wireless.

- The **external modem** stands apart from the computer and is connected by a cable to the computer's serial port. Another cable connects the modem to the telephone wall jack.
- The **internal modem** consists of a plug-in circuit board inside the system unit. A telephone cable connects the modem to the telephone wall jack. (See Figure 7-11.)
- The **wireless modem** is very similar to the external modem. It connects to the computer's serial port. Unlike an external modem, it does not connect to telephone lines. Rather, wireless modems receive through the air. This is a new type of modem using new technology.

Types of Connections

Standard telephone lines and conventional modems provide what is called a **dial-up service.** Although still the most popular type of connection service, dial-up service is quite slow, and many users find it inadequate to meet their communication needs.

For years, large corporations have been leasing special high-speed lines from telephone companies. These lines—known as **T1, T2, T3,** and **T4 lines**—support all digital communications, do not require conventional modems, and provide very high capacity. Unfortunately, this type of connection is very expensive. For example, T1 lines provide a speed of 1.5 mbps (over 26 times as fast as a conventional modem) and cost several thousands of dollars. Some promising newer technologies include ISDN, DSL, cable modems, and satellite/air connection.

ON THE WEB EXPLORATIONS

@Home is a leading cable modem service provider. To learn more about the company, visit its Web site at **http://www.athome.net**

- **Integrated services digital network (ISDN)** is a service provided by many local telephone companies using special high-speed telephone lines. It has been available in most urban and suburban areas for the past several years. Primarily smaller organizations and individuals use ISDN. It provides data transfer rates that are more than twice as fast as conventional modems at a cost much less than that of T1 lines.
- **Digital subscriber line (DSL)** uses existing telephone lines to provide high-speed connections as fast as a T1 connection at less cost. This is a very new and rapidly evolving technology. Although presently limited to a few large cities, DSL is expected to become widely available in the next few years.

- **Cable modems** use existing television cables to provide high-speed connections as fast as a T1 or DSL connection, at a lower cost. Although cable connections reach 90 percent of the homes in America, all cable companies do not support cable modems. Industry observers, however, predict 100 percent availability within the next few years.
- **Satellite/air connection services** use satellites and the air to download or send data to users at a rate seven times faster than dial-up connections. Unfortunately, users cannot upload or send data to satellites and must rely on a dial-up connection. While slower than DSL and cable modems, satellite/air connections are available almost anywhere that a satellite-receiving disk can be aimed at the southern skies.

Type	Cost/Year	Speed	Seconds to Receive Image
Dial-up	250	56 kbps	45.0 seconds
T1	17,150	1.5 mbps	1.7 seconds
ISDN	750	128 kbps	19.9 seconds
DSL	4,150	1.5 mbps	1.7 seconds
Cable modem	650	1.5 mbps	1.7 seconds
Satellite/air	1,050	400 kbps	6.3 seconds

FIGURE 7-12
Typical user connection costs and speeds
(Cost/Year includes equipment and connection charges. Image based on Figure 7-9.)

For a comparison of typical user connection costs and speeds, see Figure 7-12.

CONCEPT CHECK

✔ Telephones typically send/receive ________ signals; computers send/receive ________ signals.

✔ What do modems do?

✔ Communications speed is typically measured in ________ ____ ________.

✔ Name four newer connection technologies.

Communications Channels

Data may flow through five kinds of communications channels: telephone lines, coaxial cable, fiber-optic cable, microwave, and satellite.

The two ways of connecting microcomputers with each other and with other equipment are through a cable and through the air. Specifically, five kinds of technology are used to transmit data. These are telephone lines (twisted pair), coaxial cable, fiber-optic cable, microwave, and satellite.

Telephone Lines

Most telephone lines you see strung on poles consist of **twisted pair** cable, which is made up of hundreds of copper wires. A single twisted pair culminates in a wall jack into which you can plug your phone. (See Figure 7-13.) Telephone lines have been the standard transmission medium for years for both voice and data. However, they are now being phased out by more technically advanced and reliable media.

FIGURE 7-13
Twisted pair cable

FIGURE 7-14
Coaxial cable

Coaxial Cable

Coaxial cable, a high-frequency transmission cable, replaces the multiple wires of telephone lines with a single solid-copper core. (See Figure 7-14.) In terms of number of telephone connections, a coaxial cable has over 80 times the transmission capacity of twisted pair. Coaxial cable is often used to link parts of a computer system in one building.

Fiber-Optic Cable

In **fiber-optic cable,** data is transmitted as pulses of light through tubes of glass. (See Figure 7-15.) In terms of number of telephone connections, fiber-optic cable has over 26,000 times the transmission capacity of twisted pair. However, it is significantly smaller. Indeed, a fiber-optic tube can be half the diameter of a human hair. Although limited in the distance they can carry information, fiber-optic cables have several advantages. Such cables are immune to electronic interference, which makes them more secure. They are also lighter and less expensive than coaxial cable and are more reliable at transmitting data. They transmit information using beams of light at light speeds instead of pulses of electricity, making them far faster than copper cable. Fiber-optic cable is rapidly replacing twisted pair telephone lines.

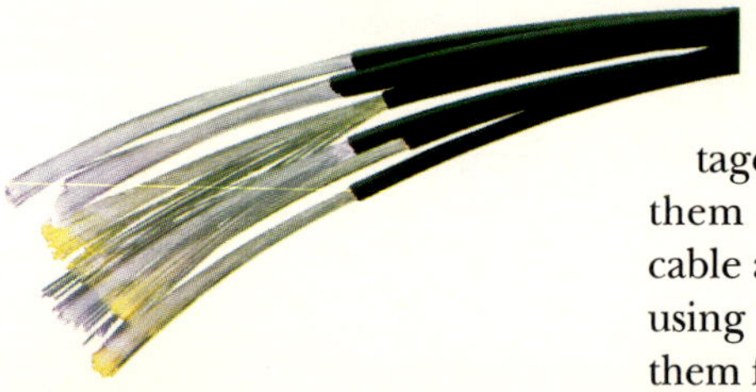

FIGURE 7-15
Fiber-optic cable

Microwave

In the case of the microwave communications channel, the medium is not a solid substance but rather the air itself. **Microwave communication** uses high-frequency radio waves that travel in straight lines through the air. Because the waves cannot bend with the curvature of the earth, they can be transmitted only over short distances. Thus, microwave is a good medium for sending data between buildings in a city or on a large college campus. For longer distances, the waves must be relayed by means of "dishes," or antennas. These can be installed on towers, high buildings, and mountaintops, for example. (See Figure 7-16.)

FIGURE 7-16
Microwave dish

Satellite

Satellite communication uses satellites orbiting about 22,000 miles above the earth as microwave relay stations. (See Figure 7-17.) Many of these are offered by Intelsat, the *In*ternational *Tel*ecommunications *Sat*ellite Consortium, which is owned by 114 governments and forms a worldwide

FIGURE 7-17
Satellite

Channel	Description
Twisted pair	Copper wire, standard voice telephone line
Coaxial cable	Solid copper core, more than 80 times capacity of twisted pair
Fiber-optic	Light carries data, more than 26,000 times capacity of twisted pair
Microwave	High-frequency radio waves carry data, travels in straight line through the air
Satellite	Microwave relay station in the sky, rotates at fixed point above the earth

FIGURE 7-18
Types of communications channels

communications system. Satellites rotate at a precise point and speed above the earth. This makes them appear stationary, so they can amplify and relay microwave signals from one transmitter on the ground to another. Thus, satellites can be used to send large volumes of data. Their major drawback is that bad weather can sometimes interrupt the flow of data.

For a summary of the five kinds of communication channels, see Figure 7-18.

CONCEPT CHECK

- ✔ List five kinds of communications channels.
- ✔ Which is the fastest form of cable communications channels?
- ✔ What is one limitation of microwave communications?

Data Transmission

Several technical matters affect data communications. They are bandwidth, serial versus parallel transmission, direction of flow, modes of transmission, and protocols.

Several factors affect how data is transmitted. They include bandwidth, serial or parallel transmission, direction of data flow, modes of transmitting data, and protocols.

Bandwidth

The different communications channels have different data transmission speeds. This bits-per-second transmission capability of a channel is called its **bandwidth.**

Bandwidth may be of three types:

- **Voiceband: Voiceband** is the bandwidth of a standard telephone line and used often for microcomputer transmission; typical speeds are 9,600 to 56 kbps, although with special equipment much higher speeds are possible.

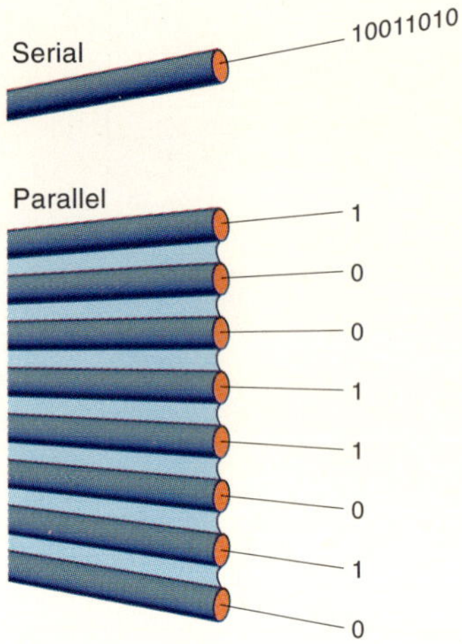

FIGURE 7-19
Serial versus parallel transmission

- **Medium band:** The **medium band** is the bandwidth of special leased lines used mainly with minicomputers and mainframe computers; the speed is 56 kbps to 264 mbps.
- **Broadband:** The **broadband** is the bandwidth that includes microwave, satellite, coaxial cable, and fiber-optic channels. It is used for very high speed computers whose processors communicate directly with each other. It is in the range of 264 mbps to 30 gbps.

Serial and Parallel Transmission

Data travels in two ways: serially and in parallel. (See Figure 7-19.)

- In **serial data transmission,** bits flow in a series or continuous stream, like cars crossing a one-lane bridge. Serial transmission is the way most data is sent over telephone lines. For this reason, external modems typically connect to a microcomputer through a serial port. More technical names for the serial port are **RS-232C connector** and **asynchronous communications port.**
- With **parallel data transmission,** bits flow through separate lines simultaneously. In other words, they resemble cars moving together at the same speed on a multilane freeway. Parallel transmission is typically limited to communications over short distances and typically is not used over telephone lines. It is, however, a standard method of sending data from a computer's CPU to a printer.

Direction of Data Transmission

There are three directions or modes of data flow in a data communications system. (See Figure 7-20.)

FIGURE 7-20
Simplex, half-duplex, and full-duplex communication

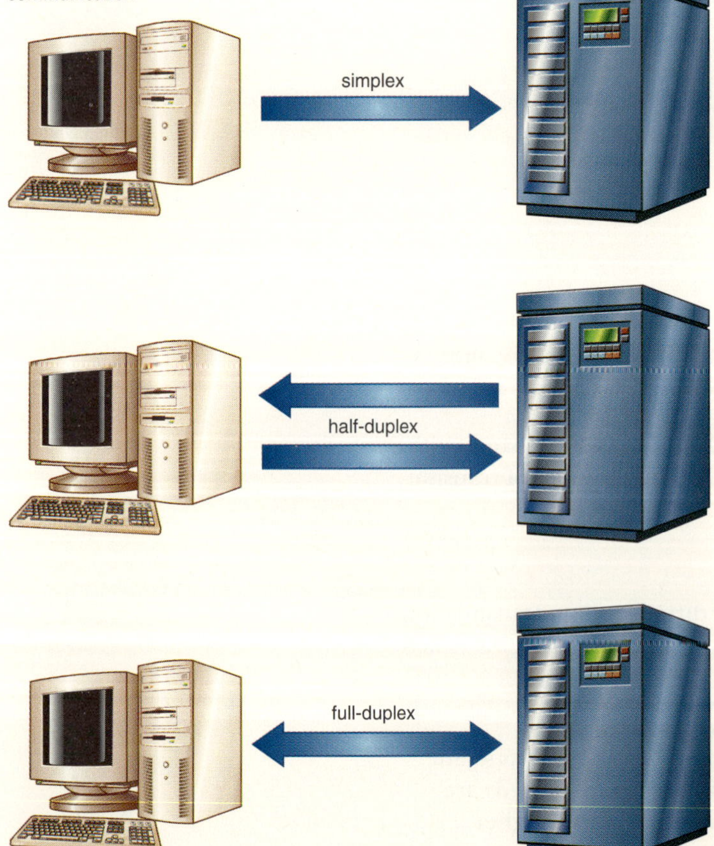

- **Simplex communication** resembles the movement of cars on a one-way street. Data travels in one direction only. The simplex mode is not frequently used in data communications systems today. One instance in which it is used may be in point-of-sale (POS) terminals in which data is being entered only.
- In **half-duplex communication,** data flows in both directions, but not simultaneously. That is, data flows in only one direction at any one time. This resembles traffic on a one-lane bridge. Half-duplex is very common and frequently used for linking microcomputers by telephone lines to other microcomputers.
- In **full-duplex communication,** data is transmitted back and forth at the same time, like traffic on a two-way street. It is clearly the fastest and most efficient form of two-way communication. Full-duplex has been widely used for mainframe communications for years. Now, it is becoming the standard mode for microcomputers as well.

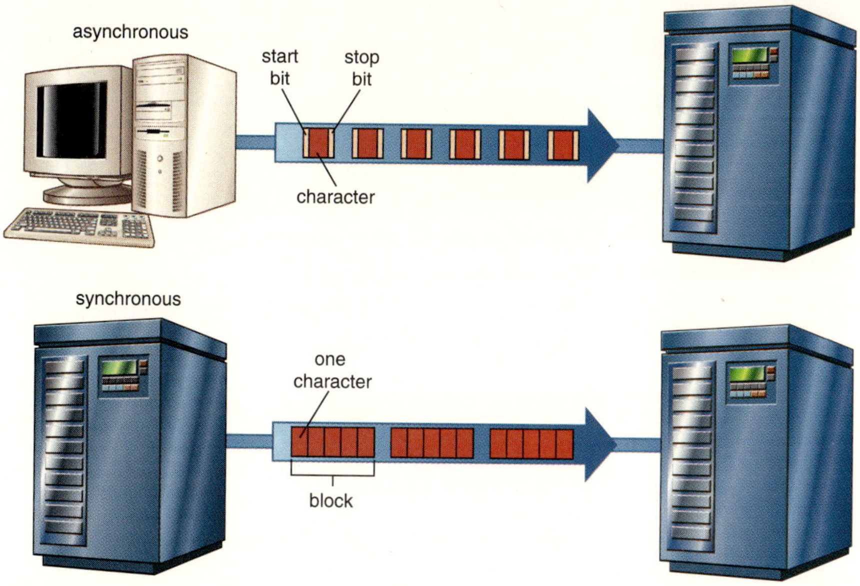

FIGURE 7-21
Asynchronous and synchronous communication

Modes of Data Transmission

Data may be sent by asynchronous or synchronous transmission. (See Figure 7-21.)

- In **asynchronous transmission,** the method frequently used with microcomputers, data is sent and received one byte at a time. Asynchronous transmission is often used for terminals with slow speeds. Its advantage is that the data can be transmitted whenever convenient for the sender. Its disadvantage is a relatively slow rate of data transfer.
- **Synchronous transmission** is used to transfer great quantities of information by sending several bytes or a block at a time. For the data transmission to occur, the sending and receiving of the blocks of bytes must occur at carefully timed intervals. Thus, the system requires a synchronized clock. Its advantage is that data can be sent very quickly. Its disadvantage is the cost of the required equipment.

Protocols

For data transmission to be successful, sender and receiver must follow a set of communication rules for the exchange of information. These rules for exchanging data between computers are known as the line **protocol.** A communications software package like Crosstalk helps define the protocol, such as speeds and modes, for connecting with another microcomputer.

When different types of microcomputers are connected in a network, the protocols can become very complex. Obviously, for the connections to work, these network protocols must adhere to certain standards. The first commercially available set of standards was IBM's Systems Network Architecture (SNA). This works for IBM's own equipment, but other machines won't necessarily communicate with them.

The International Standards Organization has defined a set of communications protocols called the Open Systems Interconnection (OSI). The purpose of the OSI model is to identify functions provided by any network. It separates each network's functions into seven "layers" of protocols, or communication rules. When two network systems communicate, their corresponding layers may exchange data. This assumes that the microcomputers and other equipment on each network have implemented the same functions and interfaces.

CONCEPT CHECK

- ✔ Bits-per-second transmission capability of a channel is called ________.
- ✔ Data travels in two ways: ________ and ________.
- ✔ Data may be sent by ________ or ________ transmission.
- ✔ For data transmission to be successful, sender and receiver must follow ________, or rules for exchanging data between computers.

Network Architecture

Network architecture describes how a computer network is configured and what strategies are used.

Communications channels can be connected in different arrangements, or **networks,** to suit different users' needs. A **computer network** is a communications system connecting two or more computers that work together to exchange information and share resources. **Network architecture** describes how the network is arranged and how the resources are coordinated and shared.

Terms

There are a number of specialized terms that describe computer networks. Some terms often used with networks are:

- **Node:** A **node** is any device that is connected to a network. It could be a computer, printer, or data storage device.
- **Client:** A **client** is a node that requests and uses resources available from other nodes. Typically, a client is a user's microcomputer.
- **Server:** A **server** is a node that shares resources with other nodes. Depending on the resources shared, it may be called a file server, printer server, communication server, Web server, or database server.
- **Network Operating System (NOS):** Microcomputer operating systems interact with an application and a computer. On the other hand, **network operating systems (NOS)** control and coordinate the activities between computers on a network. These activities include electronic communication and the sharing of information and resources.
- **Distributed processing:** In a **distributed processing** system, computing power is located and shared at different locations. This type of system is common in decentralized organizations where divisional offices have their own computer systems. The computer systems in the divisional offices are networked to the organization's main or centralized computer.
- **Host computer:** A **host computer** is a large centralized computer, usually a minicomputer or a mainframe.

A network may consist only of microcomputers, or it may integrate microcomputers or other devices with larger computers. Networks can be controlled by all nodes working together equally or by specialized nodes coordinating and supplying all resources. Networks may be simple or complex, self-contained or dispersed over a large geographical area.

CONCEPT CHECK

- ✔ What is meant by the term *network architecture?*
- ✔ What are some of the specialized terms that describe networks?

Configurations

A network can be arranged or configured in several different ways. This arrangement is called the network's **topology.** The four principal network topologies are star, bus, ring, and hierarchical.

In a **star network,** a number of small computers or peripheral devices are linked to a central unit. (See Figure 7-22.) This central unit may be a *host computer* or a *file server.*

All communications pass through this central unit. Control is maintained by **polling.** That is, each connecting device is asked ("polled") whether it has a message to send. Each device is then in turn allowed to send its message.

One particular advantage of the star form of network is that it can be used to provide a **time-sharing system.** That is, several users can share resources ("time") on a central computer. The star is a common arrangement for linking several microcomputers to a mainframe that allows access to an organization's database.

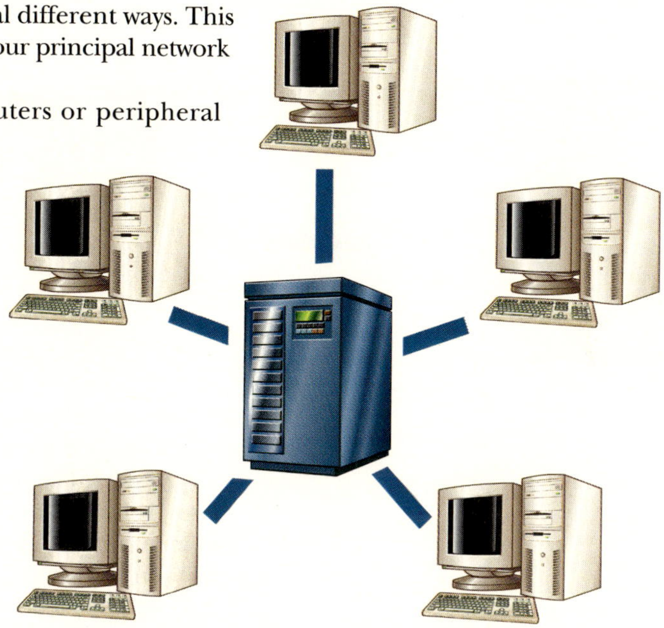

FIGURE 7-22
Star network

In a **bus network,** each device in the network handles its own communications control. There is no host computer. All communications travel along a common connecting cable called a **bus.** (See Figure 7-23.) As the information passes along the bus, it is examined by each device to see if the information is intended for it.

The bus network is typically used when only a few microcomputers are to be linked together. This arrangement is common in systems for electronic mail or for sharing data stored on different microcomputers. The bus network is not as efficient as the star network for sharing common resources. (This is because the bus network is not a direct link to the resource.) However, a bus network is less expensive and is in very common use.

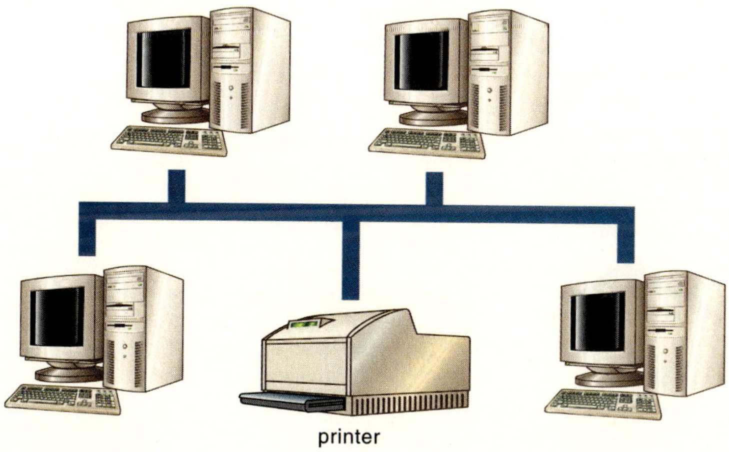

FIGURE 7-23
Bus network

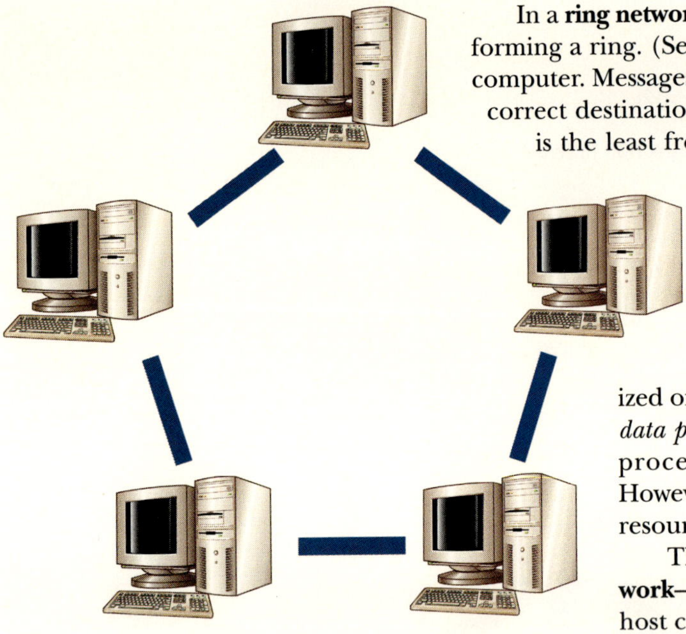

FIGURE 7-24
Ring network

In a **ring network,** each device is connected to two other devices, forming a ring. (See Figure 7-24.) There is no central file server or computer. Messages are passed around the ring until they reach the correct destination. With microcomputers, the ring arrangement is the least frequently used of the four networks. However, it often is used to link mainframes, especially over wide geographical areas. These mainframes tend to operate fairly autonomously. They perform most or all of their own processing and only occasionally share data and programs with other mainframes.

A ring network is useful in a decentralized organization because it makes possible a *distributed data processing system.* That is, computers can perform processing tasks at their own dispersed locations. However, they can also share programs, data, and other resources with each other.

The **hierarchical network**—also called a **hybrid network**—consists of several computers linked to a central host computer, just like a star network. However, these other computers are also hosts to other, smaller computers or to peripheral devices. (See Figure 7-25.)

Thus, the host at the top of the hierarchy could be a mainframe. The computers below the mainframe could be minicomputers, and those below, microcomputers. The hierarchical network allows various computers to share databases, processing power, and different output devices.

A hierarchical network is useful in centralized organizations. For example, different departments within an organization may have individual microcomputers connected to departmental minicomputers. The minicomputers in turn may be connected to the corporation's mainframe, which contains data and programs accessible to all.

For a summary of the network configurations, see Figure 7-26.

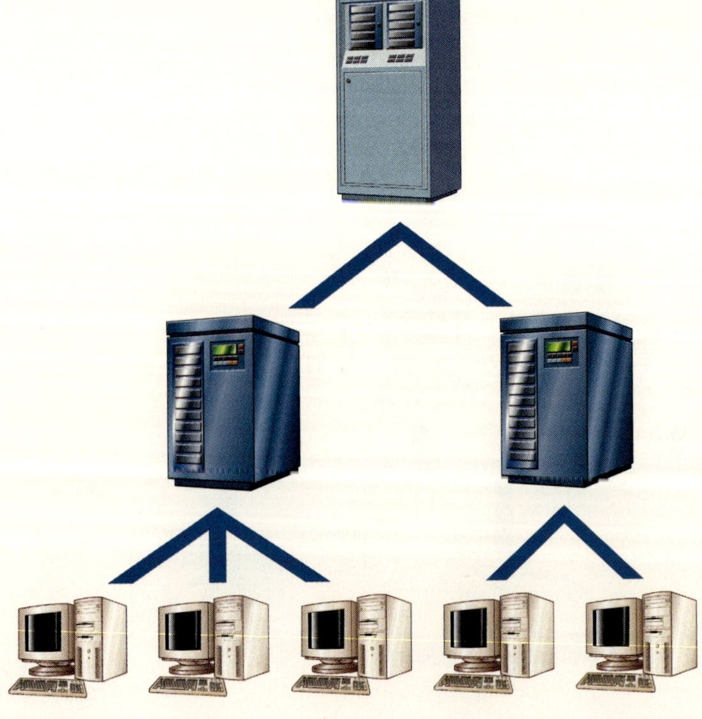

FIGURE 7-25
Hierarchical network

Type	Description
Star	Several computers connected to a central server or host; all communications travel through central server; good for sharing common resources
Bus	Computers connected by a common line; communication travels along this common line; less expensive than star
Ring	Each computer connected to two others forming a ring; communications travel around ring; often used to link mainframe computers in decentralized organizations
Hierarchical	One top-level host computer connected to next-level computers, which are connected to third-level computers; often used in centralized organizations

FIGURE 7-26
Principal network configurations

CONCEPT CHECK

- ✔ What is a network topology? List the four principal network topologies.
- ✔ What is one advantage of the star network topology?
- ✔ A ring network is useful because it makes possible a ________ ________ ________ ________.
- ✔ Where might you find a hierarchical network?

Strategies

Every network has a *strategy,* or way of coordinating the sharing of information and resources. The most common network strategies are terminal, peer-to-peer, and client/server systems.

In a **terminal network system,** processing power is centralized in one large computer, usually a mainframe. The nodes connected to this host computer are terminals with little or no processing capabilities. (See Figure 7-27.) The star and hierarchical networks are typical configurations with Unix as the operating system.

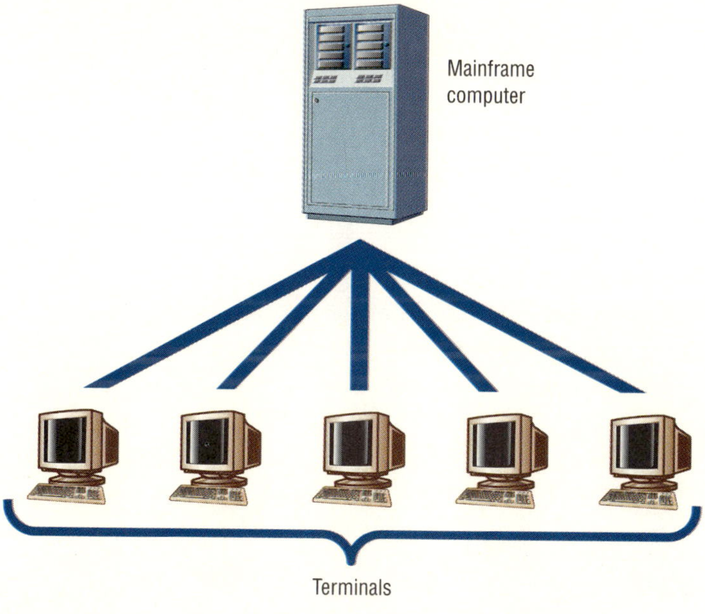

FIGURE 7-27
Terminal network system

Many airline reservation systems are terminal systems. A large central computer maintains all the airline schedules, rates, seat availability, and so on. Travel agents use terminals to connect to the central computer and use it to schedule reservations. Although the tickets may be printed along with travel itineraries at the agent's desk, nearly all processing is done at the central computer.

One advantage of terminal network systems is the centralized location and control of technical personnel, software, and data. One disadvantage is the lack of control and flexibility for the end user. Another disadvantage is that terminal systems do not use the processing power available with microcomputers. Though the terminal strategy was once very popular, most new systems do not use it.

In a **peer-to-peer network system,** nodes can act as both servers and clients. For example, one microcomputer can *obtain* files located on another microcomputer and can also *provide* files to other microcomputers. (See Figure 7-28.) A typical configuration for a peer-to-peer system is the bus network. Commonly used network operating systems are Novell's NetWare Lite, Microsoft's Windows NT, and Apple's Macintosh Peer-to-Peer LANs.

There are several advantages to using this type of strategy. The networks are inexpensive and easy to install, and they usually work well for smaller systems with fewer than 10 nodes. As the number of nodes increases, however, the performance of the network declines. Another disadvantage is the lack of powerful management software to effectively monitor a large network's activities. For these reasons, peer-to-peer networks are typically used by small networks.

Client/server network systems use one powerful computer to coordinate and supply services to all other nodes on the network. The server provides access to centralized resources such as databases, application software, and hardware. (See Figure 7-29.) This strategy is based on specialization. Server nodes coordinate and supply specialized services, and client nodes request the services. Commonly used network operating systems are Novell's NetWare, Microsoft's Windows NT, IBM's LAN Server, and Banyan Vines.

One advantage of client/server network systems is their ability to handle very large networks efficiently. Another advantage is the powerful network management software that monitors and controls the network's activities. The major disadvantages are the cost of installation and maintenance.

For a summary of the network strategies, see Figure 7-30.

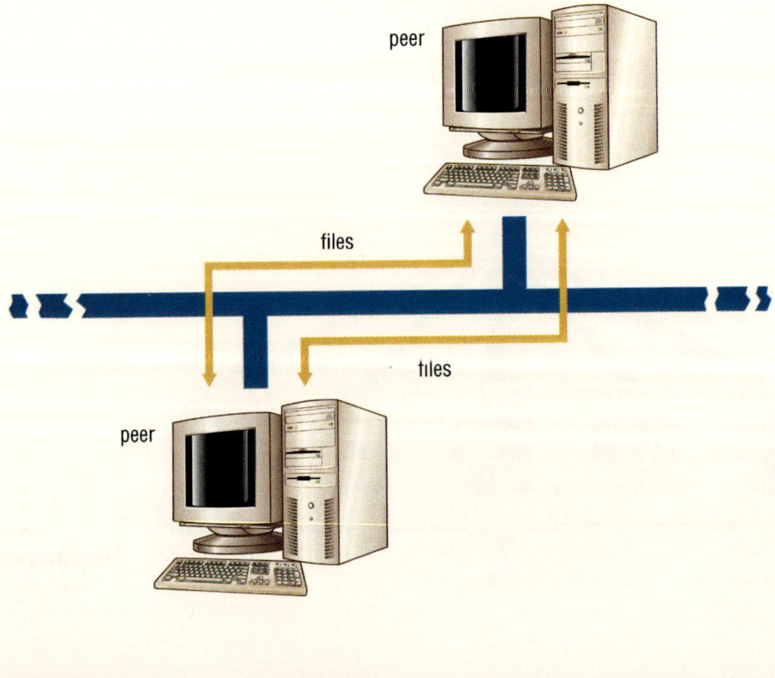

FIGURE 7-28
Peer-to-peer network system

Type	Description
Terminal	One large computer provides all processing, strong central control, limited flexibility and control for users
Peer-to-peer	Computers act as both servers and clients, inexpensive and easy to install, works well in small networks
Client/server	Several clients or computers depend upon one central server or computer to coordinate and supply services

FIGURE 7-30
Common network strategies

FIGURE 7-29
Client/server network system

Computer networks in organizations have evolved over time. Most large organizations have a wide range of different network configurations, operating systems, and strategies. These organizations are moving toward integrating or connecting all of these networks together. That way, a user on one network can access resources available throughout the company. This is called **enterprise computing.**

CONCEPT CHECK

- ✔ The most common network strategies are: ________, ________, and ________.
- ✔ What are the advantages of each network strategy?

Network Types

Communications networks differ in geographical size. Three important types are LANs, MANs, and WANs.

Clearly, different types of channels—cable or air—allow different kinds of networks to be formed. Telephone lines, for instance, may connect communications equipment within the same building. In fact, many new buildings—called *smart buildings*—have coaxial or fiber-optic cable installed inside the walls. This makes it easy to form communications networks.

Networks may also be citywide and even international, using both cable and air connections. Here let us distinguish among three types: *local area networks, metropolitan area networks,* and *wide area networks.*

Local Area Networks

Networks with computers and peripheral devices in close physical proximity—within the same building, for instance—are called **local area networks (LANs).** Linked by cable—telephone, coaxial, or fiber-optic—LANs often use a bus form of organization.

Our illustration shows an example of a LAN. (See Figure 7-31.) This typical arrangement has two benefits. People can share different equipment, which lowers the cost of equipment. For instance, here the four microcomputers share the laser printer and the file server, which are expensive pieces

MAKING IT WORK FOR YOU

Home Networking

Computer networks are not just for corporations and schools anymore. If you have more than one computer, you can use a home network to share files and printers, to allow multiple users access to the Internet at the same time, and to play interactive computer games.

How It Works

Computers can be connected using a variety of ways including electrical wiring, special cables, and radio frequencies. One of the simplest ways, however, is to use your home's existing telephone wiring system. Using this approach, telephone network adapter cards are installed on each computer. The adapter cards are connected to the telephone wiring system using standard telephone connections. Without affecting normal telephone use, your computers are connected and can share resources.

Installing the Network

Various telephone home networking kits are available. These kits typically include adapter card(s), standard telephone extension lines, and installation software. Once the adapter cards have been installed and connected to the telephone wiring system, you need to run the installation software.

For example, using Intel's AnyPoint Home Network installation software, you could set up your home network as shown to the right.

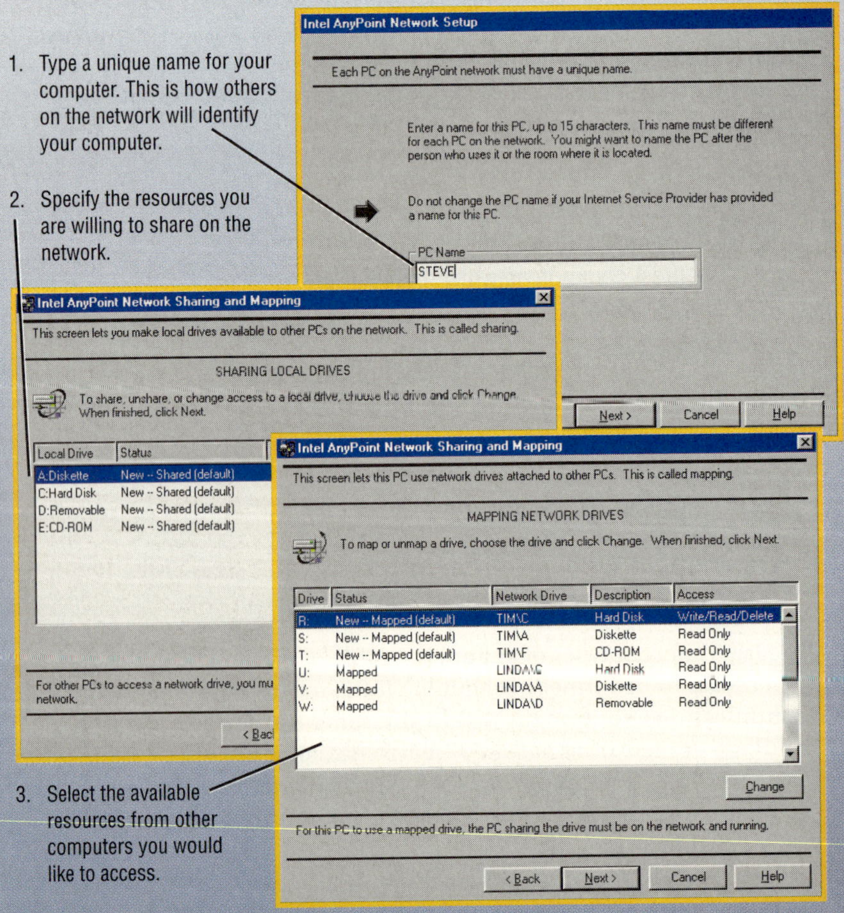

Using the Network

Now your computers are ready to share their resources. The four most common uses of a home network are to share files, printers, and Internet access, and to run multi-player computer games.

Sharing files: You are able to access files stored on other computers on your network. For example, the computer identified as TIM can access files stored on LINDA's and STEVE's hard disk drives.

Sharing printers: Any computer can print files using any printer that is connected to a computer on the network. This is handy if you have only one printer, or would like to use separate printers for different tasks. For example, you might have one inexpensive black and white printer for written materials and a more expensive color printer for graphics.

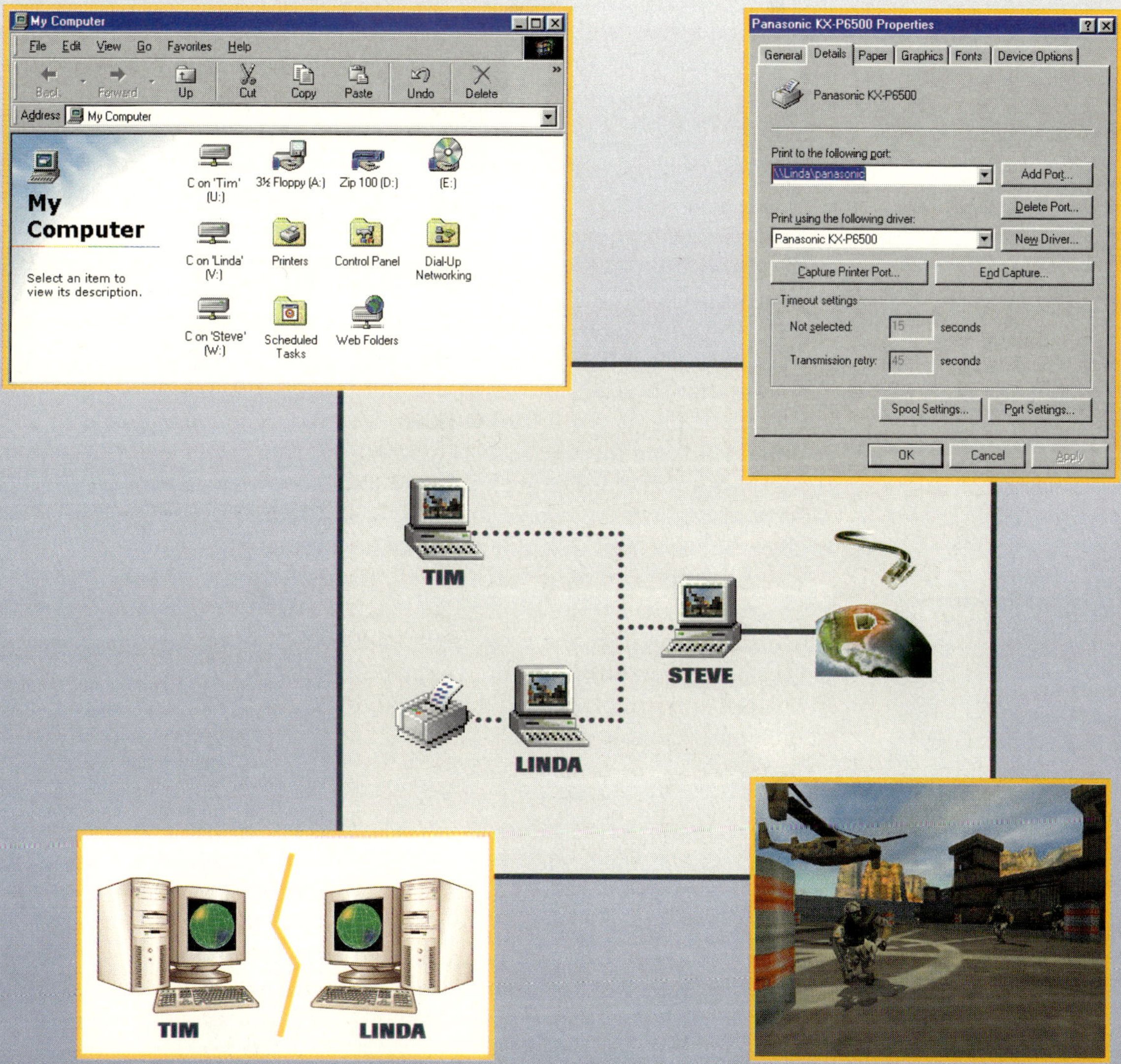

Sharing the Internet: Only one computer on the network connects directly to the Internet. It is known as the *server*. Whenever the server is connected to the Internet, each computer can surf the Internet independently at the same time. For example, you could be researching a paper on the Web using TIM while someone else is using LINDA to send and receive e-mail.

Multi-player computer games: Several computer games have options to play against other people. Players interact using different computers on the network. For example, you could be using TIM while two friends are using LINDA and STEVE.

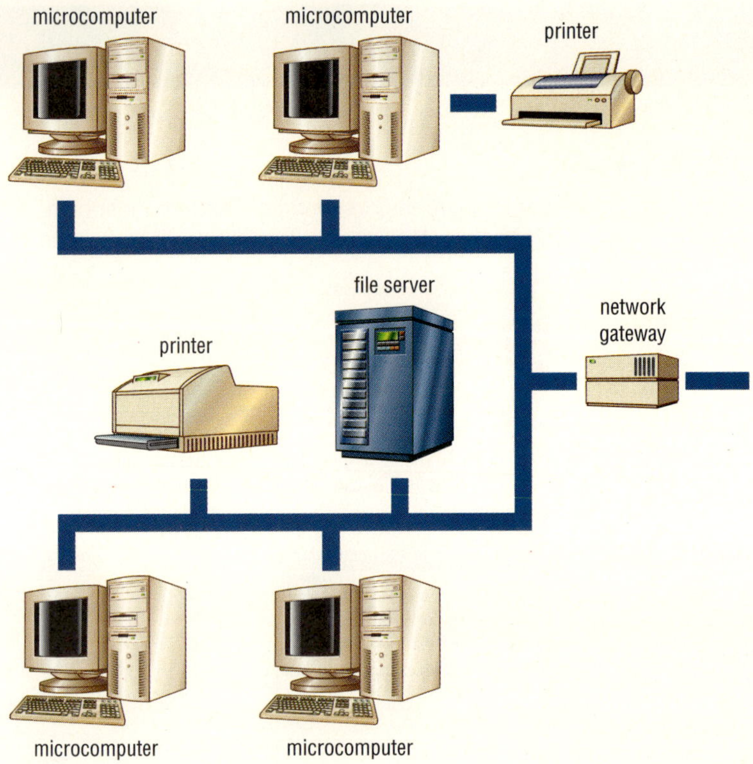

FIGURE 7-31
A local area network that includes a file server and network gateway

of hardware. (Individual microcomputers many times also have their own less expensive printers, such as the ink-jet printer shown in our illustration.) Other equipment may also be added to the LAN—for instance, mini- or mainframe computers or optical-disk storage devices.

Note that the LAN shown in our illustration also features a **network gateway.** A LAN may be linked to other LANs or to larger networks in this manner. For example, the LAN of one office group may be connected to the LAN of another office group. It may also be connected to others in the wider world, even if their configurations are different. Alternatively, a **network bridge** would be used to connect networks with the same configurations.

ON THE WEB EXPLORATIONS

What about LANs for the home? Intelogis and ShareWave are leaders in developing wireless home networks. To learn more about these companies, visit their Web sites at

http://www.intelogis.com
http://www.sharewave.com

Metropolitan Area Networks

The next step up from the LAN might be the **MAN**—the **metropolitan area network.** These networks are used as links between office buildings in a city. Cellular phone systems expand the flexibility of MANs by allowing links to car phones and portable phones.

Wide Area Networks

Wide area networks (WANs) are countrywide and worldwide networks. Among other kinds of channels, they use microwave relays and satellites to reach users over long distances—for example, from Los Angeles to Paris. (See Figure 7-32.) Of course, the widest of all WANs is the Internet, which spans the entire globe.

The primary difference between a LAN, MAN, and WAN is the geographical range. Each may have various combinations of hardware, such as microcomputers, minicomputers, mainframes, and various peripheral devices.

CONCEPT CHECK

- ✔ Distinguish the three types of networks described here.
- ✔ The primary difference between network types is the _______ _______.

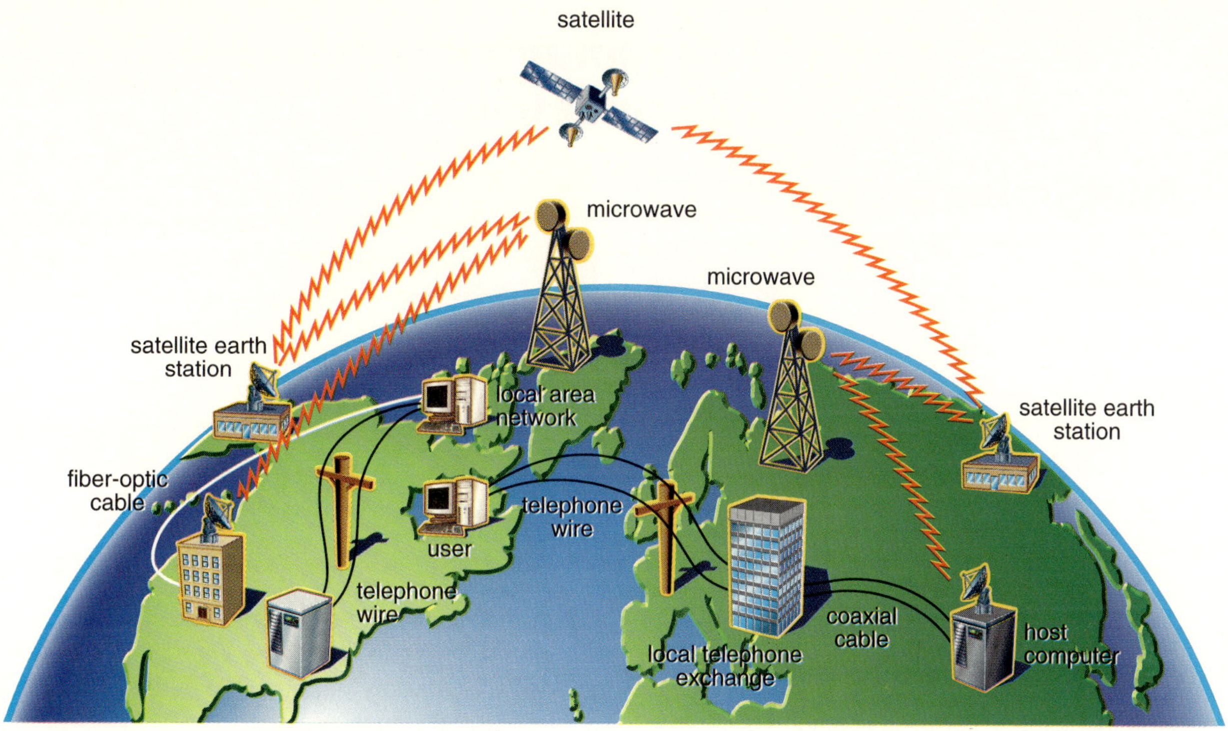

FIGURE 7-32
Wide area network

A LOOK TO THE FUTURE

Teledisc Corporation hopes to create an airborne Internet that will connect the world community.

Can you imagine what it would be like if all of the world's people could directly communicate with one another? If you wanted to know more about life in a remote African village, you could directly connect to members of that village to share experiences and explore the future. Medical researchers from every corner of the world could meet daily to coordinate and share their work. The world community could quickly react to and unite to face global crises.

Of course, that's what the Internet is all about. All the major cities in North America and Europe are wired for fast, efficient Internet access. Most of the rest of the world, however, is not. While satellites can be used to connect these other areas, most satellites orbit at such high altitudes that Internet connections are not effective. But that may be changing in the very near future.

Bill Gates from Microsoft and Craig McCaw from Cellular Communications have formed a corporation called Teledisc. This corporation is investing over $9 billion in the next two years to launch over 800 low-orbit satellites by the year 2003. These satellites will hover just 435 miles above the earth and provide direct effective Internet access. Once this airborne Internet is in place, all a user will need to link up to it from any location in the world is a microcomputer with a sender/receiver the size of a large pizza and a signal decoder.

Is there a need for this global communication system? Probably not right now. However, the Internet is growing fast and the demand for worldwide communication is growing even faster. Will Teledisc be a reality in the near future? This project requires a lot of ground-breaking technology. We will have to wait and see.

VISUAL SUMMARY Communications and Connectivity

CONNECTIVITY

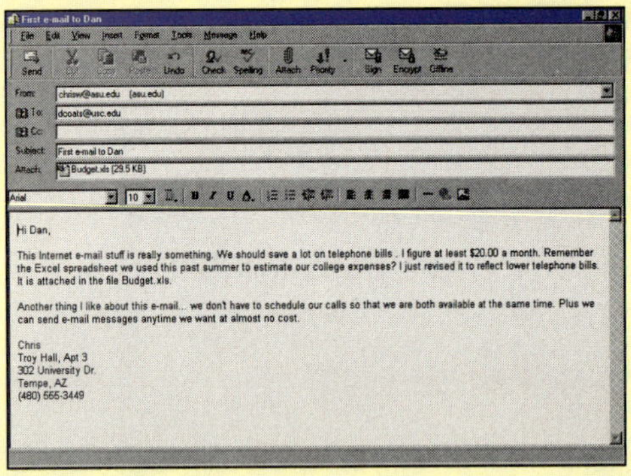

Connectivity is the act of linking computers to other electronic devices through communication systems to share access to information and data.

Available connection options include the following.

Fax Machines

Fax machines scan images and convert to signals to be transmitted over telephone lines.

E-Mail

E-mail or **electronic mail** is an electronic letter sent between individuals or computers.

Voice-Messaging Systems

Voice-messaging systems are computer systems linked to telephones that convert the human voice into digital bits.

Videoconferencing Systems

Videoconferencing systems allow people located at various geographic locations to have in-person meetings.

Shared Resources

Important aspects of connectivity are sharing expensive hardware and data.

Online Services

Online services provide a variety of services including **teleshopping, home banking, investing, travel reservations,** and **Internet access.**

USER CONNECTION

Communication Speeds

Unit	Speed
bps	bit per second
kbps	thousand bits per second
mbps	million bits per second
gbps	billion bits per second

Users often connect to communication systems using standard telephone lines. The lines typically send and receive **analog** signals. Computers send and receive **digital** signals.

Modems

Modems convert digital signals to analog signals and vice versa. There are three types of conventional modems:

- **External**—outside the system cabinet connected by cable to serial port.
- **Internal**—card that plugs into a slot on the system board.
- **Wireless**—does not connect to telephone line; receives data through the air.

Other Connections

Dial-up connections connect standard telephone line to conventional modems.

Some connections are all digital. For example, **T1, T2, T3,** and **T4** support very high speed transmission without conventional modems. Some promising new technologies include:

- **ISDN—integrated services digital network.**
- **DSL—digital subscriber line.**
- **Cable modems**—use existing cable lines.
- **Satellite/air**—use satellites to download data.

To be a competent end user you need to understand the concept of connectivity and the various connectivity options. Additionally, you need to know the essential parts of communications technology including connections, channels, transmission, network architectures, and network types.

COMMUNICATIONS CHANNELS

Communications channels connect computers either through cable or through the air. The ways or channels for transmitting data include *telephone lines, coaxial cable, fiber-optic cable, microwave,* and *satellite.*

Telephone Lines

Telephone lines—older telephone lines consist of **twisted pairs** of copper wire. Although still very common, these lines are being replaced.

Coaxial Cable

Coaxial cable replaces the multiple wires of older telephone lines with a solid-copper core to provide higher transmission capacity.

Fiber-Optic Cable

Data is transmitted as pulses of light through a **fiber-optical cable** of glass. It is lighter and faster than coaxial cable and rapidly replacing twisted pair technology.

Microwave

Data is sent short distances through the air in **microwaves** or high-frequency radio waves.

Satellite

Satellites rotating above the earth send data over long distances through the air.

DATA TRANSMISSION

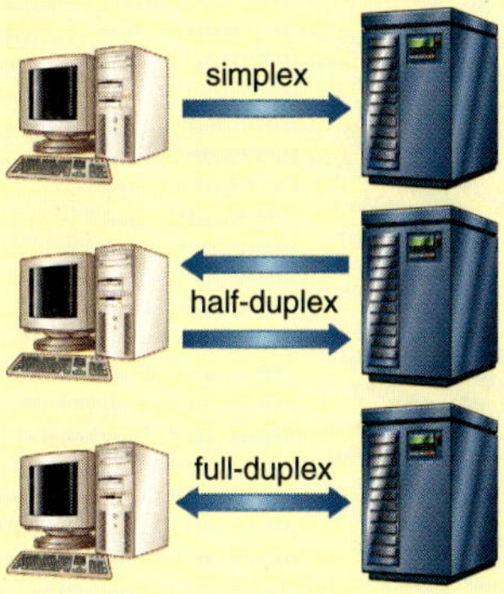

Several factors effect how data is actually transmitted from one point to another:

Bandwidth

Bandwidth is the bits-per-second transmission capability of a channel. Three bandwidths from lowest to highest are: **voiceband, medium band,** and **broadband.**

Serial and Parallel Transmission

With **serial transmission,** bits flow in a single continuous stream. With **parallel transmission,** bits flow through separate lines simultaneously.

Direction of Data Transmission

Three directions or modes of data flow are:

- **Simplex communication**—slower and older technology in which data travels in only one direction
- **Half-duplex communication**—allows data to flow in both directions but not simultaneously.
- **Full-duplex communication**—the fastest and becoming the standard for microcomputer communications. It allows data to travel in both directions simultaneously.

Modes of Data Transmission

Two modes are **asynchronous** (data is sent and received one byte at a time) and **synchronous** (several bytes, a block, are sent at a time).

Protocols

Protocols are rules for exchanging data between computers.

NETWORK ARCHITECTURE

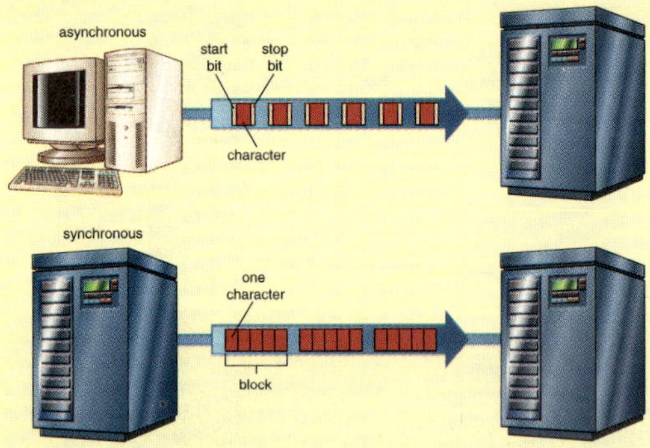

Network architecture describes how a **computer network** is configured and what strategies are used.

Terms

Terms often used with networks are: **node, client, server, network operating system, distributed processing,** and **host computer.**

Configurations

Networks can be configured in several ways:

- **Star network**—each device linked to a central unit; control maintained by **polling**.
- **Bus network**—each device handles its own communications along a common connecting cable called a **bus.**
- **Ring network**—each device connected to two other devices forming a ring.
- **Hierarchical network (hybrid network)**—connect smaller computers to a central host.

Strategies

Every network has a **strategy,** or way of sharing information and resources. Three widely used networking strategies are:

- **Terminal network system**—power is centralized in one large computer and distributed among several terminals.
- **Peer-to-peer network system**—each computer can act as both a server providing services and a client requesting services.
- **Client/server network system**—a computer is either a client requesting access to resources or a server providing access to centralized resources.

NETWORK TYPES

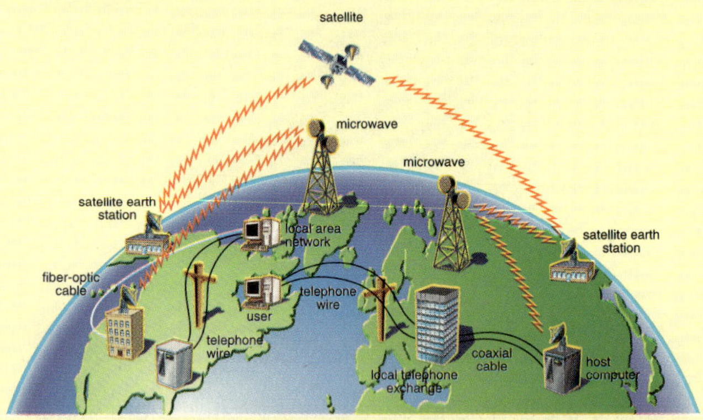

Networks can be citywide or even international using both cable and air connections. Three network types are: *local area networks, metropolitan area networks,* and *wide area networks.*

Local Area Networks

Local area networks or **LANs** connect devices that are located close to one another. Often these devices are located in the same office or floor. **Network gateways** and **bridges** link a LAN to other LANs or to larger networks.

Metropolitan Area Networks

Metropolitan area networks or **MANs** are used to link office building within a city. *Cellular phone systems* expand the flexibility of MANs by allowing links to car phones and portable phones.

Wide Area Networks

Wide Area Networks or **WANs** are the largest type. They span states and countries, or form worldwide networks. The Internet is the largest wide area network in the world.

Key Terms

analog signal (147)
asynchronous communications port (152)
asynchronous transmission (153)
bandwidth (151)
broadband (152)
bus (155)
bus network (155)
cable modem (149)
client (154)
client/server network system (158)
coaxial cable (150)
computer network (154)
data communications system (143)
demodulation (147)
dial-up service (148)
digital signal (147)
digital subscriber line (DSL) (148)
distributed processing (154)
electronic mail (144)
e-mail (144)
enterprise computing (159)
external modem (148)
fax machine (144)
fiber-optic cable (150)
full-duplex communication (152)
half-duplex communication (152)
hierarchical network (156)
host computer (154)
hybrid network (156)
integrated services digital network (ISDN) (148)
internal modem (148)
local area network (LAN) (160)
medium band (152)
metropolitan area network (MAN) (162)
microwave communication (150)
modulation (147)
network (154)
network architecture (154)
network bridge (162)
network gateway (162)
network operating system (NOS) (154)
node (154)
parallel data transmission (152)
peer-to-peer network system (158)
polling (155)
protocol (153)
ring network (156)
RS-232C connector (152)
satellite communication (150)
satellite/air connection services (149)
serial data transmission (152)
server (154)
simplex communication (152)
star network (155)
synchronous transmission (153)
terminal network system (157)
time-sharing system (155)
T1, T2, T3, T4 lines (148)
topology (155)
twisted pair (149)
videoconferencing system (145)
voiceband (151)
voice-messaging system (145)
wide area network (WAN) (162)
wireless modem (148)

Chapter Review

LEVEL 1

Reviewing Facts and Terms

Matching

Match each numbered item with the most closely related lettered item. Write your answers in the spaces provided.

1. Rules for exchanging data between computers. ____
2. In this channel, data is transmitted as pulses of light through tubes of glass. ____
3. A node that shares resources with other nodes. ____
4. In this method, data is sent and received one byte at a time. ____
5. These represent the presence or absence of an electronic pulse. ____
6. The arrangement or configuration of a network. ____
7. Very similar to the external modem, but it receives through the air. ____
8. Networks with computers and peripheral devices in very close proximity. ____
9. A way of sending an electronic letter or message between individuals or computers. ____
10. Network where a number of small computers are linked to a central unit. ____

a. Asynchronous transmission
b. Bandwidth
c. Bus network
d. Cable modem
e. Client
f. Client/server network system
g. Digital signal
h. E-mail
i. Fiber-optic cable
j. Full-duplex communication
k. ISDN
l. Local area network
m. Network

11. Data is transmitted back and forth at the same time, like traffic on a two-way street. ____
12. In this network system, nodes can act as both servers and clients. ____
13. The bits-per-second transmission capability of a channel. ____
14. Any device that is connected to a network. ____
15. A node that requests and uses resources available from other nodes. ____
16. This network system uses one powerful computer to coordinate and supply services to all other nodes on the network. ____
17. Service provided by many local telephone companies using special high-speed telephone lines. ____
18. Communications system connecting two or more computers that work together to exchange information and share resources. ____
19. Uses existing television cables to provide high-speed connections as fast as a T1 or DSL connection at a lower cost. ____
20. In this network topology, each device handles its own communications control, there is no host, and communications travel along a common connecting cable. ____

n. Node
o. Peer-to-peer network system
p. Protocol
q. Server
r. Star network
s. Topology
t. Wireless modem

True/False

In the spaces provided, write T or F to indicate whether the statement is true or false.

1. A local area network connects two or more computers within a limited area, such as within the same building. ____
2. Modems are used to convert data on a CD-ROM to an internal hard disk. ____
3. Frequently, computer communications over telephone lines require a modem. ____
4. In half-duplex communication, data flows in both directions at the same time. ____
5. In a client/server system, each node on the network has equal responsibility for coordinating the network's activities. ____
6. Voice-messaging systems are computer systems linked to telephones that convert human voice into digital bits. ____

Multiple Choice

Circle the letter of the correct answer.

1. Computer systems that allow people at different geographic locations to have in-person meetings:
   - a. voice-messaging system
   - b. online service
   - c. fax
   - d. videoconferencing system
   - e. modem
2. This technology uses existing telephone lines to provide high-speed communication comparable to T1 lines:
   - a. internal modems
   - b. ISDN
   - c. DDL
   - d. cable modem
   - e. MTV

3. What communications channel transfers data as pulses of light?
   a. telephone lines
   b. coaxial cable
   c. fiber-optic cable
   d. microwave
   e. satellite

4. Rules for exchanging data on a network:
   a. protocol
   b. asynchronous transmission
   c. configuration
   d. channel
   e. serial transmission

5. A system frequently used in decentralized organizations in which computing power is located and shared at different sites:
   a. client/server
   b. ring
   c. centralized
   d. mainframe
   e. distributed

6. A network strategy where processing power is centralized in one large computer, usually a mainframe, and the nodes connected to this host have little or no processing capability:
   a. terminal network system
   b. client/server network system
   c. peer-to-peer network system
   d. bus network
   e. data communications system

Completion

Complete each statement in the spaces provided.

1. __________ means the ability to connect your microcomputer by telecommunications links to other computers and information sources.
2. Internet access is a typical __________ service.
3. Because __________ travel in straight lines through the air and cannot bend with the curvature of the earth, they can transmit data only over short distances.
4. A __________ __________ system controls and coordinates the activities on a network.
5. __________ are countrywide and worldwide networks that connect users over long distances.
6. __________ is the process of converting from analog signals to digital signals.

Reviewing Concepts

LEVEL 2

Open-Ended

On a separate sheet of paper, respond to each question and statement.

1. Describe typical online services. Have you used any of these services? If so, which ones and how?
2. What are the differences between a terminal, a peer-to-peer, and a client/server system?
3. Describe the differences between simplex, half-duplex, and full-duplex communication.
4. Discuss the four basic network configurations. When is each used?
5. Discuss the three most common network strategies.
6. List the factors that affect data transmission.

COMPUTING ESSENTIALS 2000 2001

Concept Mapping

On a separate sheet of paper, draw a concept map or a flowchart showing how the following terms are related. Show all relationships. Include any additional terms you can think of.

analog signal
asynchronous transmission
bandwidth
broadband
bus
bus network
client
client/server network system
coaxial cable
computer network
data communications system
demodulation
digital signal
DSL
e-mail
fiber-optic cable
full-duplex communication
half-duplex communication
hierarchical network
host computer
local area network
metropolitan area network
microwave
voice-messaging system
wide area network
modulation
network
network architecture
node
parallel data transmission
peer-to-peer network system
polling
protocol
ring network
satellite
serial data transmission
server
simplex communication
star network
synchronous transmission
terminal network system
T1, T2, T3, T4 lines
topology
voiceband
twisted pair
videoconferencing system

Critical Thinking Questions and Projects

LEVEL 3

Read each exercise and answer the related questions on a separate sheet of paper.

1. *Connectivity options*: Which of the connectivity options have you used? Describe what you have used them for, when you used them, how you used them, and discuss their effectiveness. For those that you have not used, describe specific situations in which you might use them. Use personal and business examples.

2. *Home LANs:* Many new homes today are designed for local area networks or home-based computer control systems. These systems are designed to coordinate electronic devices in the home such as telephones, heating and air-conditioning systems, security systems, and more. Prepare a short report describing these systems. Discuss what they are, what they can do, who might use them, and who manufactures them. *Hint*: using either the library or the Internet check out IBM's Home Director (http://www.ibm.net), Intel's Anywhere in the Home (http://www.intel.net), Intelogis's Passport (http://www.intelogis.net), and/or ShareWave's ShareWave (http://www.sharewave.net).

3. *Ethics and privacy*: The FBI has long used court-approved wiretaps on telephone lines to monitor the communications of suspected criminals. Do you think the FBI also wiretaps electronic communications across computer networks? Do you think employers monitor e-mail sent across their internal networks? When you send e-mail or any other type of electronic information across the Internet, do you think other people could be listening in? Under what conditions do you think monitoring of electronic communications is acceptable and ethical? How might these conditions be enforced?

On the Web Exercises

1. Cable Connections

Are you tired of waiting for images and text to download from the World Wide Web? If you want to decrease the wait time, consider getting an Internet connection with a higher bandwidth. One way is to get a cable connection. To learn more about cable, visit our Web site at http://www.mhhe.com/cit/concepts/oleary 2000-2001/webex7.html to link to a site specializing in cable connections. Once connected to that site, explore and learn more about cable. Print out the Web page you find most informative. Write a paragraph on who should and who shouldn't get a cable modem and why. Consider individuals in different geographic locations, with different usage needs, and in large and small companies, and suggest alternatives to cable that might be more economical.

2. Satellite Link

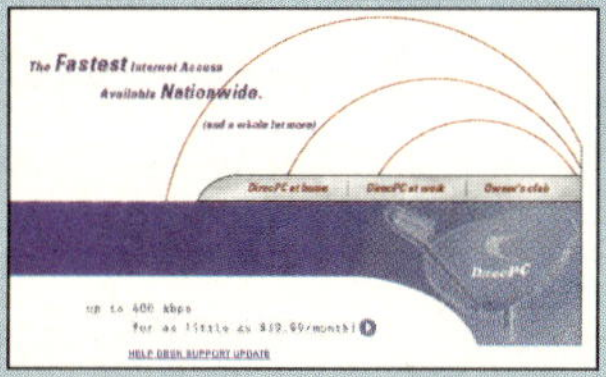

One way to speed up Internet access and delivery is by using a satellite link. All you need is a satellite service provider and satellite dish to download information from satellites and upload information via a phone line. To learn more about satellite links, visit our Web site at http://www.mhhe.com/cit/concepts/oleary2000-2001/webex7.html to link to a site specializing in satellite links. Once connected to that site, explore and print out the Web page you find most informative. Write a paragraph listing the pros and cons of using a satellite link for your Internet connection.

3. Cable Modems

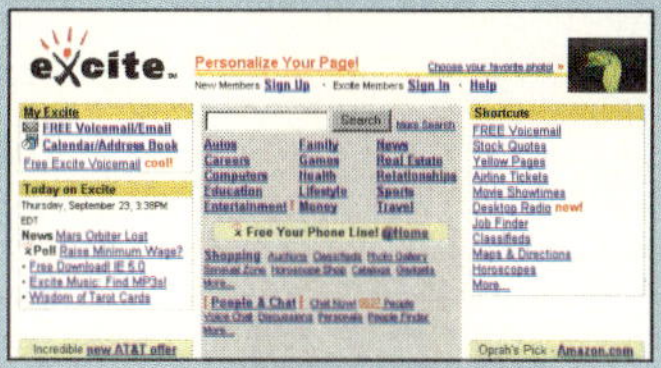

Many observers look to cable modems to greatly increase Internet access and connection capabilities. Search the Internet to learn more about cable modems and cable modem service. Visit the Excite search service at http: //www.excite.com and use keywords such as "cable internet connection" and "high bandwidth." Also use Excite's topic areas to limit your search, and take advantage of Excite's [More Like This] buttons next to each site. Print out the most informative Web page, and write a paragraph describing the site, and explaining how it is useful and how you found it. Find out whether your local cable company provides Internet access and how much it costs.

4. Travel

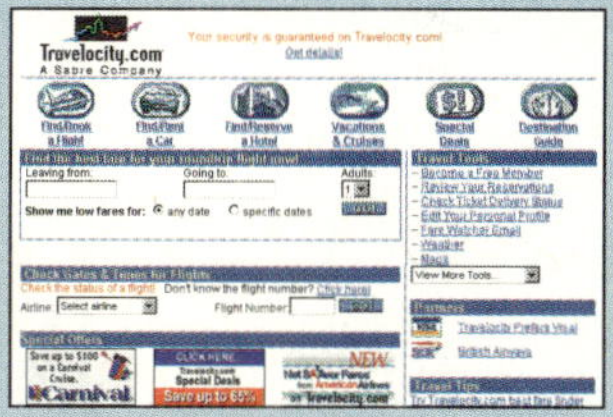

You can find all sorts of travel information and advice on the Internet. Visit our Web site at http://www.mhhe.com/cit/concepts/oleary 2000-2001/webex7.html to link to one of the best travel sites on the Web. Once connected to that site, you'll find a wide range of travel information from tickets to theatrical and sporting events to plane, hotel, and cruise schedules. Plan the vacation of your dreams. Print out the most interesting Web page, and write a paragraph describing your vacation plans, including estimated budget, destinations, airline (or cruise) departure times, and accommodations.

CHAPTER 8

The Internet and the Web

COMPETENCIES

After you have read this chapter, you should be able to:

1. **Describe Internet providers, connections, and protocols.**
2. **Discuss e-mail, mailing lists, newsgroups, chat groups, and instant messaging.**
3. **Describe electronic commerce including Web storefronts, auctions, and electronic payment.**
4. **Describe Internet services: Telnet, FTP, Gopher, and the Web.**
5. **Discuss browsers, Web pages, and Web portals.**
6. **Compare the two types of search tools: indexes and search engines.**
7. **Discuss the two types of Web utilities: plug-ins and helper applications.**
8. **Describe intranets, extranets, and firewalls.**

Want to communicate with a friend across town, in another state, or even in another country? Perhaps you would like to send a drawing, a photo, or just a letter. Looking for travel or entertainment information? Perhaps you're researching a term paper or exploring different career paths. Where do you start? For these and other information-related activities, try the Internet and the Web. They are the 21st-century information resources designed for all of us to use.

The Internet is like a highway that connects you to millions of other people and organizations. Unlike typical highways that move people and things from one location to another, the Internet moves your *ideas* and *information.* Rather than moving through geographic space, you move through **cyberspace**—the space of electronic movement of ideas and information. The Web provides an easy-to-use, exciting, multimedia interface to

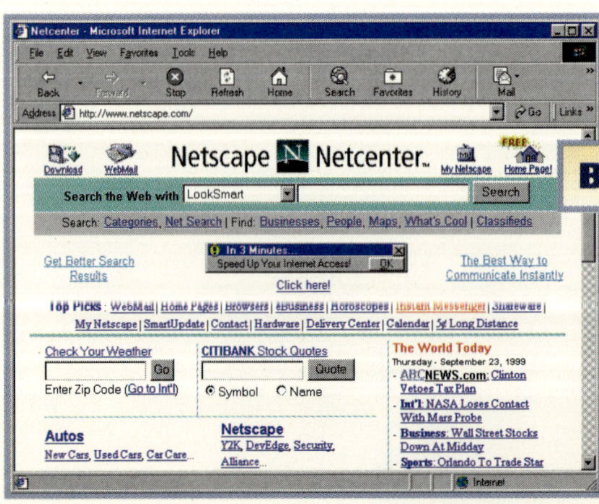

Browsers

connect to the Internet and to access the resources available in cyberspace.

The Internet was launched in 1969 when the United States funded a project that developed a national computer network called **Advanced Research Project Agency Network (ARPANET).** The **Web,** also known as **WWW** and the **World Wide Web,** was introduced in 1992 at the **Center for European Nuclear Research (CERN)** in Switzerland. Prior to the Web, the Internet was all text—no graphics, animations, sound, or video. The Web provided a multimedia interface to resources available on the Internet. From these research beginnings, the Internet and the Web have evolved as tools for all of us to use.

Competent end users need to be aware of the resources available on the Internet and the Web. Additionally, they need to know how to access these resources, to effectively communicate electronically, to understand electronic commerce, and to efficiently use Web browsers, portals, pages, search tools, and utilities. Also, competent end users need to be aware of how organizations use intranets and extranets.

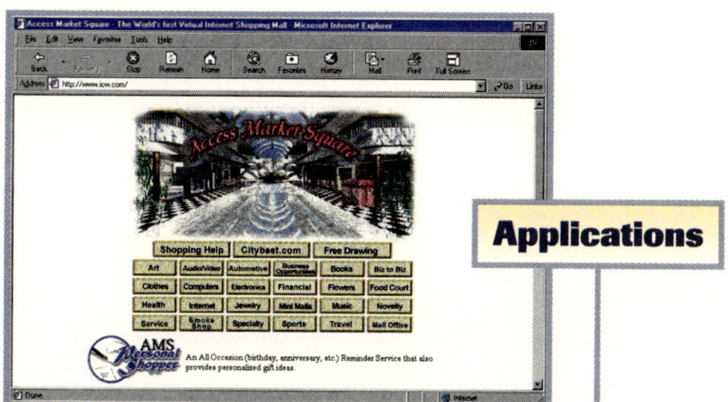

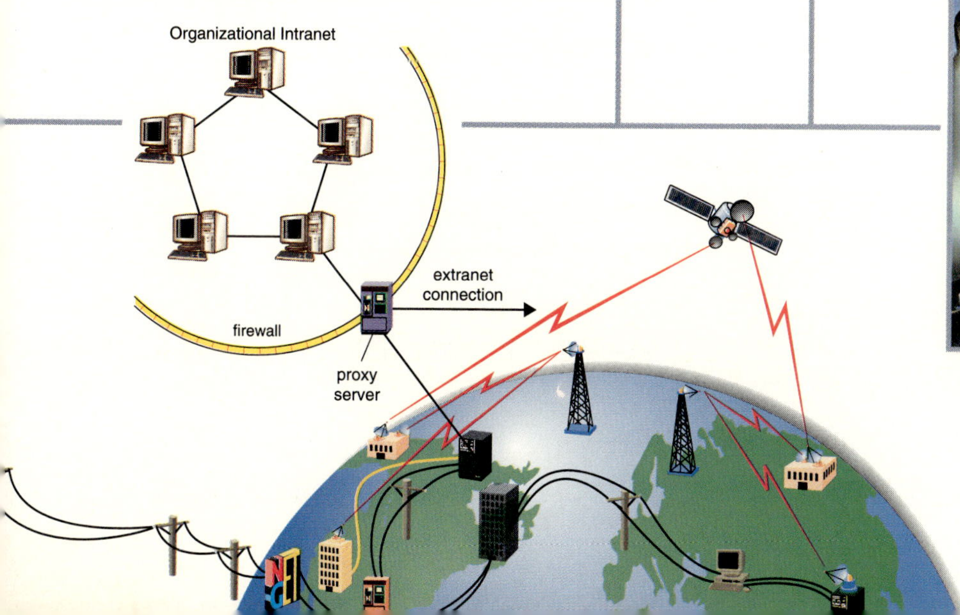

Internet Applications

The most common Internet applications are communicating, shopping, researching, and entertainment.

Every day over a billion users from every country in the world use the Internet and the Web. What are they doing? The most common uses are the following.

Communicating

Communicating via e-mail is the most popular Internet activity. You can exchange e-mail with your friends and family located almost anywhere in the world. You can also join and listen to discussions and debates on a wide variety of special-interest topics.

Shopping

One of the fastest-growing Internet applications is electronic commerce. You can visit a cybermall to windowshop at the best stores, look for the latest fashions, search for bargains, and make purchases. (See Figure 8-1.) You can purchase goods using checks, credit cards, or electronic cash.

Researching

How would you like to have one of the world's largest libraries available from home? Well, you can have several of them. By visiting virtual libraries, you can browse through the stacks, read selected items, and even check out books.

Entertainment

Do you like music, movies, books, magazines, or computer games? You'll find them all on the Internet waiting for you to locate and enjoy. You will find live concerts, movie previews, book clubs, and interactive live games. (See Figure 8-2.)

How can you get started using the Internet and the Web? The first step is to get connected, or to gain access to the Internet.

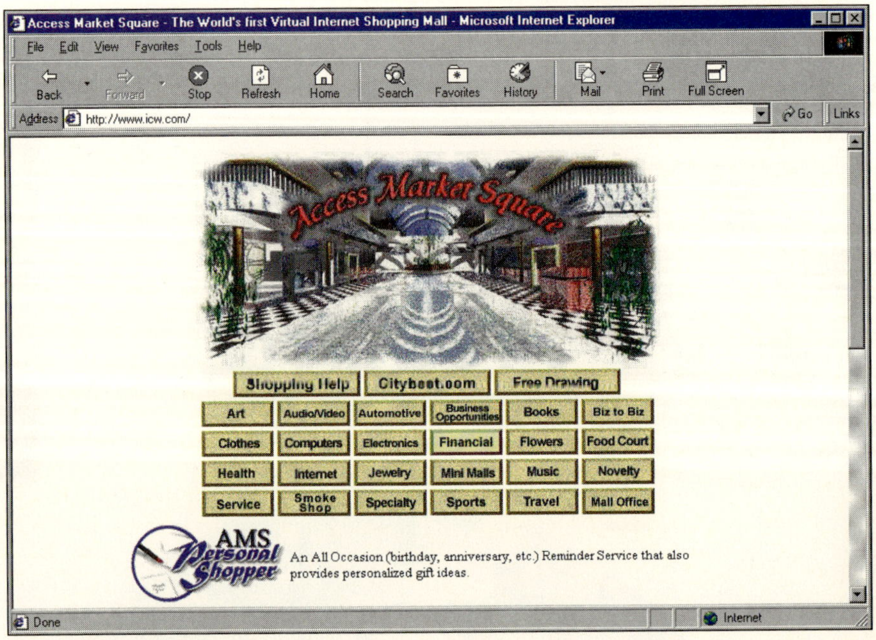

FIGURE 8-1
Cyber mall

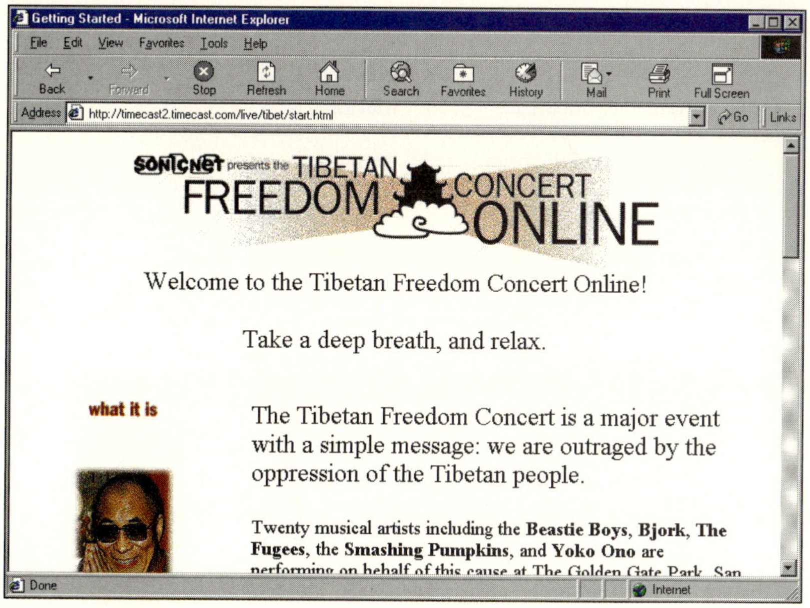

FIGURE 8-2
Entertainment

CONCEPT CHECK

✔ What are the most common applications of the Internet?

Access

Providers give us access to the Internet. Internet connections are either direct, SLIP and PPP, or by terminal connection. TCP/IP is the standard Internet protocol.

The Internet and the telephone system are similar—you can connect a computer to the Internet much like you connect a phone to the telephone system. Once you are on the Internet, your computer becomes an extension of what seems like a giant computer—a computer that branches all over the world.

Providers

The most common way to access the Internet is through a **provider** or **host computer.** The providers are already connected to the Internet and provide a path or connection for individuals to access the Internet. There are three widely used providers.

- **Colleges and universities:** Most colleges and universities provide free access to the Internet through their local area networks. You may be able to access the Internet through your school or through other local colleges and universities.
- **Internet service providers:** An **Internet service provider (ISP)** offers access to the Internet for a fee. The best-known national Internet service providers are AT&T WorldNet, IBM Internet Connection, and MindSpring. Local providers are also available in many areas at a slightly lower cost.

Type	Provider	Site
ISP	AT&T WorldNet	att.net
	IBM Internet Connection	ibm.net
	MindSpring	mindspring.net
	Earthlink	earthlink.com
Online	America Online	aol.com
	CompuServe	compuserve.com
	MSN	msn.com
	Prodigy	prodigy.com

FIGURE 8-3
Service providers

- **Online service providers:** The most widely used source for access to the Internet is through **online service providers.** Like Internet service providers, they provide access to the Internet. Additionally, online service providers offer a variety of other services as well. The best known are America Online (AOL), CompuServe, MSN (Microsoft Network), and Prodigy.

To learn more about service providers, visit some of the sites presented in Figure 8-3.

Connections

To gain access to the Internet, you must have a connection. (See Figure 8-4.) This connection can be made either directly to the Internet or indirectly through a provider. There are three types of connections:

FIGURE 8-4
Connection

- **Direct or dedicated:** To have the most efficient access to all the functions on the Internet, you need a direct or dedicated link. Individuals rarely have direct connections because they are quite expensive. However, many organizations such as colleges, universities, service providers, and corporations do have direct links.

  The primary advantages of a direct link are complete access to Internet functions, ease of connection for individual users, and fast response and retrieval of information. The primary disadvantage is cost.
- **SLIP and PPP:** Using a high-speed modem and standard telephone lines, you can connect to a provider that has a direct connection to the Internet. This type of connection requires special software such as **serial line Internet protocol (SLIP)** or **point-to-point protocol (PPP).** Using this type of connection, your computer becomes part of a client/server network. The provider or host computer is the server providing access to the Internet. Your computer is the client. Using special client software, your computer is able to communicate with server software running on the provider's computer and on other Internet computers.

  This type of connection is widely used by end users to connect to the Internet. It provides a high level of service at a lower cost than a direct or dedicated connection. Of course, it is somewhat slower and may not be as convenient.
- **Terminal connection:** Another way to access the Internet using a high-speed modem and standard telephone lines is called a **terminal connection.** Using this type of connection, your computer becomes a part of a terminal network. Unlike with a SLIP or PPP connection, your computer's operations with a terminal connection are very limited. Your computer simply displays the communication that occurs between the provider and the other computers on the Internet. Compared to a SLIP or PPP connection, terminal connection is less expensive but not as fast or convenient.

For a summary of the typical costs and users of the three types of connections, see Figure 8-5.

TCP/IP

When information is sent over the Internet, it usually travels through numerous interconnected networks. Before a message is sent, it is broken down into small parts called **packets.** Each packet is then sent separately over the Internet, possibly traveling different routes to one common destination. At the receiving end, the packets are reassembled into the correct order. As we mentioned in Chapter 7, *protocols* control how messages are broken down,

Connection	User	Cost
Direct/Dedicated	Medium to large company	$4,000 to $15,000 per year
SLIP/PPP	Individual or small company	$100 to $300 per year, plus hourly charges in some cases
Terminal connection	Individual	$0 to $50 per year

FIGURE 8-5
Typical user and connection costs

sent, and reassembled. They govern how and when computers talk to one another. The standard protocol for the Internet is called **transmission control protocol/Internet protocol (TCP/IP).**

CONCEPT CHECK

- ✔ Name some common Internet providers.
- ✔ Before information is sent over the Internet, it is broken into ________. ________ control how messages are broken down, sent, and reassembled.
- ✔ What is the standard protocol for the Internet?

E-Mail

An e-mail message has three basic elements. Internet addresses use the domain name system.

As we noted earlier, communicating via e-mail is by far the most common Internet activity. You can communicate with anyone in the world who has an Internet address or e-mail account with a system connected to the Internet. All you need is access to the Internet and an e-mail program. Two of the most widely used e-mail programs are Microsoft's Outlook Express and Netscape's Navigator.

Suppose that you have a friend, Dan Coats, who is going to the University of Southern California. You and Dan have been calling back and forth at least once a week for the past month. Your telephone bill has skyrocketed. Fortunately, you both have Internet e-mail accounts through your schools. To save money, you and Dan agree to communicate via the Internet instead of the telephone. After exchanging e-mail addresses, you are ready to send your first Internet e-mail message to Dan.

Basic Elements

A typical e-mail message has three basic elements: header, message, and signature. (See Figure 8-6.) The **header** appears first and typically includes the following information:

- **Subject:** A one-line description, used to present the topic of the message. Subject lines typically are displayed when a person checks his or her mailbox.
- **Addresses:** Addresses of the persons sending, receiving, and, optionally, anyone else who is to receive copies.
- **Attachments:** Many e-mail programs allow you to attach files such as documents and worksheets. If a message has an attachment, the file name appears on the attachment line.

TIPS Did you know that a lot of e-mail never gets read? Busy people quickly scan their e-mail to select which messages to read. Here are a few simple tips to help ensure that your e-mail messages are read:

1. *Make the subject line precise.* Many people screen their e-mail by looking at the subject line. If the subject is unclear or appears to be unimportant, the e-mail may never be read.
2. *Write in short paragraphs.* It's also a good idea to skip a line between paragraphs. This will make your e-mail easier to read and more likely to be read.
3. *Be careful what you write.* You could be held criminally liable for messages that could be interpreted to be abusive, threatening, harassing, or bigoted.
4. *DO NOT TYPE IN ALL UPPERCASE CHARACTERS.* This is called shouting and is perceived as very aggressive. Also, do not type in all lowercase characters. This is perceived as very timid. Use a normal combination of uppercase and lowercase characters.
5. *Check spelling, punctuation, and grammar.* Also, think twice about the content of your message. Once it is sent, you can't get it back.
6. *Don't forward or copy unnecessary material.* This contributes to spam, the electronic equivalent to junk mail. Often used for commercial purposes, spam clutters inboxes and slows down the Internet.

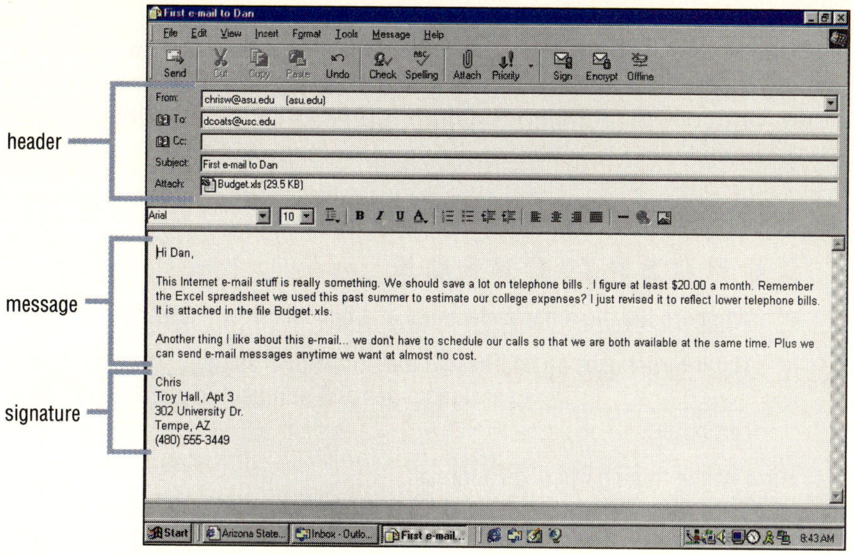

FIGURE 8-6
Basic elements of an e-mail message

The letter or **message** comes next. It is typically short and to the point. Finally, the **signature line** provides additional information about the sender. Typically, this information includes the sender's name, address, and telephone number.

Addresses

One of the most important elements of an e-mail message is the address of the person who is to receive the letter. The Internet uses an addressing method known as the **domain name system (DNS)** to assign names and numbers to people and computers. This system divides an address into three parts: user name, domain name, and domain code. (See Figure 8-7.)

Internet addresses typically are read backwards. The last part of the address, the **domain code,** identifies the geographical description or organizational identification. For example, *edu* in Figure 8-7 indicates an address at an educational and research institution. (For other codes, see Figure 8-8.)

Separated from the domain code by a dot (.) is the **domain name.** It is a reference to the particular organization. In this case, *usc* represents the

ON THE WEB EXPLORATIONS

Almost all ISPs and online service providers offer e-mail service to their customers. But you can get this service for free from Hotmail, Juno Online Services, USA Net Inc., and Yahoo. To learn more about free e-mail service, visit one or more of the following sites:

http://www.hotmail.com
http://www.juno.com
http://www.usa.net
http://www.yahoo.com

FIGURE 8-7
Parts of an Internet address

Domain	Identification
com	Commercial
edu	Educational and research
org	Other organizations
net	Major network centers
gov	Government

FIGURE 8-8
Common Internet domain codes

TIPS What if you don't know or have forgotten someone's e-mail address? You can go to e-mail address directories, also known as e-mail "white pages." These directories can be used much like you would use the telephone white pages. Here are three e-mail address directories you might try:

www.bigfoot.com

www.people.yahoo.com

www.infospace.com

University of Southern California. Separated from the domain name by an "at" (@) symbol, the **user name** identifies a unique person or computer at the listed domain. The address shown in Figure 8-7 is for Dan Coats (dcoats) at the University of Southern California (usc), which is an education and research (edu) organization.

CONCEPT CHECK

✔ What are the three basic elements of a typical e-mail message?

✔ The Internet uses an addressing method known as the ________ ________ ________ to assign names and numbers to people and computers.

✔ List the three parts of an address.

Discussion Groups

Mailing lists send e-mail to all members. Newsgroups use the UseNet. Chat groups support live conversations. Instant messaging provides greater control and flexibility. Lurking is good.

You can also use e-mail to communicate with people you do not know but with whom you wish to share ideas and interests. You can participate in discussions and debates that range from general topics like current events and movies to specialized forums like computer troubleshooting and Star Trek.

Mailing Lists

Mailing lists are one type of discussion group available on the Internet. Members of a mailing list communicate by sending messages to a **list address.** Each message is then copied and sent via e-mail to every member of the mailing list.

There are thousands of different mailing lists. To participate in one, you must first subscribe by sending an e-mail request to the mailing list **subscription address.** (See Figure 8-9.) Once you are a member of a list, you can expect to receive e-mail from others on the list. You may find the number of messages to be overwhelming. If you want to cancel a mailing list, send an e-mail request to "unsubscribe" to the subscription address.

Description	Subscription Address
Music and bands	dbird@netinfo.com.au
Movies	moviereview-request@cuenet.com
Jokes	dailyjoke@lists.ivillage.com
Travel	tourbus@listserv.aol.com

FIGURE 8-9
Popular mailing lists

Newsgroups

Newsgroups are a widely used type of discussion group. Unlike mailing lists, **newsgroups** use a special network of computers called the **UseNet.** Each of these computers maintains the newsgroup listing. There are over 10,000 different newsgroups organized into major topic areas that are further subdivided into subtopics.

This hierarchy system is similar to the domain name system. For example, the newsgroup specializing in motion picture discussions is categorized under the major topic *rec* (for "recreational"), then the subtopic *arts,* and then the further subdivision *cinema.* (See Figure 8-10.)

Contributions to a particular newsgroup are sent to one of the computers on the UseNet. This computer saves the messages on its system and periodically shares all its recent messages with the other computers on the UseNet. Unlike mailing lists, a copy of each message is not sent to each member of a list. Rather, interested individuals check contributions to a particular newsgroup, reading only those of interest.

There are thousands of newsgroups covering a wide variety of topic areas. (See Figure 8-11.)

Chat Groups

Chat groups are becoming a very popular type of discussion group. While mailing lists and newsgroups rely on e-mail, chat groups allow direct "live" communication. To participate, you join a chat group, select a **channel** or topic, and communicate live with others by typing words on your computer. Other members of your channel immediately see those words on their computers and can respond in the same manner.

By far the most popular chat service is called **Internet Relay Chat (IRC).** To participate, you need access to a server or computer that supports IRC. This is done using special chat-client software. This software is available free from several locations on the Internet. Using the chat-client software, you log on to the server, select a channel or topic in which you are interested, and begin chatting.

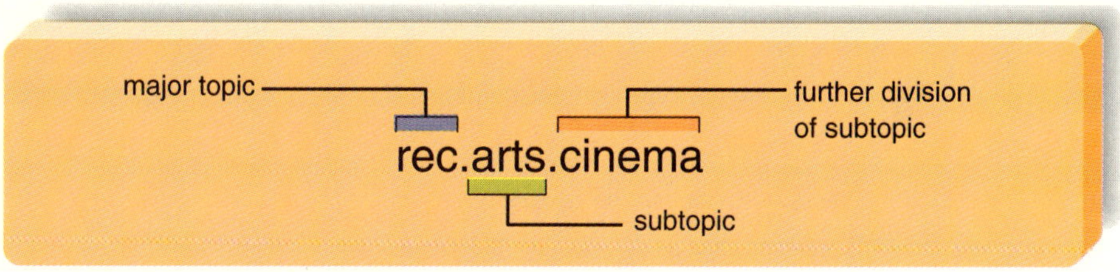

FIGURE 8-10
Newsgroup hierarchy

Description	Newsgroups
Aerobics fitness	misc.fitness.aerobic
Cinema	rec.arts.movies
Mountain biking	rec.bicycles.off-road
Music	rec.music.hip-hop
Clip art	alt.binaries.clip-art

FIGURE 8-11
Popular newsgroups

Instant Messaging

Although **instant messaging** has been around for a while, it has recently become much more popular as a tool for communicating and collaborating with others. Like chat groups, instant messaging allows one or more people to communicate via direct, "live" communication. Instant messaging, however, provides greater control and flexibility than chat groups.

To use instant messaging, you specify a list of friends, or "buddies," and register with an instant messaging server. Whenever you connect to the Internet, you use special software to tell your messaging server that you are online too. It notifies you if any of your buddies are online. At the same time, it notifies your buddies that you are online. You can then send messages back and forth to one another instantly.

MAKING IT WORK FOR YOU

Instant Messaging

Do you enjoy chatting with your friends? Are you working on a project and need to collaborate with others in your group? Perhaps instant messaging is just what you're looking for. It's easy and free with an Internet connection and the right software.

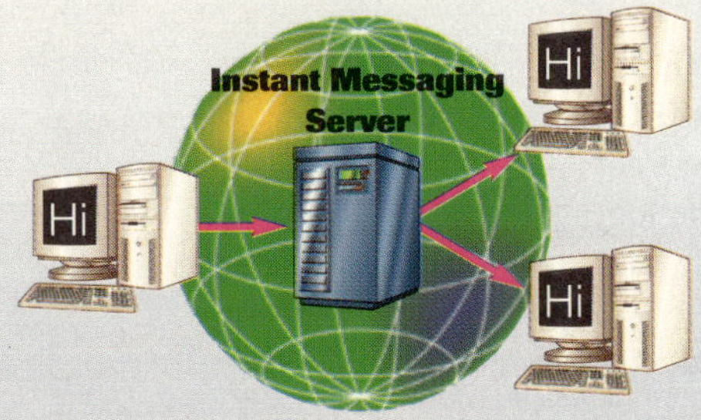

How It Works

Users register with an instant messaging server and identify friends and colleagues (buddies). Whenever a user is online, the instant messaging server notifies the user of all buddies who are also online and provides support for direct "live" communication.

Getting Started

The first step is to connect to one of the many Web sites that support instant messaging. Once at the site, register, download, and install instant messaging software, and create your buddy list.

For example, you can set up AOL Instant Messenger as shown below.

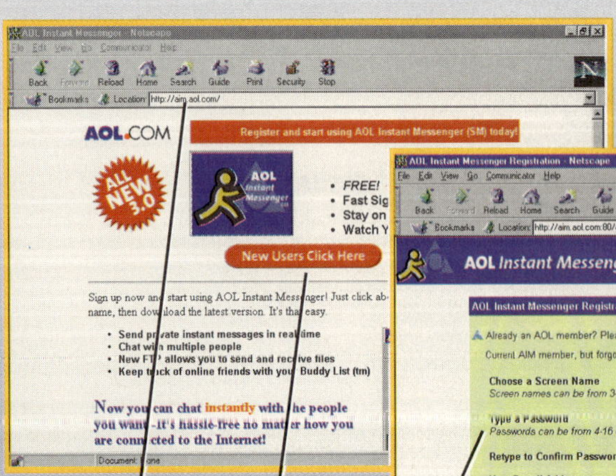

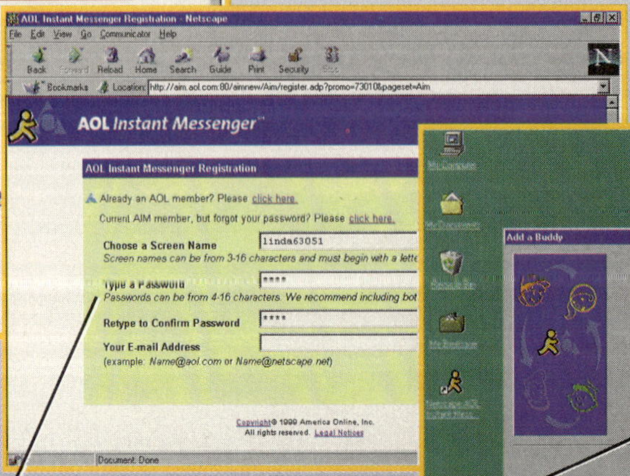

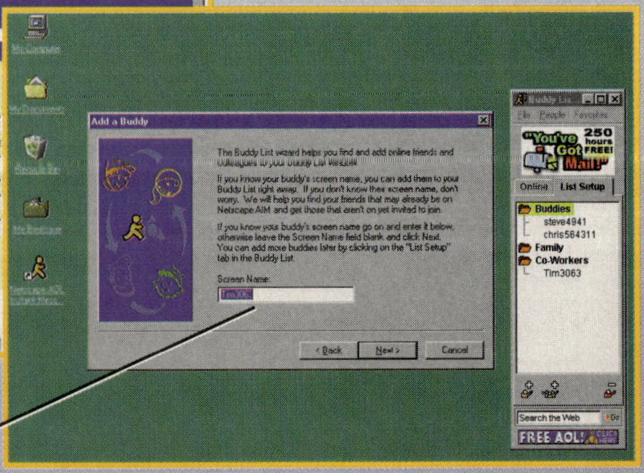

1. Enter aim.aol.com in the Location box of your browser.
2. Select the link to register as a new user.
3. Complete the registration form.
4. After installing the instant messaging software, create your "buddy list."

Communicating with a Friend

Once you have set up your instant messaging software, you can use it to communicate, live, with your online buddies. For example, you could use AOL Instant Messenger as follows:

1. Click the Instant Messenger icon on the desktop.
2. Enter your screen name and password into the Sign On window.
3. Click the *Sign In* button.
4. Double-click the screen name of the friend with whom you want to communicate.
5. Type your message in the message window.
6. Click the *Send* button to transmit the message directly to your friend's computer screen.
7. Your message appears in the main part of the message window followed by the reply you receive from your friend. The text of your conversation scrolls in the window as you continue to communicate.

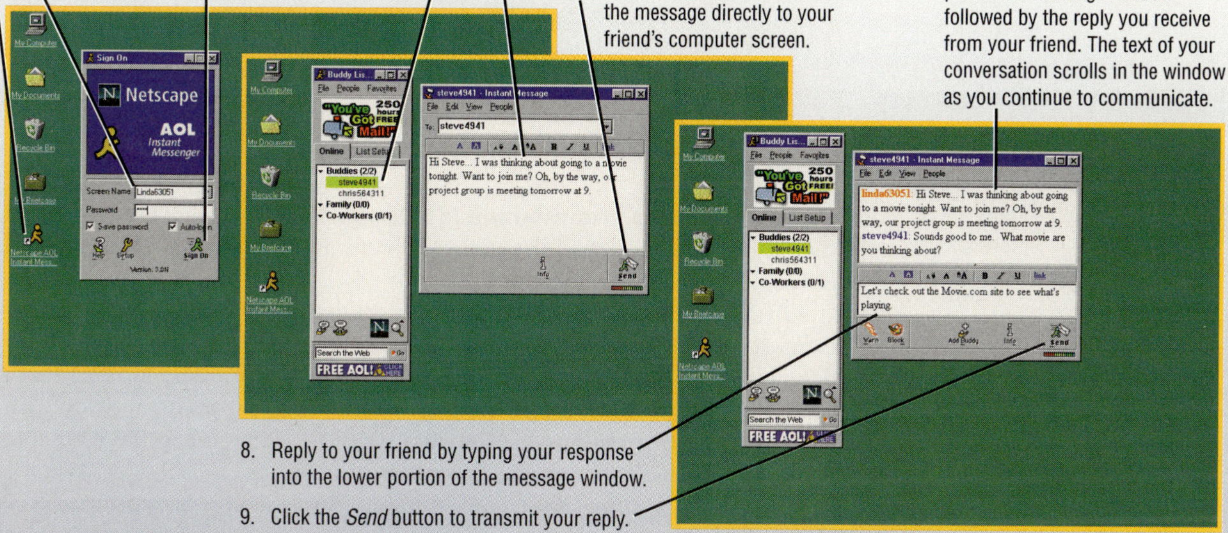

8. Reply to your friend by typing your response into the lower portion of the message window.
9. Click the *Send* button to transmit your reply.

Collaborating with a Group

You can just as easily communicate or collaborate with a group of people. To conduct a virtual group meeting, all group participants must be signed on and one participant acts as the coordinator.

For example, with AOL Instant Messenger, the coordinator begins as follows:

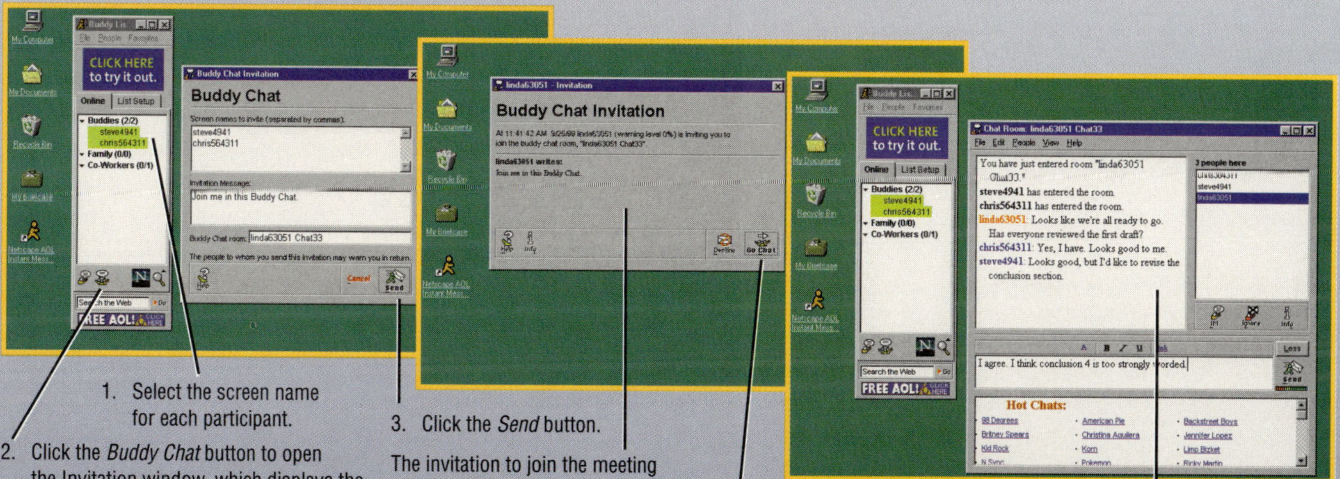

1. Select the screen name for each participant.
2. Click the *Buddy Chat* button to open the Invitation window, which displays the screen name for each participant.
3. Click the *Send* button.

The invitation to join the meeting appears on each invited member's computer screen.

4. Each recipient clicks the *Go Chat* button to join the virtual meeting.

While the meeting is in progress, the message window on each participant's screen displays the text of the conversation of all members.

Most instant messaging servers require that all participants use the same instant messaging software. However, as standards evolve this limitation will likely be overcome.

Term	Description
FAQ	Frequently asked question
Flaming	Insulting, putting down, or attacking
Lurking	Reading news but not joining in to contribute
RFD	Request for discussion
Saint	Someone who aids new users by answering questions
Thread	A sequence of ongoing messages on the same subject
Wizard	Someone who has comprehensive knowledge about a subject

FIGURE 8-12
Selected discussion-group terms

Terms

Before you submit a contribution to a discussion group, it is recommended that you observe or read the communications from others. This is called **lurking.**

By lurking, you can learn about the culture of a discussion group. For example, you can observe the level and style of the discussions. You may decide that a particular discussion group is not what you were looking for—in which case, unsubscribe. If the discussions are appropriate and you wish to participate, try to fit into the prevailing culture. Remember that your contributions will likely be read by hundreds of people.

For a list of some other commonly used discussion group terms, see Figure 8-12.

CONCEPT CHECK

- ✔ Give examples of the types of discussion groups you can find on the Internet.
- ✔ What is the most popular chat service on the Internet?

Electronic Commerce

Web storefronts offer goods and services. Web auctions are like traditional auctions. Electronic payment options include check, credit card, and electronic cash.

Electronic commerce, also known as **e-commerce,** is the buying and selling of goods over the Internet. Have you ever bought anything over the Internet? If you have not, there is a very good chance that you will within the next year or two. Shopping on the Internet is growing rapidly and there seems to be no end in sight. (See Figure 8-13.)

Web Storefronts

Web storefronts are virtual stores where shoppers can go to inspect merchandise and make purchases. (See Figure 8-14.) A new type of program

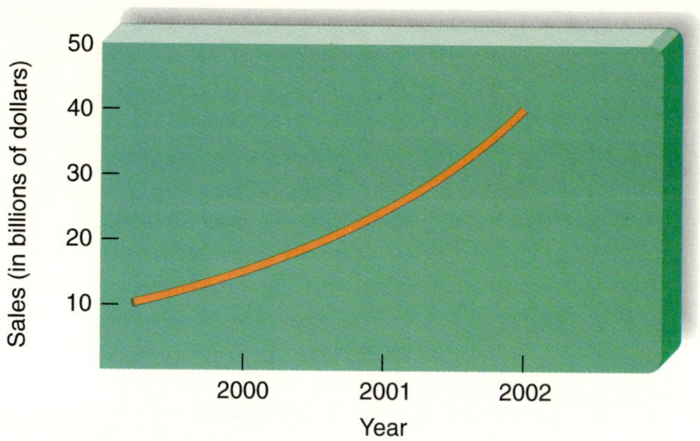

Source: Jupiter Communications

FIGURE 8-13
Online shopping

called **Web storefront creation packages** or **commerce servers** has recently evolved to help businesses create virtual stores. These packages create Web sites that allow visitors to register, browse, place products into virtual shopping carts, and purchase goods and services.

These programs do even more behind the scenes. They calculate taxes and shipping costs, handle a variety of payment options, update and replenish inventory, and ensure reliable and safe communications. Additionally, the storefront sites collect data about visitors and generate reports to evaluate the site's profitability. For a list of some of the most popular Web storefronts, see Figure 8-15.

FIGURE 8-14
Web storefront

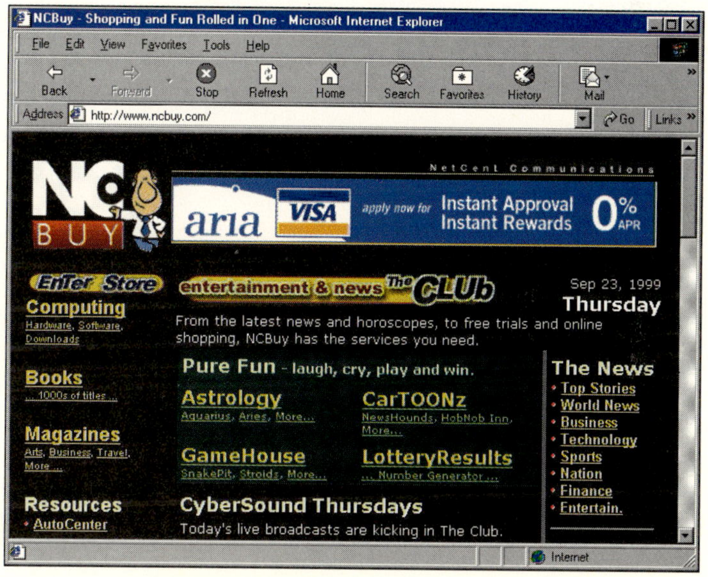

Web Auctions

A recent trend in electronic commerce is the growing popularity of Web auctions. **Web auctions** are similar to traditional auctions except that buyers and sellers seldom, if ever, meet face-to-face. Sellers post descriptions of products at a Web site and buyers submit bids electronically. Like traditional auctions, sometimes the bidding becomes highly competitive and enthusiastic. There are two basic types of Web auction sites:

- **Auction house sites** sell a wide range of merchandise directly to bidders. The auction house owner presents merchandise that is typically from a company's surplus stock. These sites operate like a traditional auction, and bargain prices are not uncommon. Auction house sites are generally considered safe places to shop.
- **Person-person auction sites** operate more like flea markets. The owner of the site provides a forum for numerous buyers and sellers to gather. While the owners of these sites typically facilitate the bidding process, they are not involved in completing transactions or in verifying the authenticity of the goods sold. As with purchases at a flea market, buyers and sellers need to be cautious.

Description	Site
Books	www.amazon.com
Music	www.cdnow.com
Computers and more	www.ncbuy.com
Gifts	www.buy.com
Alaskan products	www.alaskan.com

FIGURE 8-15
Web storefronts

FIGURE 8-16
Electronic payment

Electronic Payment

The single greatest challenge for electronic commerce is the development of fast, secure, and reliable payment methods for purchased goods. (See Figure 8-16.) The three basic payment options are check, credit card, and electronic cash.

- Checks are the most traditional and perhaps the safest. Unfortunately, check purchases require the longest time to complete. After selecting an item, the buyer sends a check through the mail. Upon receipt of the check, the seller verifies that the check is good. If it is good, then the purchased item is sent out.
- Credit card purchases are faster and more convenient than check purchases. Credit card fraud, however, is a major concern for both buyers and sellers. Criminals known as **carders** specialize in stealing, trading, and using stolen credit cards over the Internet.
- **Electronic cash,** or **e-cash,** is the Internet's equivalent to traditional cash. It is also known as **cybercash** and **digital cash**. Buyers purchase e-cash from a third party (a bank that specializes in electronic currency) by transferring funds from their banks. Buyers purchase goods using e-cash. Sellers convert the e-cash to traditional currency through the third party. Although not as convenient as credit card purchases, e-cash is more secure.

CONCEPT CHECK

✔ What is electronic commerce?

✔ What is the single greatest challenge for electronic commerce?

Internet Services

Telnet runs programs on remote computers. FTP transfers files. Gopher provides menus for available resources. The Web provides a multimedia interface to available resources.

There are numerous services available on the Internet. Four commonly used services are Telnet, FTP, Gopher, and the Web. (See Figure 8-17.)

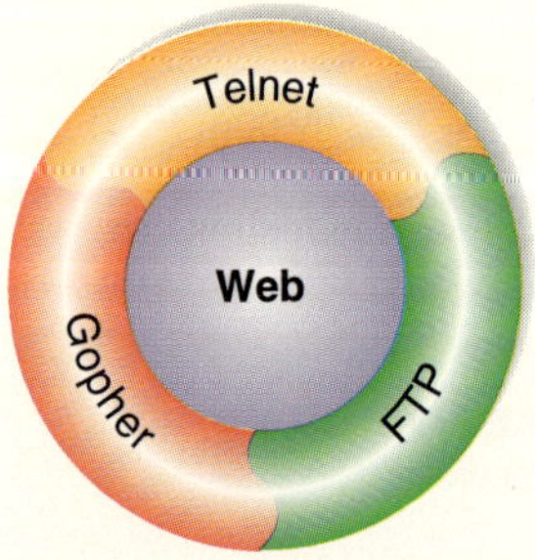

FIGURE 8-17
Available services

Telnet

Many computers on the Internet will allow you to connect to them and to run selected programs on them. **Telnet** is the Internet service that helps you to connect to another computer (host) on the Internet and log on to that computer as if you were on a terminal in the next room. There are hundreds of computers on the Internet that you can connect to. Some allow limited free access, and others charge fees for their use.

FTP

File transfer protocol (FTP) is an Internet service for transferring files. Many computers on the Internet allow you to copy files to your computer. This is called **downloading.** You can also use FTP to copy files from your computer to another computer on the Internet. This is called **uploading.**

Gopher

Gopher is a software application that provides menu-based search and retrieval functions for a particular computer site. It was originally developed at the University of Minnesota in 1991. Internet **Gopher sites** are computers that provide menus describing their available resources and direct links to the resources. Essentially, these menus are a "table of contents" for organizing and locating information. In addition, these sites typically handle transferring of files (FTP) and connecting to other computers (Telnet).

The Web

The Internet service receiving the most attention today is the Web. It is easy to get the Internet and the Web confused, but they are not the same thing. The Internet is the actual physical network. It is made up of wires, cables, and satellites. It connects computers and resources throughout the world. The Web is a multimedia interface to resources available on the Internet.

See Figure 8-18 for a summary of Internet services.

Service	Description
Telnet	Runs programs on remote computers
FTP	Uploads and downloads files
Gopher	Provides menus for available resources for one computer site
Web	Uses a multimedia interface to link to resources located worldwide

FIGURE 8-18
Internet services

CONCEPT CHECK

✔ What are examples of common Internet services?

Browsers

Browsers connect to Web sites using URL addresses. Web portals offer services.

The Web is accessed through your computer using special software known as a **browser.** As we discussed in Chapter 3, this software connects you to remote computers, opens and transfers files, displays text and images, and provides in one tool an uncomplicated interface to the Internet and Web documents. Two well-known browsers are Netscape Navigator and Microsoft Internet Explorer. (See Figure 8-19.)

FIGURE 8-19
Browser: Netscape Communicator

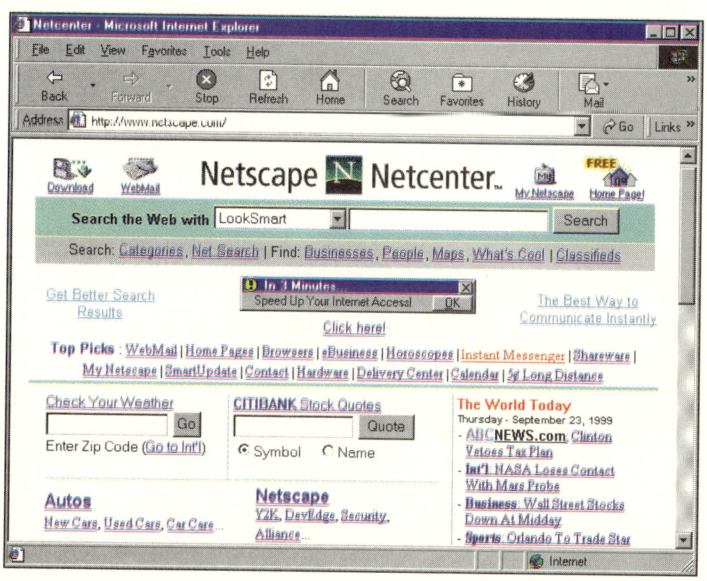

Uniform Resource Locators

For browsers to connect to other resources, the location or address of the resources must be specified. These addresses are called **uniform resource locators (URLs).** (See Figure 8-20.)

All URLs have at least two basic parts. (See Figure 8-21.) The first part presents the protocol used to connect to the resource. The protocol *http://*, is by far the most common. The second part presents the domain name or the name of the server where the resource is located. In Figure 8-21 the server is identified

FIGURE 8-20
URL address

FIGURE 8-21
Two basic parts of a URL

as *www.netscape.com.* (Many URLs have additional parts specifying directory paths, file names, and pointers.)

The URL *http://www.netscape.com* connects your computer to a computer that provides information about Netscape. These informational locations on the Web are called **Web sites.** Moving from one Web site to another is called **surfing.**

Type	Site
Horizontal	www.excite.com
Horizontal portal	www.aol.com
Vertical for sports	www.cbs.sportsline.com
Vertical for news	www.usatoday.com
Vertical for computers	www.zdnet.com

FIGURE 8-22
Popular Web portals

Web Portals

Web portals are sites that offer a variety of services, typically including e-mail, sports updates, financial data, news, and links to selected Web sites. They are designed to encourage you to visit them each time you are on the Web, to act as your home base, and to use as a gateway to their resources. There are two types of portals. **Horizontal portals** are designed to appeal to mass audiences. They offer general-interest services and links. **Vertical portals** present focused content to appeal to special-interest groups. For a list of some popular portals, see Figure 8-22.

CONCEPT CHECK

- ✔ What is a browser?
- ✔ How do browsers locate/connect to other resources?
- ✔ What are Web portals?

Web Pages

Browsers interpret HTML documents to display Web pages.

Once the browser has connected to a Web site, a document file is sent to your computer. This document contains **Hypertext Markup Language (HTML)** commands. The browser interprets the HTML commands and displays the document as a **Web page.** Typically, the first page of a Web site is referred to as its home page. (See Figure 8-23.) The **home page** presents information about the site along with references and **hyperlinks,** or connections to other documents that contain related information—text files, graphic images, audio, and video clips.

These documents may be located on a nearby computer system or on one located halfway around the world. The references appear as underlined and

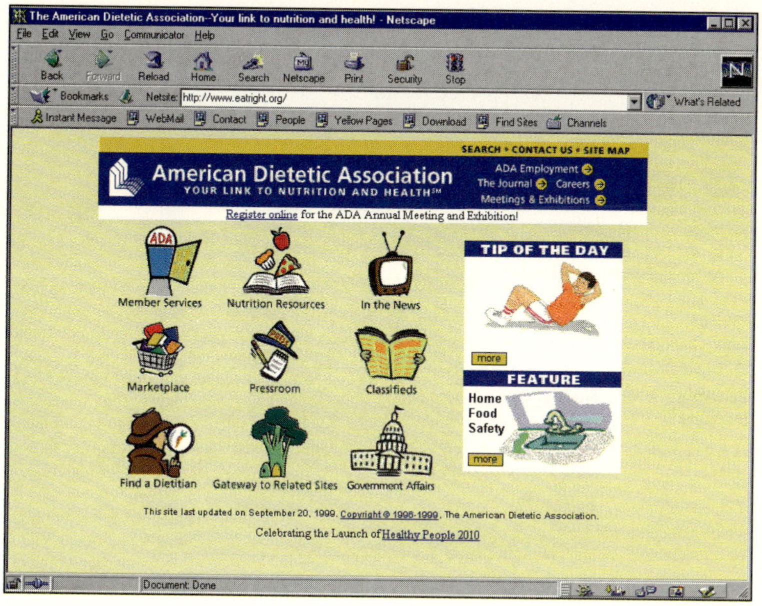

FIGURE 8-23
The American Dietetic Association home page

colored text and/or images on the Web page. To access the referenced material, all you do is click on the highlighted text or image. A link is automatically made to the computer containing the material, and the referenced material appears.

Applets and Java

Web pages can also contain links to special programs, called **applets,** written in a programming language called **Java.** These programs can be quickly downloaded and run by most browsers. Java applets are widely used to add interest and activity to a Web site by presenting animation, displaying graphics, providing interactive games, and much more.

CONCEPT CHECK

- ✔ Browsers interpret _______ documents to display Web pages.
- ✔ What are Java applets?

Search Tools

Indexes are organized by categories. Search engines are organized like a database.

The Web is a massive collection of interrelated Web pages. (See Figure 8-24.) With so much available information, locating the precise information you need can be difficult. Fortunately, a number of **search tools** have been developed and are available to you on certain Web sites. There are basically two types: indexes and search engines.

FIGURE 8-24
Entering the Web

Indexes

Indexes, also known as **Web directories,** are organized by categories such as art, computers, entertainment, news, science, sports, and so on. Each category is further organized into subcategories. Using your browser, you select

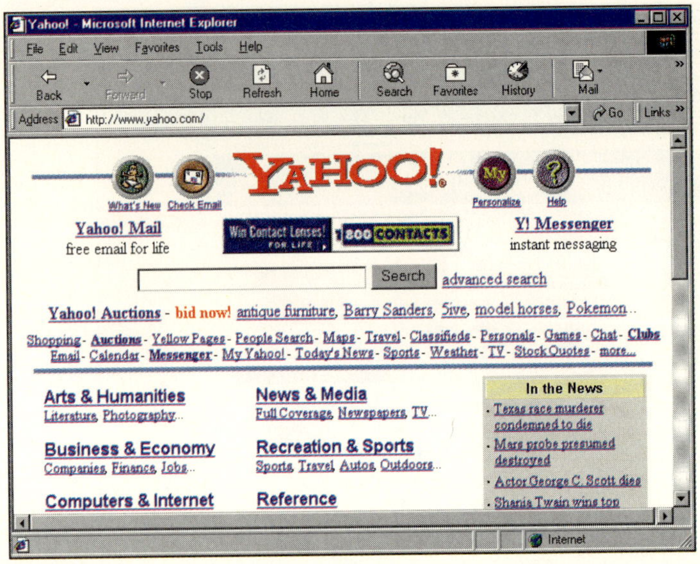

FIGURE 8-25
Index: Yahoo

> **TIPS** Are you going to use a search tool to locate some information? Here are a few tips that might help.
>
> 1. *Start with the right tool.* For general information, use an index like Yahoo. For specific information, use a search engine like Hotbot.
> 2. *Be as precise as possible.* Use specific key words that relate directly to the topic.
> 3. *Use multiple words.* Use quotation marks to identify key words.
> 4. *Use Boolean operators.* Typically, these include words such as "and," "not," "or."
> 5. *Check your spelling.* Misspelling is one of the most common problems.
> 6. *Keep moving.* Look only at the first page of search results. If necessary, try another search using different key words.

a category and continue to select subcategories until your search has been narrowed and a list of relevant documents appears. By selecting a document, you cause the appropriate links to be made and the document appears. One of the best known and most widely used indexes is Yahoo! (See Figure 8-25.)

Search Engines

Search engines are also known as **Web crawlers** and **Web spiders.** Information is not organized by major categories. Rather, search engines are organized like a database, and you search through them by entering key words and phrases. These databases are maintained by special programs called **agents, spiders,** or **bots.** They automatically search for new information on the Web and update the databases. Three widely used search engines are HotBot, WebCrawler, and Alta Vista. (See Figure 8-26).

CONCEPT CHECK

✔ What are some of the search tools available on the Web?

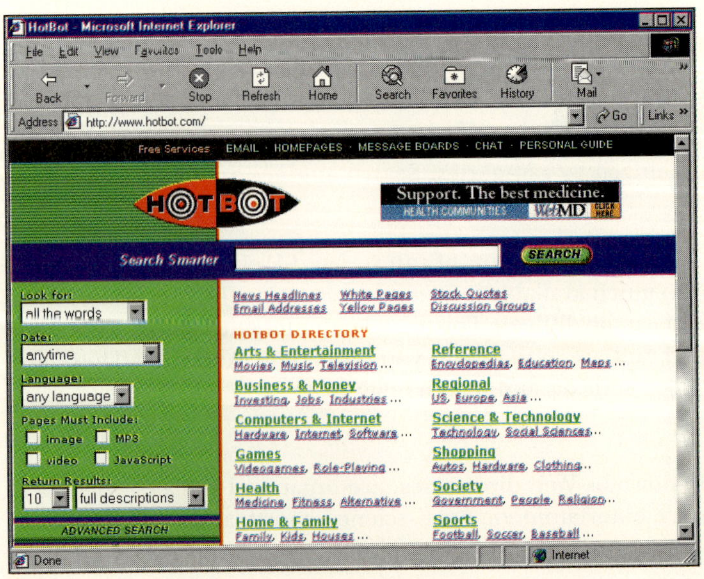

FIGURE 8-26
Search engine: HotBot

Web Utilities

Plug-ins are automatically loaded by your browser. Helper applications are independent programs executed from your browser.

Web utilities are programs that work with a browser to increase your speed, productivity, and capabilities. Many utilities are found in the latest versions of browsers, and others are available free or for a nominal charge. There are two categories of utilities: plug-ins and helper applications.

Plug-ins

Plug-ins are programs that are automatically loaded and operate as a part of your browser. Many Web sites require you to have one or more plug-ins to fully experience their content. Some widely used plug-ins include:

- Shockwave from Macromedia, used for a variety of Web-based games, live concerts, and dynamic animations.
- Quicktime from Apple, required by over 20,000 Web sites to display video and play audio.
- Cosmos from Silicon Graphics, displaying three-dimensional graphics and used in sites displaying virtual reality.

To learn more about plug-ins, visit some of the sites listed in Figure 8-27.

Source	Site
Shockwave	www.macromedia.com
Quicktime	www.quicktime.apple.com
Cosmos Player	www.cosmo.sgi.com

FIGURE 8-27
Plug-in sites

Helper Applications

Also known as **add-ons, helper applications** are independent programs that can be executed or launched from your browser. There are hundreds of helper applications, most of them designed to maximize your efficiency. Four of the most common types are off-line browsers, information pushers, off-line search utilities, and filters.

Off-Line Browsers

In order for a Web page to appear on your screen, its HTML document has to be downloaded from the Web site to your computer and executed. When the Internet is busy and/or the document is large, you spend a fair amount of time waiting. (See Figure 8-28.) Off-line browsers offer a solution.

FIGURE 8-28
Waiting for download

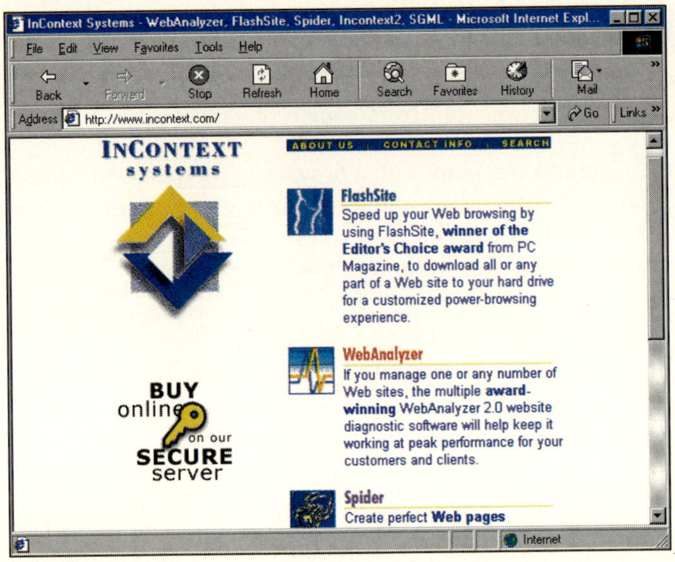

FIGURE 8-29
Off-line browser: InContext FlashSite

Off-line browsers, also known as **Web-downloading utilities** and **pull products,** are programs that automatically connect to selected Web sites, download HTML documents, and save them to your hard disk. You can view the Web pages later without being connected to the Internet and without waiting for documents to be downloaded. Two popular off-line browsers are InContext FlashSite and Teleport Pro. (See Figure 8-29.)

Information Pushers

Imagine a personalized newspaper containing only those articles that interested you the most. That is the basic idea behind information pushers.

You select topic areas known as *channels* that you are interested in. **Information pushers,** which are also known as **Web broadcasters** and **push products,** gather information on your topics and send it to your hard disk, where you can read it whenever you want. Two well-known information pushers are PointCast Network and BackWeb client.

Metasearch Utilities

One way to research a topic is to visit the Web site for several individual indexes and search engines. At each site, the search instructions are entered, and the search begins. After a few moments (or longer, depending on the particular search and the level of activity on the Internet), a list appears. This process can be quite time-consuming, and duplicate responses from the different search tools are inevitable. Metasearch utilities offer a solution.

Metasearch utilities are programs that automatically submit your search request to several indexes and search engines. They receive the results, sort them, eliminate duplicates, and create an index for your review. Three popular metasearch utilities are MetaCrawler, Dogpile, and SavvySearch. (See Figure 8-30.)

TIPS Do your children or little brother or sister use the Internet a lot? While you may want them to be able to take advantage of the educational and entertainment side of the Internet, you also want to protect them from the negative side. To help protect them from viewing inappropriate material, consider the following suggestions:

1. *Locate.* Place the computer in a common area where children can be easily supervised.
2. *Discuss.* Discuss browsing with children to explain what types of content you consider to be appropriate.
3. *Filter.* Use a filter program and/or investigate your browser's filtering capabilities.

Recent versions of Internet Explorer, for example, include a Content Advisor program.

Filters

The Internet is an interesting and multifaceted arena. But one of those facets is a dark and seamy one. Parents, in particular, are concerned

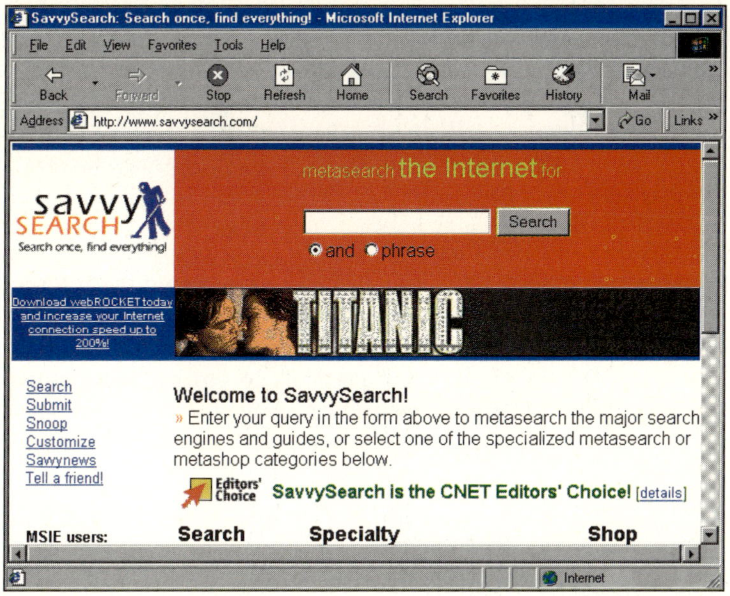

FIGURE 8-30
Metasearch utility: SavvySearch

about children roaming unrestricted across the Internet. **Filter** programs allow parents as well as organizations to block out selected sites and set time limits. Additionally, these programs can monitor use and generate reports detailing the total time spent on the Internet, and time spent at individual Web sites, chat groups, and newsgroups. Three well-known filters are Cyber Patrol, Cybersitter, and Net Nanny.

To learn more about helper applications, explore some of the sites presented in Figure 8-31.

CONCEPT CHECK

- ✔ What are Web utilities?
- ✔ What are the two categories of utilities?

Type	Source	Site
Off-line browsers	Incontext FlashSite	www.incontext.com
	Teleport Pro	www.tenmax.com
Information pushers	Entry Point	www.entrypoint.com
	BackWeb Client	www.backweb.com
Metasearch utilities	MetaCrawler	www.metacrawler.com
	Dogpile	www.dogpile.com
Filters	Cyber Patrol	www.cyberpatrol.com
	Cybersitter	www.cybersitter.com

FIGURE 8-31
Helper application sites

Organizational Internets: Intranets and Extranets

Intranets are private networks within an organization. Extranets are private networks connecting organizations. Firewalls use proxy servers to provide security.

Nearly every organization today uses the Internet to promote its products and to service its customers. These organizations have found the Internet and the Web to be powerful yet very easy to use tools for reaching the public. They have also found that they can apply Internet technologies within their organizations to connect their own employees and to connect to other organizations. (See Figure 8-32.) These networks are called intranets and extranets.

FIGURE 8-32
Connecting people and organizations

Intranets

An **intranet** is a *private* network within an organization that resembles the Internet. Like the *public* Internet, intranets use browsers, Web sites, and Web pages. Intranets typically provide e-mail, mailing lists, newsgroups, and FTP services accessible only to those within the organization.

Organizations use intranets to provide information to their employees. Typical applications include electronic telephone directories, e-mail addresses, employee benefit information, internal job openings, and much more. Employees find surfing their organizational intranets to be as easy and as intuitive as surfing the Internet.

Extranets

An **extranet** is a *private* network that connects *more than one* organization. Many organizations use Internet technologies to allow suppliers and others limited access to their networks. The purpose is to increase efficiency and reduce costs. For example, General Motors has thousands of suppliers for the parts that go into making an automobile. By having access to the production schedules, suppliers can schedule and deliver parts as they are needed at the General Motors assembly plants. In this way, General Motors can be assured of having adequate parts without maintaining large inventories.

Firewalls

Organizations have to be very careful to protect their information systems. A **firewall** is a security system designed to protect an organization's network against external threats. It consists of hardware and software that control access to a company's intranet or other internal networks.

Typically a firewall includes a special computer called a **proxy server.** This computer is a gatekeeper. All communications between the company's internal networks and the outside world must pass through it. By evaluating the source and the content of each communication, the proxy server decides whether it is safe to let a particular message or file pass into or out of the organization's network. (See Figure 8-33.)

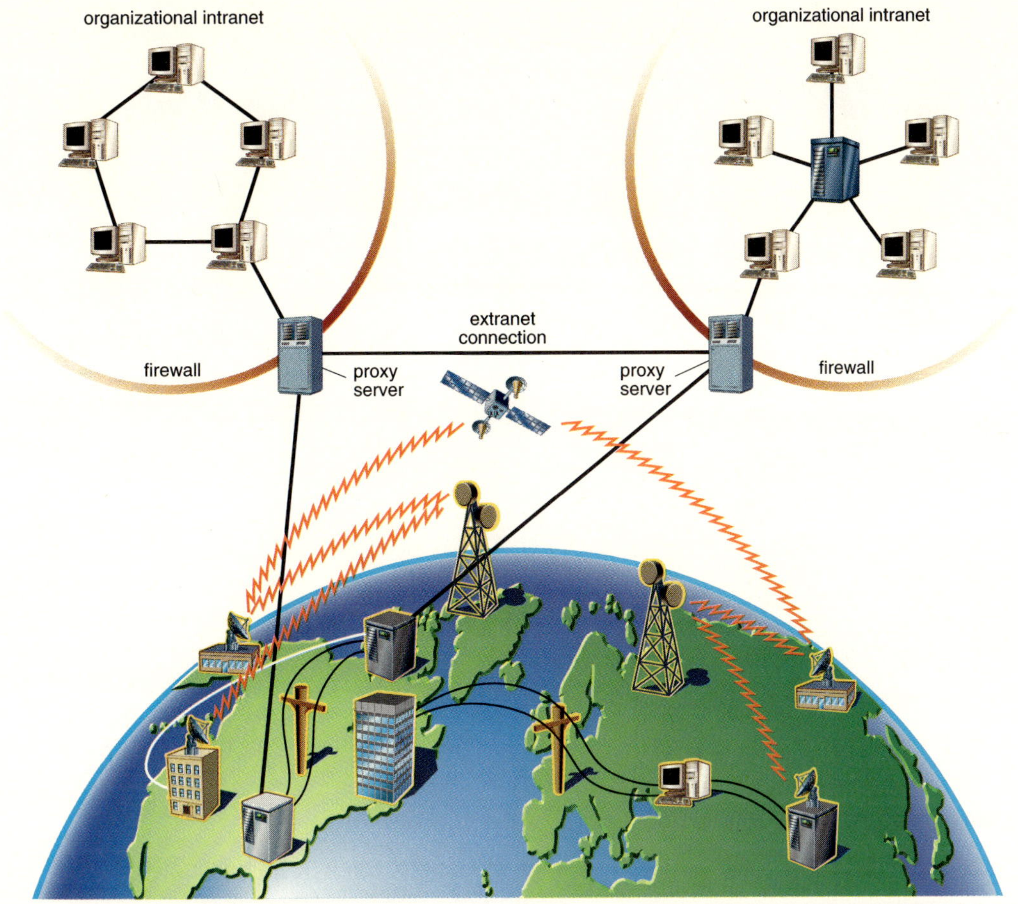

FIGURE 8-33
Intranets, extranets, firewalls, and proxy servers

A LOOK TO THE FUTURE

Internet2 will be a private high-performance Internet.

Have you ever been unable to connect to the Internet? Have you ever had a long wait before a Web page or a graphic appeared on your screen? Almost all of us have experienced busy servers and slow access. Unfortunately, Internet service is expected to get worse. For organizations that depend on the Internet to reach customers and conduct other business activities, this trend is very concerning.

To address this concern, a separate, private Internet called Internet2 is being developed. It will be a high-speed network capable of dazzling feats that far exceed today's Internet capabilities. Expected to be fully operational by 2002, Internet2 will have limited access to those willing to pay more to get more. Access to today's Internet will remain public and available for a nominal fee.

The primary beneficiaries of Internet2 will be federal agencies and major corporations. Each will pay an annual fee of $500,000 for access to this network that combines high performance with tightly controlled security. One of the first to take advantage of Internet2 will be online publishers of books, photographs, and original artwork. Advanced virtual reality interfaces, called **nanomanipulators,** are expected to be available. Researchers from different parts of the world will be able to share devices such as atomic microscopes and to jointly study, experience, and move within realistic virtual subatomic environments.

Will moving power users to Internet2 increase the performance of the public Internet? We will have to wait and see.

VISUAL SUMMARY The Internet and the Web

INTERNET APPLICATIONS

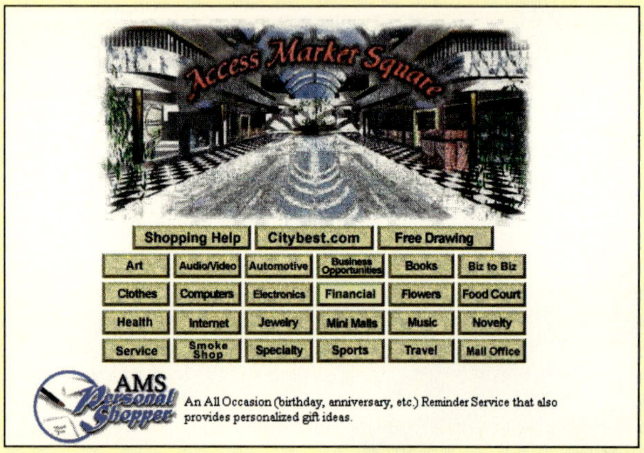

The most common Internet applications are **communicating, shopping, researching,** and **entertainment.**

ACCESS

Once connected to the Internet, your computer seemingly becomes an extension of a giant computer that branches all over the world.

Providers

The most common access is through a **provider** or **host computer.** Three widely used providers are:

- **Colleges and universities**—often offer free Internet access through their LANs.
- **Internet service providers (ISPs)**—offer access for a fee.
- **Online service providers**—offer access and a variety of other services for a fee.

Connections

To access the Internet, you need to connect to a provider. Three types of connections are **direct (dedicated), SLIP** and **PPP,** and **terminal.**

TCP/IP

TCP/IP is the standard **protocol** of the Internet.

E-MAIL

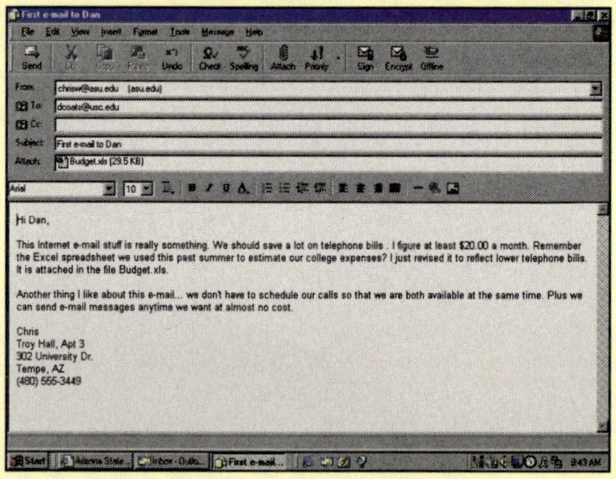

Sending and receiving **e-mail** is the most common Internet activity.

Basic Elements

E-mail messages have three basic elements:

- **Subject**—one line description.
- **Addresses**—sender, receiver, and anyone else receiving copies.
- **Attachments**—files.

Addresses

The Internet uses the **domain name system (DNS)** for e-mail. The first part is the **user name,** followed by the **domain name,** and then the **domain code.**

DISCUSSION GROUPS

Discussion groups support electronic communication between individuals. Four types exist:

- **Mailing lists** use e-mail **subscription** and **list addresses.**
- **Newsgroups** are organized by major topic areas and use the **UseNet** network.
- **Chat groups** allow direct "live" communication.
- **Instant messaging** is for communicating and collaborating.

To be a competent end user you need to be aware of the basic Internet applications, to be able to access resources, to effectively communicate electronically, to understand electronic commerce, and to efficiently use Web browsers, pages, search tools, and utilities. Also, competent end users need to be aware of organizational intranets and extranets.

ELECTRONIC COMMERCE

Electronic commerce, or **e-commerce**, is the buying and selling of goods over the Internet.

Web Storefronts

Web storefronts are virtual stores for viewing and selecting goods. **Web storefront creation packages** or **commerce servers** are specialized packages for creating virtual stores.

Web Auctions

Web auctions are similar to traditional auction except that buyers and seller rarely meet face-to-face. Two basic types are **auction house sites** and **person-to-person sites.**

Electronic Payment

Three basic payment options are check, credit card, and **electronic cash (e-cash).**

SERVICES

There are four basic types of Internet services: **Telnet, FTP, Gopher,** and the **Web.**

Telnet	Runs programs on remote computers
FTP	Uploads and downloads files
Gopher	Provides menus for available resources for one computer site
Web	Uses a multimedia interface to link to resources located worldwide

BROWSERS

Browsers are programs used to access the Web and provide other Internet services.

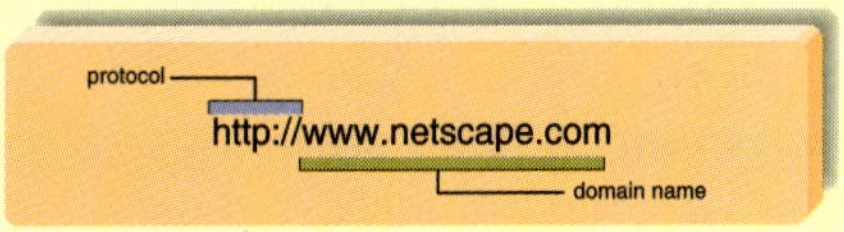

Uniform Resource Locators

Uniform Resource Locators (URLs) are addresses of Web resources. The first part is the **protocol,** followed by the **domain name.** Moving from one site to another is called **surfing.**

Web Portals

Web portals are sites that provide a variety of services. **Horizontal portals** appeal to mass audiences. **Vertical portals** appeal to special interest groups.

WEB PAGES

Web pages are created in **HTML**. The first page at a Web site is its **home page. Hyperlinks** are connections to related sites and documents.

Applets and Java

Java is a programming language for creating special programs called **applets**.

SEARCH TOOLS

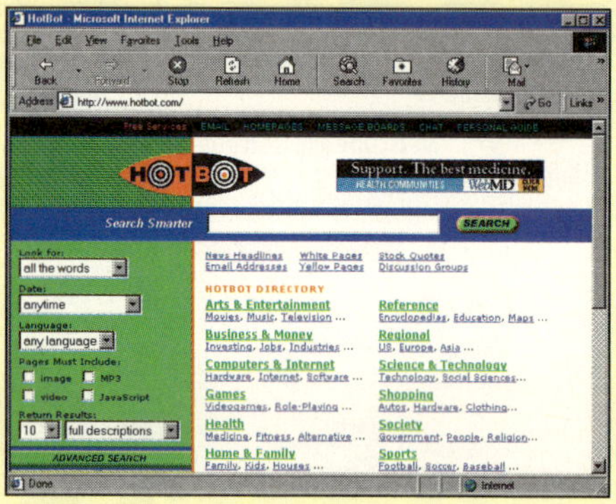

Search tools are used to locate information on the Web. There are two basic types:

- **Indexes (Web directories)** are organized by categories.
- **Search engines (Web crawlers** and **Web spiders)** are organized like a database.

WEB UTILITIES

Web utilities are programs that increase the performance of browsers. Two categories are: *plug-ins* and *helper applications.*

Plug-ins

Plug-ins are automatically loaded with the browser and are designed to better experience a Web site's contents.

Helper Applications

Helper applications (add-ons) are independent applications that can be launched from the browser.

Four types of helper applications exist: **off-line browsers, information pushers, metasearch programs,** and **filters.**

ORGANIZATIONAL INTERNETS

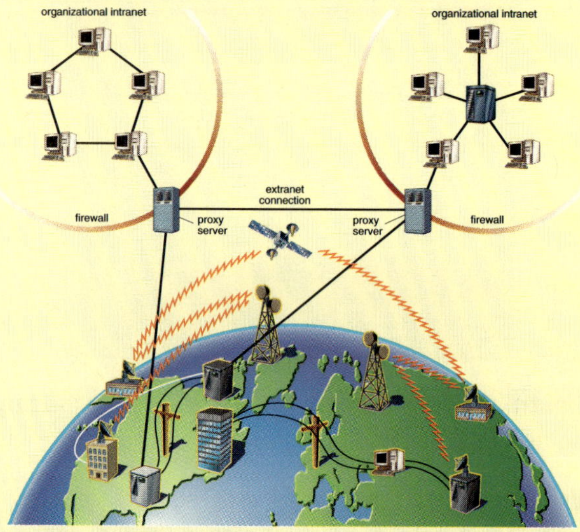

Many **organizations** use Internet technologies in their private networks. These include *Intranets, extranets,* and *firewalls.*

Intranets

Intranets are *private* networks within an organization that resemble the Internet. They use browsers, Web sites, and Web pages that are available only to those within the organization.

Extranets

Extranets are similar to intranets, except that extranets connect more than one organization. Extranets are often used to connect suppliers and producers.

Firewalls

A **firewall** is a security system to protect against external threats. It consists of both hardware and software. All communications into and out of an organization pass through a special security computer called a **proxy server**.

Key Terms

add-on (191)
Advanced Research Project Agency Network (ARPANET) (173)
agents (190)
applets (189)
auction house sites (185)
bots (190)
browser (187)
carders (186)
Center for European Nuclear Research (CERN) (173)
channel (181)
chat groups (181)
commerce servers (185)
cybercash (186)
cyberspace (172)
digital cash (186)
domain code (179)
domain name (179)
domain name system (179)
downloading (187)
e-cash (186)
e-commerce (184)
electronic cash (186)
electronic commerce (184)
extranet (194)
file transfer protocol (FTP) (186)
filter (193)
firewall (194)
Gopher (187)
Gopher site (187)
header (178)
helper application (191)
home page (188)
horizontal portal (188)
host computer (175)
hyperlinks (188)
Hypertext Markup Language (HTML) (188)
Internet Relay Chat (IRC) (181)
indexes (189)
information pusher (192)
instant messaging (182)
Internet service provider (ISP) (175)
intranet (194)
Java (189)
list address (180)
lurking (184)
mailing list (180)
message (179)
metasearch utility (192)
nanomanipulator (195)
newsgroup (181)
off-line browser (192)
online service provider (176)
packet (177)
person-to-person auction site (185)
plug-in (191)
point-to-point protocol (PPP) (177)
proxy server (194)
provider (175)
pull product (192)
push product (192)
search engines (190)
search tools (189)
serial line Internet protocol (SLIP) (177)
signature line (179)
spider (190)
subscription address (180)
surfing (188)
Telnet (186)
terminal connection (177)
transmission control protocol/Internet protocol (TCP/IP) (178)
uniform resource locator (URL) (187)
uploading (187)
UseNet (181)
user name (180)
vertical portal (188)
Web (173)
Web auction (185)
Web broadcaster (192)
Web crawler (190)
Web directory (189)
Web-downloading utility (192)
Web page (188)
Web portal (188)
Web site (188)
Web spiders (190)
Web storefront (184)
Web storefront creation package (185)
World Wide Web (173)
WWW (173)

Chapter Review

LEVEL 1

Reviewing Facts and Terms

Matching

Match each numbered item with the most closely related lettered item. Write your answers in the spaces provided.

1. The space of electronic movement of ideas and information. ____
2. The standard protocol for the Internet. ____
3. Security system designed to protect an organization's network against external threats. ____
4. Special software used by your computer to access the Web. ____
5. Identifies a unique person or computer at the listed domain. ____
6. Programs that are automatically uploaded and operate as part of your browser to view certain Web content. ____
7. Informational locations on the Web. ____
8. Addressing method used by the Internet to assign names and numbers to people and computers. ____
9. Copying files from your computer to another computer on the Internet. ____
10. Widely used Internet programs that add interest and activity to a Web site by presenting animation, displaying graphics, providing interactive games, and more. ____
11. The buying and selling of goods over the Internet. ____
12. The type of commands interpreted by a browser to display Web pages. ____
13. Programming language used to create applets. ____
14. Internet service that helps you connect to another computer (host) on the Internet and log on to that computer. ____
15. A private network within an organization that resembles the Internet. ____
16. One type of discussion group available on the Internet. ____
17. Connections to other documents that contain related information. ____
18. The small parts a message is broken into before it is sent over the Internet. ____
19. Organized like a database, you search through them by entering key words and phrases. ____
20. All communications between a company's internal networks and the outside world must pass through this special gatekeeping computer. ____

a. Applets
b. Browser
c. Cyberspace
d. DNS
e. E-commerce
f. Firewall
g. HTML
h. Hyperlinks
i. Intranet
j. Java
k. Mailing list
l. Packets
m. Plug-in
n. Proxy server
o. Search engine
p. TCP/IP
q. Telnet
r. Uploading
s. User name
t. Web site

True/False

In the spaces provided, write T or F to indicate whether the statement is true or false.

1. The Internet is a huge network that connects computers worldwide. ____
2. Newsgroups use a special network of computers called the NewsNet. ____
3. URLs are used to route e-mail. ____
4. Spiders are special programs that automatically search for new information on the Web. ____
5. Intranet, extranet, and Internet all mean the same thing. ____

Multiple Choice

Circle the letter of the correct answer.

1. If you wanted to window-shop on the Internet, you would visit a:
   - **a.** chat group
   - **b.** discussion group
   - **c.** Telnet
   - **d.** cybermall
   - **e.** FTP
2. In an e-mail message, the __________ provides a brief description of the message.
   - **a.** subject
   - **b.** closing
   - **c.** signature
   - **d.** message
   - **e.** attachment
3. The most popular chat service is:
   - **a.** Talk Today
   - **b.** Internet Relay Chat
   - **c.** browser
   - **d.** Yahoo!
   - **e.** Internet Explorer
4. The Web is accessed using a:
   - **a.** browser
   - **b.** newsgroup
   - **c.** WAIS
   - **d.** filter
   - **e.** search tool
5. Yahoo! is a(n):
   - **a.** information pusher
   - **b.** browser
   - **c.** chat group
   - **d.** home page
   - **e.** search tool

Completion

Complete each statement in the spaces provided.

1. __________ is the electronic movement of ideas and information.
2. SLIP and __________ connections are widely used to access the Internet.
3. The three parts of an Internet address are user name, domain name, and __________.
4. Off-line search utilities, information pushers, off-line browsers, and filters are __________ __________.
5. __________ is an Internet service that runs programs on remote computers.

Reviewing Concepts

LEVEL 2

Open-Ended

On a separate sheet of paper, respond to each question and statement.

1. Discuss four frequently used Internet services.
2. Describe how addresses are assigned under the domain name system.
3. What are the two types of Internet search tools? How do they differ?
4. Describe some typical Web utilities and how they can help you.
5. Discuss the similarities and differences between intranets and extranets.

Concept Mapping

On a separate sheet of paper, draw a concept map or a flowchart showing how the following terms are related. Show all relationships. Include any additional terms you can think of.

applets	FTP	plug-ins
browsers	host computer	TCP/IP
chat groups	HTML	Telnet
cyberspace	hyperlinks	uploading/downloading
e-mail	intranets	Web site
end user	ISP	World Wide Web
firewall	mailing lists	

Critical Thinking Questions and Projects

LEVEL 3

Read each exercise and answer the related questions on a separate sheet of paper.

1. *Going on an Internet scavenger hunt*: Use the Internet to find information about the following topics. (Record the URLs where you found the information, and write a short description of your findings.)
   - **a.** Hotels in London
   - **b.** Cast members for one of your favorite television programs
   - **c.** MTV's news for this week
   - **d.** Employment opportunities in a career of your choice
   - **e.** Painting known as the *Mona Lisa*
   - **f.** The weather conditions for your city (or the nearest large city)
2. *Ethics and privacy*: While visiting a Web site, it is not uncommon for the site to be collecting information about you. This information is saved in a file that is typically stored on your hard disk to be retrieved and used again the next time you visit that Web site. What type of information do you think is being collected? Why do you suppose it is being collected? Do you think the site has an ethical obligation to inform visitors that it is collecting information? Is there an ethical obligation to inform visitors before using their computer resources? Do you see this activity as an invasion of your privacy? Why or why not?
3. *Privacy and security*: Some who cite the right to free speech and personal privacy argue that the Internet should be totally unencumbered and uncensored by government restrictions and legislation. Do you agree with this position? Do you think religious groups should be allowed to distribute information over the Internet? What about doomsday cult groups? Do you think vendors of pornographic materials should be allowed to use the Internet? What about child pornography? If you think some regulation is required, who should determine what and how restrictions are to be imposed and enforced?

On the Web Exercises

1. Off-Line Browsing

Off-line browsing offers a great promise of increased productivity. What could be better than to have your computer searching the Web for you while you sleep? To learn more about off-line browsing, visit our site at http://www.mhhe.com/cit/concepts/oleary2000-2001/webex8.html to link a site that specializes in off-line browsing. Once connected, explore and learn more about off-line browsing. Print out the most informative Web page you find and write a brief paragraph summarizing the pros and cons of off-line browsing.

2. E-Cash

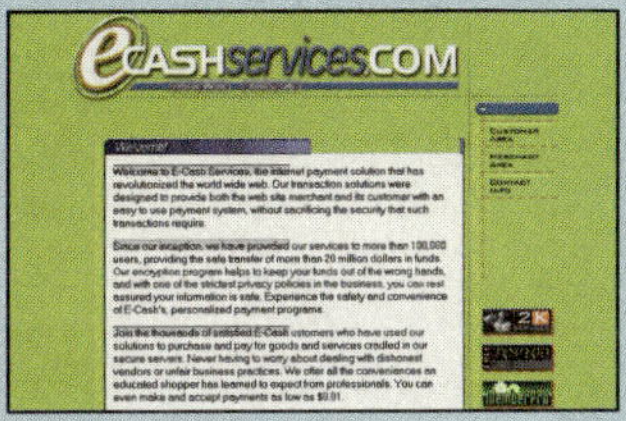

Several companies, including CyberCash and DigiCash, are working on different variations of e-cash. Visit our site at http://www.mhhe.com/cit/concepts/oleary2000-2001/webex8.html to link to a site that specializes in e-cash. Once connected, explore and learn more about e-cash and its alternatives. Print out the most informative Web page you find and write a brief paragraph describing how e-cash works.

3. Searching

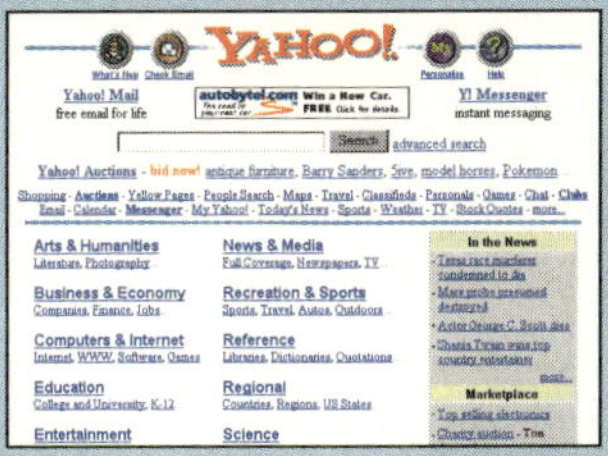

Finding relevant information quickly on the Web can be both rewarding and frustrating. Each search tool is a unique resource. Knowing which search tool to use and how to use it can save you a lot of time. To learn more about the different search tools and search techniques, visit the Yahoo site at http://www.yahoo.com and look at the subject area "Computers and Internet: Internet: Searching the Net: World Wide Web." Explore and learn more about different search tools and search techniques. Print out the Web page you find the most informative, and write a brief paragraph describing what you learned.

4. Adventure Tours

Travel to exotic places around the world without ever leaving home. To do this, visit our site at http://www.mhhe.com/cit/concepts/oleary2000-2001/webex8.html to link to a site specializing in exotic virtual travel. Once connected to the site, explore and learn more about adventure tours. Print out the Web page you find the most informative, and write a brief paragraph describing a virtual tour and discuss what you think the future is for this type of activity.

CHAPTER 9

Multimedia, Web Authoring, and More

COMPETENCIES

After you have read this chapter, you should be able to:

1. **Describe multimedia, including story boards and authoring programs.**
2. **Explain Web authoring, Web site design, and Web authoring programs.**
3. **Describe desktop publishing, image editors, and illustration programs.**
4. **Define virtual reality, VRML, and V-R authoring programs.**
5. **Discuss artificial intelligence: robotics and knowledge-based systems.**
6. **Define project management, Gantt charts, and PERT charts.**

Expect surprises—exciting ones, positive ones. This is the view to take in achieving computer competency. If at first the surprises worry you, that's normal. Most people wonder how well they can handle something new. But the latest technological developments also offer you new opportunities to vastly extend your range. As we show in this chapter, software that for years was available only for mainframes has recently become available for microcomputers. Here's a chance to join the competent computer users of tomorrow.

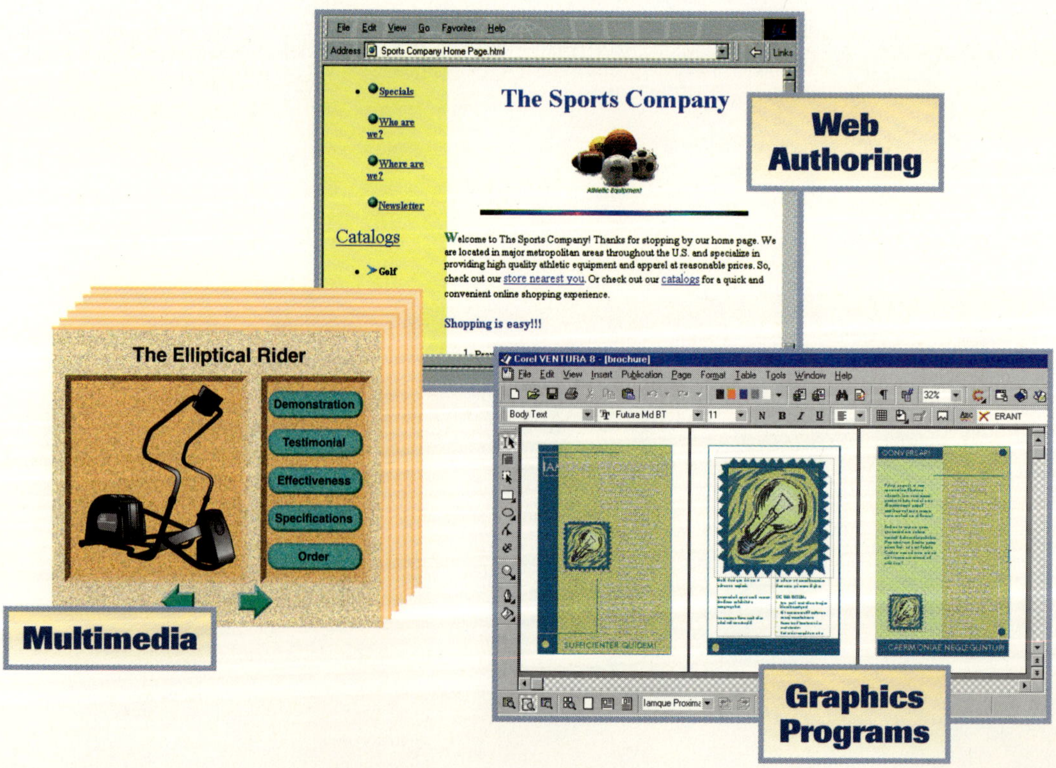

Specialized applications: This is the characterization we have given to a whole new generation of software only recently available for microcomputers. Is there really a need to know anything about these new developments? There is if you want to be like those professionals in every area who are at the forefront of their disciplines. They are there because they have found more efficient ways to use their time and talents. You owe it to yourself, therefore, to at least be aware of what this software and hardware can do.

Competent end users need to be aware of specialized applications. They need to know who uses them, what they are used for, and how they are used. These advanced applications include multimedia, Web authoring, graphics programs, virtual reality, artificial intelligence, and project managers.

Aritificial Intelligence

Virtual Reality

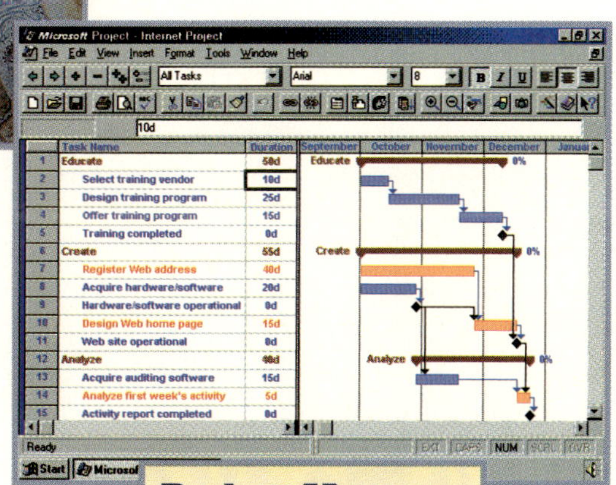

Project Manager

Multimedia

Multimedia integrates all kinds of information. Pages are linked by buttons. Story boards show logic, flow, and structure. Authoring programs create presentations.

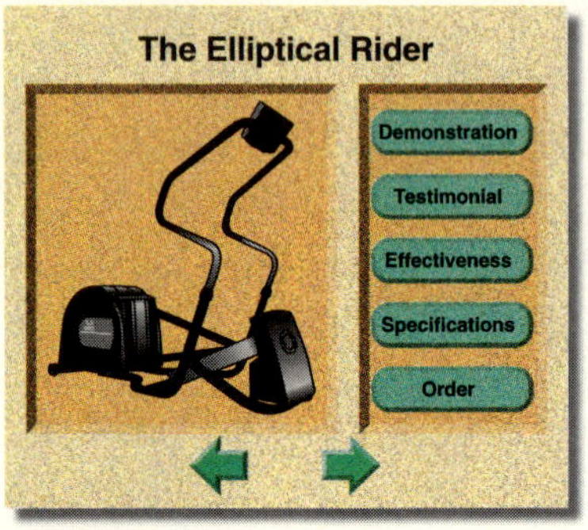

FIGURE 9-1
Opening page of a multimedia presentation

Multimedia, also called **hypermedia,** is the integration of all sorts of media into one presentation. These media may include video, music, voice, graphics, and text. An essential and unique feature of multimedia is user participation, or **interactivity.** When experiencing a multimedia presentation, users typically can control the flow and content by selecting options that customize the presentation to their needs. (See Figure 9-1.)

Once used almost exclusively for computer games, multimedia is now widely used in business, education, and the home. Business uses include high-quality interactive presentations, product demonstrations, and Web page design. In education, multimedia is used for in-class presentation as well as individual study. In the home, multimedia is primarily used for entertainment. In the very near future, however, higher-end multimedia applications such as interactive home shopping are expected to be commonplace.

Links and Buttons

A multimedia presentation is typically organized as a series of related pages. Each page presents information and provides **links** or connections to related information. These links can be to video, sound, graphics, and text files, to other pages, and to other resources.

By clicking special areas called **buttons** on a page, you can make appropriate links and "navigate" through a presentation to locate and discover information. Typically, there are several buttons on a page. You can select one, some, or none of them. You are in control. You direct the flow and content of the presentation.

ON THE WEB EXPLORATIONS

Macromedia Inc. is one of the leaders in the development of multimedia authoring programs. To learn more about the company, visit its web site at **http://www.macromedia.com**

Story Boards

Story boards are used in the early planning phase of a multimedia project. They are a design tool used to record the intended overall logic, flow, and structure of a multimedia presentation. (See Figure 9-2.) Individual story

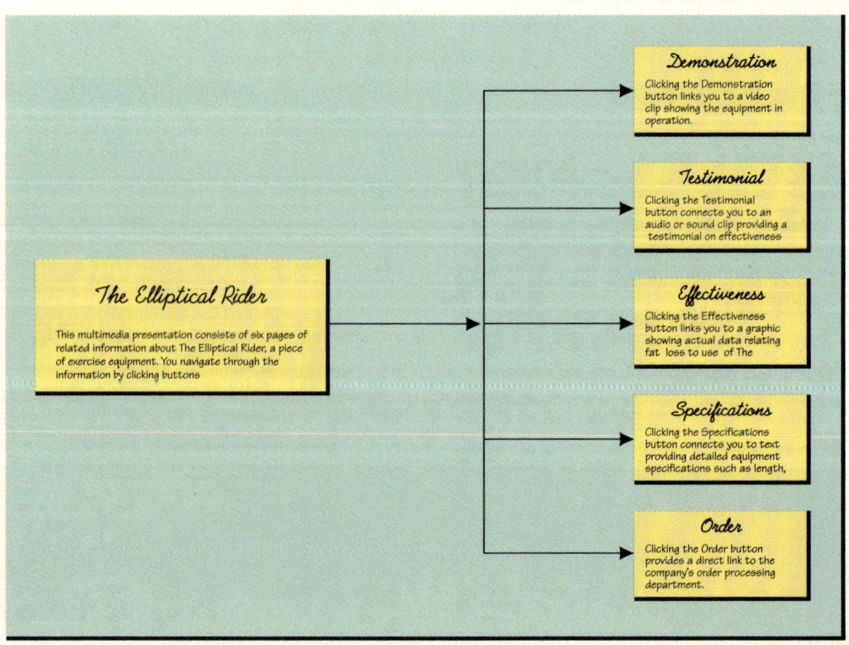

FIGURE 9-2
Partial story board for multimedia project

boards specify the content, style, and design of each display along with the links to video, audio, graphics, text, or any other media.

Multimedia Authoring Programs

Multimedia authoring programs are special programs used to create multimedia presentations. They bring together all the video, audio, graphics, and text elements into an interactive framework. Widely used authoring programs include Macromedia Director, Authorware, and Toolbook.

To learn more about multimedia applications, study Figure 9-3.

TIPS Do you think you might ever be involved with creating a multimedia presentation? Here are a few suggestions:

1. *Design.* Use story boards to graphically represent flow, style, and content. Large projects use design teams consisting of a content expert, a multimedia specialist, and a multimedia programmer.
2. *Produce.* Create and integrate media using a multimedia authoring program. Commands or scripts link and control the various types of media.
3. *Distribute.* Use CDs or DVD-ROMs to distribute completed presentation.

CONCEPT CHECK

- ✔ What is meant by the term *multimedia?*
- ✔ Name an essential and unique feature of multimedia.

FIGURE 9-3
How multimedia presentations work

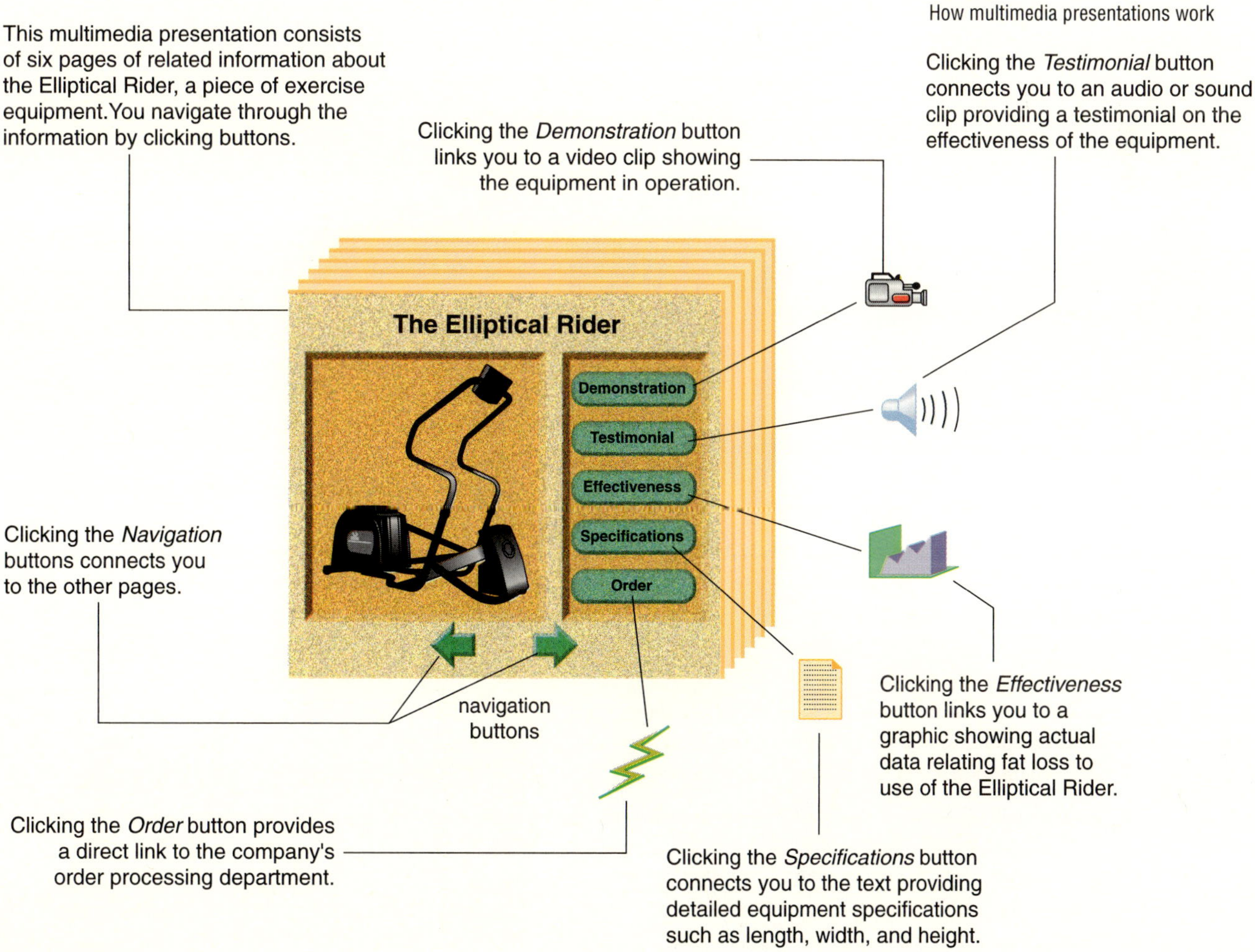

Web Authoring

Creating Web sites is called Web authoring. Graphical maps present overall site design. Web authoring programs support design and HTML coding.

You cannot watch TV or read a magazine without coming across a reference to a site or location on the Web. There are over half a million commercial Web sites on the Internet, and hundreds more being added every day. Corporations use the Web to reach new customers and to promote their products. Individuals can even create their own personal sites on the Web. Have you ever wondered how these sites are created or ever thought of creating your own Web site? Creating a site is called **Web authoring.** It begins with Web site design followed by creation of a document file that displays the Web site's content. (See Figure 9-4.)

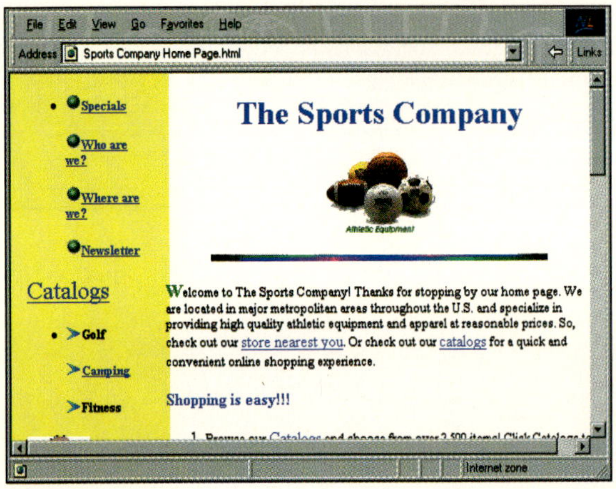

FIGURE 9-4
Web page

Web Site Design

A Web site is an interactive multimedia form of communication. Designing a Web site begins with determining the site's overall content. The content is then broken down into a series of related pieces of information. The overall site design is commonly represented in a **graphical map.** Blocks in the map represent the pieces of information. Lines joining the blocks represent the relationships between the blocks or pieces of information.

The Web site's home page or opening page serves as a table of contents. The following pages present the specific pieces or blocks of information. Links connect related blocks or pages of information. Multimedia elements including sound, video, and animation are added to individual pages to enhance interest and interactivity.

Web Authoring Programs

As we mentioned earlier, Web pages are displayed using HTML documents. With knowledge of HTML and a simple text editor, you can create Web pages. Even without knowledge of HTML you can create Web pages using one of many word processing packages.

More specialized and powerful programs, called **Web authoring programs,** are typically used to create sophisticated commercial sites. Also known as **Web page editors** and **HTML editors,** these programs provide support for Web site design and HTML coding. Widely used Web authoring programs include Adobe PageMill, Corel WebSite Builder, and Microsoft FrontPage.

To learn more about FrontPage and Web authoring, study Figure 9-5.

TIPS Are you thinking about creating your own Web page? Perhaps you already have one and would like to spruce it up a bit? Here are a few suggestions that might help.

1. *Use a common design and theme.* Consistency in the use of colors, fonts, background designs, and navigation features gives a Web site a unified feeling and makes it easier to use.
2. *Use graphics and animations to add interest.* Graphics and animations add interest and focus the user's attention. However, they take time to download and the wait time frustrates users. Be selective and limit the size of graphics. Also reuse graphics from one page to another.
3. *Make navigating your Web site easy.* Create a simple method of navigating that allows users to get to their desired information as quickly as possible. None of your content should be more than three clicks from the home page.
4. *Design your page to fit on a standard 800 × 600 display.* To maximize the impact of your site for the largest number of users, design it to be viewed by a monitor with a standard 800 × 600 resolution.

CONCEPT CHECK

- ✔ What steps are involved in Web authoring?
- ✔ What is a Web site?

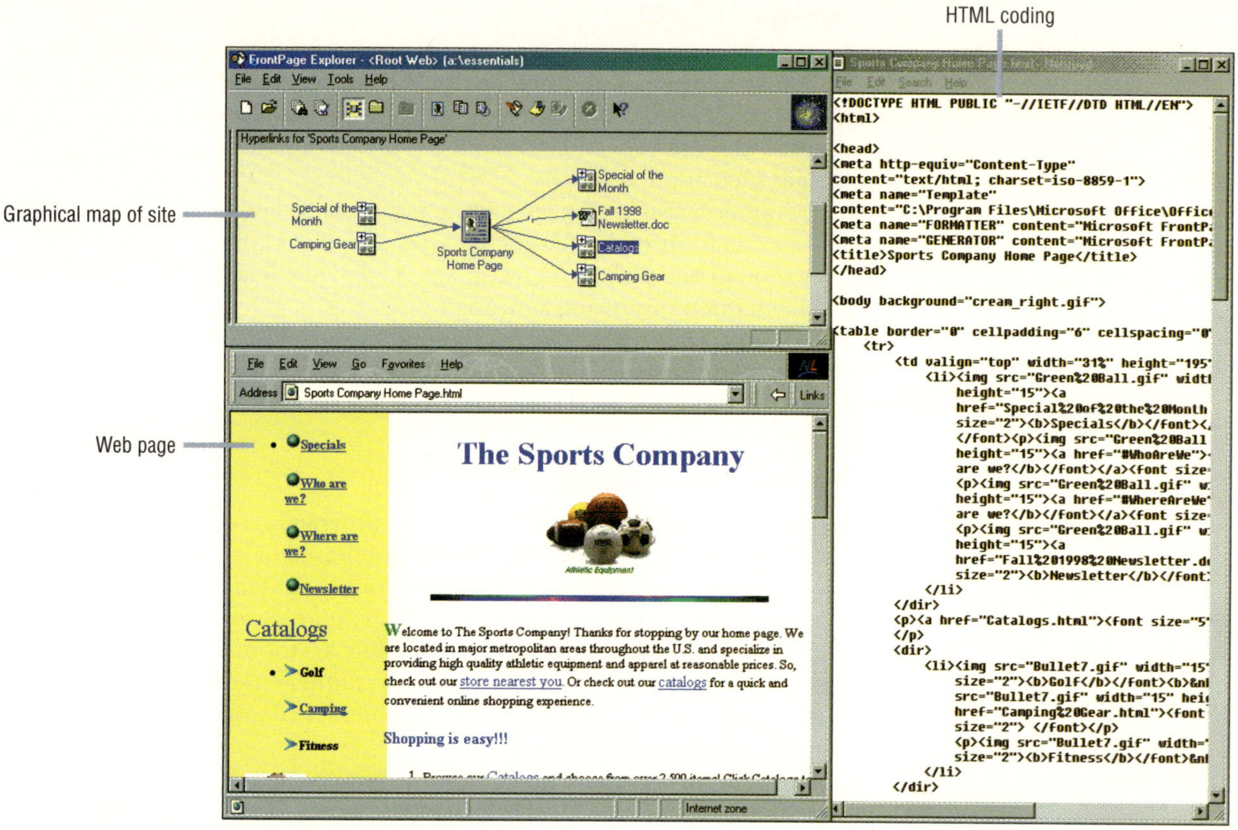

FIGURE 9-5
Web authoring program: Microsoft FrontPage

Graphics Programs

Desktop publishers mix text and graphics. Image editors modify bitmap image files. Illustrators modify vector files. Graphics suites bundle separate programs.

In Chapter 2, we discussed analytical and presentation graphics; which are widely used to analyze data and to create professional-looking presentations. Here we focus on more specialized graphics programs used by professionals in the graphic arts profession. These graphics programs are desktop publishing, image editors, and illustration programs. While desktop publishing is used to produce professional publications, image editors and illustration programs are used to modify graphic images.

Desktop Publishing

Desktop publishing programs allow you to mix text and graphics to create publications of professional quality. While *word processors* focus on creating text and have the ability to combine text and graphics, *desktop publishers* focus on page design and layout and provide greater flexibility.

Desktop publishing programs are widely used by graphic artists to create brochures, newsletters, newspapers, and textbooks. Popular desktop publishing programs include Adobe FrameMaker, Adobe PageMaker, Corel Ventura, and QuarkXPress. (See Figure 9-6.)

FIGURE 9-6
Desktop publisher: Corel Ventura

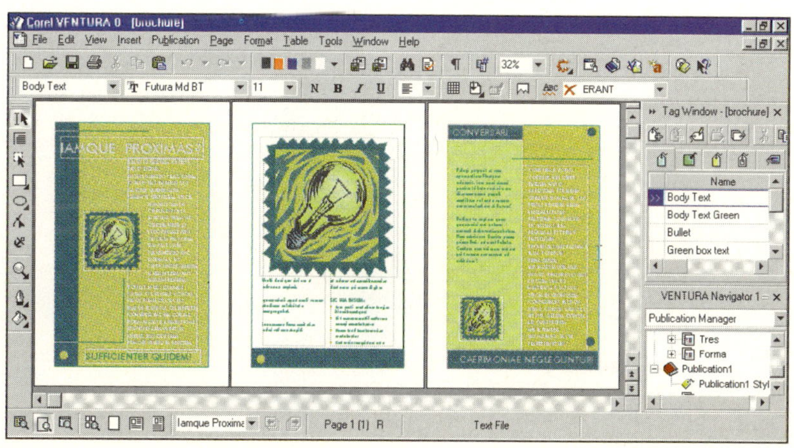

Image Editors

Image editors, also known as **paint programs,** are used to create and to modify bitmap image files. In a **bitmap file,** the image is made up of thousands of dots or pixels—much like how a computer screen displays images. Bitmapped graphic files are very common and are ideally suited to represent realistic images such as photographs.

Graphic artists use image editing programs to correct or change colors and to create special effects. One type of special effect called **morphing** allows you to smoothly blend two images so that one image seems to melt into the next, often producing amusing results.

Paintbrush for Windows is a low-end image editor. Popular professional image editor programs include Adobe Photoshop, Corel Photo, and Macromedia xRes. (See Figure 9-7.)

Illustration Programs

Illustration programs, also known as **draw programs,** are used to modify **vector images.** In a vector file, the image is composed of a collection of objects such as lines, rectangles, and ovals. A vector file contains all the shapes, colors, and starting and ending points necessary to recreate the image. Graphic artists use illustration programs to create line art for magazines, books, and special publications. Engineers and programmers use them to create 3-D models. One exciting application is to create virtual worlds or virtual reality, as we describe later in this chapter.

Popular professional illustration programs include Adobe Illustrator, CorelDraw, Macromedia FreeHand, and Micrografx Designer. (See Figure 9-8.)

ON THE WEB EXPLORATIONS

Adobe Systems Inc. is one of the leaders in the development of powerful graphics programs. To learn more about the company, visit its Web site at

http://www.adobe.com

Graphics Suites

Some companies are combining or bundling their separate graphics programs as a group called **graphics suites.** The advantage of the graphics suites is that you can buy a larger variety of graphics programs at a lower cost than if purchased separately.

The most popular suite is from the Corel Corporation. The suite, called CorelDraw, includes five individual Corel graphics programs plus a large library of clip art, media clips, and fonts. Two other popular suites are Corel's Graphics Pack and Micrografx's ABC Graphics Suite.

FIGURE 9-7
Image editor: Corel Photo

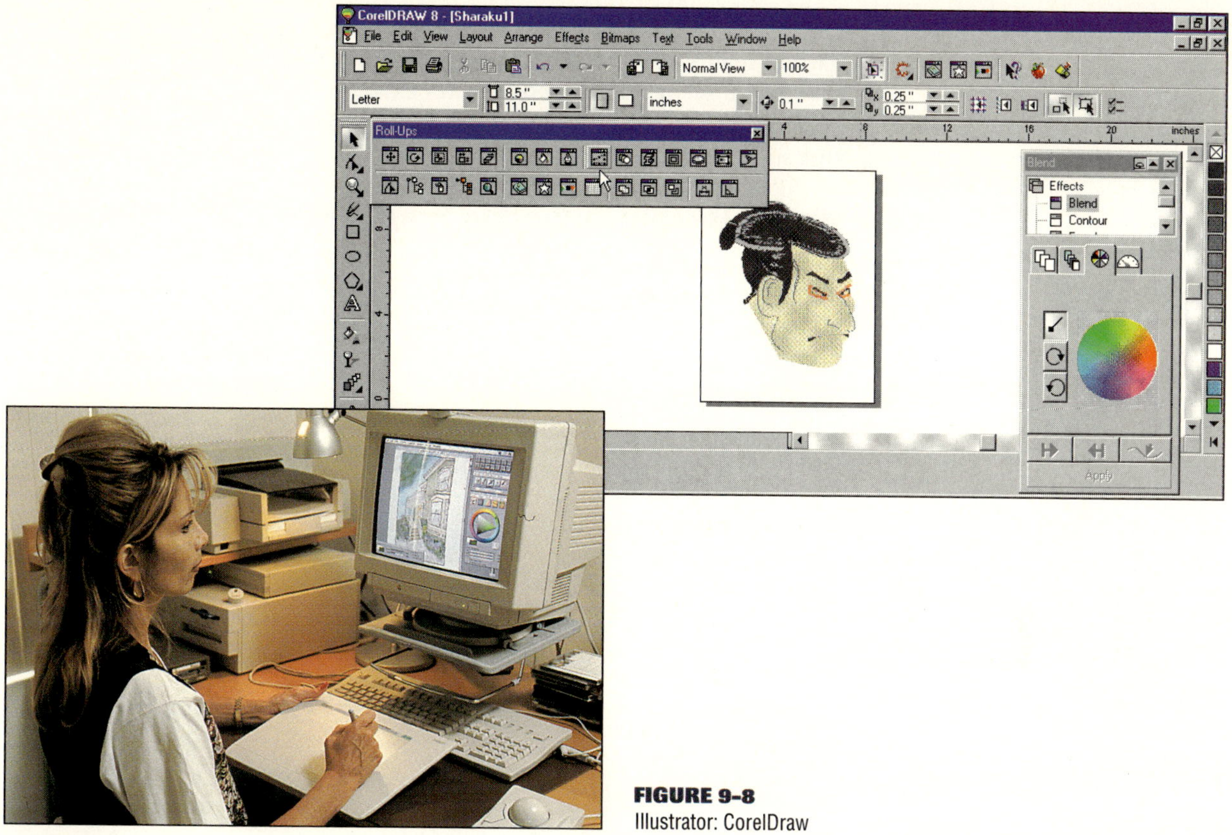

FIGURE 9-8
Illustrator: CorelDraw

CONCEPT CHECK

- ✔ List different types of specialized graphics programs.
- ✔ What are graphics suites?

Virtual Reality

Virtual reality creates simulated environments. VRML is a programming language to produce virtual reality applications. Virtual reality authoring programs are used to create applications.

Suppose you could create and virtually experience any new form of reality you wished. You could see the world through the eyes of a child, a robot—or even a lobster. You could explore faraway resorts, the moon, or inside a nuclear waste dump, without leaving your chair. This simulated experience is possible with *virtual reality.*

Virtual reality is also known as **VR, artificial reality,** or **virtual environments.** Virtual reality hardware includes headgear and gloves. The headgear (one type is called Eyephones) has earphones and three-dimensional stereoscopic screens. The gloves (DataGlove) have sensors that collect data about your hand movements. Coupled with software (such as a program called Body Electric), this interactive sensory equipment lets you immerse yourself in a computer-generated world.

ON THE WEB EXPLORATIONS

Cosmo Software is one of the leaders in the development of virtual reality on the Web. To learn more about the company, visit its Web site at

http://www.virtualstudio.com.hk

VRML

Virtual reality modeling language (VRML), is used to create real-time animated 3-D scenes. Hundreds of sites exist on the Web with virtual reality applications. Users are able to experience these applications with browsers that support VRML.

Virtual Reality Authoring Programs

Creating virtual reality programs once required very high end software costing several thousands of dollars. Recently, several lower-cost yet powerful authoring programs have been introduced. These programs utilize VRML and are widely used to create Web-based virtual reality applications. Three of the best known are Cosmo Worlds from Cosmo Software, Platinum VRCreator from Platinum Technology, and V-Realm Builder from Ligos Corporation.

Applications

An example of virtual reality is shown in Figure 9-9. In the photo is a person wearing an interactive sensory headset and glove. The rest of the photo shows what the person is actually seeing—in this instance a molecular view of a human cell. In Figure 9-10, two colleagues share this dynamic world.

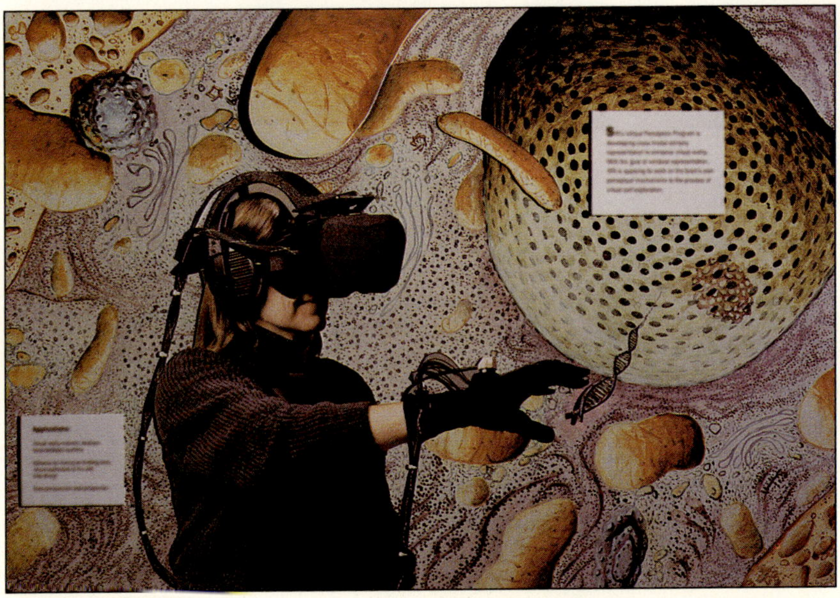

FIGURE 9-9
Virtual reality: looking inside a molecule

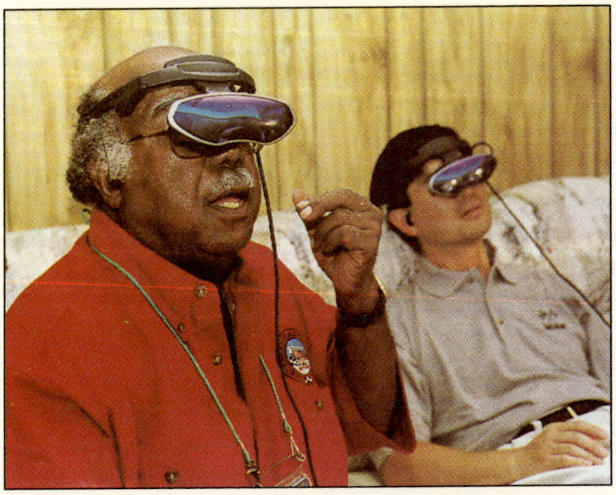

FIGURE 9-10
Virtual reality: sharing the view

There are any number of possible applications for virtual reality. The ultimate recreational use might be something resembling a giant virtual amusement park. More serious applications can simulate important experiences or training environments such as aviation, surgical operations, spaceship repair, or nuclear disaster cleanup.

CONCEPT CHECK

- ✔ What is virtual reality?
- ✔ The language used to create real-time 3-D scenes is ________.

Artificial Intelligence

Artificial intelligence attempts to simulate human thought processes and actions. Two areas are knowledge-based (expert) systems and robotics.

Does human intelligence really need the presence of "artificial intelligence," whatever that is? Indeed, you might worry, do we need the competition? Actually, the goal of artificial intelligence is not to replace human intelligence, which is probably not replaceable. Rather, it is to help people be more productive.

In the past, computers used calculating power to solve *structured* problems, which can be broken down into a series of well-defined steps. People—using intuition, reasoning, and memory—were better at solving *unstructured* problems, whether building a product or approving a loan. Organizations have long been able to computerize the tasks once performed by clerks. Now, knowledge-intensive work, such as that performed by many managers, is being automated.

The field of computer science known as **artificial intelligence (AI)** is moving into the mainstream. AI attempts to develop computer systems that can mimic or simulate human thought processes and actions. These include reasoning, learning from past actions, and using senses such as vision and touch. True artificial intelligence that corresponds to human intelligence is still a long way off. However, several tools that emulate human problem solving and information processing have been developed. Many of these tools have practical applications for business, medicine, law, and so on.

Let us now consider two areas in which human talents and abilities have been enhanced with "computerized intelligence": knowledge-based systems and robotics.

Knowledge-Based (Expert) Systems

People who are expert in a particular area—certain kinds of law, medicine, accounting, engineering, and so on—are generally well paid for their specialized knowledge. Unfortunately for their clients and customers, they are expensive, not always available, and hard to replace when they move on.

What if you were to somehow *capture* the knowledge of a human expert and make it accessible to everyone through a computer program? This is exactly what is being done with so-called *knowledge-based* or *expert systems*. **Expert systems** are computer programs that provide advice to decision makers who would otherwise rely on human experts. These expert systems use **knowledge bases** that contain specific facts, rules to relate these facts, and user

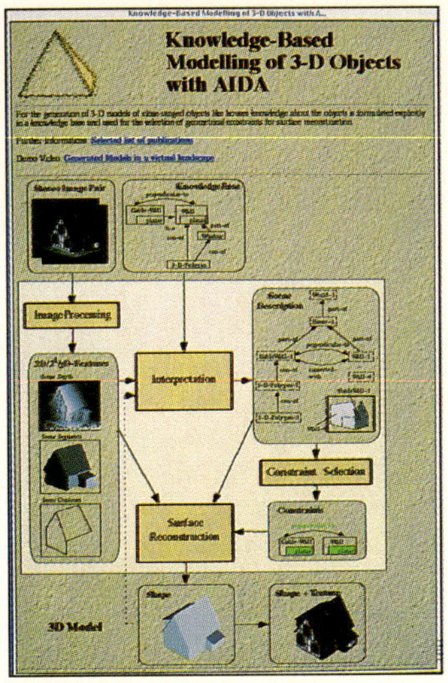

FIGURE 9-11
Knowledge-based system: creating 3-D images

input to formulate recommendations and decisions. The rules are used only when needed. The sequence of processing is determined by the interaction of the user and the knowledge base.

Many expert systems use so-called **fuzzy logic,** which allows users to respond to questions in a very humanlike way. For example, if an expert system asked how your classes were going, you could respond, "great," "OK," "terrible," and so on.

Over the past decade, expert systems have been developed in areas such as medicine, geology, chemistry, photography, and architecture. (See Figure 9-11.) There are expert systems with such names as Oil Spill Advisor, Bird Species Identification, and even Midwives Assistant. A system called Grain Marketing Advisor helps farmers select the best way to market their grain. Another, called Senex, shows how to treat breast cancer based on advanced treatment techniques.

Robotics

Robotics is the field of study concerned with developing and using robots. **Robots** are computer-controlled machines that mimic the motor activities of humans. Some toylike household robots (such as the Androbots) have been made for entertainment purposes. (See Figure 9-12.) Most, however, are used in factories and elsewhere. They differ from other assembly-line machines in that they can be reprogrammed to do more than one task. Robots are often used to handle dangerous, repetitive tasks. There are three types of robots:

- **Perception systems:** Perception system robots imitate some of the human senses. For example, robots with television-camera vision systems are particularly useful. They can be used for guiding machine tools, for inspecting products, for identifying and sorting parts, and for welding. (See Figure 9-12.) Other kinds of perception systems rely on a sense of touch, such as those used on microcomputer assembly lines to put parts into place.

FIGURE 9-12
Perception system: vision-system robot, used for welding

FIGURE 9-13
Industrial robot: painting and polishing on car plant production line

- **Industrial robots:** Industrial robots are used in factories to perform certain assembly-line tasks. Examples are machines used in automobile plants to do painting and polishing. (See Figure 9-13.) In the garment industry, robot pattern cutters create pieces of fabric for clothing. Some types of robots have claws for picking up objects.
- **Mobile robots:** Mobile robots act as transporters, such as "mailmobiles." They carry mail through an office, following a preprogrammed route. Specialized mobile robots with perception capabilites are used for military and police applications such as locating and disarming explosive devices. (See Figure 9-13.)

CONCEPT CHECK

- ✔ What does artificial intelligence attempt to simulate?
- ✔ Name two areas in which human talents and abilities have been enhanced with artificial intelligence.

Project Management

Project management software allows you to plan projects, schedule people, and control resources.

There are many occasions in business where managers need to watch projects to avoid delays and cost overruns. A **project** may be defined as a one-time operation composed of several tasks that must be completed during a stated period of time. Examples of large projects are found in construction, aerospace, and political campaigns. Examples of smaller jobs might occur in advertising agencies, corporate marketing departments, and management information systems departments. As a student, you may have projects like term papers and lab experiments.

Project Managers

Project managers are programs designed to assist in planning, scheduling, and controlling the people, resources, and costs needed to complete a project on time. For instance, a contractor building a housing development might use it to keep track of the materials, dollars, and people required for success.

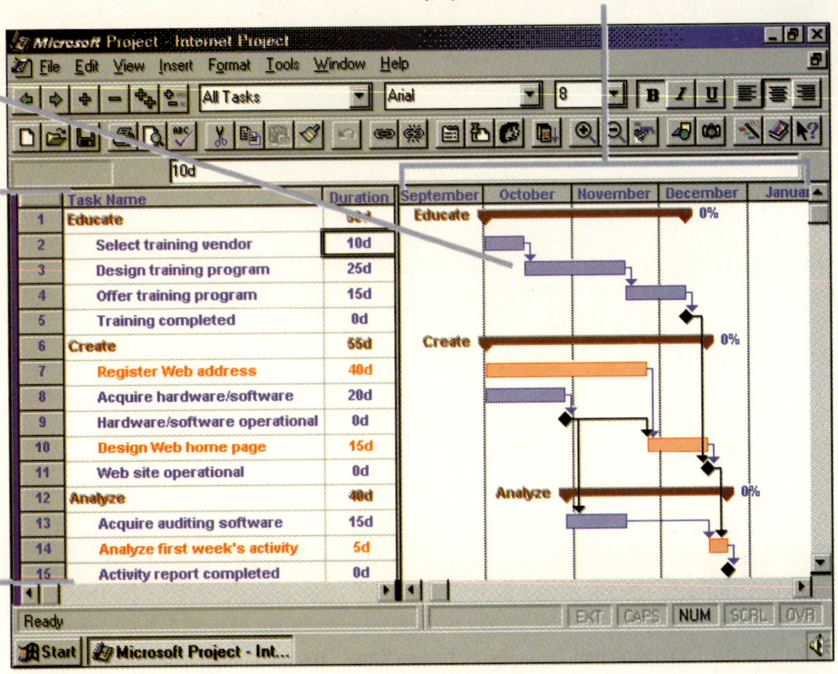

FIGURE 9-14
Gantt chart: Microsoft Project

Examples of project management software are Harvard Project Manager, Microsoft Project, Project Scheduler, SuperProject, and Time Line.

A typical use of project management software is to show the scheduled beginning and ending dates for each task in order to complete a particular project on time. It then shows the dates when each task was actually completed. Two important tools found in project management software are Gantt charts and PERT charts.

Gantt Charts

A **Gantt chart** uses bars and lines to represent a project. It has two parts. The first part is a table that lists information about each task. The second part is a bar chart that displays task durations, start dates, and finish dates on a timeline. The relative positions of the task bars reflect the order in which each task is to be performed. (See Figure 9-14.)

PERT Charts

A **Program Evaluation Review Technique (PERT) chart** uses boxes and lines to represent a project. A PERT chart shows not only the timing of a project but also the relationships among its tasks. The chart identifies which tasks must be completed before others can begin. The relationships are represented by lines that connect boxes stating the tasks, completion times, and dates. The **critical path,** the sequence of tasks that takes the longest to complete, is also identified. (See Figure 9-15.)

CONCEPT CHECK

✔ What are the functions of project management software?

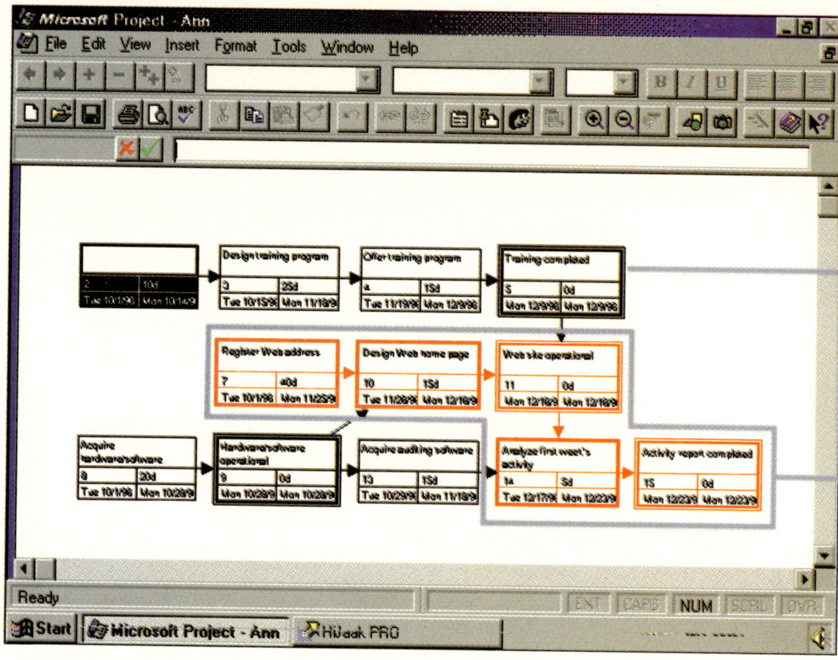

FIGURE 9-15
PERT chart: Microsoft Project

A LOOK TO THE FUTURE

IPIX, a new immersive photographic technique, may allow you to take virtual tours and exotic vacations.

There are few applications with more exciting potential than virtual reality. Although some virtual reality applications do exist, few present lifelike images and fluid motion. This is due in part to the expense and difficulty in capturing 3-D data.

Some experts predict that we will see an explosion of high-quality, photo-realistic virtual reality applications in the near future. One key is a recently released immersive photographic technique called IPIX.

Using a special fish-eye (180-degree) camera, two opposite facing images are recorded digitally and stored in memory. IPIX software takes the two images, corrects for distortion, and joins them into a single image.

Using special software, you can view this image on a computer screen, changing the angle, looking up, down, left, and right. You see almost exactly what you would see if you were standing in one location and looking in every direction. Data for a virtual tour of any environment can be readily captured by taking successive photographs while walking through that environment.

Will we be able to take realistic tours of famous museums, explore classical architecture, or even take exotic vacations without leaving our home? Who knows, but some observers say we will within the next two years.

VISUAL SUMMARY Multimedia, Web Authoring, and More

MULTIMEDIA

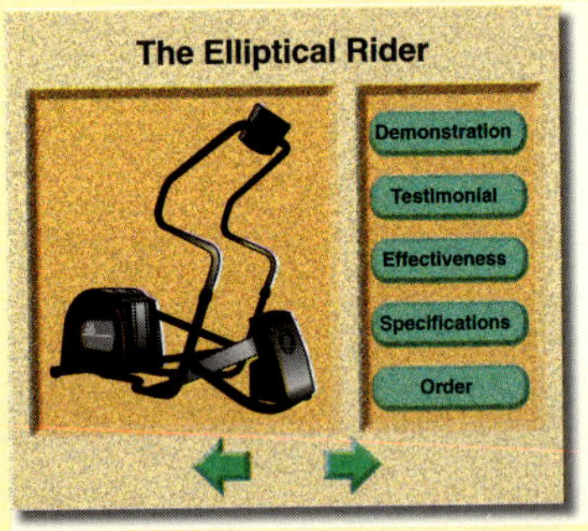

Multimedia or **hypermedia** integrates all sorts of media into an interactive presentation. This media may include video, music, voice, graphics, and text.

An essential feature is user participation or **interactivity.**

Links and Buttons

A multimedia presentation is organized as a series of related pages. Pages are **linked,** or connected, by **buttons.**

Story Boards

Story boards are design tools to record the intended overall logic, flow, and structure of a multimedia presentation. Individual storyboards specify links, content, style, and design of each display.

Multimedia Authoring Programs

Multimedia authoring programs are special programs to create multimedia presentations. They bring together all the video, audio, graphics, and text elements in an interactive framework.

WEB AUTHORING

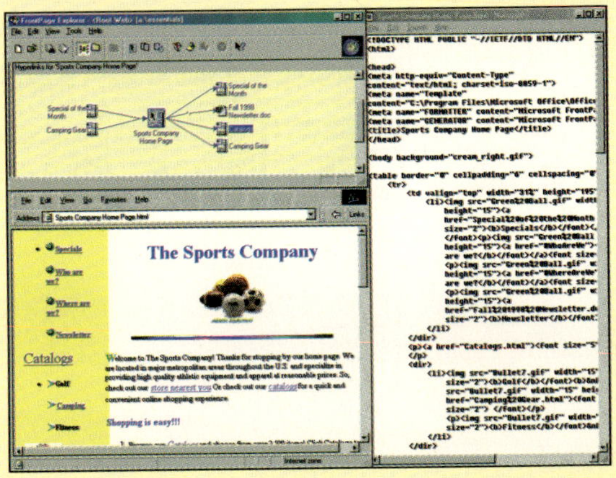

Creating Web sites is called **Web authoring.** It begins with Web site design followed by creating a document file that displays the Web site content.

Web Site Design

Web site design begins with determining overall content.

Graphical maps present overall Web site design. The home page presents overall content much like a table of contents. Links connect related blocks or pages of information.

Web Authoring Programs

Web sites can be created using a simple text editor or word processor. **Web authoring programs,** also known as **Web page editors** or **HTML editors,** are more powerful and specialized. They provide support for Web site design and HTML coding.

To be a competent end user you need to be aware of advanced applications. You need to know who uses them, what they are used for, and how they are used. Advanced applications include multimedia, Web authoring, graphics programs, virtual reality, artificial intelligence, and project managers.

GRAPHICS PROGRAMS

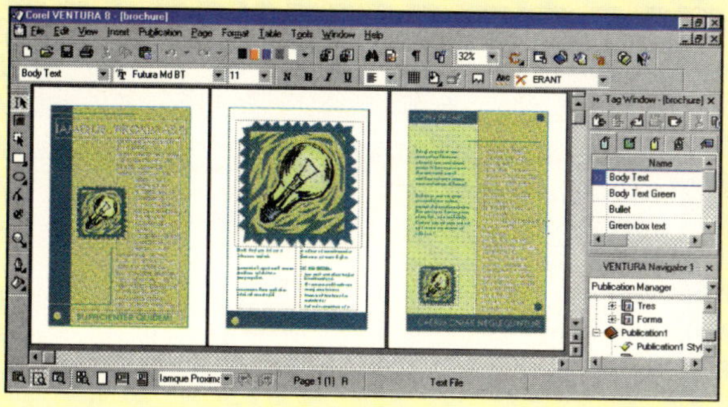

Professionals in graphic arts use specialized **graphics programs.** These programs are desktop publishers, image editors, and illustration programs.

Desktop Publishers

Desktop publishers mix text and graphics to create professional publications. They are widely used by graphic artists to create brochures, newsletters, newspapers, and textbooks.

Image Editors

Image editors, also known as **paint programs**, create and modify **bitmap image files**. In bitmap files, images are recorded as thousands of dots or pixels. **Morphing** is a special effect that blends two images into one.

Illustration Programs

Illustration programs, also known as **draw programs**, modify vector images. In a vector file, images are recorded as a collection of objects such as lines, rectangles, and ovals.

Graphics Suites

A **graphics suite** is a collection of individual graphics programs sold as a unit.

VIRTUAL REALITY

Virtual reality is also known as **VR, artificial reality,** or **virtual environments.** It consists of interactive sensory equipment to simulate alternative realities to the physical world. VR creates computer-generated simulated environments.

VRML

VRML (virtual reality modeling language) is used to create real-time virtual reality applications on the Web.

VR Authoring Programs

Virtual reality authoring programs use VRML and are widely used to create Web-based virtual reality applications.

Applications

Applications include virtual amusement parks, aviation, surgical operations, spaceship repairs, and nuclear disaster cleanup.

ARTIFICIAL INTELLIGENCE

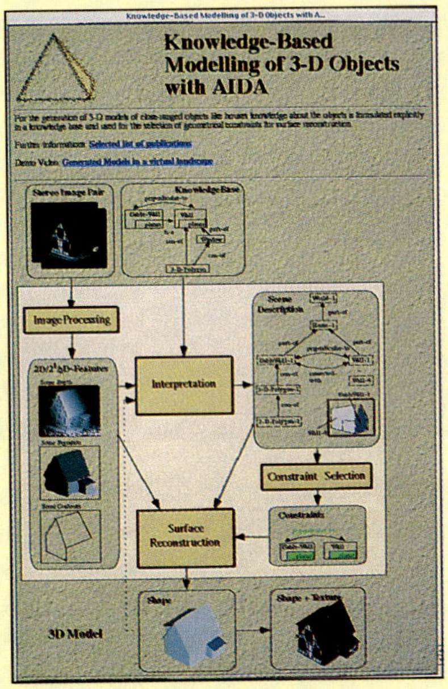

Artificial intelligence is a research field to develop computer systems that simulate human thought processes and actions. Two areas are knowledge-based systems and robotics.

Knowledge-Based (Expert) Systems

Knowledge-based (expert) systems are programs that duplicate the knowledge humans have for performing specialized tasks.

Expert systems provide advice to users who would normally rely on human experts. **Knowledge bases** contain specific facts and rules to relate to these facts. **Fuzzy logic** is used to allow humanlike input and output.

Robotics

Robots are computer-controlled machines that mimic the motor activities of humans. Three types are:

- Industrial robots—widely used in factories.
- Perception systems—simulate human senses.
- Mobile robots—act as transporters.

PROJECT MANAGEMENT

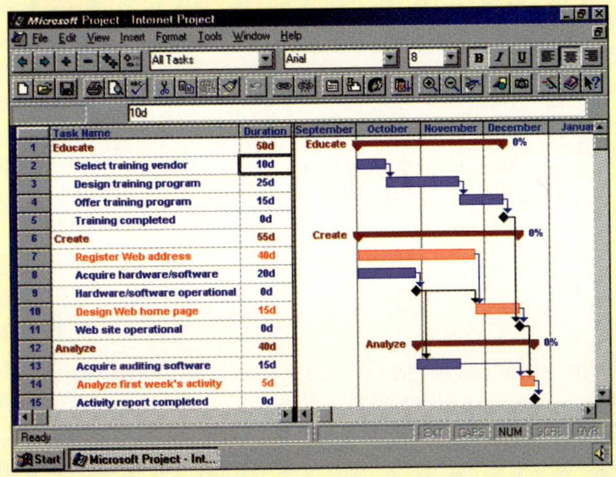

A **project** can be defined as one-time operation composed of several tasks that must be completed during a stated period of time. Project management is a common business activity.

Project Managers

Project managers are programs designed to assist in the planning, scheduling, and controlling of people, resources, and costs of a project. Two important tools are Gantt and PERT charts.

Gantt Charts

A **Gantt chart** uses bars and lines to represent a project. Bars represent the length of time to complete each task and their starting and ending dates. The lines connecting the bars indicate the order that the tasks must be completed.

PERT Charts

A **Program Evaluation Review Technique (PERT) chart** uses boxes and lines to represent a project. Each box includes a description of the task, projected completion times, and dates. Lines between boxes represent the order of completion. The **critical path** is the sequence of tasks that takes the longest to complete.

Key Terms

artificial intelligence (AI) (213)
artificial reality (211)
bitmap file (210)
button (206)
critical path (216)
desktop publishing (209)
draw program (210)
expert system (213)
fuzzy logic (214)
Gantt chart (216)
graphical map (208)
graphics suite (210)
HTML editor (208)
hypermedia (206)
illustration program (210)
image editor (210)
interactivity (206)
knowledge base (213)
link (206)
morphing (210)
multimedia (206)
multimedia authoring program (207)
paint program (210)
Program Evaluation Review Technique (PERT) chart (216)
project (215)
project managers (215)
robot (214)
robotics (214)
story board (206)
vector images (210)
virtual environment (211)
virtual reality (VR) (211)
Virtual reality programming language (VRML) (212)
Web authoring (208)
Web authoring program (208)
Web page editor (208)

Chapter Review

LEVEL 1

Reviewing Facts and Terms

Matching

Match each numbered item with the most closely related lettered item. Write your answers in the spaces provided.

1. Creates simulated environments. ____
2. Images composed of a collection of objects such as lines, rectangles, and ovals. ____
3. Programs designed to assist in planning, scheduling, and controlling the people, resources, and costs needed to complete a project on time. ____
4. Used in the early planning phase of a multimedia - project. ____
5. Uses bars and lines to represent a project. ____
6. An essential and unique feature of multimedia. ____
7. Field of study concerned with developing and using robots. ____
8. Program used to modify vector images. ____
9. Creating a Web site. ____
10. Uses boxes and lines to represent a project. ____
11. Programs that allow you to mix text and graphics to create publications of professional quality. ____
12. Computer programs that provide advice to decision makers who would otherwise rely on human experts. ____
13. In this file type, the image consists of thousands of pixels. ____
14. Used to create sophisticated Web sites while providing support for Web site design and HTML coding. ____
15. Attempts to simulate human thought processes and actions. ____

a. Artificial intelligence
b. Bitmap file
c. Buttons
d. Desktop publishing
e. Expert systems
f. Fuzzy logic
g. Gantt chart
h. Graphics suite
i. Illustration program
j. Image editor
k. Interactivity
l. Multimedia
m. PERT chart
n. Project managers
o. Robotics
p. Story board
q. Vector images
r. Virtual reality
s. Web authoring
t. Web page editors

16. Bundle of graphics programs—you can buy a larger variety at a lower cost this way. ____
17. The integration of different media into one presentation. ____
18. Special areas on a Web page that can link you to related Web sites or to additional areas within a Web page. ____
19. Used to create and modify bitmap image files. ____
20. Allows computer users to respond to questions in a very humanlike way. ____

True/False

In the spaces provided, write T or F to indicate whether the statement is true or false.

1. Desktop publishing programs combine text and graphics to create professional-quality publications. ____
2. Illustrators are used to create HTML code. ____
3. Image editors are used to create Web pages. ____
4. Virtual reality employs various sensory equipment to allow you the experience of a computer-generated world. ____
5. Expert systems are programs that give advice to individuals who would otherwise rely on human experts. ____

Multiple Choice

Circle the letter of the correct answer.

1. The application that can link all sorts of media into one form of presentation:
   - **a.** image editor
   - **b.** word processor
   - **c.** multimedia
   - **d.** spreadsheet
   - **e.** virtual reality
2. __________ are a multimedia design tool.
   - **a.** story boards
   - **b.** bitmaps
   - **c.** VRML
   - **d.** video clips
   - **e.** animations
3. __________ is a research field that develops computer systems to simulate human thought processes.
   - **a.** cyberspace
   - **b.** illustrators
   - **c.** AI
   - **d.** cybernetics
   - **e.** cryonics
4. A one-time operation composed of several tasks that must be completed during a stated period:
   - **a.** plan
   - **b.** image editor
   - **c.** manager
   - **d.** schedule
   - **e.** project
5. The __________ chart uses bars and lines to represent a project.
   - **a.** Gantt
   - **b.** analytical
   - **c.** directional
   - **d.** presentational
   - **e.** pie
6. An area of artificial intelligence that simulates certain experiences using special headgear, gloves, and software that translates data into images:
   - **a.** virtual reality
   - **b.** expert system
   - **c.** natural language processing
   - **d.** hypermedia
   - **e.** knowledge-based systems

Completion

Complete each statement in the spaces provided.

1. __________ __________ are used to modify bitmap images.
2. __________ is a programming language used to create Web pages.
3. __________ is the integration of text, graphics, animation, video, music, and voice into one presentation.
4. Unlike most assembly-line machines, __________ can be reprogrammed to do more than one task.
5. __________ systems are programs that duplicate the knowledge of highly trained people.

Reviewing Concepts

LEVEL 2

Open-Ended

On a separate sheet of paper, respond to each question and statement.

1. What is multimedia? What is it used for?
2. What are Web authoring programs? What are they used for?
3. Describe desktop publishers, image editors, and illustration programs. How do they differ?
4. What are the two areas of artificial intelligence? Describe each.
5. Explain what project management software does. Give an example of how one might be used.

Concept Mapping

On a separate sheet of paper, draw a concept map or a flowchart showing how the following terms are related. Show all relationships. Include any additional terms you can think of.

artificial intelligence
bitmap file
button
desktop publishing
draw program
expert system
fuzzy logic
Gantt chart
graphical map
graphics suite
HTML editor
hypermedia
illustration program
image editor
interactivity
knowledge base
link
multimedia
multimedia authoring program
paint program
PERT chart
project managers
robotics
story board
vector images
virtual reality
VRML
Web authoring programs
Web page editor

Critical Thinking Questions and Projects

LEVEL 3

Read each exercise and answer the related questions on a separate sheet of paper.

1. *New areas for expert systems:* There are numerous expert systems designed to pick winning stocks in the stock market. However, not everyone using these systems has become rich. Why? List and discuss three other areas in which you think it would be difficult to devise an expert system.
2. *Tools for entrepreneurs:* Have you ever thought of starting a new business? More and more people are doing so. Advanced applications like multimedia, Web authoring,

graphics programs, expert systems, artificial intelligence, and project management provide tools for entrepreneurs to get a business off the ground and moving toward success. Think of a new business. It can be almost anything, from an auto parts store to a catering service to a consulting company. Briefly describe the business and then discuss how you might use any or all of the specialized applications discussed in this chapter to start and to run the business.

3. *Ethics:* One way to learn how to create interesting and dynamic Web sites is to study how professionals create their sites. Once connected to a Web site, you can examine the HTML code used to create that site. With Netscape, for example, select Document Source from the View submenu. Do you see any ethical issues that relate to examining the HTML code? What about copying part of parts of that code? What about copying all of the code? Defend your position(s).

On the Web Exercises

1. Multimedia

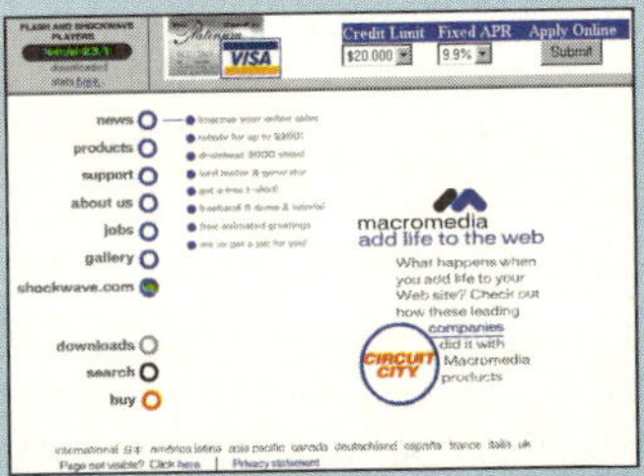

Macromedia Corporation is a leader in multimedia software. Visit our Web site at http://www.mhhe.com/cit/concepts/oleary2000-2001/webex9.html to link to their site. Once connected to that site, preview the latest software and choose a program that would be useful for creating multimedia presentations. Print out a page from the site that describes the software and write a paragraph discussing how you could use this software to create or enhance a multimedia presentation.

2. Creating Web Pages

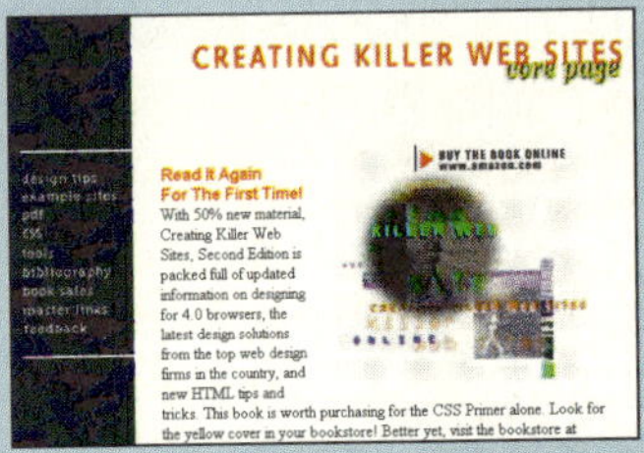

Nearly every organization today has a Web site, and it is very likely that you will be involved with either creating Web sites or modifying them. Perhaps you will work with a specialist or work on your own. In either case, it is worthwhile to know what makes a site interesting and attractive. Visit our Web site at http://www.mhhe.com/cit/concepts/oleary2000-2001/webex9.html to link to a site that provides guidance for Web page design, style, and content. Print out the first page of this site, explore the site, and write a paragraph describing some of the programs for creating Web pages.

3. Virtual Reality

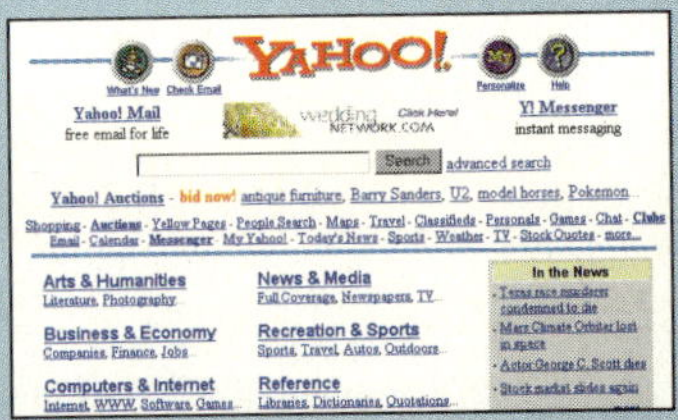

Everyone looks forward to the day when we can interact with computers in a more natural manner. Many expect virtual reality to make this happen. To get the latest information on virtual reality, connect to the Yahoo site http://www.yahoo.com, and search with key words such as "virtual reality," "immersive environments technology," and "VR"; or use categories to look in "Computers and Internet: Multimedia: Virtual Reality" and explore from there. Print out the Web page you find most informative, write a paragraph listing companies and industries that are using virtual reality, and explain how they use it.

4. Shareware and Freeware

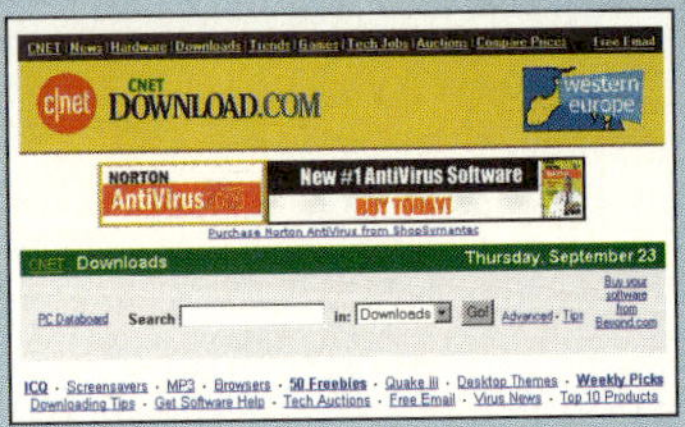

Shareware and freeware are application programs available to the public at little or no cost. Visit our site at http://www.mhhe.com/cit/concepts/oleary2000-2001/webex9.html for a link to a site providing an extensive list of shareware and freeware that you can download to your computer system. Once connected to this site, find a list of the most popular downloads for your operating system. Print out the list and write a paragraph detailing the three most interesting programs you found at this site.

The Evolution of the Computer Age

Many of you probably can't remember a world without computers, but for some of us, computers were virtually unknown when we were born and have rapidly come of age during our lifetime

Although there are many predecessors to what we think of as the modern computer—reaching as far back as the 18th century, when Joseph Marie Jacquard created a loom programmed to weave cloth and Charles Babbage created the first fully modern computer design (which he could never get to work)—the Computer Age did not really begin until the first computer was made available to the public in 1951.

The modern age of computers spans almost 50 years (thus far), which is typically broken down into five generations. Each generation is marked by a significant advancement in technology:

- **First Generation (1951–57):** During this generation, computers were built with vacuum tubes—electronic tubes that were made of glass and were about the size of light bulbs.

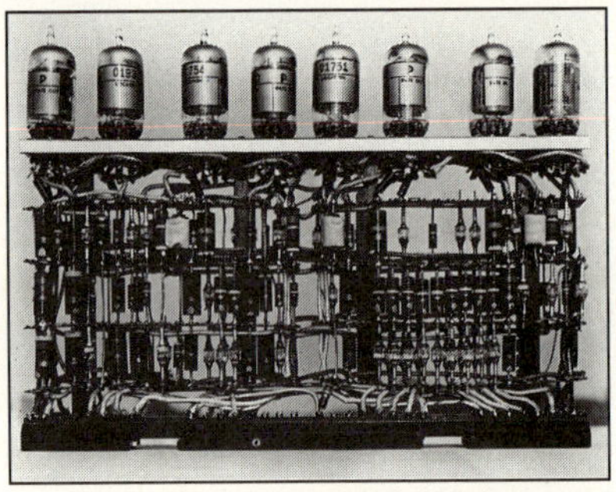

- **Second Generation (1958–63):** This generation begins with the first computers built with transistors—small devices that transfer electronic signals across a resistor. Because transistors are much smaller, use less power, and create less heat than vacuum tubes, the new computers were faster, smaller, and more reliable than the first-generation machines were.

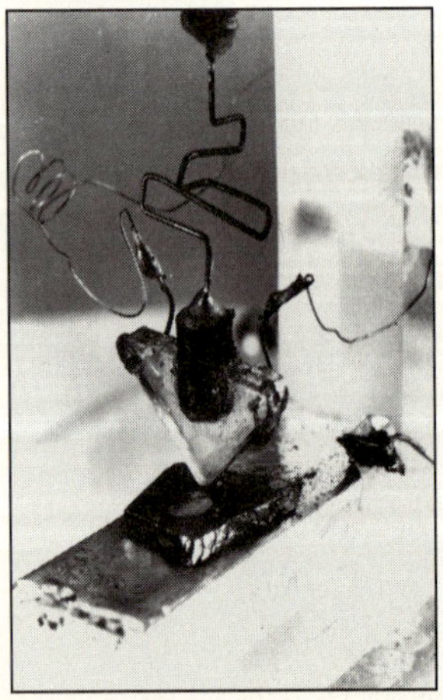

- **Third Generation (1964–69):** In 1964, computer manufacturers began replacing transistors with integrated circuits. An integrated circuit (IC) is a complete electronic circuit on a small chip made of silicon (one of the most abundant elements in the earth's crust). These computers were more reliable and compact than computers made with transistors, and they cost less to manufacture.
- **Fourth Generation (1970–90):** There are many key advancements that were made during this generation, the most significant of which was the use of the microprocessor—a specialized chip developed for computer memory and logic. This revolutionized the computer industry by making it possible to use a single chip to create a smaller "personal" computer (as well as digital watches, pocket calculators, copy machines, and so on).

- **Fifth Generation (1991–2000 and beyond):** Our current generation has been referred to as the "Connected Generation" because of the industry's massive effort to increase the connectivity of computers. The rapidly expanding Internet, World Wide Web, and intranets have created an information superhighway that has enabled both computer professionals and home computer users to communicate with others across the globe.

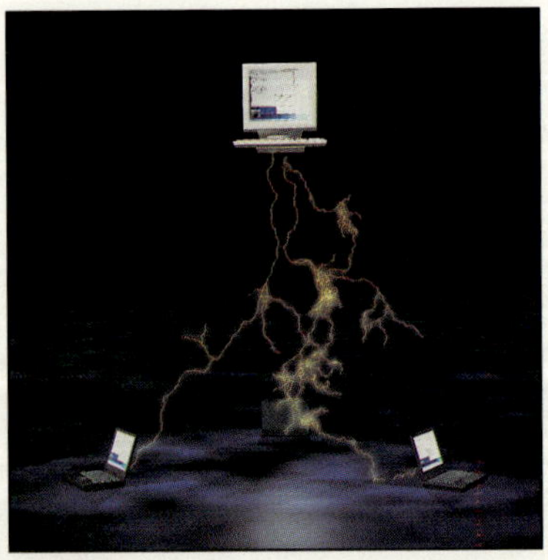

This appendix provides you with a timeline that describes some of the most significant events in each generation.

First Generation
The Vacuum Tube Age

1951: Dr. John W. Mauchly and J. Presper Eckert, Jr., introduce the first commercially available electronic digital computer—the UNIVAC—built with vacuum tubes. This computer was based on their earlier ENIAC (Electronic Numerical Integrator and Computer) design completed in 1946.

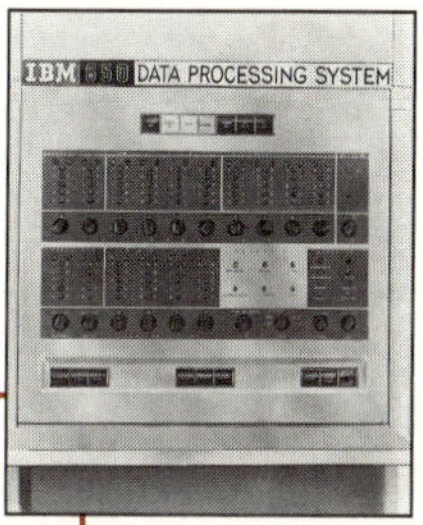

1951–53: IBM adds computers to its business equipment products and sells over 1,000 IBM 650 systems.

1951 1952 1953 1954 1955 1956 1957

1957: Introduction of first high-level programming language—FORTRAN (FORmula TRANslator).

1952: Development team led by Dr. Grace Hopper, former U.S. Navy programmer, introduces the A6 Compiler—the first example of software that converts high-level language symbols into instructions that a computer can execute.

Second Generation
The Transistor Age

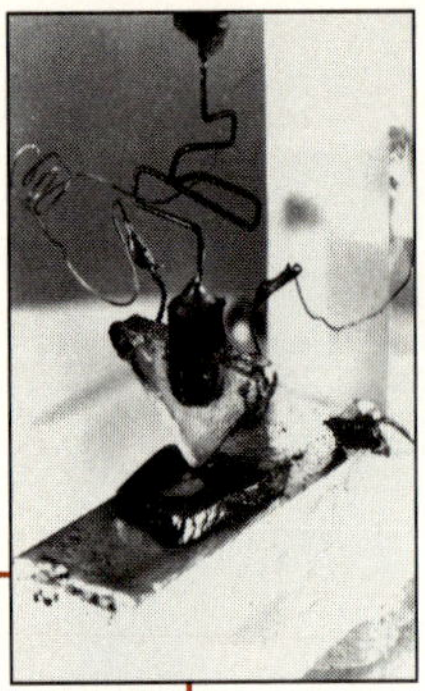

1958: Introduction of computers built with transistors—a 1947 Bell Laboratories invention.

1959: Introduction of the removable disk pack, providing users with fast access to stored data.

1960: Introduction of first business application programming language—COBOL (Common Business Oriented Language)—based on English-like phrases.

1958 1959 1960 1961 1962 1963

1963: Introduction of the first computer industry standard character set—ASCII (American Standard Code for Information Interchange) that enables computers to exchange information.

1959: General Electric Corporation introduces ERMA (Electronic Recording Machine Accounting)—the first technology that can read special characters, such as digitized information.

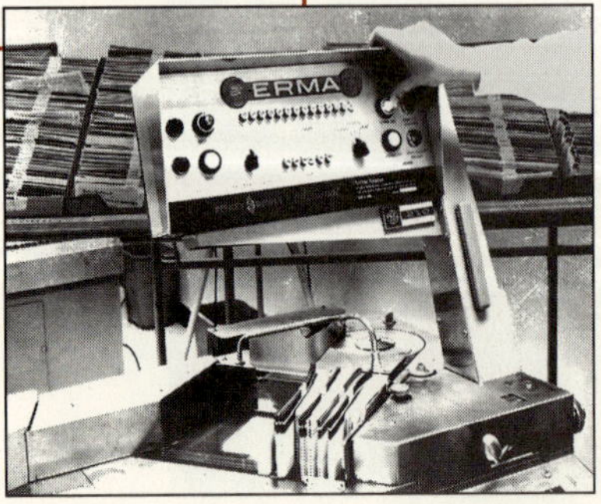

Third Generation
The Integrated Circuit Age

1964: Introduction of computers built with an integrated circuit (IC), which incorporates multiple transistors and electronic circuits on a single silicon chip.

1965: Digital Equipment Corporation (DEC) introduces the first minicomputer.

1969: Introduction of ARPANET and the beginning of the Internet.

1964 1965 1966 1967 1968 1969

1965: Introduction of the BASIC programming language.

1969: IBM announces its decision to offer unbundled software, priced and sold separately from the hardware.

1964: IBM introduces its System/360 line of compatible computers, which can all use the same programs and peripherals.

Fourth Generation
The Microprocessor Age

1970: Introduction of computers built with chips that used LSI (large-scale integration).

1975: First local area network (LAN) —Ethernet—developed at Xerox PARC (Palo Alto Research Center).

1977: Apple Computer, Inc., founded by Steve Wozniak and Steve Jobs, and Apple I introduced as an easy-to-use "hobbyist" computer.

1970 1971 1972 1973 1974 1975 1976 1977 1978 1979

1971: Dr. Ted Hoff of Intel Corporation develops a microprogrammable computer chip—the Intel 4004 microprocessor.

1975: The MITS, Inc. Altair becomes the first commercially successful microcomputer, selling for less than $400 a kit.

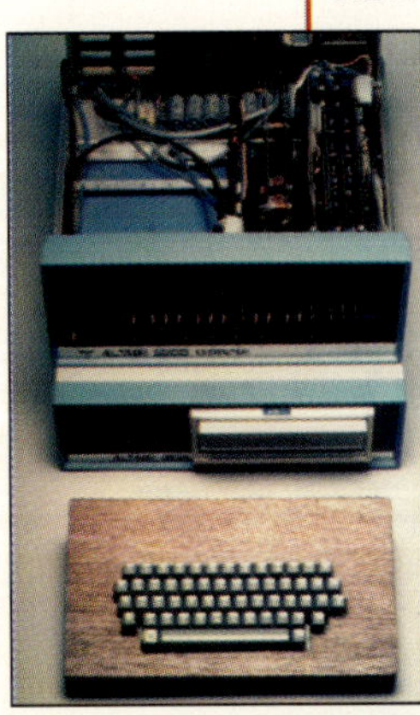

1979: Introduction of the first public information services—Compuserve and the Source.

1980: IBM asks Microsoft founder, Bill Gates, to develop an operating system—MS DOS—for the soon-to-be released IBM personal computer.

1981: Introduction of the IBM PC, which contains an Intel microprocessor chip and Microsoft's MS-DOS operating system.

1989: Introduction of Intel 486—the first 1,000,000 transistor microprocessor.

1980 1981 1982 1983 1984 1985 1986 1987 1988 1989 1990

1984: Apple introduces the Macintosh Computer, with a unique, easy-to-use graphical user interface.

1985: Microsoft introduces their Windows graphical user interface.

1990: Microsoft releases Windows 3.0, with an enhanced graphical user interface and the ability to run multiple applications.

Fifth Generation
The Age of Connectivity

1991: Release of World Wide Web standards that describe the framework of linking documents on different computers.

1992: Apple introduces the Newton MessagePad—a personal digital assistant (PDA) that incorporates a pen interface and wireless communications.

1993: Introduction of computer systems built with Intel's Pentium microprocessor.

1995: Intel begins shipping the Pentium Pro microprocessor.

1991 1992 1993 1994 1995

1991: Linus Torvalds, a graduate student at the University of Helsinki, develops a version of UNIX called the Linux operating system.

1993: Introduction of the Mosaic graphical Web browser, which led to the organization of Netscape Communications Corporation.

1995: Microsoft releases Windows 95, a major upgrade to its Windows operating system.

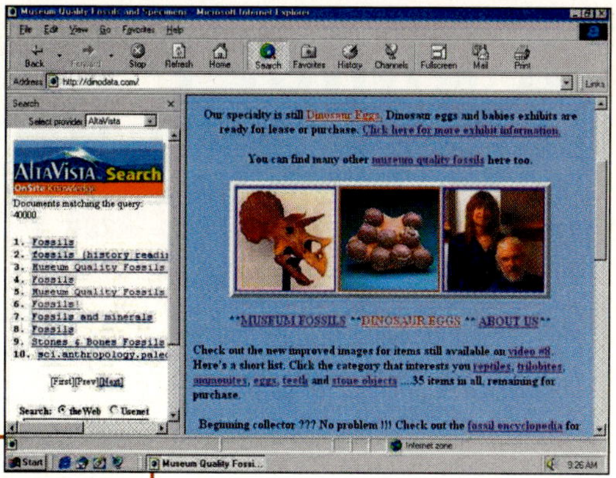

1998: Microsoft releases Office 98 integrated with Internet Explorer 4.0—antitrust legislation intensifies.

1997: Microsoft releases Office 97 with major Web enhancements integrated into its applications.

By 2002: A private Internet—Internet2—expected to be completed with higher speed, limited access, and tighter security—expected to include advanced virtual reality interfaces called nanomanipulators.

1996 — 1997 — 1998 — 1999 — 2000+

1997: The number of Internet and World Wide Web users estimated at 50 million.

1999: Microsoft releases Office 2000 featuring extensive Web integration and document collaboration—soon followed by Windows 2000.

1996: More than 50 million PCs sold and more than 250 million PCs in use worldwide.

The Buyer's Guide

How to Buy Your Own Microcomputer System

Some people make snap judgments about some of the biggest purchases in their lives: cars, college educations, houses. People have been known to buy such things based solely on an ad, a brief conversation, or a one-time look. And they may be making an impulsive decision about something costing thousands of dollars. Who is to blame, then, if they are disappointed later? They simply didn't take time to check it out.

The same concerns apply in buying a microcomputer system. You can make your choice on the basis of a friend's enthusiasm or a salesperson's promises. Or you can proceed more deliberately, as you would, say, in looking for a job.

Four Steps in Buying a Microcomputer System

The following is not intended to make buying a microcomputer an exhausting experience. Rather, it is to help you clarify your thinking about what you need and can afford.

The four steps in buying a microcomputer system are presented on the following pages. We divided each step into two parts on the assumption that your needs may change, but so may the money you have to spend on a microcomputer. For instance, later in your college career or after college graduation, you may want a far more powerful computer system than you need now. At that point you may have more money to spend. Or you may not need to spend money at all, if your employer provides you with a computer.

STEP 1
What Needs Do I Want a Computer to Serve?

The trick is to distinguish between your needs and your wants. Sure, you *want* a cutting-edge system powerful enough to hold every conceivable program you'll ever need. And you want a system fast enough to process them all at the speed of light. But do you *need* this? Your main concern is to address the two-part question:

- What do I need a computer system to do for me today?
- What will I need it to do for me in another year or two?

The questionnaire at the end of this guide will help you determine the answers to both questions.

Suggestions

The first thing to establish is whether you need a computer at all. Some colleges offer computer facilities at the library or in some dormitories. Or perhaps you can borrow a roommate's. The problem, however, is that when you are up against a term-paper deadline, many others may be also. Then the machine you want may not be available. To determine the availability of campus computers and network support, call the computer center or the dean of students' office.

Another matter on which you might want advice is what type of computer is popular on campus. Some schools favor Apple Macintoshes, others favor IBMs or IBM-compatibles. If you own a system that's incompatible with most others on campus, you may be stuck if your computer breaks down. Ask someone knowledgeable who is a year or two ahead of you if your school favors one system over another.

Finally, look ahead and determine whether your major requires a computer. Business and engineering students may find one a necessity, physical education and drama majors may not. Your major may also determine the kind of computer that's best. A journalism major may want an IBM or IBM-compatible notebook that can be set up anywhere. An architecture major may want a powerful desktop Macintosh with a laser printer that can produce elaborate drawings. Ask your academic advisor for some recommendations.

Example

Suppose you are a college student beginning your sophomore year, with no major declared. Looking at the courses you will likely take this year, you decide you will probably need a computer mainly for word processing. That is, you need a system that will help you write short (10- to 20-page) papers for a variety of courses.

By this time next year, however, you may be an accounting major. Having talked to some juniors and seniors, you find that courses in this major, such as financial accounting, will require you to use elaborate spreadsheets. Or maybe you will be a fine arts or architecture major. Then you may be required to submit projects for which drawing and painting desktop publishing software would be helpful. Or perhaps you will be out in the job market and will be writing application letters and résumés. In that case, you'll want them to have a professional appearance.

STEP 2
How Much Money Do I Have to Spend on a Computer System?

When you buy your first computer, you are not necessarily buying your last. Thus, you can think about spending just the bare-bones amount for a system that meets your needs while in college. Then you might plan to get another system later on. After all, most college students who own cars (quite often used cars) don't consider those the last cars they'll own.

You know what kind of money you have to spend. Your main concern is to answer this two-part question:

- How much am I prepared to spend on a computer system today?
- How much am I prepared to spend in another year or two?

The questionnaire at the end of this guide asks you this.

Suggestions

You can probably buy a good used computer of some sort for under $400 and a printer for under $100. On the other hand, you might spend $1,500 to $3,500 on a new state-of-the-art system. When upgraded, this computer could meet your needs for the next five years.

There is nothing wrong with getting a used system, if you have a way of checking it out. For a reasonable fee, a computer-repair shop can examine it prior to your purchase. Look at newspaper ads and notices on campus bulletin boards for good buys on used equipment. Also try the Internet. Often the sellers will include a great deal of software and other items (disks, reference materials) with the package. If you stay with recognized brands such as Apple, IBM, Compaq, or Dell, you probably won't have any difficulties. The exception may be with printers, which, since they are principally mechanical devices, may get a lot of wear and tear. This is even more reason to tell the seller you want a repair shop to examine the equipment before you buy.

If you're buying new equipment, be sure to look for student discounts. Most college bookstores, for instance, offer special prices to students. Mail-order houses also steeply discount their products. These firms run ads in such periodicals as *Computer Shopper* (sold on newsstands) and other magazines as well as the Internet. However, using mail and telephone for repairs and support can be a nuisance. Often you can use the prices advertised by a mail-order house to get local retail computer stores to lower their prices.

Example

Perhaps you have access to a microcomputer at the campus student computing center, the library, or the dormitory. Or you can borrow a friend's. However, this computer isn't always available when it's convenient for you. Moreover, you're not only going to college but also working, so both time and money are tight. Having your own computer would enable you to write papers when it's convenient for you. Spending more than $500 might cause real hardship, so a new microcomputer system may be out of the question. You'll need to shop the newspaper classified ads or the campus bulletin boards to find a used but workable computer system.

Or, maybe you can afford to spend more now—say, between $1,000 and $2,000—but probably only $500 next year. By this time next year, however, you'll know your major and how your computer needs have changed. For example, if you're going to be a finance major, you need to have a lot more computer memory (primary storage). This will hold the massive amounts of data you'll be working with in your spreadsheets. Or maybe you'll be an architecture major or graduating and looking for a job. In that case, you'll need a laser printer to produce attractive-looking designs or application letters. Thus, whatever system you buy this year, you'll want to upgrade it next year.

STEP 3
What Kind of Software Will Best Serve My Needs?

Most computer experts urge that you determine what software you need before you buy the hardware. The reasoning here is that some hardware simply won't run the software that is important to you. This is certainly true once you get into *sophisticated* software. Examples include specialized programs available for certain professions (such as certain agricultural or retail-management programs). However, if all you are interested in today are the basic tools of software—word processing, spreadsheet, and communications programs—these are available for nearly all microcomputers. The main caution is that some more recent versions of application software won't run on older hardware. Still, if someone offers you a free computer, don't say no because you feel you have to decide what software you need first. You will no doubt find it sufficient for many general purposes, especially during the early years in college.

That said, you are better served if you follow step 3 after step 2—namely, finding the answers to the two-part question:

- What kind of software will best serve my needs today?
- What kind will best serve my needs in another year or two?

The questionnaire at the end of this guide may help you determine your answers.

Suggestions

No doubt some kinds of application software are more popular on your campus—and in certain departments on your campus—than others. Are freshman and sophomore students mainly writing their term papers in Word, WordPerfect, or Word Pro? Which spreadsheet is most often used by business students: Excel, Lotus 1-2-3, or Quattro Pro? Which desktop publishing program is most favored by graphic arts majors: PageMaker, Ventura Publisher, or Freehand? Do many students use their microcomputers to access the Internet, and, if so, which communications software is the favorite? Do engineering and architecture majors use their own machines for CAD/CAM applications? Start by asking other students and your academic advisor.

If you're looking to buy state-of-the-art software, you'll find plenty of advice in various computer magazines. Several of them rate the quality of newly issued programs. Such periodicals include *InfoWorld, PC World, PC/Computing,* and *MacWorld.*

Example

Suppose you determine that all you need is software to help you write short papers. In that case, nearly any kind of word processing program would do. You could even get by with some older versions or off-brand kinds of word processing software. This might happen if such software was included in the sale of a used microcomputer that you bought at a bargain price.

But will this software be sufficient a year or two from now? Looking ahead, you guess that you'll major in theater arts, and minor in screenwriting, which you may pursue as a career. At that point a simple word processing program won't do. You learn from juniors and seniors in that department that screenplays are written using special screenwriting programs. This is software that's not available for some computers. Or, as an advertising and marketing major, you're expected to turn word-processed promotional pieces into brochures. For this, you need desktop publishing software. Or, as a physics major, you discover you will need to write reports on a word processor that can handle equations. In short, you need to look at your software needs not just for today but also for the near future. You especially want to consider what programs will be useful to you in building your career.

STEP 4
What Kind of Hardware Will Best Serve My Needs?

A bare-bones hardware system might include a three-year-old desktop or notebook computer with a 3½-inch floppy disk drive and a hard-disk drive. It should also include a monitor and a printer. With a newer system, the sky's the limit. On the one hand, as a student—unless you're involved in some very specialized activities—it's doubtful you'll really need such things as voice-input devices, touch screens, scanners, and the like. On the other hand, you will probably need speakers and a CD-ROM or DVD-ROM drive. The choices of equipment are vast.

As with the other steps, the main task is to find the answers to a two-part question:

- What kind of hardware will best serve my needs today?
- What kind will best serve my needs in another year or two?

There are several questions on the questionnaire at the end of this guide to help you determine answers to these concerns.

Suggestions

Clearly, you should let the software be your guide in determining your choice of hardware. Perhaps you've found that the most popular software in your department runs on a Macintosh rather than an IBM-compatible. If so, that would seem to determine your general brand of hardware.

Whether you buy IBM or Macintosh, a desktop or a notebook, we suggest you get a 3½-inch floppy disk drive, a hard-disk drive with at least 2 gigabytes of storage, a DVD-ROM drive, at least 128 megabytes of memory, and an ink-jet printer.

As with software, several computer magazines not only describe new hardware but also issue ratings. See *InfoWorld, PC World,* and *MacWorld,* for example.

Example

Right now, let's say, you're mainly interested in using a computer to write papers, so almost anything would do. But you need to look ahead.

Suppose you find that Word seems to be the software of choice around your campus. You find that Word 97 will run well on a Pentium machine with 8 megabytes of memory and a 1-gigabyte hard disk. Although this equipment is now outdated, you find from looking at classified ads that there are many such used machines around. Plus, they cost very little—well under $500 for a complete system.

If you're a history or philosophy major, maybe this is all the hardware and software you need. Indeed, this configuration may be just fine all the way through college. However, some majors, and the careers following them, may require more sophisticated equipment. Your choice then becomes: Should I buy an inexpensive system now that can't be upgraded, then sell it later and buy a better one? Or should I buy at least some of the components of a good system now and upgrade it over the next year or so?

As an advertising major, you see the value of learning desktop publishing. This will be a useful if not essential skill once you embark on a career. In exploring the software, you learn that Word includes some desktop publishing capabilities. However, the hardware you previously considered simply isn't sufficient. Moreover, you learn from reading about software and talking to people in your major that there are better desktop publishing programs. Specialized desktop publishing programs like Ventura Publisher are considered more versatile than Word. Probably the best software arrangement, in fact, is to have Word as a word processing program and Ventura Publisher for a desktop publishing program.

To be sure, the campus makes computers that will run this software available to students. If you can afford it, however, you're better off having your own. Now, however, we're talking about a major expense. A computer running a Pentium III microprocessor, with 256 megabytes of memory, a 3½-inch disk drive, a DVD-ROM disk drive, and a 10-gigabyte hard disk, plus a modem, color monitor, and laser printer, could cost in excess of $1,500.

Perhaps the best idea is to buy now, knowing how you would like your system to grow in the future. That is, you will buy a microcomputer with a Pentium III microprocessor. But at this point, you will buy only an ink-jet printer and not buy a DVD-ROM drive. Next year or the year following, you might sell off the less sophisticated peripheral devices and add a DVD-ROM drive and a laser printer.

Developing a Philosophy about Computer Purchasing

It's important not to develop a case of "computer envy." Even if you bought the latest, most expensive microcomputer system, in a matter of months, something better will come along. Computer technology is still in a very dynamic state, with more powerful, versatile, and compact systems constantly hitting the marketplace. So what if your friends have the hottest new piece of software or hardware? The main question is: Do you need it to solve the tasks required of you or to keep up in your field? Or can you get along with something simpler but equally serviceable?

VISUAL SUMMARY The Buyer's Guide: How to Buy Your Own Microcomputer System

NEEDS

What do I need a computer system to do for me today? In another year or two?

I wish to use the computer for:

	Today	1–2 years
Word processing—writing papers, letters, memos, or reports	❑	❑
Business or financial applications—balance sheets, sales projections, expense budgets, or accounting problems	❑	❑
Record-keeping and sorting—research bibliographies, scientific data, or address files	❑	❑
Graphic presentations—of business, scientific, or social science data	❑	❑
Online information retrieval—to campus networks, service providers, or the Internet	❑	❑
Publications, design, or drawing—for printed newsletters, architectural drawing, or graphic arts	❑	❑
Multimedia—for video games, viewing, creating, presenting, or research	❑	❑
Other—(specify): ______________	❑	❑

BUDGET

How much am I prepared to spend on a system today? In another year or two?

I can spend:

	Today	1–2 years
Under $500	❑	❑
Up to $1,000	❑	❑
Up to $1,500	❑	❑
Up to $2,000	❑	❑
Up to $2,500	❑	❑
Over $3,000 (specify): ________________	❑	❑

Buying a Microcomputer System

Step	Questions
1	*My needs:* What do I need a computer system to do for me today? In another year or two?
2	*My budget:* How much am I prepared to spend on a system today? In another year or two?
3	*My software:* What kind of software will best serve my needs today? In another year or two?
4	*My hardware:* What kind of hardware will best serve my needs today? In another year or two?

To help clarify your thinking about buying a microcomputer system, complete the questionnaire below by checking the appropriate boxes.

SOFTWARE

What kinds of software will best serve my needs today? In another year or two?

The application software I need includes:

	Today	1–2 years
Word processing—Word, WordPerfect, Word Pro, or other (specify): ______	❑	❑
Spreadsheet—Excel, Lotus 1-2-3, Quattro Pro, or other (specify): ______	❑	❑
Database—Access, Paradox, Approach, or other (specify): ______	❑	❑
Presentation graphics—PowerPoint, Freelance, CorelPresentations, or other (specify): ______	❑	❑
Browsers—Netscape Navigator, Microsoft Internet Explorer, or other (specify): ______	❑	❑
Other—integrated packages, software suites, graphics, multimedia, Web Authoring, CAD/CAM, other (specify): ______	❑	❑

The system software I need:

	Today	1–2 years
Windows 95	❑	❑
Windows 98	❑	❑
Windows 2000	❑	❑
Mac OS	❑	❑
Unix	❑	❑
Other (specify): ______	❑	❑

HARDWARE

What kinds of hardware will best serve my needs today? In another year or two?

The hardware I need includes:

	Today	1–2 years
Microprocessor—Pentium III, Pentium II, Power PC, other (specify): ______	❑	❑
Memory—(specify amount): ______	❑	❑
Monitor—size (specify): ______	❑	❑
Floppy disk drives—3½" and/or Zip (specify): ______	❑	❑
Optical disk drive—CD-ROM, DVD-ROM (specify type, speed, and capacity): ______	❑	❑
Hard-disk drive—(specify capacity): ______	❑	❑
Portable computer—laptop, notebook, subnotebook, personal digital assistant (specify): ______	❑	❑
Printer—ink-jet, laser, color (specify): ______	❑	❑
Other—modem, speakers, fax, surge protector (specify): ______	❑	❑

The Upgrader's Guide

How to Upgrade Your Microcomputer System

If you own a microcomputer, chances are that your machine is not the latest and greatest. Microcomputers are always getting better—more powerful and faster. While that is a good thing, it can be frustrating trying to keep up.

What can you do? If you have lots of money, you can simply buy a new one. Another alternative is to upgrade or add new components to increase the power and speed of your current microcomputer. You probably can increase your system's performance at a fraction of the cost of a new one.

Three Steps in Upgrading a Microcomputer System

The following is not intended to detail specific hardware upgrades. Rather, it is intended to help you clarify your thinking about what you need and can afford.

The three steps in upgrading a microcomputer system are presented on the following pages. Each step begins by asking a key question and then provides some suggestions or factors to consider when responding to the question.

STEP 1
Is It Time to Upgrade?

Almost any upgrade you make will provide some benefit; the trick is determining if it is worth the monetary investment. It is rarely practical to rebuild an older computer system into a newer model piece by piece. The cost of a complete upgrade typically far exceeds the purchase price of a new system. But if your system is just a piece or two away from meeting your needs, an upgrade may be in order.

Clearly defining what you hope to gain with an upgrade of some of your system's hardware will enable you to make the most relevant and cost-effective selections. Before deciding what to buy, decide what goal you hope to accomplish. Do you want to speed up your computer's performance? Do you need more space to save your files? Is it a new component you'd like to add, such as a DVD-ROM drive?

Suggestions

A good place to start is the documentation on the packaging of any software you use or plan to use. Software manufacturers clearly label the minimum requirements to use their product. These requirements are usually broken down into categories that relate to specific pieces of hardware. For instance, how much RAM (random access memory) does a new program require? How much hard disk space is needed? Keep in mind these ratings are typically the bare minimum. If your system comes very close to the baseline in any particular category, you should still consider an upgrade.

Another thing to investigate is whether there is a software solution that will better serve your needs. For instance, if you are looking to enhance performance or make more room on your hard disk, there are diagnostic and disk optimization utility programs that may solve your problem. In Chapter 3, we discuss a variety of utility programs, such as Norton SystemWorks, that monitor, evaluate, and enhance system performance and storage capacity.

Typical objectives of an upgrade are to improve system performance, increase storage capacity, or add new technology.

STEP 2
What Should I Upgrade?

Once you have clearly defined your objectives, the focus shifts to identifying specific components to meet those objectives.

Suggestions

If your objective is to improve *performance,* three components to consider are RAM, the microprocessor, and expansion cards. If your objective is to increase *storage capacity,* two components to consider are hard disk drive and Zip disk drive. If you are adding *new technology,* consider the capability of your current system to support new devices.

Performance

If you want to increase the speed of your computer, consider increasing the amount of RAM. In most cases, this upgrade is relatively inexpensive and will yield the highest performance result per dollar invested. How much your system's performance will increase depends on how much RAM you start with, the size of programs you run, and how often you run large programs.

Another way to increase speed is to replace your system's microprocessor. Processor speed is measured in megahertz (MHz). This rating is not a direct measurement of how fast the processor works, but rather gives you a general idea of how it compares to other processors. (Computing magazines such as *PC World* often publish articles comparing the relative effectiveness of different processors.) The concept behind a microprocessor upgrade is simple: a faster processor will process faster. This is often an expensive upgrade and not as cost-effective as increasing RAM.

If you are looking at upgrading for a specific type of application, perhaps an expansion card is your answer. Expansion cards connect to slots on the system board, provide specialized support, and often free up resources and increase overall system performance. For example, if you run graphics-intensive programs, such as a drafting program or a video game, a video-card upgrade may be a good buy. An upgraded video card can be used to support higher resolution displays, handle all video data, and speed up overall system performance.

Storage Capacity

It's not hard to know when it's time to upgrade your storage capacity. If you frequently have to delete old files to make way for new ones, then it is probably time for more space. A larger or an additional hard drive is usually the solution. Two things to consider when comparing new hard drives are (1) size, which is usually rated in gigabytes (GB) of data the drive can hold, and (2) seek time, which is a rating of the average time it takes the drive to access any particular piece of data.

If you are storing a lot of data that you no longer use, such as old term papers, you might consider adding a Zip drive. This is usually cheaper and is a good way to archive and transport data. Access time is slower than from a hard drive, so this is an option best suited for infrequently used data or for backing up data.

New Technology

Perhaps you are not looking to modify existing hardware, but would like to add a new device. Examples include large high-resolution monitors, DVD-ROM drives, and high-speed printers.

The key consideration is whether the new device will work with your existing hardware. The requirements for these devices are typically printed on the outside packaging. If not, then refer to the product's operating manuals. Obviously, if your current system cannot support the new technology, you need to evaluate the cost of the new device plus the necessary additional hardware upgrades.

STEP 3
Who Should Do the Upgrade?

Once you've decided that the cost of the upgrade is justified and you know what you want to upgrade, the final decision is who is going to do it. Basically, there are two choices. You can either do it yourself or pay for professional installation.

Suggestions

The easiest way, and many times the best way, is to have a professional perform the upgrade. If you select this option, be sure to include the cost of installation in your analysis. If you have had some prior hardware experience or are a bit adventurous, you may want to save some money and do it yourself.

Visit a few computer stores that carry the upgrades you have selected. Most stores that provide the parts will install them as well. Talk with their technical people, describe your system (better yet, bring your system unit to the store), and determine the cost of professional installation. If you are thinking of doing it yourself, ask for their advice. Ask if they will provide assistance if you need it.

If you decide to have the components professionally installed, get the total price in writing and inquire about any guarantees that might exist. Before leaving your system be sure that it is carefully tagged with your name and address. After the service has been completed, pay by credit card and thoroughly test the upgrade. If it does not perform satisfactorily, contact the store and ask for assistance. If the store's service is not satisfactory, you may be able to have your credit card company help to mediate any disputes.

VISUAL SUMMARY The Upgrader's Guide: How to Upgrade Your Microcomputer System

Upgrading a Microcomputer System

Step	Questions
1	*Needs:* Is it time to upgrade? What do I need that my current system is unable to deliver?
2	*Analysis:* What should I upgrade? Will the upgrade meet my needs and will it be cost-effective?
3	*Action:* Who should do the upgrade? Should I pay a professional or do it myself?

NEEDS

Is it time to upgrade? What do I need that my current system is unable to deliver?

I am considering an upgrade to:

- ❑ **Improve performance because**
  - ❑ My programs run too slow
  - ❑ I cannot run some programs I need
- ❑ **Increase storage capacity because:**
  - ❑ I don't have enough space to store all my files
  - ❑ I don't have enough space to install new programs
  - ❑ I need a secure place to back up important files
  - ❑ I'd like to download large files from the Internet
- ❑ **Add new technology:**
  - ❑ Zip Drive
  - ❑ DVD-ROM
  - ❑ High-performance monitor
  - ❑ Printer
  - ❑ TV tuner card
  - ❑ Enhanced video card
  - ❑ Enhanced sound card
  - ❑ Other ______________________________

ANALYSIS

What should I upgrade? Will the upgrade meet my needs and will it be cost effective?

I will improve:

- ❑ **Performance by**
  - ❑ Adding random-access memory (RAM)
    - Current RAM (MB) ____________
    - Upgrade to ____________
    - Cost $____________
    - Expected improvement ____________
    - Other factors ________________
  - ❑ Replacing the current microprocessor
    - Current processor ____________
    - Upgrade processor ____________
    - Cost $____________
    - Expected improvement ____________
    - Other factors ________________
  - ❑ Adding an expansion card
    - Type ________________________
    - Purpose ______________________
    - Cost $____________
    - Expected improvement ____________
    - Other factors ________________
- ❑ **Storage capacity by**
  - ❑ Adding a hard disk drive
    - Current size (GB) ____________
    - Upgrade size (GB) ____________
    - Cost $____________
    - Expected improvement ____________
    - Other factors ________________
  - ❑ Adding a Zip disk drive
    - Upgrade size (GB) ____________
    - Cost $____________
    - Type ________________________
    - Expected improvement ____________
    - Other factors ________________
- ❑ **Functionality by adding**
  - New technology ____________
  - System requirements ____________
  - Cost $____________
  - Expected improvement ______________
  - Other factors ____________________

To help clarify your thinking about upgrading a microcomputer system, complete the questionnaire below by checking the appropriate boxes.

ACTION

Who should do the upgrade? Should I do it myself or should I pay a professional?

The two choices are:

❑ **Professional installation**

The easiest way, and many times the best way, is to have a professional perform the upgrade. If you select this option, be sure to include the cost of installation in you analysis. Pay with a credit card, and make sure your system is tagged with your name and address before you part with it.

❑ **Do-it-yourself installation**

If you have had some prior hardware experience or are a bit adventurous, you may want to save some money and do it yourself. Avoid touching sensitive electronic parts and be sure to ground yourself by touching an unpainted metal surface in your computer.

GLOSSARY

Access: Refers to the responsibility of those having data to control who is able to use that data.

Access time: The period between the time the computer requests data from a secondary storage device and the time the transfer of data is completed.

Accounts payable: The activity that shows the money a company owes to its suppliers for the materials and services it has received.

Accounts receivable: The activity that shows what money has been received or is owed by customers.

Accuracy: Relates to the responsibility of those who collect data to ensure that the data is correct.

Active desktop: The Windows dektop view in which "active content" from Web pages is displayed.

Active-matrix monitor: Monitor in which each pixel is independently activated. More colors with better clarity can be displayed.

Ada: Procedural language named after an English countess regarded as the first programmer; was originally designed for weapons systems but has commercial uses as well. Because of its structured design, modules of a large program can be written, compiled, and tested separately before the entire program is put together.

Adapter card: *See* Expansion card.

Add-on: *See* Helper applications.

Advanced Research Project Agency Network (ARPANET): A national computer network from which the Internet developed.

Agent: Program for updating search engine. Also called bot or spider.

ALU: *See* Arithmetic-logic unit.

American Standard Code for Information Interchange: *See* ASCII.

Analog signal: Signal that represents a range of frequencies, such as the human voice.

Analytical graphs: Form of graphics used to put numeric data into forms that are easier to analyze, such as bar charts, line graphs, and pie charts.

Animation: Feature involving special visual and sound effects.

Antivirus programs: Programs that guard a computer system from viruses or other damaging programs.

Applets: Java programs used on Web pages.

Application generator: Software with modules that have been preprogrammed to accomplish various tasks, such as calculation of overtime pay.

Applications: Programs such as word processing and spreadsheets.

Application software: Software that can perform useful work, such as word processing, cost estimating, or accounting tasks.

Arithmetic-logic unit (ALU): The part of the CPU that performs arithmetic and logical operations.

ARPANET: *See* Advanced Research Project Agency Network.

Artificial intelligence (AI): A field of computer science that attempts to develop computer systems that can mimic or simulate human thought processes and actions.

Artificial reality: *See* Virtual reality.

ASCII (American Standard Code for Information Interchange): Binary coding scheme widely used on all computers, including microcomputers.

Assembly language: Second generation of programming languages. These languages use abbreviations for program instructions.

Asynchronous communications port: *See* Serial port.

Asynchronous transmission: Method whereby data is sent and received one byte at a time.

Auction house sites: Web sites that operate like a traditional auction to sell merchandise to bidders.

Automated design tool: Software package that evaluates hardware and software alternatives according to requirements given by the systems analyst.

Backup programs: Programs that make copies of files to be used in case the originals are lost or damaged.

Backup tape cartridge unit: *See* Magnetic tape streamer.

Bandwidth: Bits-per-second transmission capability of a channel.

Bar code: Code consisting of vertical zebra-striped marks printed on product containers; read with a bar-code reader.

Bar-code reader: Photoelectric scanner that reads bar codes for processing.

BASIC (Beginner's All-purpose Symbolic Instruction Code): Easy-to-learn procedural programming language widely used on microcomputers.

Basic applications: *See* General-purpose applications.

Batch processing: Processing performed all at once on data that has been collected over several days.

Binary system: Numbering system in which all numbers consist of only two digits—0 and 1.

Bit (binary digit): A 0 or 1 in the binary system.

Bitmap file: Graphic file in which image is made up of thousands of dots (pixels).

Bot: *See* Agent.

Broadband: Bandwidth that includes microwave, satellite, coaxial cable, and fiber-optic channels. It is used for very high speed computers.

Browser: Special Internet software that allows users to effortlessly jump from one computer's resources to another computer's resources.

Browsing: Surfing or navigating the Web.

Bus: A data roadway along which bits travel.

Bus line: Electronic data roadway, connecting the parts of the CPU to each other and linking the CPU with other important hardware, along which bits travel. Also, the common connecting cable in a bus network.

Bus network: Network in which all communications travel along a common path. Each device in the network handles its own communications control. There is no host computer or file server.

Button: A special area you can click to make links and "navigate" through a presentation.

Byte: Unit consisting of eight bits. There are 256 possible bit combinations in a byte.

C: General-purpose procedural language originally designed for writing operating systems. Widely used and portable.

C++: One of the most widely used object-oriented programming languages.

Cable: Cords used to connect input and output devices to the system unit.

Cable modem: Allows all digital communication; speed of 27 million bps.

Cache memory: Area of random-access memory (RAM) set aside to store the most frequently accessed information. Acts as a temporary high-speed holding zone between memory and CPU.

CAD: *See* Computer-aided design.

CAM: *See* Computed-aided manufacturing.

Carder: Criminal who steals credit cards over the Internet.

Carpal tunnel syndrome: Disorder found among frequent computer users, consisting of damage to nerves and tendons in the hands. *See also* Repetitive strain injury.

CASE tool: *See* Automated design tool.

Cathode-ray tube (CRT): Desktop-type monitor built in the same way as a television set. The most common type of monitor for the office and the home. These monitors are typically placed directly on the system unit or on the top of the desk.

CD: *See* compact disc.

CD-R: Optical disk that can be written to once. After that it can be read many times without deterioration and cannot be written on or erased.

CD-ROM (compact disc–read-only memory): Optical disk that allows data to be read but not recorded.

CD-RW (compact disc–rewritable): Optical disk that is not permanently altered when data is recorded.

Center for European Nuclear Research (CERN): In Switzerland; where the Web was introduced in 1992.

Central processing unit (CPU): Part of the computer that holds data and program instructions for processing the data. The CPU consists of the control unit and the arithmetic-logic unit. In a microcomputer, the CPU is on a single electronic component, the microprocessor chip.

Channel: Topic for discussion in a chat group.

Character: A single letter, number, or special character such as a punctuation mark or $.

Checklist: List of questions that helps in guiding the systems analyst and end user through key issues for the present system.

Child node: A node one level below the node being considered in a hierarchical database or network.

Chip: A tiny circuit board etched on a small square of sandlike material called silicon.

Chlorofluorocarbons (CFCs): Toxic chemicals found in solvents and cleaning agents. Chlorofluorocarbons can travel into the atmosphere and deplete the earth's ozone layer.

CISC: *See* complex instruction set computer chip.

Client: A node that requests and uses resources available from other nodes.

Client/server network system: Network in which one powerful computer coordinates and supplies services to all other nodes on the network. Server nodes coordinate and supply specialized services, and client nodes request the services.

Closed architecture: Computer manufactured in such a way that users cannot easily add new devices.

CMOS: *See* complementary metal-oxide semiconductor.

Coaxial cable: High-frequency transmission cable that replaces the multiple wires of telephone lines with a single solid-copper core.

COBOL (Common Business-Oriented Language): Procedural language most frequently used in business.

Coding: Actual writing of a program.

Cold site: Special emergency facility in which hardware must be installed but which is available to a company in the event of a disaster to its computer system. *Compare* Hot site.

Combination key: Keys such as the *Ctrl* key that perform an action when held down in combination with another key.

Commerce server: *See* Web storefront creation packages.

Common operational database: Integrated collection of records that contain details about the operations of a company.

Common user database: Company database that contains selected information both from the common operational database and from outside (proprietary) databases.

Communications hardware: Sends and receives data and programs from one computer or secondary storage device to another.

Compact disc (CD): Widely used optical disk format.

Company database: Collection of integrated records shared throughout a company or other organization.

Compiler: Software that converts the programmer's procedural-language program (source code) into machine language (object code).

Complementary metal-oxide semiconductor (CMOS): A CMOS chip provides flexibility and expandability for a computer system; unlike RAM, it does not lose its contents if power is turned off; unlike ROM, its contents can be changed.

Complex instruction set computer (CISC) chip: The most common type of microprocessor that has thousands of programs written specifically for it.

Computer Abuse Amendments Act of 1994: Outlaws transmission of viruses and other harmful computer code.

Computer-aided design (CAD): Type of program that manipulates images on a screen.

Computer-aided manufacturing (CAM): Type of program that controls automated factory equipment, including machine tools and robots.

Computer-aided software engineering (CASE) tool: *See* Automated design tool

Computer competent: Being able to use a computer to meet one's information needs.

Computer crime: Illegal action in which a perpetrator uses special knowledge of computer technology. Criminals may be employees, outside users, hackers and crackers, and organized crime members.

Computer Fraud and Abuse Act of 1986: Law allowing prosecution of unauthorized access to computers and databases.

Computer Matching and Privacy Protection Act of 1988: Law setting procedures for computer matching of federal data for verifying eligibility for federal benefits or for recovering delinquent debts.

Computer network: Communications system connecting two or more computers and their peripheral devices.

Computer trainer: Computer professional who provides classes to instruct users.

Connectivity: Capability of the microcomputer to use information from the world beyond one's desk. Data and information can be sent over telephone or cable lines and through the air.

Context-sensitive help: Feature of most application software that locates and displays reference information directly related to the task the user is performing.

Continuous-speech recognition system: Voice-recognition system used to control a microcomputer's operations and to issue commands to special application programs.

Controller card: *See* Expansion card.

Control unit: Section of the CPU that tells the rest of the computer how to carry out program instructions.

Conversion: *See* Systems implementation.

Cookies: Programs that record information on Web site visitors.

CPU: *See* Central processing unit.

Cracker: One who gains unauthorized access to a computer system for malicious purposes.

Critical path: In a PERT chart, sequence of tasks that takes the longest to complete.

CRT monitor: *See* Cathode-ray tube (CRT) monitor.

Cumulative trauma disorder: *See* Repetitive strain injury.

Cybercash: *See* Electronic cash.

Cyberspace: The space of electronic movement of ideas and information.

Data: Raw, unprocessed facts that are input to a computer system.

Database: A collection of related files.

Database administrator (DBA): Person responsible for structuring, coordinating, linking, and maintaining databases.

Database file: File containing highly structured and organized data.

Database management system (DBMS): *See* Database manager.

Database manager: Software package used to set up, or structure, a database.

Data bus: *See* Bus line.

Data communications system: Electronic system that transmits data over communications lines from one location to another.

Data dictionary: Dictionary containing a description of the structure of the data in a database.

Data flow diagram: Diagram showing the data or information flow within an information system.

Data integrity: A database characteristic relating to the consistency and accuracy of data.

Data mining: Technique of searching data warehouses for related information and patterns.

Data processing system (DPS): Transaction processing system that keeps track of routine operations and records these events in a database.

Data redundancy: A common database problem in which data is duplicated and stored in different files.

Data security: Protection of software and data from unauthorized tampering or damage.

Data warehouse: Special type of database that supports data mining.

DAT drive: *See* Digital audiotape (DAT) drive.

Debugging: Programmer's word for testing and then eliminating errors in a program.

Decision model: Strategic, tactical, or operational model that gives the decision support system its analytical capabilities.

Decision support system (DSS): Flexible tool for analysis that helps managers make decisions about unstructured problems, such as the effect of events and trends outside the organization.

Decision table: Table showing the decision rules that apply when certain conditions occur and what action should take place as a result.

Demand report: The opposite of a scheduled report. A demand report is produced on request.

Demodulation: Process performed by a modem in converting analog signals to digital signals.

Desk checking: Process of checking out a computer program by studying the program listing line by line, looking for syntax and logic errors.

Desktop: Windows user interface.

Desktop computer: Computer small enough to fit on top or along the side of a desk and yet too big to carry around.

Desktop managers: Programs that provide electronic organizational tools.

Desktop publishing: Program that allows you to mix text and graphics to create publications of professional quality.

Device driver: Specialized program designed to allow particular input or output devices to communicate with the rest of the computer program.

Dial-up service: Method of accessing the Internet using a high-speed modem and standard telephone lines.

Digital audiotape (DAT) drive: Backup technology that uses 2- by 3-inch cassettes that store 1.3 gigabytes or more.

Digital camera: Similar to a traditional camera except that images are recorded digitally in the camera's memory rather than on film.

Digital cash: *See* Electronic cash.

Digital notebook: An input device that records and stores pen movements.

Digital signal: Signal that represents the presence or absence of an electronic pulse.

Digital subscriber line (DSL): Provides high-speed connection using existing telephone lines.

Digital video camera: Input device that records motion digitally.

Digital video disc: *See* DVD (digital versatile disc).

Digitizer: Device that can be used to trace or copy a drawing or photograph. The shape is converted to digital data that can be represented on a screen or printed on paper.

Digitizing tablet: Device that enables the user to create images using a special stylus.

Direct approach: Approach for systems implementation whereby the old system is simply abandoned for the new.

Direct entry: Form of input that does not require data to be keyed by someone sitting at a keyboard. Direct-entry devices create machine-readable data on paper or magnetic media or feed it directly into the CPU.

Direct file organization: File organization that makes use of key fields to go directly to the record being sought rather than reading records one after another.

Direct-imaging plotter: Plotter that creates images using heat-sensitive paper and electrically heated pins.

Disaster recovery plan: Plan used by large organizations describing ways to continue operations following a disaster until normal computer operations can be restored.

Discrete-speech recognition system: Voice-recognition system that allows users to dictate directly into a microcomputer using a microphone.

Disk: *See* Floppy disk; Hard disk; Optical disk.

Disk caching: Method of improving hard-disk performance by anticipating data needs. It requires a combination of hardware and software.

Disk cleanup: Windows utility that eliminates nonessential files.

Disk defragmenter: Windows utility that optimizes disk performance by eliminating unnecessary fragments and by rearranging files.

Diskette: *See* Floppy disk.

Distributed database: Database that can be made accessible through a variety of communications networks, which allows portions of the database to be located in different places.

Distributed processing: System in which computing power is located and shared at different locations.

Document: Any kind of text material.

Documentation: Written descriptions and procedures about a program and how to use it.

Document file: File created by a word processor to save documents such as letters, research papers, and memos.

Domain code: Last part of an Internet address, which identifies the geographical description or organizational identification.

Domain name: Part of an Internet address, separated from the domain code by a dot (.), that is a reference to a particular organization.

Domain name system (DNS): Internet addressing method that assigns names and numbers to people and computers.

DO UNTIL structure: Loop structure in programming that appears at the end of a loop. The DO UNTIL loop means that the loop statements will be executed at least once.

DO WHILE structure: Loop structure in programming that appears at the beginning of a loop. The DO WHILE loop will keep executing as long as there is information to be processed.

Downloading: Process of transferring information from a remote computer to the computer one is using.

Draw program: Program used to help create artwork for publications. *See also* Illustration program.

DSS: *See* Decision support system.

Dual-scan monitor: *See* Passive-matrix monitor.

Dumb terminal: Terminal that can be used to input and receive data but cannot process data independently.

DVD (digital versatile, or video, disc): Similar to CD-ROMs except that more data can be packed into the same amount of space.

DVD-R: DVD-recordable.

DVD-RAM: DVD–random-access memory.

DVD-ROM: Digital versatile disc–read-only memory.

DVD-RW: DVD-rewritable

EBCDIC (Extended Binary Coded Decimal Interchange Code): Binary coding scheme that is a standard for minicomputers and mainframe computers.

Economic feasibility: Condition in which costs of designing a new sytem will be justified by the benefits it will provide.

EIS: *See* Executive information system.

Electronic cash (e-cash): Currency for Internet purchases.

Electronic commerce (e-commerce): Buying and selling of goods over the Internet.

Electronic Communications Privacy Act of 1986: Law protecting the privacy of users on public electronic-mail systems.

Electronic mail (e-mail): Similar to an electronic bulletin board, but provides confidentiality and may use special communications rather than telephone lines.

Electronic spreadsheet: *See* Spreadsheet.

Electrostatic plotter: Plotter that uses electrostatic charges to create images made up of tiny dots on specially treated paper.

E-mail: *See* Electronic mail.

Encrypting: Coding information so that only the user can read or otherwise use it.

End user: Person who uses microcomputers or has access to larger computers.

Energy Star: Program created by the Environmental Protection Agency to discourage waste in the microcomputer industry.

Enter key: Key used to enter a command after it has been typed into the computer.

Enterprise computing: Integrating an organization's networks.

Erasable optical disk: Optical disk on which the disk drive can write information and also erase and rewrite information.

Ergonomics: Study of human factors related to things people use.

ESS: *See* Executive support system.

Ethics: Standards of moral conduct.

Exception report: Report that calls attention to unusual events.

Executive information system (EIS): Sophisticated software that can draw together data from an organization's databases in meaningful patterns.

Executive support system (ESS): *See* Executive information system.
Expansion card: Optional device that plugs into a slot inside the system unit. Ports on the board allow cables to be connected from the expansion board to devices outside the system unit.
Expert system: Computer program that provides advice to decision makers who would otherwise rely on human experts.
Extended Binary Coded Decimal Interchange Code: *See* EBCDIC.
External modem: Modem that stands apart from the computer and is connected by a cable to the computer's serial port. Another cable connects the modem to the telephone wall jack.
Extranet: Private network that connects more than one organization.
Facsimile transmission machine: *See* Fax machine.
Fair Credit Reporting Act of 1970: Law prohibiting credit agencies from sharing credit information with anyone but authorized customers and giving consumers the right to review and correct their credit records.
Fax machine: Device that scans an image and sends it electronically over telephone lines to a receiving fax machine, which converts the electronic signals back to an image and recreates it on paper.
Fax/modem board: Expansion board that provides the independent capabilities of a fax and a modem.
Fiber-optic cable: Special transmission cable made of glass tubes that are immune to electronic interference. Data is transmitted through fiber-optic cables in the form of pulses of light.
Field: Each column of information within a record is called a field. A field contains a set of related characters.
File: A collection of related records.
File compression: Process of reducing the storage requirements for a file.
File compression programs: Programs that reduce the size of files.
File decompression: Process of expanding a compressed file.
File transfer protocol (FTP): Internet service for transferring files.
Filter: Program to block selected Web sites, set time limits, monitor use, and generate reports on use.
Find: In word processing, a command that allows the user to locate any character, word, or phrase in a document.
Firewall: Security hardware and software.
FireWire port: Used to connect high-speed printers and even videocameras to system unit.
Firmware: *See* ROM.
Fixed disk: *See* Internal hard disk.
Flash memory: *See* Flash RAM.
Flash RAM: RAM chips that retain data even when power is disrupted.
Flatbed scanner: An input device similar to a copying machine.
Flat-panel monitor: Monitor that lies flat instead of standing upright.
Flexible disk: *See* Floppy disk.
Floppy: *See* Floppy disk.
Floppy disk: Flat, circular piece of magnetically treated mylar plastic that rotates within a jacket.
Floppy-disk cartridge: Include Zip disks, SuperDisks, and HiFD disks, all competing to become the next higher capacity floppy disk standard.
Formatting toolbar: A collection of buttons used as shortcuts to commands that enhance the appearance of a document.
Formula: Instructions for calculations in a spreadsheet.
FORTRAN (FORmula TRANslation): Most widely used scientific and mathematical procedural language.
Freedom of Information Act of 1970: Law giving citizens the right to examine data about them in federal government files, except for that restricted for national security reasons.
FTP: *See* File transfer protocol.
Full-duplex communication: Mode of communication in which data is transmitted back and forth at the same time.
Function: In a spreadsheet, a built-in formula that performs calculations automatically.
Fuzzy logic: Used by expert systems to allow users to respond by using qualitative terms such as *great* and *OK*.
Gantt chart: Chart using bars and lines to indicate the time scale of a series of tasks.
General ledger: Activity that produces income statements and balance sheets based on all transactions of a company.
General-purpose applications: Applications designed to be used by most people doing the most common tasks, such as browsers and word processors.
Generations of programming languages: The five generations are machine languages, assembly languages, procedural languages, problem-oriented languages, and natural languages.
Gopher: Program that helps individuals on the Internet to access other computers on the Internet.
Gopher site: Internet computer that provides menus describing its available resources and direct links to the resources.
Grammar checker: In word processing, a tool that identifies poorly worded sentences and incorrect grammar.
Graphical map: Diagram of a Web site's overall design.
Graphical user interface (GUI): Special screen that allows software commands to be issued through the use of graphic symbols (icons) or pull-down menus.
Graphics suite: Group of graphics programs offered at lower cost than if purchased separately.
Green PC: Microcomputer industry concept of an environmentally friendly, low-power-consuming machine.
Grid chart: Chart that shows the relationship between input and output documents.
Group decision support system (GDSS): System used to support the collective work of a team addressing large problems.

GUI: *See* Graphical user interface.

Hacker: Person who gains unauthorized access to a computer system for the fun and challenge of it.

Half-duplex communication: Mode of communication in which data flows in both directions, but not simultaneously.

Handheld computer: *See* Personal digital assistant (PDA).

Hard copy: Images output on paper by a printer or plotter.

Hard disk: Enclosed disk drive that contains one or more metallic disks. A hard disk has many times the capacity of a floppy disk.

Hard-disk cartridge: Hard disk that is easily removed.

Hard-disk pack: Several platters aligned one above the other, thereby offering much greater storage capacity.

Hardware: Equipment that includes a keyboard, monitor, printer, the computer itself, and other devices.

Hashing: Program that uses mathematical operations to convert the key field's numeric value to a particular storage address.

Head crash: Occurs when the surface of the read-write head or particles on its surface contact the magnetic disk surface.

Header: The first element of an e-mail message.

Help: A feature in most application software providing options that typically include an index, a glossary, and a search feature to locate reference information about specific commands.

Helper applications: Independent programs that can be executed by a browser. Also called add-ons.

Hierarchical database: Database in which fields or records are structured in nodes.

Hierarchical network: Network consisting of several computers linked to a central host computer. The computers linked to the host are themselves hosts to other computers or devices.

HiFD disk: High-capacity floppy disk manufactured by Sony.

High-definition television (HDTV): All-digital television that delivers a much clearer and more detailed wide-screen picture.

History file: Created by browser to store information on Web sites visited.

Home page: Top-level or opening page of Web site.

Home PC: Specialized large-screen system with high-quality audio.

Horizontal portal: Web portal designed to appeal to mass audiences.

Host computer: A large centralized computer. A common way of accessing the Internet. The host computer is connected to the Internet and provides a path or connection for individuals to access the Internet.

Hot site: Special emergency facility consisting of a fully equipped computer center available to a company in the event of disaster to its computer system. *Compare* Cold site.

HTML: *See* Hypertext Markup Language (HTML).

HTML editor: *See* Web authoring program.

Hybrid network: *See* Hierarchical network.

Hyperlink: A hypertext link.

Hypermedia: *See* Multimedia.

Hypertext link: These create connections between information references within a document or between documents.

Hypertext Markup Language (HTML): Programming language for the document files that are used to display Web pages.

Icon: Graphic object on the desktop used to represent commonly used features.

IF-THEN-ELSE structure: Logical selection structure whereby one of two paths is followed according to IF, THEN, and ELSE statements in a program.

Illustration program: Used to modify vector images and thus create line art, 3-D models, and virtual reality. Also called draw program.

Image editor: Used to create and modify bitmap files. Also called paint program.

Image scanner: Device that identifies images on a page and automatically converts them to electronic signals that can be stored in a computer.

Index sequential file organization: Compromise between sequential and direct file organization. Records are stored sequentially, but an index is used to access a group of records directly.

Individual database: Collection of integrated records useful mainly to just one person.

Industry Standard Architecture (ISA): Bus-line standard developed for the IBM Personal Computer. It first consisted of an 8-bit-wide data path, then a 16-bit-wide data path.

Information: Data that has been processed by a computer system.

Information pusher: Program that automatically gathers information on topics of your choice and saves it on your hard disk. Also called push product and Web Broadcaster utility.

Information system: Collection of hardware, software, people, data, and procedures that work together to provide information essential to running an organization.

Information worker: Employee that creates, distributes, and communicates information.

Ink-jet plotter: Plotter that forms images by spraying droplets of ink onto paper.

Ink-jet printer: Printer that sprays small droplets of ink at high speed onto the surface of the paper.

Input device: Piece of equipment that puts data into a form a computer can process.

Instant messaging: Communication and collaboration tool for direct, "live," connections over the Internet.

Integrated circuit: *See* Silicon chip.

Integrated package: Collection of computer programs that work together and share information.

Integrated services digital network (ISDN): Connection service provided by local telephone companies using special high-speed telephone lines.

Intelligent terminal: Terminal that includes a processing unit, memory, secondary storage, communications software, and a telephone hookup or other communications link.

Interactivity: User participation in a multimedia presentation.

Interface card: *See* Expansion card.

Internal hard disk: Storage device consisting of one or more metallic platters sealed inside a container. Internal hard disks are installed inside the system cabinet of a microcomputer.

Internet: A huge computer network available to nearly everyone with a microcomputer and a means to connect to it. It is a resource for information about an infinite number of topics.

Internet relay chat (IRC): Leading type of chat group service.

Internet service provider (ISP): Provides access to the Internet.

Internet terminal: Provides access to the Internet and displays Web pages on a standard television set. Also called Web terminal.

Interpreter: Software that converts a procedural language one statement at a time into machine language just before the statement is executed.

Intranet: Like the Internet but privately owned by an organization.

Inventory: Material or products that a company has in stock.

ISA: *See* Industry Standard Architecture.

ISDN: *See* Integrated services digital network.

ISP: *See* Internet service provider.

Java: A portable programming language.

Joystick: Popular input device for computer games.

Keyboard: Input device that looks like a typewriter keyboard but has additional keys.

Key field: The common field by which tables in a database are related to each other.

Knowledge base: *See* Expert system.

Knowledge work system (KWS): Specialized information system used to create information in a specific area of expertise.

Label: Column or row heading in a spreadsheet.

Lands and pits: Flat and bumpy areas, respectively, that represent 1s and 0s on the optical disk surface to be read by a laser.

LAN: *See* Local area network.

Language translator: Converts programming instructions into a machine language that can be processed by a computer.

Laser printer: Printer that creates dotlike images on a drum, using a laser beam light source.

Layout files: Sample presentation files.

LCD: *See* Liquid crystal display.

Levels of programming languages: Levels used by computer professionals to describe programming languages. A lower-level language is one closer to the language the computer uses itself. A higher-level language is closer to the language humans use.

Light pen: Light-sensitive penlike device used with a special monitor to enter commands by touching the monitor with the pen.

Link: A connection to related information.

Linux: Type of Unix operating system initially developed by Linus Torvalds.

Liquid crystal display (LCD): Display consisting of liquid crystal molecules whose optical properties can be altered by an applied electric field.

List address: Internet mailing list address. Members of a mailing list communicate by sending messages to the list address.

Local area network (LAN): Network consisting of computers and other devices that are physically near each other, such as within the same building.

Logic error: Error that occurs when a programmer has used an incorrect calculation or left out a programming procedure.

Logic structure: Structure that controls the logical sequence in which computer program instructions are executed. The three structures are sequence, selection, and loop.

Loop structure: Logic structure in which a process may be repeated as long as a certain condition remains true.

Lurking: Observing or reading communications from others on an Internet discussion group without participating.

Machine language: Language in which data is represented in 1s and 0s.

Mac OS: Operating system designed for Macintosh computers.

Magnetic-ink character recognition (MICR): Direct-entry scanning device used in banks. This technology is used to automatically read the futuristic-looking numbers on the bottom of checks.

Magnetic tape drive: Device used to read data from and store data on magnetic tape.

Magnetic tape streamer: Device that allows duplication (backup) of the data stored on a microcomputer hard disk.

Magnetic tape unit: *See* Magnetic tape drive.

Mailing list: Type of discussion group available on the Internet.

Main board: *See* System board.

Mainframe: Computer that can process several million program instructions per second. Large organizations rely on these room-size systems to handle large programs with lots of data.

MAN: *See* Metropolitan area network.

Management information system (MIS): Computer-based information system that produces standardized reports in summarized, structured form. It is used to support middle managers.

Mark sensing: *See* Optical-character recognition.

Master file: Complete file containing all records current up to the last update.

Medium band: Bandwidth of special leased lines, used mainly with minicomputers and mainframe computers.

Megahertz (MHz): Unit representing 1 million beats (cycles) per second.

Memory: Part of the microcomputer that holds data for processing, instructions for processing the data, and information (processed data) waiting to be output or sent to secondary storage.

Menu: List of commands.

Message: The content portion of e-mail correspondence.

Metasearch utility: Program that automatically submits your search request to several indices and search engines, then creates an index from received information. Also called metasearch program.

Metropolitan area network (MAN): Network linking office buildings in a city.

MHz: *See* Megahertz.

MICR: *See* Magnetic-ink character recognition.

Microcomputer: Small, low-cost computer designed for individual users.

Microcomputer database: *See* Individual database.

Microprocessor: The central processing unit of a microcomputer. The microprocessor is contained on a single integrated circuit chip.

Microsecond: One-millionth of a second.

Microwave communication: Communication using high-frequency radio waves that travel in straight lines through the air.

Middle-level manager: Manager dealing with control and planning. The manager implements the long-term goals of the organization.

Midrange computer: *See* Minicomputer.

Minicomputer: Desk-sized machine falling in between microcomputers and mainframes in processing speed and data-storing capacity.

MIS: *See* Management information system.

Modem: Communications device that translates the electronic signals from a computer into electronic signals that can travel over a telephone line.

Modulation: Process of converting digital signals to analog signals.

Module: *See* Program module.

Monitor: Output device like a television screen that displays data processed by the computer.

Morphing: Special effect in which one image seems to melt into another.

Motherboard: *See* System board.

Mouse: Device that typically rolls on the desktop and directs the cursor on the display screen.

Multimedia: Technology that can link all sorts of media into one form of presentation.

Multimedia authoring program: Program to create a multimedia presentation by bringing together text, graphics, audio, and other elements into an interactive framework.

Multitasking: Operating system that allows a single user to run several application programs at the same time.

Nanomanipulator: Advanced virtual reality interface.

National Information Infrastructure Protection Act of 1996: Provides penalties for trespassing on computer systems, threats made against computer networks, and theft of information.

Natural language: Language designed to give people a more human connection with computers.

Navigating: Moving from one Web site to another.

Net personal computer (Net PC): Low-cost type of intelligent terminal that typically has only one type of secondary storage and no expansion slots.

Network adapter card: Connects the sytem unit to a cable that connects to other devices on the network.

Network architecture: Describes how a network is arranged and how the resources are shared.

Network bridge: Connects networks of the same configuration.

Network computer: *See* Network terminal.

Network database: Database with a hierarchical arrangement of nodes, except that each child node may have more than one parent node.

Network gateway: Connection by which a local area network may be linked to other local area networks or to larger networks.

Network manager: Computer professional who ensures that existing information and communication systems are operating effectively and that new ones are implemented as needed. Also responsible for meeting security and privacy requirements.

Network operating system (NOS): Software that interacts with applications and computers, and also coordinate activities between computers on a network.

Network terminal: Low-cost alternative to intelligent terminal; relies on host computer or server for software. *Also* called network computer.

Newsgroup: Most popular type of Internet discussion group. Newsgroups use a special network of computers called the UseNet. Each of these computers maintains the newsgroup listing. The newsgroups are organized into major topic areas that are further subdivided into hierarchies.

Node: Any device connected to a network. Also, points in a hierarchical database connected like the branches of an upside-down tree.

No Electronic Theft (NET) Act of 1997: Provides penalties for unathorized distribution of copyrighted materials (software) on the Internet.

Nonvolatile storage: Permanent storage used to preserve data and programs.

Norton AntiVirus: Collection of antivirus programs from Symantec.

Norton CleanSweep: Collection of programs to safely remove files and programs from Symantec.

Norton CrashGuard: Collection of programs that protect against system crashes from Symantec.

Norton Utilities: Collection of 17 troubleshooting utilities from Symantec.

Norton Web Services: Service from Symantec that monitors a computer system for out-of-date software.

Notebook: Portable computer weighing between 5 and 10 pounds.

Object linking and embedding (OLE): Powerful feature of many application programs that allows sharing of information.

Object-oriented database: Keep track of objects, which are entities that contain both data and the action that can be taken on data.

Object-oriented programming (OOP): Methodology in which a program is organized into objects, each containing both the data and processing operations necessary to perform a task.

Object-oriented software development: Software development approach that focuses less on the tasks and more on defining the relationships between previously defined procedures or objects.

OCR: *See* Optical-character recognition.

Off-line browser: Program that automatically connects to selected Web sites, downloads HTML documents, and saves them to your hard disk. Also called pull product and Web-downloading utility.

Office automation system (OAS): System designed primarily to support data workers. It focuses on managing documents, communicating, and scheduling.

OMR: *See* Optical-mark recognition.

1.44 MB 3½-inch disk: The most widely used floppy disk.

Online service provider: Provides access to Internet plus other services.

OOP: *See* Object-oriented programming.

Open architecture: Microcomputer architecture allowing users to expand their systems by inserting optional devices known as expansion cards.

Operating system: Software that interacts between application software and the computer. The operating system handles such details as running programs, storing data and programs, and processing data.

Operational feasibility: Condition in which the design of a new system will be able to function within the existing framework of an organization.

Optical-character recognition (OCR): Scanning device that uses special preprinted characters, such as those printed on utility bills, that can be read by a light source and changed into machine-readable code.

Optical disk: Storage device that can hold 650 megabytes of data. Lasers are used to record and read data on the disk.

Optical-mark recognition (OMR): Device that senses the presence or absence of a mark, such as a pencil mark.

Organization chart: Chart showing the levels of management and formal lines of authority in an organization.

Output device: Equipment that translates processed information from the central processing unit into a form that can be understood.

Packet: Before a message is sent on the Internet, it is broken down into small parts called packets. Each packet is then sent separately over the Internet. At the receiving end, the packets are reassembled into the correct order.

Paint program: *See* Image editor.

Palmtop computer: *See* Personal digital assistant (PDA).

Parallel approach: Systems implementation in which old and new systems are operated side by side until the new one has shown it is reliable.

Parallel data transmission: Data transmission in which bits flow through separate lines simultaneously.

Parallel port: Used to connect external devices that send or receive a lot of data over a short distance. Mostly used to connect printers to system unit.

Parent node: Node one level above the node being considered in a hierarchical database or network.

Pascal: Procedural programming language widely used on microcomputers.

Passive-matrix monitor: Monitor that creates images by scanning the entire screen.

Password: Special sequence of numbers or letters that limits access to information, such as electronic mail.

Payroll: Activity concerned with calculating employee paychecks.

PC card: *See* PCMCIA card.

PC/TV: The merger of microcomputers and television.

Peer-to-peer network system: Network in which nodes can act as both servers and clients. For example, one microcomputer can obtain files located on another microcomputer and can also provide files to other microcomputers.

Pen plotter: Plotter that creates plots by moving a pen or pencil over drafting paper.

Periodic report: Report generated at regular intervals.

Peripheral Component Interconnect (PCI): Bus architecture that combines the capabilities of MCA and EISA with the ability to send video instructions at speeds to match the microprocessor.

Personal Computer Memory Card International Association (PCMCIA) card: Credit card–sized expansion cards developed for portable computers.

Personal digital assistant (PDA): A device that typically combines pen input, writing recognition, personal organizational tools, and communication capabilities in a very small package. Also called Handheld PC and palmtop computer.

Personal information managers (PIMs): Programs that provide electronic organizational tools.

Personal laser printer: Inexpensive laser printer widely used by single users to produce black-and-white documents.

Phased approach: Systems implementation in which the new system is implemented gradually over a period of time.

Physical security: Activity concerned with protecting hardware from possible human and natural disasters.

Pilot approach: Systems implementation in which the new system is tried out in only one part of the organization. Later it is implemented throughout the rest of the organization.

Pits: *See* Lands and pits.

Pixel: Smallest unit on the screen that can be turned on and off or made different shades.

Platform scanner: Handheld direct-entry device used to read special characters on price tags.

Plotter: Special-purpose output device for producing bar charts, maps, architectural drawings, and three-dimensional illustrations.

Plug and Play: Set of hardware and software standards developed to create operating systems, processing units, and expansion cards, as well as other devices, that are able to configure themselves.

Plug-in: Program that is automatically loaded and operates as part of a browser.

Plug-in board: *See* Expansion card.

Pointer: For a monitor, a pointer is typically displayed as an arrow and controlled by a mouse. For a database, a pointer is a connection between parent node and child node in a hierarchical database.

Pointing stick: Device used to control the pointer by directing the stick with your finger.

Point-of-sale (POS) terminal: Terminal that consists of a keyboard, screen, and printer. It is used like a cash register.

Point-to-point protocol (PPP): Software that allows your computer to become part of a client/server network.

The provider or host computer is the server providing access to the Internet. Your computer is the client. Using special client software, your computer is able to communicate with server software running on the provider's computer and on other Internet computers.

Polling: Process whereby a host computer or file server asks each connecting device whether it has a message to send and then allows the message to be sent.

Port: Connecting socket on the outside of the system unit. Used to connect input and output devices to the system unit.

Portable language: Language that can be run on more than one kind of computer.

Portable scanner: Handheld input device for scanning images and text.

POS terminal: *See* Point-of-sale (POS) terminal.

Preliminary investigation: First phase of systems analysis and design. It involves defining the problem, suggesting alternative systems, and preparing a short report.

Presentation file: A file created by presentation graphics programs to save presentation materials.

Presentation graphics: Graphics used to communicate a message or to persuade other people.

Printer: Device that produces printed paper output.

Privacy: Computer ethics issue concerning the collection and use of data about individuals.

Privacy Act of 1974: Law designed to restrict the way federal agencies share information about American citizens. It prohibits federal information collected for one purpose from being used for a different purpose.

Problem-oriented language: Programming language designed to solve specific problems.

Procedural language: Programming language designed to express the logic that can solve problems.

Procedures: Rules or guidelines to follow when using hardware, software, and data.

Processing rights: Refers to which people have access to what kind of data.

Processor: *See* Central processing unit.

Program: List of instructions for the computer to follow to process data. *See also* Software.

Program analysis: *See* Program specification.

Program definition: *See* Program specification.

Program design: Creation of a solution using programming techniques such as top-down program design, pseudocode, flowcharts, logic structures, object-oriented programming, and CASE tools.

Program Evaluation Review Technique (PERT) chart: Chart showing the timing of a project and the relationships among its tasks. The chart identifies which tasks must be completed before others can begin.

Program flowchart: Flowchart graphically presenting the detailed sequence of steps needed to solve a programming problem.

Program maintenance: Activity of updating software to correct errors, improve usability, standardize, and adjust to organizational changes.

Programmer: Computer professional who creates new software or revises existing software.

Programming: Six-step procedure for creating a program.

Program module: Logically related program statements.

Program specification: Programming step in which objectives, outputs, inputs, and processing requirements are determined.

Project: One-time operation composed of several tasks that must be completed during a stated period of time.

Project manager: Software that enables users to plan, schedule, and control the people, resources, and costs needed to complete a project on time.

Property: Computer ethics issue relating to who owns data and rights to software.

Proprietary database: Enormous database an organization develops to cover certain particular objects. Access to this type of database is usually offered for a fee.

Protocol: Rules for exchanging data between computers.

Prototyping: Building of a model (prototype) that can be modified before the actual system is installed. It allows users to find out right away how a change in the system can help their work.

Provider: *See* Host computer.

Proxy server: Computer that acts as a gateway or checkpoint in an organization's firewall.

Pseudocode: Narrative form of the logic of a computer program.

Pull product: *See* Off-line browser.

Purchasing: Buying of raw materials and services.

Push product: *See* Information pusher.

Query language: Easy-to-use language understandable to most users. It is used to search and generate reports from a database.

RAD: *See* Rapid applications development.

RAM (random-access memory): Volatile storage that holds the program and data the CPU is presently processing.

RAM cache: *See* Cache memory.

Random-access memory (RAM): *See* RAM (random-access memory).

Rapid applications development (RAD): Involves the use of powerful development software and specialized teams as an alternative to the systems development life cycle approach.

Reader/sorter: A special purpose input device that reads characters made of ink containing magnetized particles.

Read-only memory (ROM): *See* ROM (read-only memory).

Real-time processing: Processing that occurs when data is processed at the same time the transaction occurs.

Record: Each line of information in a database is a record. A record is a collection of related fields.

Reduced instruction set computer (RISC) chip: Powerful microprocessor chip found in workstations.

Redundant arrays of inexpensive disks (RAIDs): Groups of inexpensive hard-disk drives related or grouped together using networks and special software. They improve performance by expanding external storage.

Relation: Table in a relational database in which data elements are stored.

Relational database: A widely used database structure, in which data is organized into related tables.

Repetitive motion injury: *See* Repetitive strain injury.

Repetitive strain injury (RSI): Category of injuries resulting from fast, repetitive work that causes neck, wrist, hand, and arm pain.

Replace: In word processing, command that enables the user to search for a word and replace it with another.

Resolution: A measurement in pixels of a monitor's clarity.

Right to Financial Privacy Act of 1979: Law setting strict procedures that federal agencies must follow when seeking to examine customer records in banks.

Ring network: Network in which each device is connected to two other devices, forming a ring. There is no host computer, and messages are passed around the ring until they reach the correct destination.

Robot: Machine used in factories and elsewhere that can be reprogrammed to do more than one task.

Robotics: Field of study concerned with developing and using robots.

Roller ball: *See* Trackball.

ROM (read-only memory): Refers to chips that have programs built into them at the factory. The contents of such chips cannot be changed by the user.

RS-232C connector: Serial port, a port set up for serial data transmission.

RSI: *See* Repetitive strain injury.

Sales order processing: Activity that records the demands of customers for a company's products or services.

Satellite/air connection services: Connection services that use satellites and the air to download or send data to users at a rate seven times faster than dial-up connections.

Satellite communication: Communication using satellites as microwave relay stations.

Scanner: *See* Image scanner.

Search engine: Search tool that lets you search by entering key words or phrases.

Search tools: Help you locate information on the Web; there are two basic kinds: indexes and search engines.

Secondary storage: Permanent storage used to preserve programs and data, including floppy disks, hard disks, and magnetic tape.

Sector: Section shaped like a pie wedge that divides the tracks on a disk.

Security: The protection of information, hardware, and software.

Selection structure: Logic structure that determines which of two paths will be followed when a decision must be made by a program.

Semiconductor: Silicon chip through which electricity flows with some resistance.

Sequence structure: Logic structure in which one program statement follows another.

Sequential file organization: File organization in which records are stored physically one after another in predetermined order.

Serial data transmission: Method of transmission in which bits flow in a series, one after another.

Serial line Internet protocol (SLIP): Internet protocol that enables your computer to become part of a client/server network. The provider or host computer is the server providing access to the Internet. Your computer is the client.

Serial port: Used to connect external devices that send or receive data one bit at a time over a long distance. Used for mouse, keyboard, modem, and many other devices.

Server: A connection to the Internet that stores document files used to display pages.

Service program: *See* Utility.

Shared laser printer: More expensive laser printer used by a group of users to produce black-and-white documents.

Sherlock: A search feature in Mac OS 8.5 operating system.

Signature line: Provides additional information about a sender of an e-mail message, such as name, address, and telephone number.

Silicon chip: Tiny circuit board etched on a small square of sandlike material called silicon. Chips are mounted on carrier packages, which then plug into sockets on the system board.

Simplex communication: Mode of communication in which data travels in one direction only.

Slot: Area on a system board that accepts cards to expand a computer system's capabilities.

Small computer interface (SCSI) card: This card uses only one slot and can connect as many as seven devices to the system unit.

Smart card: Card about the size of a credit card containing a tiny built-in microprocessor. It can be used to hold such information as frequent flier miles.

Snoopware: Programs that record virtually every activity on a computer system.

Soft copy: Images or characters output on a monitor screen.

Software: Computer program.

Software Copyright Act of 1980: Law allowing owners of programs to make copies for backup purposes, and to modify them to make them useful, provided they are not resold or given away.

Software development: *See* Programming.

Software piracy: Unauthorized copying of programs for personal gain.

Software suite: Individual application programs that are sold together as a group.

Sorting: Arranging objects numerically or alphabetically.

Source document: Original version of a document before any processing has been performed on it.

Spelling checker: Program used with a word processor to check the spelling of typed text against an electronic dictionary.

Spider: *See* Agent.

Spike: *See* Voltage surge.

Spreadsheet: Computer-produced spreadsheet based on the traditional accounting "worksheet" that has rows and columns that can be used to present and analyze data.

Standard toolbar: A collection of buttons used as shortcuts to the most frequently used menu commands.

Star network: Network of computers or peripheral devices linked to a central computer through which all communications pass. Control is maintained by polling.

Start menu: A Windows menu listing commands used to gain access to information, change hardware settings, find information, get online help, run programs, log off a network, and shut down the computer system.

Story boards: Design tool for planning and structuring a multimedia presentaiton.

Structured programming techniques: Techniques that consist of top-down program design, pseudocode, flowcharts, and logic structures.
Structured query language (SQL): Program control language used to create sophisticated database applications.
Stylus: A special input device that traces images.
Subnotebook: Handheld or pocket-size portable computer.
Subscription address: Mailing list address. To participate in a mailing list, you must first subscribe by sending an e-mail request to the mailing list subscription address.
Supercomputer: Fastest calculating device ever invented, processing billions of program instructions per second.
SuperDisk: High-capacity floppy disk manufactured by Imation.
SVGA: Refers to a resolution standard that displays 800 by 600 pixels.
Supervisor: Manager responsible for managing and monitoring workers. Supervisors have responsibility for operational matters.
Surfing: Moving from one Web site to another.
Surge protector: Device separating the computer from the power source of the wall outlet. When a voltage surge occurs, a circuit breaker is activated, protecting the computer system.
SXGA: Refers to a resolutuion standard of 1,280 by 1,024 pixels.
Synchronous transmission: Method whereby data is transmitted several bytes or a block at a time.
Syntax error: Violation of the rules of whatever language a computer program is written in.
System: Collection of activities and elements designed to accomplish a goal.
System board: Flat board that usually contains the CPU and some memory chips.
System clock: Clock that controls how fast all the operations within a computer take place.
System flowchart: Flowchart that shows the kinds of equipment used to handle the data or information flow.
System software: "Background" software that enables the application software to interact with the computer. It includes programs that help the computer manage its own internal resources.
System unit: Part of a microcomputer that contains the CPU.
Systems analysis: Determining the requirements for a new system. Data is collected about the present system, analyzed, and new requirements are determined.
Systems analysis and design: Six-phase problem-solving procedure for examining an information system and improving it.
Systems analyst: Computer professional who studies an organization's systems to determine what actions to take and how to use computer technology to assist them.
Systems audit: A systems audit compares the performance of a new system to the original design specifications to determine if the new procedures are actually improving productivity.
Systems design: Phase consisting of designing alternative systems, selecting the best system, and writing a systems design report.
Systems development: Phase consisting of developing software, acquiring hardware, and testing the new system.
Systems implementation: Process of changing from the old system to the new and training people to use it.
Systems life cycle: Phases of systems analysis and design.
Systems maintenance: Consists of a systems audit and periodic evaluation.
Table (in database): The list of records in a database.
Technical feasibility: Condition in which hardware, software, and training will be available to facilitate the design of a new system.
Technical writer: Computer professional who explains in writing how a computer program works.
Technostress: Tension that arises when humans must unnaturally adapt to computers.
Television board: Contains a TV tuner and video converter that changes the TV signal into one that can be displayed on your monitor.
Telnet: Internet service that helps to connect computers on the Internet and to run programs on remote computers.
Templates: Model presentations.
Terminal: Form of input (and output) device that consists of a keyboard, a monitor, and a communications link.
Terminal connection: Method of accessing the Internet using a high-speed modem and standard telephone lines.
Terminal network system: Network system in which processing power is centralized in one large computer, usually a mainframe. The nodes connected to this host computer are terminals with little or no processing capabilities.
Thermal printer: Printer that uses heat elements to produce images on heat-sensitive paper.
Thin client: *See* Network terminal.
Thin film transistor (TFT): Type of flat-panel monitor that activates each pixel independently.
Time-sharing system: System that allows several users to share resources in the host computer.
Toggle key: On-off key.
T1, T2, T3, T4 lines: High-speed lines that support all digital communications, provide very high capacity, and are very expensive.
Toolbar: Bar located typically below the menu bar. It contains icons or graphical representations for commonly used commands.
Top-down analysis method: Method used to identify the top-level component of a system and break this component down into smaller components for analysis.
Top-down program design: Process of identifying the top element (module) for a program and then breaking the top element down into smaller pieces in a hierarchical fashion.
Top-level manager: Manager concerned with long-range (strategic) planning. Top-level managers supervise middle-level managers.

Topology: The configuration of a network.
Touch screen: Monitor screen that allows actions or commands to be entered by the touch of a finger.
Track: Closed, concentric ring on a disk on which data is recorded.
Trackball: Device used to control the pointer by rotating a ball with your thumb.
Transaction: Event recorded in a database.
Transaction file: File containing recent changes to records that will be used to update the master file.
Transaction processing system (TPS): System that records day-to-day transactions.
Transmission control protocol/Internet protocol (TCP/IP): The two standard protocols for all communications on the Internet.
Troubleshooting programs: Programs that recognize and correct computer related problems.
Twisted pair: Copper-wire telephone line.
2HD: Two-sided, double-density disk.
Unicode: A 16-bit code designed to support international languages like Chinese and Japanese.
Uniform resource locator (URL): Addresses of resources on the Web.
Unix: An operating system originally developed for minicomputers. It is now important because it can run on many of the more powerful microcomputers.
Uploading: Process of transferring information from the computer the user is operating to a remote computer.
Uninstall program: Programs that safely and completely remove unwanted programs and related files.
Universal serial bus (USB) port: Expected to replace serial and parallel ports.
UseNet: Special network of computers that support newsgroups.
User: *See* End user.
User interface: Means by which users interact with programs and hardware.
User name: The part of an Internet address that identifies a unique person or computer at the listed domain.
Utility: Performs specific tasks related to managing computer resources or files.
Utility program: Program that performs common repetitious tasks, such as keeping files orderly, merging, and sorting.
UXGA: Refers to a resolution standard of 1,600 by 1,200 pixels.
Value: Number contained in a cell in a spreadsheet.
Vector image: Graphics file made up of a collection of objects such as lines, rectangles, and ovals.
Vertical portal: Web portal designed to appeal to special-interest groups.
VGA (video graphics array): Circuit board that may be inserted into a microcomputer and offers up to 256 colors.
Videoconferencing systems: Computer systems that allow people located at various geographic locations to have in-person meetings.
Video display screen: *See* Monitor.
Video Privacy Protection Act of 1988: Law preventing retailers from selling or disclosing video-rental records without the customer's consent or a court order.
Virtual environment: *See* Virtual reality.
Virtual memory: Feature of an operating system that increases the amount of memory available to run programs.
Virtual reality: Interactive sensory equipment (headgear and gloves) that allows users to experience alternative realities to the physical world.
Virtual reality modeling language (VRML): Used to create real-time animated 3-D scenes.
Virus: Hidden instructions that migrate through networks and operating systems and become embedded in different programs. They may be designed to destroy data or simply to display messages.
Visual BASIC: A widely used programming language created by Microsoft.
Voiceband: Bandwidth of a standard telephone line.
Voice-input device: Direct-entry device that converts speech into a numeric code that can be processed by a computer.
Voice-messaging system: Computer system linked to telephones that converts human voice into digital bits.
Voice-output device: Device that makes sounds resembling human speech that are actually prerecorded vocalized sounds.
Voice recognition system: *See* Voice-input device.
Volatile storage: Temporary storage that destroys the current data when power is lost or new data is read.
Voltage surge (spike): Excess of electricity, which may destroy chips or other electronic computer components.
WAN: *See* Wide area network.
Wand reader: Special-purpose handheld device used to read OCR characters.
Web: A service that provides a multimedia interface to resources on the Internet. *See also* World Wide Web.
Web auction: Similar to traditional auctions except that buyers and sellers meet only on the Web.
Web authoring: Creating a Web site.
Web authoring program: Word processing program for generating Web pages. Also called HTMLeditor; Web page editor.
Web broadcaster: *See* Information pusher.
Web crawler: *See* Search engine.
Web directory: *See* Index.
Web-downloading utility: *See* Off-line browser.
Webmaster: Person who designs, creates, monitors, and evaluates corporate Web sites.
Web page: Browsers interpret HTML documents to display Web pages.
Web page editor: *See* Web authoring program.
Web portal: Site that offers a variety of services such as e-mail, news, and sports updates.
Web site: A location on a server.
Web spider: *See* Search engine.
Web storefront creation packages: Programs for creating Web sites for virtual stores.
Web storefronts: Virtual stores where shoppers can go to inspect goods and make purchases.
Web terminal: *See* Internet terminal.

What-if analysis: Spreadsheet feature in which changing one or more numbers results in the automatic recalculation of all related formulas.

Wide area network (WAN): Countrywide network that uses microwave relays and satellites to reach users over long distances.

Window: A rectangular area containing a document or message.

Windows: An operating environment that extends the capability of DOS.

Wireless modem: Modem that connects to the serial port but does not connect to telephone lines. It receives through the air.

Word: Unit that describes the number of bits in a common unit of information.

Word processing: Use of a computer to create, edit, save, and print documents composed of text.

Word wrap: Feature of word processing that automatically moves the cursor from the end of one line to the beginning of the next.

Worksheet file: File created by an electronic spreadsheet.

World Wide Web (WWW, the Web): Internet service that uses hypertext to jump from document to document and from computer to computer. The Web is accessed by browsers.

Worm: Variant on computer virus, a destructive program that fills a computer system with self-replicating information, clogging the system so that its operations are slowed or stopped.

WORM (write once, read many): Form of optical disk that allows data to be written only once but read many times without deterioration.

Write-protect notch: Notch on a floppy disk used to prevent the computer from destroying data or information on the disk.

WWW: *See* World Wide Web.

XGA (extended graphics array): Circuit board that can be inserted into a microcomputer and offers up to 256 colors under normal circumstances and more than 65,000 colors with special equipment.

Zip disk: High capacity floppy disk manufactured by Sony.

CREDITS

01-01 a: © PhotoDisc, Inc.
01-01 b © Jose L. Pelaez, Inc/The Stock Market
01-01 c: © Mark Harme/Tony Stone Images
01-01 d: © AP/Wide World Photos, Inc.
01-01 e: © Jon Riley/Tony Stone Images
01-07: Courtesy of International Business Machines Corporation. Unauthorized use not permitted
01-08: © AP/Wide World Photos, Inc.
01-09: © PhotoDisc, Inc.
01-10: © Don Mason/The Stock Market
01-14: © Jeff Zaruba/The Stock Market
01-18: © Masami Sano/The Stock Market
03-01a © AP/Wide World Photos, Inc.
03-14: © Seth Affoumado
04-00: © Wides+Holl/FPG International
04-05 a: © AP/Wide World Photos, Inc.
04-06: Courtesy of Intel Corporation
04-13: Courtesy of Phoebe Micro, Inc.
04-14: Courtesy of 3Com Corporation
04-15: © PhotoDisc, Inc.
05-01: © Michael Newman/PhotoEdit
05-03: Courtesy of Microsoft Corporation
05-04: © AP/Wide World Photos, Inc.
05-06: © AP/Wide World Photos, Inc.
05-07: © William Whitehurst/The Stock Market
05-08: Courtesy of International Business Machines Corporation. Unauthorized use not permitted
05-09: © Jose L. Pelaez, Inc./The Stock Market
05-10: © David K. Crow/PhotoEdit
05-11: Courtesy of HEI , Inc.
05-12: © Richard Pasley/Stock, Boston
05-13: Courtesy of Casio
05-14: Courtesy of Cross Pen Computing
05-15: © Eric Neurath/Stock, Boston
05-16: © Richard Pasley/Stock, Boston
05-17: © John Blaustein/The Gamma Liaison Network
05-18: Courtesy of Symbol Technologies
05-19: Courtesy of Dragon Systems
05-20: Courtesy of Dragon Systems
05-23: © Cindy Charles/PhotoEdit
05 24: © PhotoDisc, Inc.
05-25: Courtesy of Hewlett Packard
05-28: Courtesy of Cal-Comp Technology
05-29: Courtesy of Hewlett Packard Company
05-30: Courtesy of Bose
05-31: © Tony Stone Images
06-01: © PhotoDisc, Inc.
06-02: Scott Goodwin Photography
06-07: Courtesy of Seagate Technologies
06-08: Scott Goodwin Photography
06-09: Courtesy of International Business Machines Corporation. Unauthorized use not permitted
06-12: © PhotoDisc, Inc.
06-14: © PhotoDisc, Inc.
06-16: © PhotoDisc, Inc.
06-17: Scott Goodwin Photography
07-01: © PhotoDisc, Inc.
07-02: © Masami Sano/The Stock Market
07-03: © Bob Daemmrich/The Image Works, Inc.
07-05: © Corbis-Bettmann
07-11a: Courtesy of 3Com Corporation
07-13: © PhotoDisc, Inc.
07-14: © PhotoDisc, Inc.
07-15: © PhotoDisc, Inc.
07-16: © PhotoDisc, Inc.
07-17: © PhotoDisc, Inc.
08-04: © Denis Scott/FPG International
08-16: © PhotoDisc, Inc.
08-20: © PhotoDisc, Inc.
08-24: © PhotoDisc, Inc.
08-28: © V.C.G./FPG International
08-32: © Ron Chapple/FPG International
09-08a: © Young-Wolf/PhotoEdit
09-09: Courtesy of SRI International
09-09a: © AP/Wide World Photos, Inc.
09-10: © Tom Pantages
09-11: © AP/Wide World Photos, Inc.
09-12: © Corbis-Bettmann
10-01: © Bob Daemmrich/Stock, Boston
10-02: © P. Crowther/S. Carter/Tony Stone Images
10-05: © Michael Shay/FPG International
10-09: © Tony Stone Images
10-10: © AP/Wide World Photos, Inc.
10-12: © PhotoDisc, Inc.
10-13: © AP/Wide World Photos, Inc.
10-16: © PhotoDisc, Inc.
10-17: © Eric Pearle/FPG International
11 13: © V.C.G./FPG International
12-07: © Jim Cummins/FPG International
12-12: © Corbis-Bettmann
12-13: © V.C.G./FPG International
13-01b: © PhotoDisc, Inc.
13-03: © PhotoDisc, Inc.
13-04: © Michael Krasowitz/FPG International

13-15: © Gary Buss/FPG International
13-17: © PhotoDisc, Inc.
13-18: © PhotoDisc, Inc.
13-21: © PhotoDisc, Inc.
13-24: © PhotoDisc, Inc.
14-02: © Tim Brown/ Tony Stone Images
15-01 © Tim Crosby/ The Gamma Liaison Network
15-02: © Jeff Greenberg/PhotoEdit
15-03: © Ed Taylor Studio/FPG International
15-04: © Adam Smith/FPG International
15-05: © Ed Taylor Studio/FPG International
15-07: © AP/Wide World Photos, Inc.
15-08: © Young-Wolf/PhotoEdit
15-09: © John Colett/Stock, Boston
15.10: ©Bruce Ayers/Tony Stone Images
15.11: © Terry Vine/Tony Stone Images
15.12: © Keith Wood/Tony Stone Images
First Generation: Courtesy of International Business Machines Corporation. Unauthorized use not permitted
Second Generation: Computer Museum History Center
Fourth Generation: Courtesy of International Business Machines Corporation. Unauthorized use not permitted
Fifth Generation: © Masami Sano/The Stock Market
1951 (left) & First Generation: Courtesy of International Business Machines Corporation. Unauthorized use not permitted
1951 (right): © Corbis-Bettmann
1951–1953: Courtesy of International Business Machines Corporation. Unauthorized use not permitted
1952: Computer Museum History Center
1958: Computer Museum History Center
1959: Courtesy of International Business Machines Corporation. Unauthorized use not permitted
1959 (lower): Computer Museum History Center
1964: Courtesy of International Business Machines Corporation. Unauthorized use not permitted
1965: Computer Museum History Center
1964 (lower): Courtesy of International Business Machines Corporation. Unauthorized use not permitted
1970: Computer Museum History Center
1977: Courtesy of Apple Corp.
1975: Computer Museum History Center
1980: Courtesy of Microsoft Corporation
1981: Computer Museum History Center
1989: Computer Museum History Center
1984: Courtesy of Apple Corp.
1992: Courtesy of Apple Corp.
1993: Courtesy of Intel Corporation
1995: Courtesy of Intel Corporation
1991: © Seth Affoumado
1995 (lower): Courtesy of Microsoft Corporation
1997: Courtesy of Microsoft Corporation
1998: Courtesy of Microsoft Corporation

INDEX

Working Together

Working Together

Text, data, and charts from different applications can be easily and conveniently shared among applications. One approach is to create a static copy. Another way is to create a dynamic linked copy.

Word Document

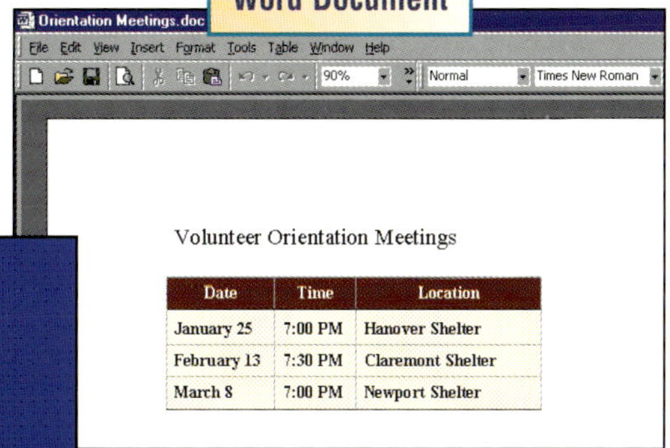

PowerPoint Slide

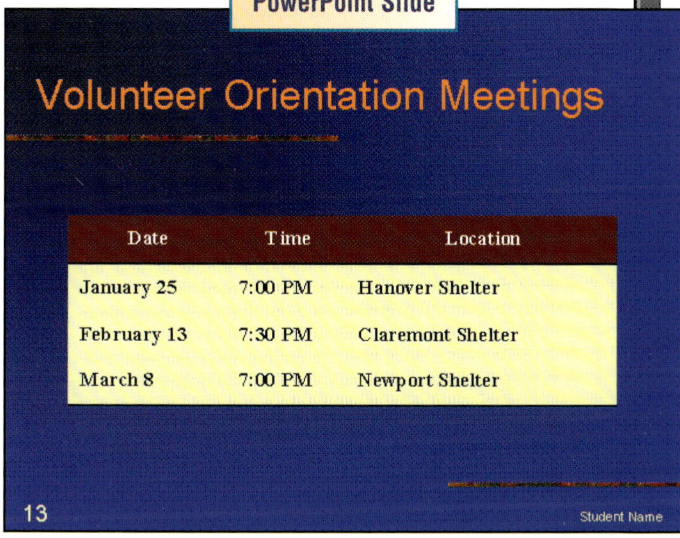

Static Copy

Information copied from a Word document and pasted into a PowerPoint presentation will not change even if the Word document is subsequently changed.

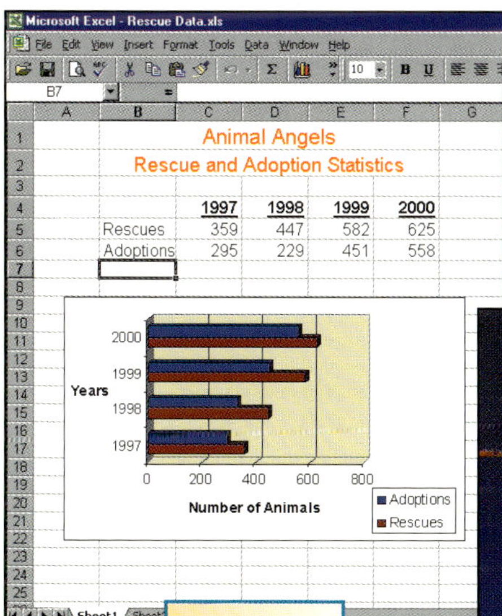

Excel Chart

Dynamic Link

Information copied from an Excel workbook and paste linked to a PowerPoint presentation can change. If the workbook changes, the PowerPoint file will be updated to reflect those changes.

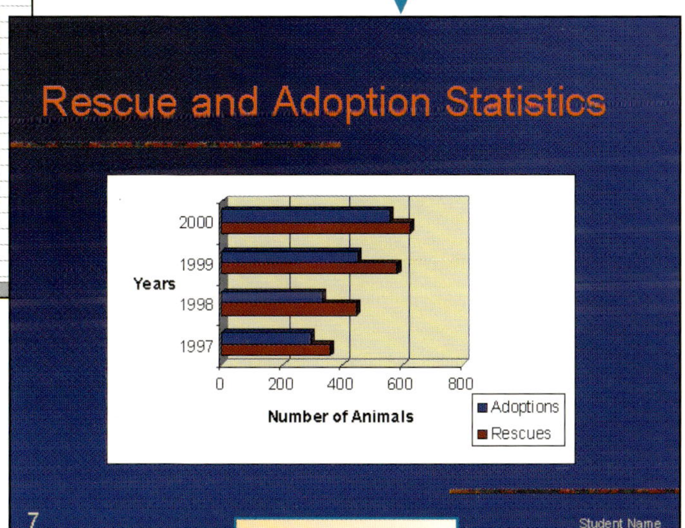

PowerPoint Slide

Support Materials

Support Materials
Two powerful support features in PowerPoint are speaker notes and audience handouts.

Speaker Notes
When giving a presentation, speaker notes help keep you organized and ensure that you present certain key topics.

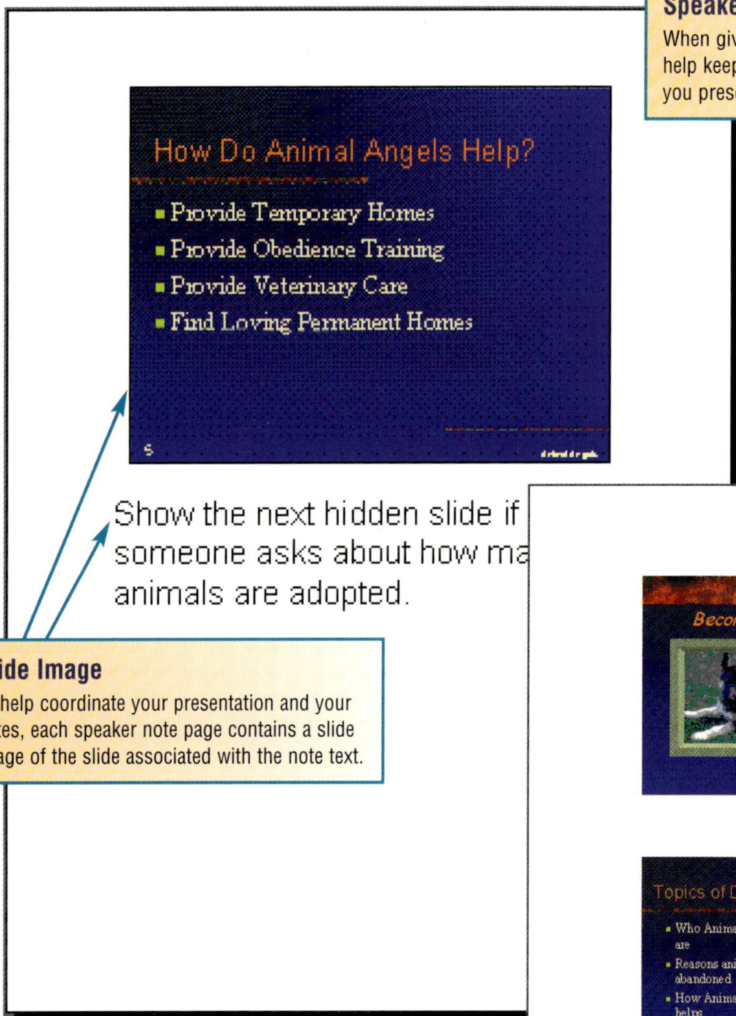

Slide Image
To help coordinate your presentation and your notes, each speaker note page contains a slide image of the slide associated with the note text.

Audience Handouts
To help your audience focus on your presentation and to encourage them to take notes, it is a good practice to provide audience handouts.

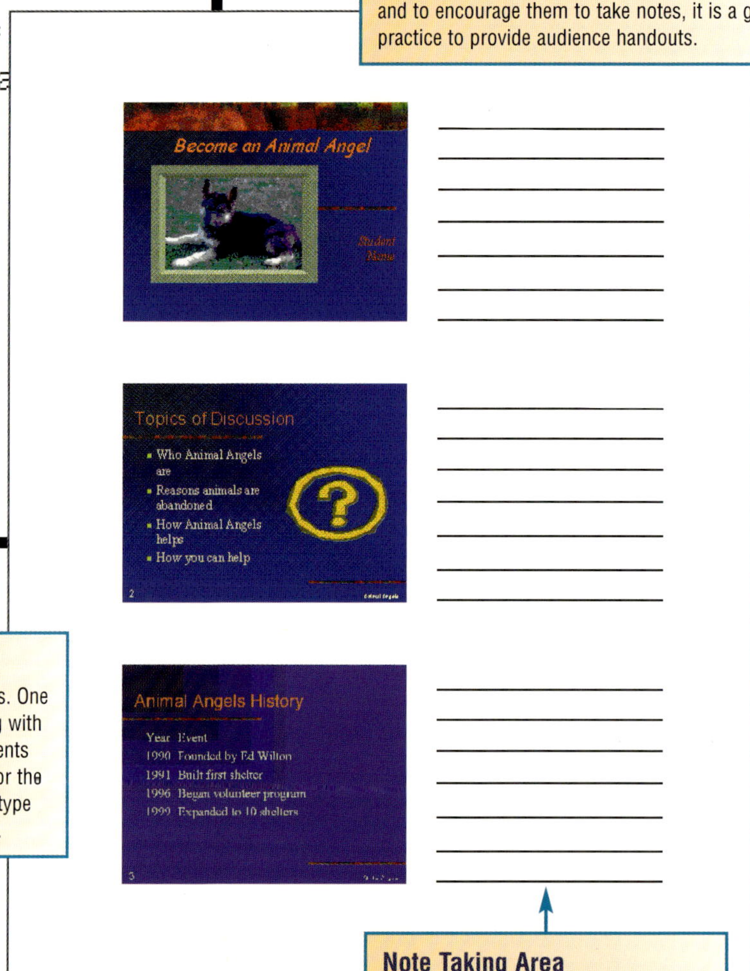

Types of Handouts
There are three basic types of handouts. One presents 3 slide images per page along with a note taking area. A second type presents only images with a variety of options for the number of images per page. The third type presents an outline of the presentation.

Note Taking Area
An area is provided for members in the audience to take personal notes.

Presentation

Presentation

Effective dramatic presentations consisting of a series of slides can be created and edited using a variety of PowerPoint features including: design templates, AutoLayouts, special effects, and master slides.

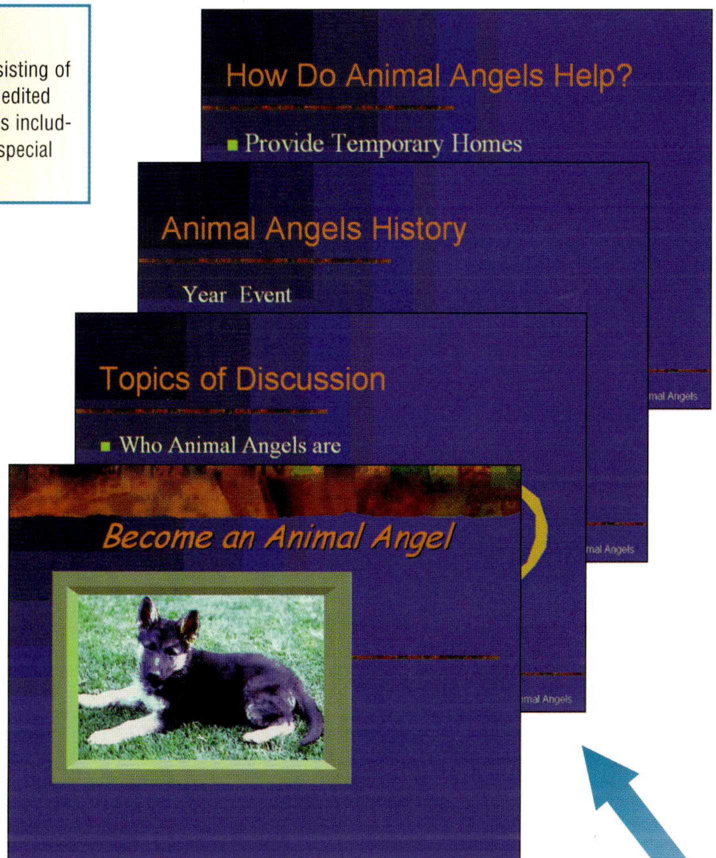

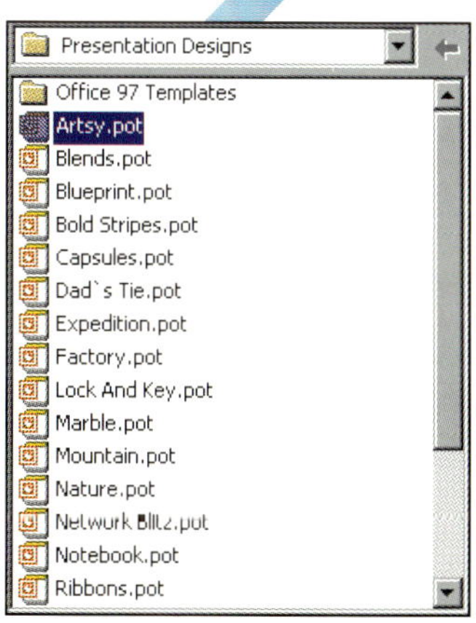

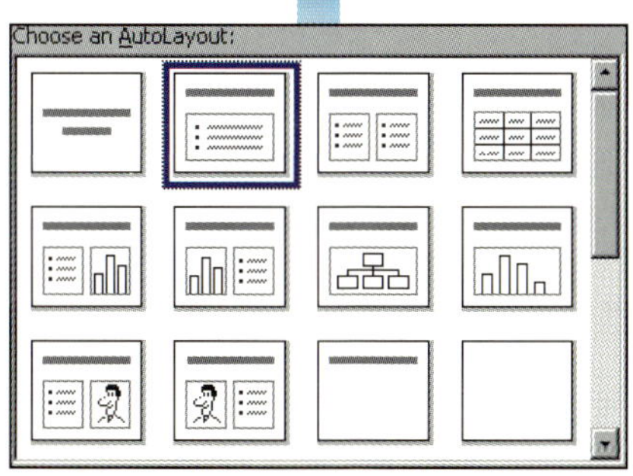

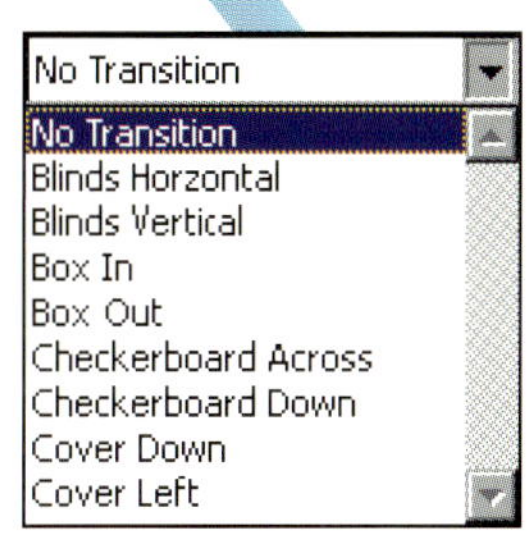

Design Templates

Design templates are professionally created slide designs that can be applied to a presentation.

AutoLayouts

PowerPoint includes 24 predefined slide layouts, called AutoLayouts. They control the placement of objects on a slide.

Special Effects

Special effects such as animation, sound, slide transitions, and build slides are used to enhance the onscreen presentation.

Masters

A master is a special slide that controls the format and placement of titles and text for all slides in your presentation.

Slides

Slide
A slide is an individual "page" in a presentation.

Fonts
A font is a set of characters with a specific design. Using fonts as a design element can add interest to your presentation.

Automatic Spelling Check
The automatic spelling checker feature advises you of misspelled words as you create and edit a presentation, and proposes possible corrections.

Graphics
A graphic object such as a drawing or picture that can be added to a slide.

AutoCorrect
As text is entered into a slide, it is checked. Certain types of errors such as incorrect punctuation are automatically corrected using the AutoCorrect feature.

Presentation Development
The development of a presentation follows several steps: plan, create, edit, enhance, and rehearse.

Types of Presentation
There are a variety of different types of PowerPoint presentations including onscreen, Web, black-and-white overheads, color overheads, and 35mm slides.

Presentation graphics create professional and exciting presentations.
To learn more about presentation graphics and POWERPOINT, see page 34.

Working Together

Working Together

Database tables and queries can be easily and conveniently shared with other applications. One approach is to create a static copy. Another way is to create a dynamic linked copy.

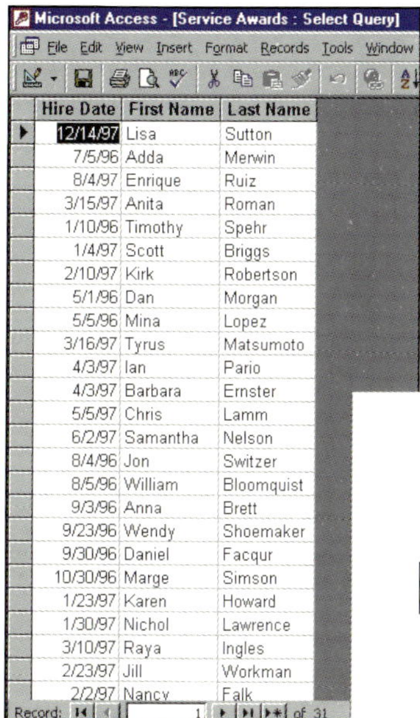

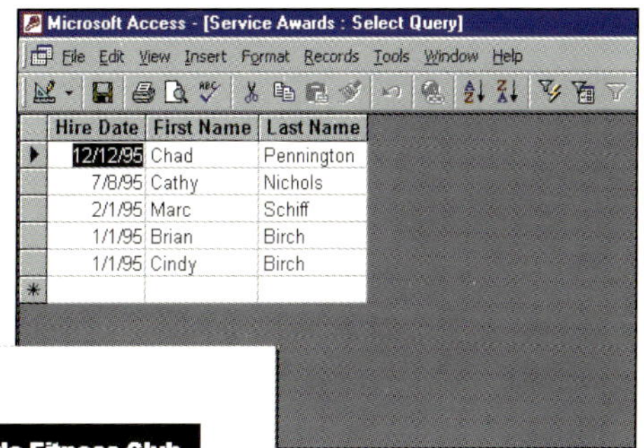

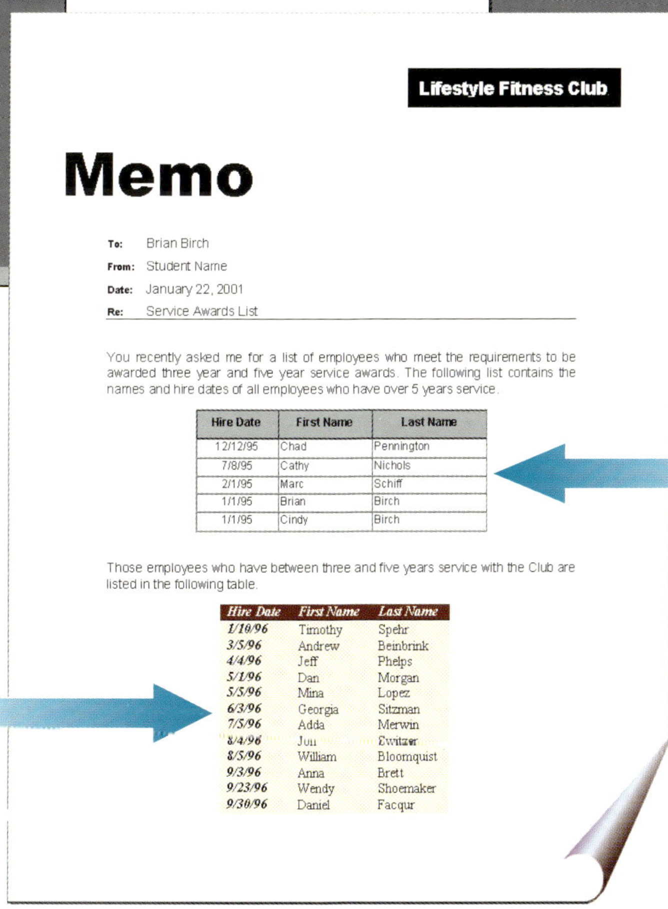

Lifestyle Fitness Club

Memo

To: Brian Birch
From: Student Name
Date: January 22, 2001
Re: Service Awards List

You recently asked me for a list of employees who meet the requirements to be awarded three year and five year service awards. The following list contains the names and hire dates of all employees who have over 5 years service.

Hire Date	First Name	Last Name
12/12/95	Chad	Pennington
7/8/95	Cathy	Nichols
2/1/95	Marc	Schiff
1/1/95	Brian	Birch
1/1/95	Cindy	Birch

Those employees who have between three and five years service with the Club are listed in the following table.

Hire Date	First Name	Last Name
1/10/96	Timothy	Spehr
3/5/96	Andrew	Beinbrink
4/4/96	Jeff	Phelps
5/1/96	Dan	Morgan
5/5/96	Mina	Lopez
6/3/96	Georgia	Sitzman
7/5/96	Adda	Merwin
8/4/96	Jon	Switzer
8/5/96	William	Bloomquist
9/3/96	Anna	Brett
9/23/96	Wendy	Shoemaker
9/30/96	Daniel	Facqur

Static Copy

Information copied from Access and pasted into a Word document will not change even if the Access database is subsequently changed.

Dynamic Link

Information copied from Access and paste linked to a Word document can change. If the linked database changes, the Word file will be updated to reflect those changes.

Reports

Report

Reports are printed output you generate from the database. Reports can be simple lists based on a single table or more complex based on queries applied to one or more tables.

Simple Table Lists

A common type of report displays a table's content in an easy to read and understand format.

Employee Address Report

First Name	Last Name	Street	City	State	Zip Code	Home Phone
Jeff	Bader	947 S. Forest St.	Fort Myers	FL	33301-1268	(941) 555-7789
Andrew	Beinbrink	45 Burr Rd.	Fort Myers	FL	33301-1268	(941) 555-5322
Brian	Birch	742 W. Lemon Dr.	Fort Myers	FL	33301-1268	(941) 555-4321
Cindy	Birch	742 W. Lemon Dr.	Fort Myers	FL	33301-1268	(941) 555-4321
William	Bloomquist	43 Kings Rd.	Forest Island	FL	33174	(941) 555-6432
Anna	Brett	23 Suffolk Ln.	Fort Myers	FL		
Scott	Briggs	45 E. Camelback Rd.	San Carlos	FL		
Erin	Burke	234 N. 1st St.	San Carlos	FL		
Gordon	Delano	8943 W. Southern Ave.	Iona	FL		
Elizabeth	DeLuca	21 W. Southern Ave.	Forest Island	FL		
Bill	Delucchi	950 S. Terrace Dr.	Cypress Lake	FL		
Barbara	Ernster	1153 S. Wilson	San Carlos	FL		
Kimberly	Fachet	923 E. Baseline Rd.	Forest Island	FL		
Daniel	Facqur	5832 Fremont St.	Forest Island	FL		
Nancy	Falk	9483 W. Island Dr.	San Carlos	FL		
Robby	Ferguson	4232 Tuller Ave.	San Carlos	FL		
Lisa	Fromthart	32 Redcoat Rd.	Cypress Lake	FL		

Sunday, March 04, 2001

Controls

The format of a report is defined by graphical objects called controls.

Query Based Report

Many reports require selected information from separate tables. A query is used to define the necessary information.

Iona to Fort Myers Car Pool Report

First Name	Last Name	City	Street	Home Phone
Bill	Delucchi	Cypress Lake	950 S. Terrace Dr.	(941) 555-8195
Lisa	Fromthart	Cypress Lake	32 Redcoat Rd.	(941) 555-0110
Nichol	Lawrence	Cypress Lake	433 S. Gaucho Dr.	(941) 555-7656
Mina	Lopez	Cypress Lake	4290 E. Alameda Dr.	(941) 555-5050
Cathy	Nichols	Cypress Lake	75 Brooklea Dr.	(941) 555-0001
Marc	Schiff	Cypress Lake	235 N. Cactus Dr.	(941) 555-0010
Eric	Helfand	Iona	4601 E. Willow Dr.	(941) 555-9101
Suzanne	Reddie	Iona	932 E. Parkway Dr.	(941) 555-1191
Name	Student	Iona	89 Any St.	(555) 555-9999
Lisa	Sutton	Iona	4389 S. Hayden Rd.	(941) 555-1950

Query

A query is a question you ask of the data contained in one or more tables. You can use queries to view data in different ways, to analyze data, and even to change existing data.

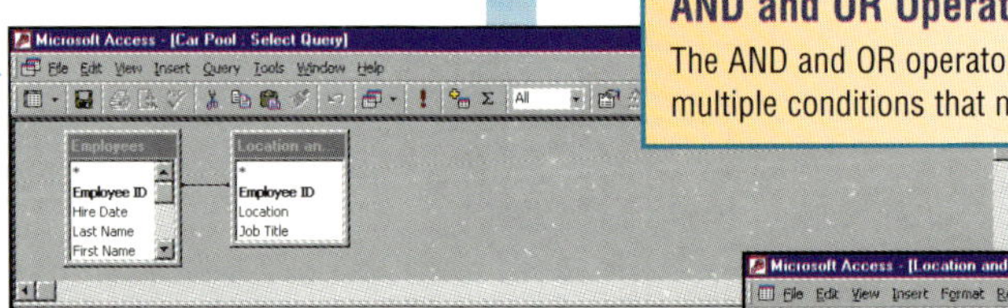

AND and OR Operators

The AND and OR operators are used to specify multiple conditions that must be met.

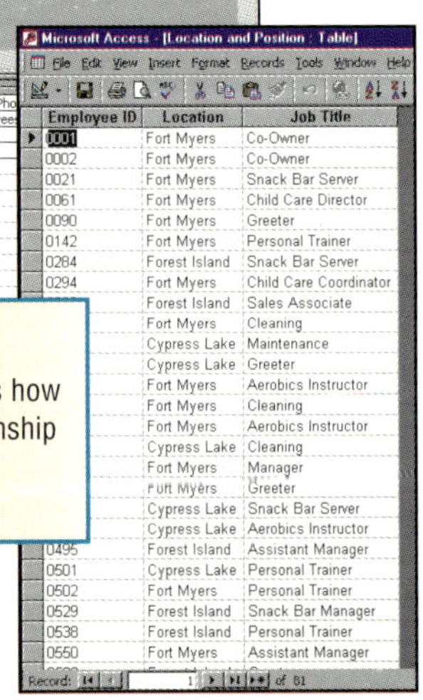

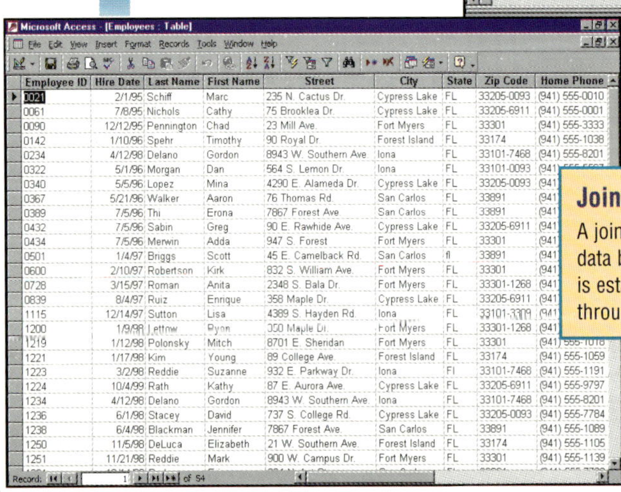

Joins and Relationships

A join is an association that tells Access how data between tables is related. A relationship is established between tables usually through at least one common field.

Forms

A form displays records one-at-a-time for printing, editing, and entering information.

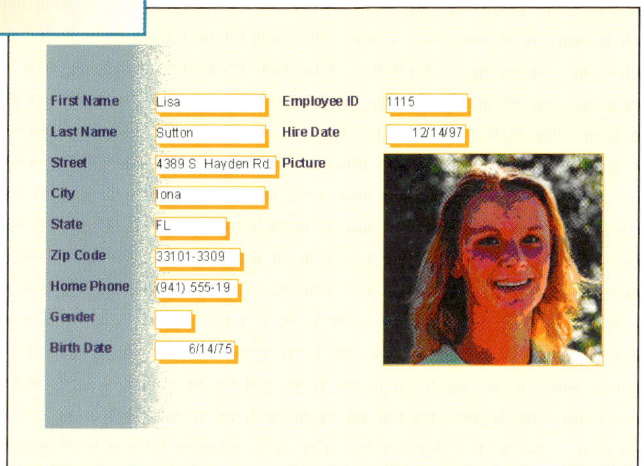

Printing

Individual records can be displayed and printed using forms.

Editing

Individual records can be retrieved from a table and displayed in a form to conveniently correct and edit information.

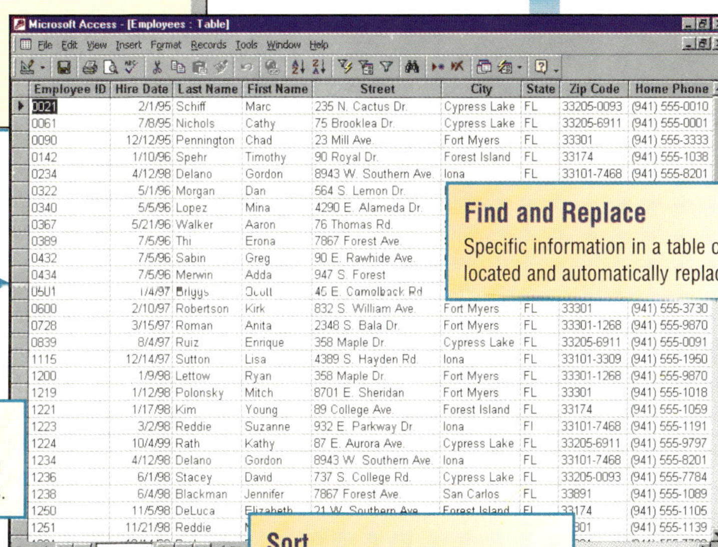

Entering

Input forms improve the accuracy and efficiency of adding new records into a table.

Find and Replace

Specific information in a table can be located and automatically replaced.

Validity Check

The accuracy of new information can be improved by using validity checks.

Sort

Data can be sorted to make it easier to locate information.

Tables

Database
A database is an organized collection of related information. Typically, the information is stored in tables.

Tables
A table arranges information in rows and columns.

Employee ID	Hire Date	Last Name	First Name	Street	
0434	7/5/96	Merwin	Adda	947 S. Forest St.	For
0728	3/15/97	Roman	Anita	2348 S. Bala Dr.	For
0839	8/4/97	Ruiz	Enrique	358 Maple Dr.	Cyp
1115	10/14/97	Sutton	Lisa	4389 Hayden Rd.	Ion
1228	4/12/98	Delano	Gordon	8943 W. Southern Ave.	Ion
9999	2/12/01	Name	Student	55 Any St.	Any

Table Development
The development of a table begins with defining the table's structure. Data can be entered into a table using the datasheet.

Table Structure
Each type of information in a table is described in the table's structure.

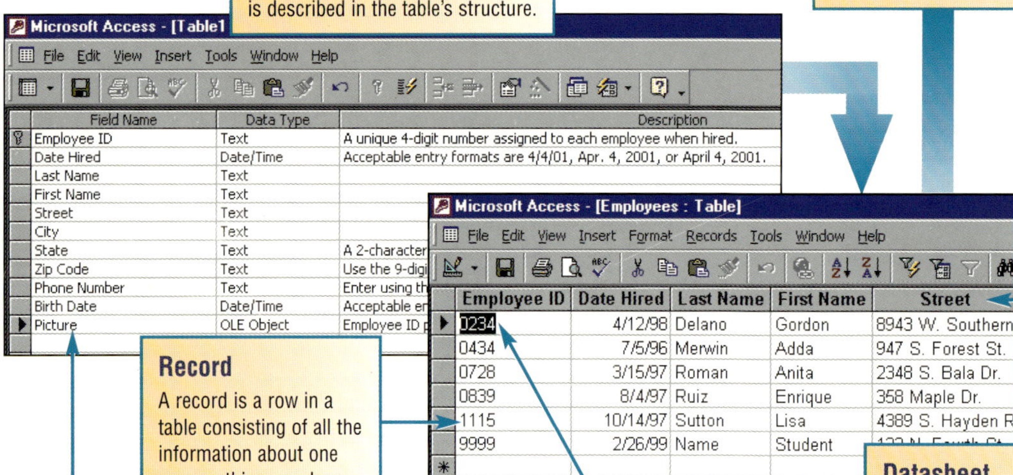

Field
A field is the smallest unit of information in a record. It is displayed in a column of a table.

Record
A record is a row in a table consisting of all the information about one person, thing, or place.

Datasheet
Before data is accepted into the datasheet, it is verified against the table's structural information.

Primary Key
Each record in a table is uniquely identified by its primary key.

Graphic Objects
Pictures and other types of graphics can be included in a table.

Database managers create databases to organize data so that information can be retrieved easily. To learn more about database managers and ACCESS, see page 32.